Lexical Semantic Gene Structure of Modern Chinese

Dan Hu

Lexical Semantic Gene Structure of Modern Chinese

華中科技大學出版社
Huazhong University of Science and Technology Press

Springer

Dan Hu
Zhongnan University of Economics
and Law
Wuhan, China

Translated by
Ziyang Hu
Wuhan University
Wuhan, China

ISBN 978-981-96-6424-5 ISBN 978-981-96-6425-2 (eBook)
https://doi.org/10.1007/978-981-96-6425-2

Jointly published with Huazhong University of Science and Technology Press
The print edition is not for sale in China Mainland. Customers from China Mainland, please order the book from Huazhong University of Science and Technology Press

The original submitted manuscript has been translated into English. The translation was done using artificial intelligence. A subsequent revision was performed by the author(s) to further refine the work and to ensure that the translation is appropriate concerning content and scientific correctness. It may, however, read stylistically different from a conventional translation.

This Springer imprint is published by the registered company Springer Nature Singapore Pte Ltd.
The registered company address is: 152 Beach Road, #21-01/04 Gateway East, Singapore 189721, Singapore

Foreword

Natural language processing technology emerged from empiricism approaches grounded in mathematics and statistics. Over its brief history of development which spans just a few decades, the technology's paradigm has been shaped by an ongoing interplay between empiricism and rationalism. Currently, big data, neural networks, and deep learning represent the most prevalent technical trends in the realm of artificial intelligence. Not surprisingly, empiricism has maintained a dominant position in natural language processing technology. Empiricism methods are indirect for the processing of natural language semantics, that is, by calculating the distribution and combination patterns of linguistic symbols in large-scale texts to infer their possible meanings. In terms of computability, the complexity of natural language lies in its integration of the concepts and facts of the objective world with the emotions and values of human subjective cognition, forming an unstructured discrete symbol system where semantic ambiguity is ubiquitous. This nature of the linguistic sign system inherently makes the precise calculation of semantics extremely challenging.

This monograph focuses on the lexicon of modern Chinese, utilizing theoretical insights from the field of biological genetics to explore the microstructure of lexical meaning, the rules governing the functioning of the semantic system, and the theory and methodology for formalizing its representation, as well as the implementation technology of large-scale semantic computing resource construction project. It aims to supply prior knowledge derived from rationalism linguistic rule parameters to empirical semantic statistical computation, and to explore potential pathways for realization of intelligent semantic computing methods based on lexical semantic rules.

This monograph primarily investigates several key issues, including:

(1) At the theoretical level, the Semantic Gene Theory is proposed, and its basic theoretical framework is elaborated.

The holographic philosophy posits that all things in the universe exhibit holographic correspondence, holographic isomorphism, or holographic identical effect relationships in terms of space, time, and process. Both natural language and biological organisms are different parts of the objective world, and their structural laws also demonstrate relationships of correlation, similarity, or isomorphism. This constitutes the fundamental premise of the proposed genetic mechanism of the natural language semantic genes, as presented in this book.

In genetics, a gene refers to the fundamental unit of genetic information that controls the phenotypic function of a specific aspect of organisms. The genetic inheritance of biological genes follows three classic genetic laws: Law of Segregation of Genes, Law of Independent Assortment, and Law of Linkage and Crossing-over. The research reveals that there exists a holographic correspondence between the semantics of natural language and biological gene structures and genetic laws. By integrating the findings from holography, biological inheritance theory, linguistic holographic theory and traditional lexical semantics, we introduced the Semantic Gene theory, which systematically elaborates on the structure of semantic genes and their laws of inheritance, recombination, and variation. Furthermore, we have demonstrated the feasibility of applying the Semantic Gene theory to the construction of large-scale lexical semantic resource for artificial intelligence computation.

The semantic gene is a basic structural unit of lexical semantics that controls certain semantic features of words and can construct new words through inheritance and recombination. The meaning of a word possesses different structural dimensions, each dimension being a semantic function composed of a number of semantic genes arranged in a certain semantic relationship.

Based on the morphological characteristics of the semantic gene and the structural information it carries, they can be categorized into: free semantic genes and bound semantic genes, explicit semantic genes and implicit semantic genes, family semantic genes and individual semantic genes. According to the functional role played by the semantic genes in the semantic feature function, they are divided into semantic constant genes, semantic dimension genes, and semantic variable assignment genes. Among them, the semantic dimension genes can be further classified into finite semantic genes and infinite semantic genes based on the range of the variable value set of the semantic feature function. And according to the distributional structure of the variable value set of the semantic feature function, they are divided into five different types: symmetric, opposit, parallel, gradual and discrete types. Each type of semantic gene has different properties, which serve as the foundation for our linguistic analysis and formal computational representation of the semantic structure.

The arrangement of semantic genes follows certain structural rules. Words with the same or similar meanings share a unified semantic information knowledge domain, which can be represented as a knowledge domain framework. By analyzing and describing the specific elements within the domain framework, the formal representation of the microstructure of the semantic genes can be achieved.

The emergence of new words is the result of the inheritance, recombination, and variation of semantic genes. The inheritance, recombination, and variation of semantic genes follow the fundamental laws of biological gene inheritance from a macro perspective, while at the micro level, they possess their own unique, intrinsic laws that differ from those of biological gene inheritance. These laws serve as significant bases for computer-based semantic reasoning.

(2) At the engineering technological level, we delve into the detailed exploration of the extraction of lexical semantic genes and the formal description technology for the structure of lexical semantic genes.

As one of the core issues in artificial intelligence, natural language intelligence is essentially a symbolic intelligence. Therefore, investigating the structure rules, the paradigmatic and syntagmatic rules and the logical rules of linguistic symbols, and representing these knowledge in a formal way that meets the requirements of computational processing, is the foundation for achieving natural language intelligence computation.

Under the premise of balancing the concurrent requirements of semantic computation in artificial intelligence with integration of informatization and intelligence into traditional language teaching, language research and lexicography, a metalanguage system for lexical semantic genes description, the strategies, methods, and operational procedures for the structural analysis and extraction of lexical semantic genes have been designed through a large amount of linguistic fact analysis.

(3) At the data level, through genetic structure analysis of a subset of representative words, the process of implementing word meaning genetic engineering is elucidated.

Taking the three basic word classes of modern Chinese (nouns, verbs, and adjectives) as examples, the process of analyzing and describing the structure of semantic genes, as well as the processes of extracting and optimizing semantic genes are systematically introduced. By integrating the theoretical viewpoints of traditional lexical semantics on the subclassification within the three word classes, we select subclasses such as nouns referring to people, nouns referring to objects, and nouns referring to event within nouns; displacement verbs, action verbs, cognitive verbs, and change verbs within verbs; and adjectives related to physical properties, adjectives related to human properties, and adjectives related to event properties within adjectives. Within each subclass, representative subsets of words are chosen for detailed analysis. An initial set of semantic genes is extracted, and through de-duplication and statistical analysis, the high-frequency semantic genes are obtained, forming a sample dataset of semantic genes in Modern Chinese.

(4) At the application level, the methods of computational application and traditional application of the semantic gene database are discussed.

In the realm of computational applications, in response to the demand of computation in artificial intelligence for large-scale semantic resources, an initial overview is introduced to the automatic generation methods of language ontology and semantic network, as well as algorithms for semantic distance calculation that rely on the semantic gene database which do not rely on large-scale text corpora. In the fields of traditional language studies, the application methods of the semantic gene database in the automatic generation of lexical semantic knowledge graph, informatization and intellectualization of language studies, and compilation of new-style philological dictionaries are briefly introduced.

The main viewpoints of this monograph are:

(1) The internal micro-structural components of word meaning exhibit holographic isomorphism with the genetic structure of organisms. The operational mechanism of the semantic system follows similar genetic inheritance, recombination, and variation laws as biological systems.
(2) Semantic genes are the fundamental structural units of lexical meaning, controlling certain semantic features of words and capable of constructing new words through inheritance, recombination, and variation. Several semantic genes with relatively stable semantic relationships can be combined into a semantic gene cluster. Similar to the genetic inheritance in biology, semantic genes, gene chains, and gene clusters can all undergo inheritance, recombination, and variation, thereby generating new words. There exists a relationship of genetic inheritance and variation among the multiple pleremes of a single word.
(3) Each plereme of a word is a multidimensional semantic space composed of multiple semantic features, with each dimension characterized by a feature function. By combining the weights of these features, a feature vector is formed, and the computational attributes of the entire semantics manifest as a multidimensional vector space. Each semantic feature function is a semantic gene chain composed of several semantic genes arranged according to certain structural rules. These gene chains, further combined in a structured manner, constitute the entire semantic space of the plereme.
(4) The number of words in a language is open and infinite, whereas the set of semantic genes that constitute meanings of all the words is finite and controllable in terms of quantity. Words of different semantic types exhibit distinct genetic structures. The framework for describing the semantic domain of word meanings serves as the fundamental rule of the semantic gene structure and also the norm we adhere to when describing the expression of semantic gene structures. Through predefining and analyzing the semantic gene structure of a mount of words, we can extract all the semantic genes present in a language.
(5) The lexical family is analogous to a biological family, where all members within a family share a common set of semantic genes, while each individual within the family possesses its own unique semantic genes. The development and evolution of the lexical system, as well as the emergence of new words and meanings, are the outcomes of the inheritance, recombination, and variation of these semantic genes.

Dan Hu
Wuhan, P. R. China

Ziyang Hu
Wuhan University
Wuhan, Hubei, China

Contents

Chapter 1
Introduction

In the era of artificial intelligence, semantic issues have transcended being merely a linguistic or philosophical concern. Artificial intelligence has permeated into every aspect of human daily life, becoming one of the most prominent disciplines in today's society. The advanced application stage of artificial intelligence technology is inseparable from natural language processing (NLP). Feng冯志伟 (2018) even pointed out: "In the field of artificial intelligence, those who master language will master the world." Semantic computation is at the core of NLP.

NLP falls under the category of symbolic intelligence in artificial intelligence. To achieve intelligent computation of language, it is first necessary to address the formal description of linguistic symbols and their structures, which represents a new historical mission for linguistics in the era of artificial intelligence. Both the linguistic circle and the artificial intelligence circle have been exploring the formal description technologies for the natural language semantics. Guided by the holographic philosophy, it has been discovered that there exist holographic structural characteristics within the language system and the entire world. Research findings in bio-linguistics indicate that there is a certain degree of holographic similarity and correspondence between the operational principles of the language system and the laws of biological inheritance and evolution. Therefore, from a genetic perspective, drawing upon the laws of biological inheritance and evolution to interpret the semantic rules of natural language, and seeking new formal description technologies for natural language semantics, is a beneficial exploration that offers a solution to the problem.

D. Hu, *Lexical Semantic Gene Structure of Modern Chinese*,
https://doi.org/10.1007/978-981-96-6425-2_1

1.1 Artificial Intelligence and Natural Language

1.1.1 Artificial Intelligence and Human Language Intelligence

The ultimate task of artificial intelligence is to develop and manufacture machines that possess human's language ability and thinking ability (Zheng郑捷, 2017: 2).

Although many scholars claim that artificial intelligence is a simulation of natural intelligence, the distinction between the two is significant. Simulation primarily occurs at the level of running results, rather than the underlying mechanisms.

1.1.1.1 The Classification of Artificial Intelligence

It is generally believed that intelligence originates from the brain of organisms. Intelligence can be further categorized into individual intelligence and swarm intelligence. Individual intelligence, also known as brain intelligence, refers to the intelligence manifested at the macroscopic level of the brain (primarily referring to the human brain). Swarm intelligence, also known as system intelligence or social intelligence, pertains to the intelligence exhibited in the group behavior of creatures, such as the intelligent behaviors demonstrated by social creatures like ant colonies and bee swarms during activities such as living together and foraging. These two types belong to different levels, leading to the emergence of two branches in the simulation of artificial intelligence: symbolic intelligence and computational intelligence. The former simulates brain intelligence, while the latter simulates swarm intelligence. The applications they generate are also different (Zhang张国英 & He何元娇, 2010).

Computational intelligence primarily focuses on bionic imitation and biological group behavior simulation, utilizing mathematical computational models as its foundation. The fields of interest encompass natural physical phenomena (such as the movement state of internal particles during the annealing and cooling of solid), biological evolutionary mechanisms, and social behaviors of creatures. It seeks new methods to solve complex problems from these natural laws. Computational intelligence boasts high efficiency and optimization, independent of specific information about the problem to be solved, and has garnered intense interest across numerous disciplines, leading to its widespread application (Ge葛宏伟, 2006). Currently, many mature computational intelligence technologies have emerged from these two aspects, including bionic algorithms such as genetic algorithms simulating the evolution of life, immune algorithms simulating biological immune mechanisms, and particle swarm optimization algorithms such as the fruit fly optimization algorithm (simulating the foraging behavior trajectory of fruit flies), wolf pack algorithm (simulating the hunting strategies of wolf packs), bat algorithm (simulating the foraging behavior of bats), ant colony algorithm (simulating ant populations tracking pheromones to find the shortest path), and firefly algorithm (simulating fireflies communicating through light signals) (Jiang姜照昶 et al., 2019; Liu刘伟 et al., 2016; Peng彭业飞 et al., 2017; Zhang张勇 et al., 2017).

The foundation of computational intelligence lies in data computation, which is based on mathematical computation models. By employing specific algorithms such as distributed computing, parallel computing, and bionic computing, it aims to reveal and characterize various intelligent rules. The foundation of symbolic intelligence, on the other hand, is rooted in symbolic processing, which is based on a knowledge bank. It establishes models for knowledge representation, knowledge reasoning, and knowledge utilization through logical deductions of discrete symbols arranged in a certain order (Ge葛宏伟, 2006). The machine simulation of human language intelligence discussed in this section belongs to symbolic intelligence.

1.1.1.2 Symbolic Intelligence and Human Thinking

In the annals of scientific history, the quest for unraveling the mysteries of human nature has never ceased. Cognitive sciences, which are concerned with consciousness, thought, and intelligence, have emerged as hotspots of research across various disciplines in the contemporary era. Cognitive psychology and neurophysiology, in their attempts to explain the operational mechanisms of human intelligence, have found it challenging to provide a clear explanation of the functioning patterns of the human brain, let alone simulate and map them in the design of intelligent machines. The number of neurons in the human brain, the robustness of the neuronal system, the highly random nature of neural network connections, and the systemic collaboration of a vast number of neurons all represent insurmountable chasms in the design and simulation of current artificial intelligence systems.

Since the 1980s, the rise of computational philosophy has provided a new approach to problem-solving.

The Canadian cognitive scientist Zenon W. Pylyshyn proposed a renowned "computational metaphor", suggesting that cognition is essentially a form of computation. He posits that Human beings and other intelligent life forms are fundamentally cognitive entities, akin to sophisticated computing systems. The process of encoding semantic content within cognitive systems is fundamentally analogous to encoding computational representations (Pylyshyn, 1986: 2). Pylyshyn's thought reflects a fundamental assumption in cognitive science: the mind possesses a certain psychological representational structure, and cognitive activities are computational operations based on this structure. Consequently we can use the data structures of computers to simulate the representational structure of the mind and use computer programs to simulate the processes of cognitive activities. In this way, the core issue that has long troubled the field of artificial intelligence, "whether computers have the ability to think", has evolved into the question of "whether thinking is a computational process".

The proposition that "mind is computation" has already become a core tenet of computational philosophy. In the fundamental concepts and research methods of contemporary cognitive science, computation holds a dominant position. People aspire to utilize computation to unveil the mysteries of mind, consciousness, and even the entire brain. From this perspective, artificial intelligence (whether computational or symbolic) may potentially discover problem-solving approaches in operation (Hao 郝宁湘, 2003).

The symbolic intelligence thought posits that humans can be regarded as an intelligent information processing system, which can be termed as the Symbol Operation System or the Physical Symbol System. The fundamental task of this system is to identify and differentiate various symbols, and to discern their essential differences. A comprehensive symbolic system should encompass six fundamental operations: symbol input, symbol output, symbol storage, symbol replication, construction of symbol structures, and conditional transfer. It is assumed that any intelligent system is capable of executing these six functions; or, any system that possesses these six functions is bound to demonstrate intelligence (Cai蔡自兴 & Xu徐光祐, 2004: 12).

This hypothesis is the Physical Symbol System Hypothesis proposed by psychologists Simon and Newell (1976). This hypothesis is accompanied by three corollaries:

> Corollary 1. Since humans possess intelligence, then humans are a physical symbol system.
> Corollary 2. Since computers are physical symbol systems, then computers are capable of exhibiting intelligence.
> Corollary 3. Since both humans and computers are physical symbol systems, then the intelligent activities of humans can be simulated using computers.

Although both humans and computers are physical symbol systems and can possess intelligence, their principles and modes of operation may not necessarily be the same. Consequently, computers can solve equations through complex calculations performed by programs, which does not necessarily simulate the process of human thought (Cai蔡自兴 & Xu徐光祐, 2004: 13).

1.1.1.3 Symbolic Intelligence and Natural Language

If computers attain intelligence simulation via computation, the computational aspect of human intelligence is realized through the process of thinking. Language serves as the material shell of thought and the medium for its realization. Human intelligence activities are facilitated by language, which also serves as the primary means for the representation, documentation, and recreation of human intelligence. Therefore, language intelligence is the core of human intelligence, and the realization of artificial intelligence inevitably involves the study of language intelligence.

Natural language itself is a symbolic system that combines sound and meaning, which is a fundamental consensus within the linguistic circle. Studying natural language through the lens of symbol intelligence entails examining the processes of input, output, storage, and replication of language symbols, as well as the structural organization of the language symbol system and the logical connections of conditional transfer within it.

The Input of Linguistic Symbols: Linguistic symbols are input into the human brain through the use of sensory organs such as the eyes, ears, and hands, via perceptual behaviors including reading, watching, listening, and touching (Braille). In contrast, they are input into the computer system through external devices such as keyboards, mice, touchpads, scanning recognition, and microphones.

The Output of Linguistic Symbols: Humans utilize their vocal organs, hands, limbs, and other body parts to produce linguistic symbols through means such as speaking, writing, sign language, and body language. Computers, on the other hand, output linguistic symbols via printing devices, display screens, and audio equipment.

The Storage of Linguistic Symbols: Humans store linguistic symbols in the brain through their memory systems, with these symbols being encoded within neurons. In contrast, computers store linguistic symbols on various storage devices such as floppy disks, hard drives, magnetic tapes, CDs, and flash drives.

The Replication of Linguistic Symbols: Humans replicate external linguistic symbols through sensory stimulation, transforming them into symbolic representations that are stored in neurons. Computers, on the other hand, replicate stored linguistic symbols between storage media by copying instructions.

The Establishment of Linguistic Symbol Structure: Humans acquire language information through learning, and the linguistic cognitive mechanism of the brain combines and processes linguistic symbols in different ways, establishing connections between various types of knowledge, forming a structural system of linguistic symbols, and constructing a knowledge system based on this. Computers can form a computational expression structure of linguistic symbols by utilizing the relationships among various linguistic symbols, including relationships defined by humans and relationships learned by machine learning.

Conditional Transfer of Linguistic Symbols: Humans, through their knowledge of language and logical thinking abilities, combined with encyclopedic knowledge and experience, judge the transfer conditions within the input series of linguistic symbols and make action transfer decisions. Computers, on the other hand, determine the transfer conditions within the input linguistic symbol data based on conditional statements set in their programs and execute the corresponding action instructions.

For the current NLP technology and information computing technology, the input, output, storage, and replication of symbols have already been very mature technologies, which are easily achievable. The primary challenge in simulating human linguistic intelligence within computers is the formalization of the structure and logic of language symbols. This includes the intricacies of condition-based transfer, condition judgment, and action directives within the symbolic framework of language.

Structural Representation of the Linguistic Symbol System

The surface structure rules of symbols represent a core issue that must be addressed in the computational processing of natural languages.

A natural language is a system composed of a number of individual linguistic symbols assembled according to certain rules, with strict structural regularities between the symbols. This does not contradict the arbitrariness of symbols. Saussure (1916: 102–104) pointed out that the arbitrariness of symbols refers to the fact that the connection between the signifier (the sound image) and the signified (the concept) is unarguable. A linguistic symbol is a coalition of the signifier and the signified, forming a single symbol unit. Arbitrariness is a fundamental attribute of linguistic symbols, and the denial of arbitrariness precludes the revelation of the nature of linguistic symbols (Chen陈保亚 & Yu余德江, 2017).

The structure of linguistic symbols is primarily manifested in the syntagmatic and paradigmatic relationships among multiple symbols. Such paradigme and syntagm is governed by grammatical rules and possesses strict semantic logical grounds, and is not arbitrary.

The structure and structural rules of linguistic symbols manifest themselves at various levels: morpheme, word, phrase, sentence, and discourse. Traditional linguistic theories generally hold that grammar constitutes the fundamental structural law of linguistic symbols, with grammatical units encompassing only the four levels of morpheme, word, phrase, and sentence. Consequently, the scope of grammatical rules is limited to the sentence level at most. Sentence groups, paragraphs, and discourses are units of language use, i.e., speech units, rather than language units, and thus are not subject to grammatical rules (Zhong仲崇山, 2010).

In fact, whether it be traditional linguistic research or research in NLP, the structural nature of linguistic symbol units above the sentence level, i.e., the discourse structure, cannot be overlooked.

The discourse is also an organized system of symbols, and its organization and structure are common characteristics of any type of text (Chen陈勇, 2008).

In discourse linguistics, a fundamental concept is the notion of textuality. Beaugrande and Dressler (1981) introduced seven key features that define the nature of a text, identified as: cohesion, coherence, intentionality, acceptability, informativeness, situational awareness, and intertextual relationships.

The realization of textual structure can be achieved through various linguistic means, including lexical devices marked with explicit symbols and those without explicit markers, such as semantic, pragmatic, and logical means. For instance, cohesion can be realized through reference, ellipsis, substitution, conjunction, and connective words. Coherence can be achieved through lexical chains, while informativity and situationality can be realized through the event structure of the text.

To facilitate symbolic computation in the realm of natural language, it is essential to conduct a thorough and systematic description of the constituent symbols and their interrelations within the linguistic framework. This involves delineating the basic units of language and the connections between them. To date, the linguistic circle has developed various solutions for the structural descriptions at the level of words, phrases, and sentences, which have significantly benefited NLP technologies. However, there is still no unified consensus among linguists regarding the structural units and their relationships in discourse, thus the computational processing of discourse remains a challenging task ahead.

The Logical Representation of the Linguistic Symbol System

The computational representation of linguistic logic constitutes another core issue encountered in natural language computational processing, particularly in the realm of semantic computation.

Logic is a discipline concerned with reasoning and argumentation, aiming to explore the forms and laws of thought to ensure the correctness and effectiveness of the process of thinking, thereby facilitating effective human communication. The main scope of its research is the form of thought, including concepts, judgments, reasoning, and arguments (Dong董志铁, 2018). Language, on the other hand, is the tool used by humans for thinking and expressing thought, and logic is born and developed alongside language. Although languages of different ethnic groups around the world have their own conventionally established structural rules, any natural language must adhere to basic logical principles. If logic is abandoned in language, the transmission of language information would be obstructed, and language would lose its due functions (Su苏鑫, 2019).

Therefore, the relationship between natural language and logic is innate: on one hand, logic studies the laws of human thinking and the validity of reasoning, while thinking requires expression through natural language; on the other hand, logic serves as the skeleton of language, and language acquisition, as well as the exploration of language structure and meaning, must be grounded in logic (Huang黄华新 & Hong洪峥怡, 2019). When expressing thought in natural language, one must employ conceptual description, judgment, and reasoning, ensuring a rigorous logical structure across all levels of the linguistic system (including vocabulary, syntax, semantics, and pragmatics). "Language logic is the application of modern logical methods to study the structure, meaning, and use of language, that is, the morphological, semantic, and pragmatic issues of natural language. As a result of the intersection between linguistics and logic, disciplines such as logical syntactics, logical semantics, and logical pragmatics have emerged" (Cai蔡曙山 & Zou邹崇理, 2010: 40, Zou邹崇理, 2000: 1).

In the field of logic, both formal logic and mathematical logic possess structured and standardized modes of expression, which are particularly well-suited for computational analysis. In natural languages, many logical expressions lack standardized formal markers. Instead, numerous logical structures are conveyed through means such as lexical association, grammar, and semantics. Generally, these cannot be computed directly and require processing and refinement.

The computational processing of natural language in artificial intelligence generally involves three fundamental steps: (1) describing the knowledge within natural language using formal methods; (2) expressing the formal linguistic knowledge in the form of certain algorithms; and (3) writing computational programs based on these algorithms. In other words, the key to processing natural language by computers lies in representing natural language with suitable symbolic data for computer processing, i.e., knowledge representation (Wang王芳, 2015). Therefore, the formal expression of linguistic knowledge is crucial for the computational processing of language intelligence.

In artificial intelligence, first-order predicate logic is generally used to represent knowledge. However, it has been proven that due to the uncertainty in knowledge representation, first-order logic is difficult to fully describe the knowledge system of the real world. First-order logic is oriented towards formal languages, which makes it challenging to adequately describe natural languages. Compared to formal languages, natural languages are characterized by phenomena such as ambiguity, redundancy, ellipsis, metaphor, and context dependence. These features endow natural languages with intrinsic characteristics such as connotation, ambiguity, and interactivity, which pose significant difficulties for the formal description of natural language (Wang 王芳, 2015). Exploring innovative approaches to formalize the depiction of logic knowledge in natural language, particularly focusing on the distinctive features at hand, has emerged as a crucial challenge in the advancement of artificial intelligence today.

1.1.2 NLP Technology in Artificial Intelligence

Artificial intelligence is inextricably linked with natural language at various levels, including the conceptual connotation, disciplinary structure, technology, and application.

1.1.2.1 The Origin of Computer Technology and NLP

In the nascent stage of artificial intelligence, when discussing how to achieve machine intelligence, the processing of natural language was incorporated into the scope of consideration. Turing (1950) pointed out, "*We may hope that machines will eventually compete with men in all purely intellectual fields. But which are the best ones to start with? Even this is a difficult decision. Many people think that a very abstract activity, like the playing of chess, would be best. It can also be maintained that it is best to provide the machine with the best sense organs that money can buy, and then teach it to understand and speak English. This process could follow the normal teaching of a child.*" It is evident that Turing also considered simulating human language intelligence as the starting point for artificial intelligence.

In fact, since the birth of computers, there has been an expectation for their application in processing human natural language. In 1946, the ENIAC, the first digital electronic computer in the world, was developed at University of Pennsylvania in the United States. The high-speed computational capabilities of electronic computers attracted scholars to consider the technical innovation of language translation. In the same year, A. D. Booth, a British engineer, proposed the idea of automatic translation of natural languages while discussing the scope of application of electronic computers. In 1954, a groundbreaking achievement in machine translation was accomplished when Georgetown University, in partnership with IBM Corporation, successfully developed a Russian-English machine translation system. The system at that time was quite simple; it only achieved the automatic translation of about 60 Russian sentences into English, which included only 6 grammatical rules and 250 words. However, this was a significant strategic breakthrough (Zheng郑捷, 2017: 3). In 1952, Bell Labs developed an early prototype of a speech recognition system, which could recognize 10 arbitrary numbers spoken by a single speaker with an accuracy rate of 97–99%.

From the historical perspective of the development of NLP technology, its earliest inception and insightful achievements are primarily found in the fields of speech recognition and machine translation. These two technologies with significant application value have been consistently integrated throughout the entire journey of NLP. Their technical approaches have kept pace with the evolution of artificial intelligence, continuously iterating and evolving up to the present day. As various disciplines related to artificial intelligence continue to advance, other issues in NLP have also progressively entered the academic sphere.

1.1.2.2 Technology Roadmap in NLP: Empiricism and Rationalism

"In the early stages, the technical strategy primarily focused on employing statistical or random algorithms to create probability models, aiming to decipher the structural relationships between various linguistic units. This is the technology roadmap later termed as empirical approach, as opposed to the rationalist approach.

Empiricism, or the statistical approach, grounded in corpus analysis techniques, seeks to uncover knowledge by examining vast collections of authentic textual data. This method involves the extraction of linguistic phenomena and the elucidation of their underlying statistical patterns. The empirical approach is particularly reliant on mathematics, with algorithms derived from various mathematical foundations, including optimization methods, information theory, probabilistic graphical models, deep learning, and neural networks. Its fundamental idea is to assign certain probability values to various linguistic events and to judge whether a particular linguistic phenomenon is common based on the confidence intervals of these probabilities. Therefore, empiricism focuses on the statistical description of the rules of symbol structures in actual language use reflected through corpora.

Rationalism, also known as rule-based school, is grounded in the theory of generative grammar and primarily relies on Chomsky's linguistic theories. It aims to generalize the structural principles of natural languages and employs these principles to describe and explain the combination structures at the level of linguistic symbols. The correctness of a sentence is determined by its adherence to these principles. The rational method depends on extensive research of linguistic phenomena and the induction of rules, achieving the analysis and generation of natural language through the artificial construction of complex rule sets (Zheng郑捷, 2017: 4).

The early stage of NLP originated from empiricism. The general statistical tools, represented by the Markov Model proposed by the Russian mathematician Андрей Марков, were widely applied in fields such as speech recognition, automatic part-of-speech tagging, syllables-to-words conversion, and probabilistic grammar, and they still have a profound impact on contemporary NLP. Over half a century, after repeated games between empiricism and rationalism, and through the tireless efforts of several generations of scholars, these two methods have developed side by side technically, each evolving a series of mature algorithmic technologies. Empirical methods mainly include: Hidden Markov Model, Noisy Channel Model, Probabilistic Context Free Grammar, Support Vector Machines, Weighted Automata, Minimum Edit Distance Algorithms, A* Decoding Algorithms, Viterbi Algorithms, Statistical Machine Translation Models, etc. Rational methods mainly include: Phrase Structure Grammar, Dependency Grammar, Montague Grammar, Conceptual Dependency Theory, Frame Networks, Semantic Networks, First-Order Predicate Calculus, Unification Operations, Complex Feature Analysis, Tomita Algorithm, Restricted Transfer Networks, Augmented Transfer Networks, Recursive Transfer Networks, Left Corner Analysis, etc. (Feng冯志伟, 2007). Both approaches have their own advantages and disadvantages, and no single method is omnipotent. Neither approach alone is sufficient to fully address the complexities of NLP; they should be integrated to enhance and support each other's capabilities.

Since the twenty-first century, deep learning technology, based on big data and neural networks, has become the mainstream direction of artificial intelligence. As one of the key technologies of artificial intelligence, NLP has inevitably been influenced by it. From a data science viewpoint, many scholars argue that natural language, a complex symbolic system, poses challenges in precisely quantifying the relationships between texts, with research in this area heavily relying on features crafted by humans. The feature discrimination and self-learning capabilities of deep learning technology are particularly suitable for the characteristics of natural language data with high dimension and lack of labels. The deep learning approach addresses the structural issues of natural language through three steps: (1) inputting raw text to enable machines to self-learn and obtain the distribution vectors of text features; (2) feeding the distributed vector features into a deep neural network; and (3) for different NLP tasks, selecting the corresponding deep learning models and conducting supervised training on the network weights (Lin林奕欧 et al., 2017).

In the brief history of the development of NLP, rationalism and empiricism have each dominated the field for several decades. Based on the rich linguistic facts uncovered through empirical methods, rational approaches will eventually return to the forefront after breaking through the limitations of human cognition, thus opening up new chapters for noumenon research of language and NLP (Jiang姜兆梓, 2012).

1.2 The Biological Genetic Laws and Natural Language

1.2.1 Language Studies from Holographic Perspective

The holographic theory originated from hologram photography technology. "In 1948, Dennis Gabor, a British physicist of Hungarian origin, discovered the holographic principle in optics and developed holographic technology, an achievement that earned him the Nobel Prize in Physics (Yan严春友 & Wang王存臻, 1988). Holographic photographs possess a very miraculous characteristic: when a holographic photograph is arbitrarily divided into fragments, any of these fragments can completely restore the image of the entire photograph. That is to say, any component of a holographic image contains all the information of that image. This is the core theoretical viewpoint of holographic theory: any part of a system contains the entire information of the whole system.

This discovery holds significant methodological implications and was quickly extended from physics to medicine, biology, and other disciplines. During the 1970s–1980s, holographic theory rapidly permeated into the fields of natural sciences, philosophy, and social sciences. The holographic paradigm was generalized (Shi施启良, 1991) and elevated to a philosophical level, thereby giving rise to holographic philosophy (Yan严春友, 2008).

Holography has evolved into a systematic science, with its research scope encompassing both the universal holographic theory at the philosophical level and the holographic phenomena and laws within specific scientific fields at the applied level. The central tenet of holographic theory is the systemic holographic law, which posits that all entities in the universe exhibit holographic connections across space, time, and processes, forming spatial holographic structures, temporal holographic structures, and process holographic structures. The specific manifestations of holographic phenomena include holographic correlation, holographic similarity, and holographic correspondence. Consequently, in practical applications, systems can be controlled holographically by adhering to these holographic principles (Chen陈端吕 & Li李际平, 2010). Holography is inherently intertwined with systems theory and cybernetics, uncovering a novel means and mechanism for the pervasive interconnectivity of all things. It offers fresh insights and innovative methodologies for the study of systems theory and cybernetics. Holography has three fundamental principles:

(1) **Holographic Correspondence:** Each part of the system is correspondingly related to the whole or to other parts of the system. There is an exchange of information between the parts of a thing and the whole, as well as among the various components, which transmits relevant information from the local to the whole and vice versa. Consequently, any part reflects the other parts and the overall system, thereby enabling each part to obtain information about the system as a whole.

(2) **Holographic Isostructuralism:** The components of a system exhibit morphological and structural similarities with the entire system or with other corresponding components within the system. The core features of the overall structure can be inferred from the local components, and vice versa.
(3) **Holographic Identical Effect:** Due to the information correspondence and structural isomorphism between the parts and the whole, as well as between the parts themselves, the same effects can be produced (Chen陈端吕 & Li李际平, 2010; Liu刘承华, 1994). Holographic identical effect serves as the theoretical foundation for holographic control. Holographic control is an important concept in the study of complex systems with similar structures, reflecting the control strategy of controlling the whole from the local. It has a wide range of applications in the automation control of various complicated system engineering (Wang王文庆 & Han韩崇昭, 2004; Zhang张嗣瀛 & Yang杨光红, 1996).

The objective world manifests holographic properties in both the dimensions of space and time. In the spatial dimension, various components within the holographic system, as well as their relationships with the whole, exhibit multiple connections, which are realized through information exchange. There is an ongoing exchange of matter, energy, and information between the parts and between the parts and the whole (Zhang张道民, 1995). In the temporal dimension, "the present" represents the sedimentation and preservation of the "past", being the record of time in space. The real space stores the evolutionary attributes of things that have disappeared with the passage of time, thus, there also exists a holographic relationship between reality and history (Hou侯成亚, 2003).

The perspective of bio-holographic theory has garnered attention from the linguistic circle shortly after its proposal. Ye叶眺新 and Lu陆丙甫 (1994) analyzed the holographic theory from a linguistic perspective, suggesting that Zhang's bio-holographic law merely absorbs the linguistic centripetal clustering method for the holographic segmentation of individual biological processes.

As an integral part of the objective world, natural language should inherently exist in a holographic relationship with the entire world and its other components. Within the linguistic system, there is also a holographic relationship between individual linguistic components and the entire system, as well as among the components themselves. From this perspective, Qian钱冠连 (1998, 2002a, 2002b) has proposed a new paradigm in linguistic research: the theory of language holography. The holographic nature of language refers to the mutual holographic relationship between the language system and various systems in the universe, as well as among the various subsystems within the linguistic system. This theory aims to explain the holographic states within and beyond language by using the bio-holographic law, the cosmic holography, and systems theory.

According to Qian's perspective, the holographic nature of language manifests itself in the internal holographic structure of the system, as well as in the external holographic relationship between the system and the universe.

Internal Holography of Language: It refers to the law of mutual inclusion and manifestation between the various subsystems within the language and the entire language system, as well as among the subsystems themselves, concerning the relationships between whole and part, and between parts. This encompasses three layers of meaning:

(1) Language constitutes a hierarchical system composed of morphemes, words, phrases, clauses, sentences, and discourses, where each component is holographic with the whole.
(2) Each part of a hierarchy contains the same information as each other.
(3) A holographic unit (subsystem) in a language system has corresponding parts or similar information to the whole and to other holographic units.

Let's take the definition of words in a dictionary as an example. For instance, the definition of a word A in a dictionary may require the use of additional words B, C, D, etc.; to understand B, C, or D, further explanations using words E, F, G, H, and so on are needed; and to further explain E, F, G, H, an even greater number of words I, J, K, L, M, and so forth are required, thus recursively exhausting the entire dictionary.

The process of dictionary definition is not merely accomplished by isolating words; it necessitates the construction of sentences, which, while ensuring grammatical accuracy, can also describe, limit, enrich, and supplement the meaning, incorporating a variety of subordinate clauses, participial phrases, adjective clauses, noun clauses, and so on. This process extends endlessly, until it exhausts the entire information of the language system. This reflects the holographic nature of the internal parts and the whole within the language system (Qian钱冠连, 2002b).

External Holography of Language: It refers to the isomorphism, similarity, and nesting between the structure of language and the structure of the universe. There exists a holographic relationship between language and various subsystems within the large system of the universe (Qian钱冠连, 2002a: 145). This can be demonstrated from four aspects:

(1) The various properties of language can be found outward to resonate with the harmony of the universe's structure, such as the arbitrariness, discreteness, recursiveness, ambiguity, rhythmicity, linearity, hierarchical nature, and organic nature of language, and so on.
(2) Many linguistic theories have successfully identified external sources of harmony and consistency, including Saussurean linguistics, the principle of holistic meaning in language, valency grammar, the concept of language as a systematic entity, systemic grammar, cognitive grammar, and the linguistic theory of sequencing.
(3) Language can validate the cosmic holography, such as: the universe elucidated through language, the prototypes of the universe and language models, the successive containment of the universe and language in each other, the hierarchical inclusion of higher-level attributes in both biology and language, the autoreferential law of the universe and the entangled discourse, Gödel's mathematical circle and the sentence circle, and so on.

(4) The language and culture are holographic in nature: there exists a relationship between language and cultural reality, a co-evolution of language and culture, and the compression of cultural vision within the structure of language (Qian 钱冠连, 2002b).

The theory of language holography connects the structure of language with the myriad things in the universe, mutually verifying each other, which holds significant methodological significance and manifests distinct philosophical characteristics (Zeng曾利沙, 2005). Zhao赵彦春 (2004) points out: philosophy is both the starting point and the destination of linguistics. After undergoing the development of ontology and epistemology, Western philosophy experienced a linguistic turn in the early twentieth century, entering the era of linguistic philosophy.

The proposal of theory of language holography has provided a new perspective and approach for the study of Eastern linguistic philosophy (Chen陈全献, 2009), offering a novel angle of view for linguistic research and also a new paradigm for human understanding and discussion of the structural regularities of natural language.

1.2.2 The Genetic Metaphor in the Semantics of Natural Language

Metaphor serves as a crucial means through which humans understand and navigate the world. According to Aristotle, The primary role of metaphor is to translate unfamiliar entities into familiar concepts, thereby facilitating expression and communication. This is achieved by indirectly comprehending or apprehending one entity through another, establishing a specific correspondence between the metaphorical entity and the entity being metaphorized. This correspondence involves mapping between the characteristics or attributes of the metaphorical object and those of the object being metaphorized, thereby enabling the conveyance of meaning through a more relatable and accessible framework. This thought is actually analogous to the holographic principle in holography, in that it is similar in essence.

Metaphor is ubiquitous in everyday life, not only existing in language but also prevalent in daily thinking and behavior. Our everyday conceptual system, upon which we rely for thinking and acting, is essentially metaphorical in nature (Lakoff & Johnsen, 2003: 4). As a unique conceptual mode and cognitive tool of humans, metaphor provides a new way of observing the world, a new perspective on things, and serves as a bridge and medium for transitioning from the known to the unknown, thereby enabling the acquaintance and understanding of the unknown (Sun孙毅, 2019). This is also consistent with the cosmic holography law. The computational metaphor proposed by Pylyshyn, a cognitive scientist, as previously discussed, underscores the holographic correspondence between human cognition and the computation of attributes.

The theory of language holography, which is akin to the bio-holographic theory, has discovered numerous holographic correspondences between linguistic structures and biological structures. Our research has shown that there are also multiple holographic correspondences or correlations between the operational mechanisms of natural language semantics and the biological hereditary laws in genetics. The theory of genetics has developed over several centuries and has become relatively mature. Observing and expressing the operational mechanisms of semantics in reference to the existing knowledge of genetics is consistent with the basic logical principles of metaphorical cognition. Therefore, we may refer to it as the genetic metaphor of natural language semantics.

Genetics is the science that studies heredity, aiming to explain the similarities and differences that arise among organisms with kinship (Snustad & Simmons, 2011: 3).

In the fifth century BC, Hippocrates, the founder of Western medicine and later revered as the "Father of Western Medicine", the Greek physician, proposed the first genetic theory. He believed that offspring possess the characteristics of their parents because the embryo accumulates minute representative elements from various parts of the body. Therefore, acquired traits after birth can be inherited. One hundred years later, Aristotle discovered the phenomenon that offspring are not defective while their parents are, thus he posited that the inheritance of organisms is not through the transmission of "samples" from various body parts, but through the transmission of "information" required for the development of individual embryos.

By the seventeenth century, a proliferation of genetic theories emerged, leading to a vibrant and diverse discourse. Among the most influential theories are those such as:

In 1809, the French biologist Jean-Baptiste Lamarck proposed the evolutionary theory of "use and disuse", which states that "use makes perfect and disuse makes waste" (Xu徐晋麟 et al., 2001: 1).

In 1866, the Austrian monk Gregor Johann Mendel published his seminal work *Experiments in Plant Hybridization*, which for the first time proposed the law of segregation and the law of independent assortment, thereby laying the foundation for modern genetics. At the time, this work did not receive the attention it deserved and remained largely unnoticed for nearly half a century. Xu徐晋麟 et al. (2001: 2) and He贺林 et al. (2013: 2).

In 1868, Charles Darwin proposed the hypothesis of pangenesis.

In 1885, the German biologist A. Weismann proposed the germplasm theory. He posited that cellular organisms could be divided into two parts: germplasm and somatoplasm. Germplasm is independent and continuous, capable of producing offspring that possess both germplasm and somatoplasm. Somatoplasm is discontinuous and cannot generate germplasm. Variations in germplasm lead to genetic variations, whereas variations in somatoplasm caused by the environment are not heritable (Xu徐晋麟 et al., 2001: 1–2).

In 1900, three botanists, H. de Vries, E. von Tschermark, and C. E. Correns from the Netherlands, Austria, and Germany respectively, independently rediscovered Gregor Mendel's laws of inheritance independently. In 1910, the American geneticist Thomas Hunt Morgan proposed the law of linkage & crossover. By this stage, the theoretical framework of modern genetics was essentially established, with the laws of segregation, independent assortment, and linkage & crossover being collectively recognized as the three classical laws of genetics (He贺林 et al., 2013: 2).

The Law of Segregation: Within cells, although different genetic factors can combine with each other, they do not mix together but remain independent, capable of segregating. The genetic traits of the parents can be split into different parts through the segregation of alleles on homologous chromosomes, and these parts are then inherited by different individuals of the offspring. The Law of Segregation is universally applicable in the biological world, fundamentally elucidating the mechanism of genetic variation and demonstrating the correspondence between genes and biological traits (He贺林 et al., 2013: 2–3; Lei, 2018).

The Law of Independent Assortment: Non-homologous chromosomes are mutually independent. Non-allelic genes located on non-homologous chromosomes do not interfere with each other and can combine randomly, being both divisible and combinable. The process of inheritance of biological traits begins with the separation of homologous chromosomes and their allelic genes in the parents, followed by the free combination of non-homologous chromosomes and their non-allelic genes, resulting in the offspring. The law of independent assortment, extending from the law of separation, further reveals the combination rules between genes. The free combination of different genes is an important reason for biological variation and the formation of biodiversity in the biological world (He贺林 et al., 2013: 2–3; Lei 雷子宸, 2018).

The Law of Linkage & Crossover: Chromosomes serve as the carriers of genetic material for biological heredity, and the number of chromosomes varies among different organisms. Each chromosome carries a certain number of genes, which are arranged linearly. Genes on the same chromosome are always inherited together, forming a linkage group. The linkage groups of genes on homologous chromosomes are not fixed and immutable. During the pairing and fusion of homologous chromosomes, allelic genes exchange with each other, leading to the recombination of linkage groups and the expression of new biological traits. Linkage is the foundation for the continuity of life, while exchange and recombination allow for infinite variations in gene combinations, thereby generating individual differences among organisms and forming the basis for biodiversity (He贺林et al., 2013: 3; Snustad & Simmons, 2011: 152).

The formation mechanism of natural language semantics, particularly lexical semantics, is highly analogous to the principles of genetic combination in genetics. Within the lexical system, there exists a hierarchical tree of semantics, where hypernyms and hyponyms exhibit semantic hereditary relationships. The hereditary mechanisms of these relationships are in consonance with the laws of heredity in the biological world.

Traditional linguistics posits that sememes are the smallest units of semantics that constitute semantics, which are also known as the distinguishing features of word meaning (Huang黄伯荣 & Liao廖序东, 2008: 237). The sememe analysis is also a fundamental tool for semantic analysis in traditional linguistics. According to this perspective, sememes in the structure of semantics are analogous to genes in the structure of biological organisms; genes carry the information of the traits

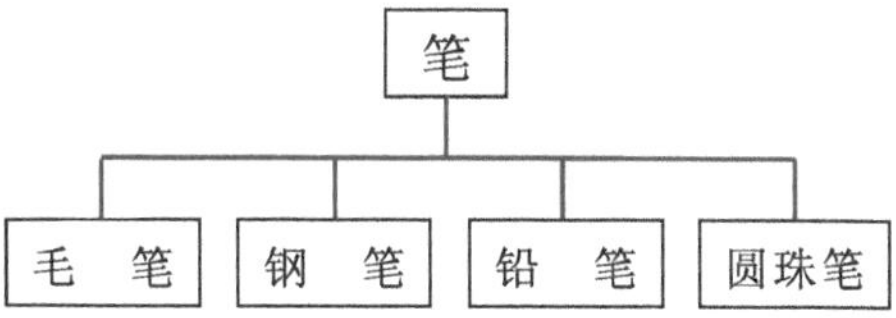

Fig. 1.1 Semantic field of "writing tools"

of organisms, which can be inherited by the next generation; similarly, sememes carry the characteristic information of semantics, which can also be inherited by hyponyms.

Let's take a simple semantic field of "writing tools" as an example to illustrate (Fig. 1.1).

Within this semantic field, "bi笔(wrting tool)" serves as the hypernym, akin to the parent generation in a biological family; while "maobi毛笔(writing brush)", "gangbi钢笔(pen)", "qianbi铅笔(pencil)", and "yuanzhubi圆珠笔(ball pen)" are the four hyponyms, corresponding to the four contemporary generations within the biological family. According to the sememe analysis, the meanings of the five words in this semantic field can be described as follows:

笔: [工具][用于写字或画图]
[Tool] [Used for writing or drawing]
毛笔: [写字或画图工具][笔头用毛制成][用墨汁书写]
[Writing or drawing tool][Tip is made of fur][Written with ink]
钢笔: [写字或画图工具][笔头用金属制成][用墨水书写]
[Writing or drawing tool][Tip is made of metal][Written with ink]
铅笔: [写字或画图工具][笔芯用石墨或彩色黏土制成][用笔芯材料书写]
[Writing or drawing tool][Refill is made of graphite or colored clay][Written with the material of the lead]
圆珠笔: [写字或画图工具][笔尖是小圆钢珠][用油墨书写]
[Writing or drawing tool][Tip is a small ball of steel][Written with ink]

In this semantic field, all the words contain the sememes [gongju工具tool] and [yongyu xiezi huo huatu用于写字或画图used for writing or drawing]. If we consider sememes as genes in the process of semantic inheritance, these two common sememes are the semantic genes possessed by the hypernym "bi笔(a wrting tool)" in this semantic field. All the hyponyms inherit these two genes from the hypernym. Moreover, during the process of semantic inheritance, these two genes combine into a linkage group [writing or drawing tool] for overall inheritance. Among the four contemporary hyponyms, this linkage group further combines freely with other semantic genes, thus forming the distinct semantic features of each hyponym. This process is consistent with the law of linkage & crossover and the law of independent assortment in the inheritance of biological organisms.

The aforementioned discussion only encompasses two of the three fundamental genetic laws, as in semantic fields constructed by hypernyms and hyponyms, the semantics of the hypernyms are fully inherited by the hyponyms, and semantic gene segregation generally does not occur during the process of inheritance. Nonetheless, this does not imply that gene segregation does not occur in any semantic inheritance. Indeed, the inheritance of semantics is fraught with complexities, and the concept of inheritance within a semantic field is just one aspect of this intricate phenomenon. To illustrate the phenomenon of gene segregation in lexical semantic inheritance, we can take the evolution of senses of words and the semantic changes of morphemes in the formation of compound words as examples.

A sense is a division of meaning for a word, originally a term used in dictionaries and lexicography (Fu符淮青, 1995). Now, it is also frequently employed as a meaning unit in semantics. A monosemy has only one sense, while a polysemy can have two or more senses. For words with multiple senses, the status of these senses is not equal; at least one sense is fundamental and commonly used, referred to as the basic meaning. Other senses are generally derived directly or indirectly from the basic meaning, and are called transferred meanings. Transferred meanings are primarily produced through extension and metaphor, which are respectively known as extended meanings and figurative meanings (Huang黄伯荣 & Liao廖序东, 2008: 235). We refer to the development from the basic meaning to the transferred meaning as the evolution of senses.

The division of senses in dictionaries is influenced by the subjective understanding of the compilers, resulting in a significant degree of subjectivity. So the division of senses for the same word across different dictionaries often exhibits certain discrepancies.

Take the verb "chi吃(eat)" as an example. Fu符淮青(1998) investigated the entries for the verb "eat" in xiandaihanyu cidian现代汉语词典*The Contemporary Chinese Dictionary*, hanyu da cidian汉语大词典*The Great Chinese Dictionary* and hanyu da zidian汉语大字典*The Grand Chinese Dictionary*. It was found that these dictionaries respectively have eight, sixteen (among which five are not modern Chinese meanings), and nine senses for "chi吃(eat)", with significant discrepancies. By synthesizing the divisions of pleremes and definitions from several dictionaries, let's choose to analyze the first few more commonly used pleremes of the word as examples.

In The *Contemporary Chinese Dictionary* (*7th Edition)*:

Plereme ❶: To place food and other substances into the mouth, chew them, and then swallow them down (including by sucking or drinking) (Marked as Sense A).

In *The Great Chinese Dictionary:*

Plereme ❶: The act of placing food and similar substances into the mouth, chewing them, and then swallowing them (Marked as Sense B).

Plereme ❷: To drink (Marked as Sense C).

Plereme ❸: To inhale, to absorb.

In fact, Plereme ❸ should be further divided into two: "xi吸(inhale)" (Marked as Sense D) and "xi shou吸收(absorb)" (Marked as Sense E). E is essentially an extension of D.

From an diachronic perspective, the verb "chi吃" did not originally carry the meaning of "ingesting". According to the interpretation in "shuowen jiezi说文解

字(origin of Chinese Characters)", "chi, yan jian nan ye吃,言蹇難也", it refers to speaking with difficulty, akin to the modern Chinese term "kou chi口吃 (stammering)". Its meaning of "jinshi进食ingesting" originated from the substitution for "chi喫"(as recorded in the Shuo Wen Jie Zi说文解字: chi, shi ye喫食也, meaning "to eat") after the medieval period. The verb "he喝" expressing the meaning of "drinking" appeared much later than "chi吃", only being documented in literature after the Song Dynasty (Lü吕鹤, 2010; Xie谢晓明, 2008). This indicates that the original usage of "chi吃" as a verb encompassed the meaning of "he喝", equivalent to Sense A (but not including the meaning of "xi吸, sucking, inhaling and absorbing"). It later differentiated into two senses: "chewing and swallowing" and "drinking", corresponding to B and C, respectively. Sense D is a usage that emerged in modern times. This represents a diachronic evolution process of senses.

Using the method of sememe analysis, the meaning of A, B, C, and D can be described as follows:

A: [人或动物][用嘴][咀嚼吞咽或者吸入][食物等]
[Human or animal] [With mouth] [Chew, swallow, or inhale] [Food and other substances]
B: [人或动物][用嘴][吞咽][固体食物等]
[Human or animal] [With mouth] [Swallow] [Solid food and the like]
C: [人或动物][用嘴][吞咽][液体或流质食物]
[Human or animal] [With mouth] [Swallow] [Liquid or semi-liquid food]
D: [人或动物][用嘴][吸入][气体]
[Human or animal] [With mouth] [Inhale] [Gases]

In the process of constructing new words (or phrases) from the morpheme "chi吃" such as "chi fan吃饭 dine", "chi jiu吃酒 drink alcohol", and "chi yan吃烟 smoke", the sememe of "chi吃" are inherited by the new words (or phrases). Among these, the sememe [chew and swallow or inhale] undergoes separation during inheritance, decomposing into three sememes: [chew and swallow], [swallow], and [inhale], which are respectively inherited by "chi fan吃饭 dine", "chi jiu吃酒 drink alcohol", and "chi yan吃烟 smoke". This process of sememe separation is analogous to the law of segregation in biological genetics.

The above analysis merely provides a rather general description of the genetic metaphor in the semantics of natural language. In reality, the sememes of words cannot be truly analogous to the genes of organisms. Sememes are characterized by their arbitrariness, uncertainty, and overly large units, necessitating a more precise units for the analysis of semantic heredity. The heredity of semantics, while adhering to the principles of biological heredity, also exhibits its own unique systematic patterns. These patterns will be further explored in subsequent chapters.

As one of the core issues in artificial intelligence, natural language intelligence is essentially a symbolic intelligence. Therefore, investigating the structure rules of linguistic symbols, the rules of their aggregation and combination, and the rules of the logic of linguistic symbols, and represent these knowledge in a formal way that meets the requirements of computational processing, is the foundation for achieving natural language intelligence computation. This book takes the formal description of the modern Chinese lexical semantic system as its research object, aiming to explore the semantic microstructure of the natural language lexical system and the dynamic laws of the operation of the semantic system, seeking new and more accurate theories, methods, and technologies to compute the representations for the intelligent processing of semantic knowledge.

In contrast to previous approaches in lexical semantics and computational lexicology, this book draws upon the research methodologies of holography and biological genetics. It constructs a theoretical framework for semantic genetic heredity based on classical genetic laws. By integrating the findings from holography, biological genetics, the theory of language holography, and biolinguistics, we put forward the following logical inferences:

Inference 1: Any constituent of the objective world can reflect the overall structure of the objective world. Since natural language is a constituent of the objective world (both material and spiritual), the structure of natural language can reflect the overall structure of the objective world.

Inference 2: Any constituent of the objective world can reflect the overall structure of the objective world. Since organisms are constituents of the objective world, the structure of organisms can, therefore, reflect the overall structure of the objective world.

Inference 3: There exist mappings of relevance, similarity, or isomorphism among the different components of a system. Since natural language and biological organisms are both components of the objective world, there is a correlation, similarity, or isomorphism between the structural laws of natural language and those of biological organisms.

These three inferences serve as the fundamental premises for the proposed natural language lexical semantic inheritance mechanism presented in this book. Based on this foundation, this study explores the computational representation models of the natural language lexical semantic system.

References

Beaugrande, R., & Dressler, W. U. (1981). *Introduction to Text Linguistic*. London: Longman.

Cai, Z., 蔡自兴 & Xu, G 徐光祐. (2004). Artificial Intelligence and Its Applications(4th ed.) 人工智能及其应用(第四版). Beijing: Tsinghua University Press.

Cai, S 蔡 曙 山 & Zou, C. 邹 崇 理 . (2010). Research on Formal Theories of Natural Language 自然语言形式理论研 究. Beijing: People's Publishing House.

Chen, B., 陈保亚 & Yu, D. 余德江. (2017). Arbitrariness of Signs: Linguistic Foundation of Cognitive Relativity 符号的任意性: 认知相对性的语言基础 *Journal of Guizhou Minzu University (Philosophy and Social Science)* 贵州民族大学学报(哲学社会科学版) (4), 82–95.

Chen, D., 陈端吕 & Li, J. 李际平. (2010). Interpretation of the Connotation of Holographic Theory 全息论的内涵解读. *Journal of Southwest University of Agriculture (Social Sciences)* 西南农业大学学报(社会科学版), *8*(1), 73–75.

Chen, Q. 陈全献. (2009). Philosophical Reflections on the Theory of Language Holography 语言全息论的哲学思考. *Data of Culture and Education* 文教资料 (1), 96–98.

Chen, Y. 陈勇. (2008). Semiotic Characteristics of Texts 篇章的符号学特征. *Journal of PLA University of Foreign Languages*解放军外国语学院学报 (5), 42–49.

de Saussure, F. (1916). *Cours de linguistique générale*. Payot.

Dong, Z. 董志铁. (2018). The Relationship Between Logic and Language from the Perspective of Ancient Chinese Dialectics 从中国古代名辩学看逻辑与语言的关系. *Chinese Journal of Language Policy and Planning*语言战略研究, *3*(1), 12–13.

Feng, Z 冯志伟. (2007). Notes on Advantages and Disadvantages of Rationalism and Experimenralism in Natural Language Processing 自然语言处理中理性主义和经验主义的利弊得失. *Yangtze River Academic*长江学术 (2), 79–85.

Feng, Z. 冯志伟. (2018). In the field of artificial intelligence, those who master language will master the world 人工智能领域:得语言者得天下. *Chinese Journal of Language Policy and Planning* 语言战略研究 *3*(5), 1.

Fu, H. 符淮青. (1995). The Division of Semantic Units and Pleremes 词义单位的划分和义项. *Lexicographical Studies* 辞书研究 (1), 75–83.

Fu, H. 符淮青. (1998). The Division of Semantic Units 词义单位的划分. *Chinese Language Learning* 汉语学习, (4), 26–32.

Ge, H. 葛宏伟. (2006).*The Research of Some Optimization Problems Based on Computational Intelligence*基于计算智能的若干优化问题研. Jilin University.

Hao, N. 郝宁湘. (2003). Philosophy of Computation: The New Tendency of the 21st Century's Philosophy of Science 计算哲学: 21世纪科学哲学的新趋向. *Journal of Dialectics of Nature* 自然辩证法通讯, *25*(6), 37–42+110.

He, L., 贺林, Ma, D., 马端 & Duan, T. 段涛. (2013). *Clinical Genetics* 临床遗传学. Shanghai: Shanghai Scientific & Technical Publisher.

Hou, C. 侯成亚. (2003). The Holistic Theory and Its Methodological Significance 全息论及其方法论意义. *New Horizons from Tianfu* 天府新论 (3), 11–13.

Huang, B., 黄伯荣 & Liao, X. 廖序东. (2008). *Modern Chinese* 现代汉语上册. Beijing: Higher Education Press.

Huang, H., 黄华新 & Hong, Z. 洪峥怡. (2019). Exploring a New Approach to Combine Language Logic with Information Processing: A Review of Logical Semantics on Natural Language Processing 探索语言逻辑与信息处理结合的新路径—《自然语言信息处理的逻辑语义学研究》评介. *Journal of Chongqing Institute of Technology (Social Science)* 重庆理工大学学报(社会科学版), *33*(4), 13–16.

Jiang, Z. 姜兆梓. (2012). The Development of Natural Language Processing from a Philosophical Perspective 哲学视阈中自然语言处理及发展. *The Northern Forum*北方论丛 (3), 47–49.

Jiang, Z., 姜照昶, Su, Y., 苏宇 & Ding, K. 丁凯孟. (2019). Advances in Multidisciplinary Methods of Swarm Computelligence 群体智能计算的多学科方法研究进展. *Computer and Digital Engineering*计算机与数字工程, *47*(12), 3053–3058.

Lakoff, G., & Johnsen, M. (2003). *Metaphors We Live by*. The University of Chicago Press.

Lei, Z. 雷子宸. (2018). Understanding and Application on the Nature of Mendel' s Law 关于孟德尔遗传定律的本质理解和应用. *Journal of Anhui Vocational College of Metallurgy and Technology* 安徽冶金科技职业学院学报, *28*(1), 72–75.

Lin, Y 林奕欧, Lei, H., 雷航, Li, X., 李晓瑜 & Wu, J.吴佳. (2017). Deep Learning in NLP: Methods and Applications 自然语言处理中的深度学习: 方法及应用. *Journal of University of Electronic Science and Technology of China*电子科技大学学报, *46*(6), 913–919.

Liu, C. 刘承华. (1994). On the Holographic Effect of the Three Major Harmonies 试论三大和谐的全息效应. *Journal of Anhui University (Philosophy and Social Sciences)* 安徽大学学报(哲学社会科学版) (3), 51–54.

Liu, W., 刘伟, Tian, E., 田娥 & Tan, M. 谭苗苗. (2016). Research and Application of Information Processing Technology Based on Computational Intelligence基于计算智能的信息处理技术的研究与应用. *Video Engineering*电视技术, *40*(12), 51–56.

Lü, H. 吕鹤. (2010). On Evolution of Meanings of Chinese word Chi 汉语"吃"字系列的古今词义演变. *Journal of Jixi University*鸡西大学学报, *10*(5), 127–128.

Newell, A. & Simon, H. A. (1976). Computer Science as Empirical Inquiry: Symbols and Search. Communications of the ACM, 19 (3): 113–126.

Peng, Y., 彭业飞, Feng, Z., 冯智鑫 & Zhang, W. 张维继. (2017). Bionic Intelligent Algorithm Research Status and Military Applications Review 仿生智能算法研究现状及军事应用综述. *Techniques of Automation and Applications* 自动化技术与应用, *36*(2), 5–8+14.

Pylyshyn, Z. W. (1986). *Computation and Cognition: Toward a Foundation for Cognitive Science*. The MIT Press.

Qian, G. 钱冠连. (1998). Outline of the Law of Language Holography 语言全息律纲要. *Foreign Languages and Their Teaching* 外语与外语教学, (8), 3–7+56.

Qian, G. 钱冠连. (2002a). *The Theory of Language Holography* 语言全息论. The Commercial Press.

Qian, G. 钱冠连. (2002b). On the Theory of Language Holography 何为语言全息论. *Foreign Languages Research* 外语研究, (2), 20–26.

Shi, Q. 施启良. (1991). Prospects for the Research of Holographic Theory 全息论研究展望. *Science, Technology and Dialectics* 科学技术与辩证法 (2), 54–55.

Snustad, D. P., & Simmons, M. J. (2011). *Principles of Genetics* (6th ed.). John Wiley & Sons.

Su, X. 苏鑫. (2019). On the Logical Relationships in Language 浅论语言中的逻辑关系. *Shenzhou* 神州 (9), 67.

Sun, Y. 孙毅. (2019). Constructing Theoretical Paradigms of Contemporary Metaphorology 当代隐喻学的理论范式构念. *Journal of HaiNan University(Humanities & Social Sciences)* 海南大学学报(人文社会科学版), *37*(6): 126–134.

Turing, A. M. (1950). Computing Machinery and Intelligence. *Mind, 59*(236), 433–460.

Wang, F. 王芳. (2015). Generation of Natural Language Logic and Knowledge Representation in Artificial Intelligence 自然语言逻辑的产生与人工智能中的知识表示. *Journal of Fujian Agriculture and Forestry University (Philosophy and Social Sciences)* 福建农林大学学报(哲学社会科学版), *18*(5), 98–101.

Wang, W., 王文庆 & Han, C. 韩崇昭. (2004). Holographic Control Design for Complex Systems Based on Fuzzy Logic Systems 基于模糊逻辑的一类复杂系统全息控制设计. *Systems Engineering and Electronics* 系统工程与电子技术, *26*(8), 1097–1101.

Xie, X. 谢晓明. (2008). *A Multi-angle Investigation of Semantically Related Verbs with Objects: A Case Study of "Eat" and "Drink" with Objects* 语义相关动词带宾语的多角度考察 "吃""喝"带宾语个案研究. Wuhan: Central China Normal University Press.

Xu, J., 徐晋麟, Xu, Q., 徐沁 & Chen, C. 陈淳. (2001). *Principles of Modern Genetics* 现代遗传学原理. Beijing: Science Press.

Yan, C. 严春友. (2008). Introduction to Holographic Philosophy 全息哲学引论. *Tribune of Social Sciences* 社会科学论坛, (23), 31–47.

Yan, C., 严春友 & Wang, C. 王存臻. (1988). Hegel and the Holographic Unity Theory 黑格尔与宇宙全息统一论. *Journal of Tianjin Normal University (Social Sciences)* 天津师大学报(社会科学版) (5), 11–20.

Ye, T., 叶眺新 & Lu, B. 陆丙甫. (1994). Linguistics and the Biological Holographic Law 语言学和生物全息律. *Journal of Hebei Normal University (Philosophy and Social Sciences)* 河北师范大学学报(社会科学版) (2), 12–19.

Zeng, L. 曾利沙. (2005). On Theoretical and Methodological Characteristics of the Theory of Language Holography: Theoretic Categorization and Innovational Academic Researches 论《语言全息论》的理论与方法论特征—也谈学术创新研究的途径: 理论范畴化. *Shandong Foreign Language Teaching Journal* 山东外语教学, (3), 15–18.

Zhang, D. 张道民. (1995). On the Principle of Correlation 论相关性原理. *Journal of Systemic Dialectics* 系统辩证学学报, *3*(1), 48–53.

Zhang, S., 张嗣瀛 & Yang, G. 杨光红. (1996). Holographic Control of Complex Systems 一类复杂控制系统的全息控制. *Control and Decision* 控制与决策 (4), 501–505.

Zhang, G., 张国英 & He, Y. 何元娇.(2010). Subject and Knowledge System Review of Artificial Intelligence人工智能知识体系及学科综述.*Computer Education*计算机教育 (8), 25–28.

Zhang, Y., 张勇, Gen, G.耿国华, Zhou, M.周明全 & Chen, L陈丽萍. (2017). Survey of Computational Intelligence计算智能研究综述. *Application Research of Computers*计算机应用研究, *34*(11), 3201–3203+3213.

Zhao, Y 赵彦春. (2004). *Philosophical Critique of Linguistics* 语言学的哲学批判. Chongqing: Chongqing Publishing House.

Zheng, J. 郑捷. (2017). *Principles and Practices of Chinese Natural Language Processing* NLP汉语自然语言处理原理与实践. Beijing:Publishing House of Electronics Industry.

Zhong, C. 仲崇山. (2010). Grammar: Structural Rule Between Language Signs 语法: 语言符号之间的结构规律. *Academic Exchange*学术交流 (10), 157–159.

Zou, C. 邹崇理. (2000). *Research on Logical Semantics of Natural Language* 自然语言逻辑研究. Beijing: Peking University Press.

Chapter 2
Construction of Lexical Semantics and Its Structural Analysis

Natural language serves as a tool for human expression of meaning, thus semantics constitutes an essential component of the linguistic system. Some scholars argue that the focus of linguistic research should not be on linguistic form but rather on meaning. The establishment of the regularities of linguistic structure entails the semantic interpretation of language fragments.

2.1 The Types of Lexical Semantics Construction

The traditional semantic studies are generally divided into two parts: lexical meaning and sentence meaning. The constitution of meaning is highly complex and can be categorized into numerous different types.

Grice (1957, 1968, 1969) initially distinguished meaning into two categories: natural meaning and non-natural meaning. Natural meaning pertains to the connection between two entities, which is unrelated to the speaker's intention. Non-natural meaning, on the other hand, concerns the relationship between linguistic symbols and their signifieds, a connection established by the speaker or the linguistic community. Then, from the standpoint of language use, the non-natural meanings are further divided into four types: timeless meaning, specified timeless meaning, occasion meaning and utterer's occasion meaning.

Kittay (1987: 41–42) distinguishes between first-order meaning and second-order meaning. The former refers to the meaning of a discourse in the default context, i.e., the literal meaning; while the latter pertains to an alternative meaning that is adopted when the first-order meaning of a discourse is inappropriate or invalid in a specific context. The second-order meaning is derived from the first-order meaning through a specific function. For instance, the sentence "He is an old gudong古董(antique)" is inexplicable in its literal meaning (first-order meaning), as "gudong古董(antique)" denotes a "precious and rare ancient object", and a person cannot be an object. Here,

D. Hu, *Lexical Semantic Gene Structure of Modern Chinese*,
https://doi.org/10.1007/978-981-96-6425-2_2

metaphor is employed, using "gudong古董 (antique)" to metaphorically describe a person as "conventional and rigid", which constitutes the second-order meaning. The metaphorical meaning of the term "gudong古董 (antique)" (second-order meaning) is obtained through the function of "metaphor" from its literal meaning (first-order meaning).

These theories of meaning classification all involve sentences and discourses, and cannot be discussed merely at the level of lexical meaning.

Modern philosophy pays little attention to the meaning of words, and the few studies that do exist have been criticized by skeptics represented by W. V. Quine. The philological community has always been interested in the study of lexical meaning, but the traditional interest of philologists has primarily been in tracing the evolution of individual word meanings. This scattered research neither belongs to logic nor to science, and therefore, it is generally not considered as part of semantic studies. The study of the meaning of linguistic symbols generally takes the word as the basic unit (Ye叶蜚声 & Xu徐通锵, 1993: 126). The research accomplishments in the study of lexical meaning within modern linguistics are predominantly derived from the structuralist linguistic school (Xu徐烈炯, 1995: 111). The discussion in this book is limited to the scope of lexical meaning, with less involvement in sentence meaning.

The nature of lexical meaning is not singular but can be categorized into various types. Regarding the classification of lexical meaning, numerous scholars have conducted extensive research. This section elucidates several notable theories.

2.1.1 The Classification by Leech

The most influential classification of meaning is attributed to the British linguist Geoffrey Leech. Leech posits that the study of meaning should not be confined to logical or conceptual meaning. From the broadest perspective, meaning can be categorized into seven types (Leech, 1974: 9–23):

I. **Conceptual Meaning:** Also known as denotative meaning or cognitive meaning, it's a core factor in linguistic communication. It expresses the distinctive features of words and is indispensable for the fundamental functions of language, which cannot be substituted by the other six types of meanings.

II. **Connotative Meaning:** The meaning attached to the conceptual meaning, which possesses communicative value based on the content referred to by the word. Social classes, strata, groups or individual entities can all ascribe connotative meaning to a word.

III. **Social Meaning:** It refers to the different stylistic meanings expressed by words due to the varying social contexts in which they are used.

IV. **Affective Meaning:** The meaning that expresses the speaker's specific emotions or attitudes. Generally, affective meaning cannot exist independently and requires dependence on other meaning categories or other linguistic components.

V. **Reflected Meaning:** There often exists a certain semantic connection between different concepts and words. When people hear or read certain words, they tend to associate them with other things or events in their minds. The characteristic of words that can evoke certain associative meanings in the listener or reader is referred to as the reflected meaning of the word.

VI. **Collocative Meaning:** The meaning that is appropriate for use in a specific context is referred to as collocative meaning. Some words, despite having common basic meanings with their synonyms, exhibit different collocational abilities, thereby resulting in different meanings. For instance, we commonly say "a beautiful girl" and "a handsome boy", but it is generally not appropriate to say "a beautiful boy" or "a handsome girl". When a positive character dies, it is generally expressed as "pass away", whereas for a negative character, it is usually stated directly as "died", or with expressions like "shang xi tian上西天(go to the hell)", "jian yan wang见阎王(met the King of Hell)", or "qiao bian zi翘辫子(croaked)", and vice versa is not acceptable. In a strict sense, what Leech refers to as "collocative meaning" should be termed "collocational restriction", as this is not a new meaning generated for collocation, but rather a limitation on the coordination of collocational combinations due to the social meaning of the words.

VII. **Thematic Meaning:** It refers to the meaning conveyed by the speaker through the organization of information, such as the arrangement of word order, means of emphasis, and focus of information. For instance, active and passive sentences with the same content express different thematic meanings. Thematic meaning is manifested through syntactic means, reflecting the structure of the entire sentence, and does not occur independently at the lexical level. It is not the main focus of this book's discussion.

VIII. Among the seven types of meaning, Leech categorizes connotative meaning, social meaning, affective meaning, reflected meaning, and collocative meaning into a single category, collectively referred to as Associative Meaning. He posits that, in comparison to conceptual meaning, these five meanings share more commonalities. They are all non-restrictive, subject to change, and capable of analysis in terms of degree and scope, rather than being as binary as conceptual meaning.

2.1.2 The Classification by Lyons

John Lyons categorizes word meanings into three types based on two distinct dimensions: semantic function and linguistic units (Lyons, 1977: 50–56, 174–125; Fu符淮青, 1996: 26–30).

I **The tripartite division from the semantic function dimension:** Verbal and non-verbal means (such as actions, expressions, etc.) have three communicative functions: conveying actual information, expressing the speaker's attitude and personality, and establishing and maintaining social connections. Based on this, meaning can be categorized into three types:

(1) Descriptive Information or Descriptive Meaning: It refers to the statement of a fact that can be objectively verified and can be affirmed or negated. For instance, "He is a doctor."

(2) Expressive Information or Expressive Meaning: This refers to the meaning that conveys the speaker's emotions, attitudes, and personal characteristics. For instance, the sentences "You may go", "You can go", and "Get out of here!" share the same conceptual meaning, yet they express the speaker's three distinct emotional attitudes.

(3) Social Information or Social Meaning: The meaning in language that is employed to establish and maintain a certain social relationship. For instance, the greeting phrase "The weather is nice today" in English does not primarily concern the literal meaning to the speaker and the listener. The primary function of such greeting expressions is to convey the speaker's friendly attitude, thereby fulfilling the communicative function of establishing and maintaining social relationships between the two parties.

Lyons refers to expressive meaning and social meaning collectively as interpersonal information, and points out that such information (meaning) is often conveyed through paralinguistic phenomena such as gestures, eye contact, and facial expressions, as well as non-prosodic vocal phenomena such as intensity, pitch, and intonation.

II. **The tripartite division from the perspective of linguistic units dimension:** Lyons distinguishes linguistic units into lexemes, forms, and expressions. In inflectional languages, the base form of a word representing a lexical unit, such as the verb "see" in English, is a lexeme; its inflectional forms, such as the past tense "saw" and the past participle "seen", are specific forms. The use of these forms in a particular context constitutes the expression in use. From this perspective, the descriptive meaning can be further divided into three categories:

(1) Sense: The meaning possessed by lexemes and words in applications.

(2) Reference: The specific entity to which the term points within the context of application.

(3) Denotation: The objective entity indicated by a lexme.

Obviously, Lyons' theory of meaning extends beyond the realm of words, encompassing elements that surpass the lexical level, extending even to sentences and discourses.

2.1.3 *The Classification by Gorovin*

The perspective from which a word's meaning is viewed can vary, leading to the possibility that the same semantic sense may simultaneously belong to different types. Regarding this issue, the examination by the Russian linguist Gorovin (Б. Н. Головин) is considered to be the most detailed in history. He has differentiated the semantic types into eleven pairs across four levels, resulting in a total of twenty-two types (Fu符准青, 1996: 32–36).

I. **The first level**: Meanings are categorized into three groups based on the relationship between word meanings, real-world entities, and imaginative concepts:

(1) Nominal reference meaning and symbolic reference meaning: Nominal reference meaning refers to the meaning of words that denote the names of things, which involves naming objects, enabling words to have reference, and allowing readers or listeners to distinguish this object from others. Symbolic reference meaning is the meaning of words that signify objects, making them into a symbolic sign of objects. Generally, only content words possess nominal reference, while the meaning of function words is symbolic reference meaning (Fu符准青, 2002).

(2) Direct meaning and transferred meaning: Direct meaning refers to the direct reflection of the meaning of a word that corresponds to its referent, while transferred meaning indirectly reflects the meaning of other objects through the mediation of certain semantic components in words. For instance, in the phrase "feed the pig with cabbage", the meanings of "pig" and "cabbage" are direct meanings. However, in the Chinese common saying "hao baicai du rang zhu gongle好白菜都让猪拱了. The good cabbage has all been rooted out by the pig (referring to beautiful things not being treated well)", the meanings of "pig" and "cabbage" are transferred meanings.

(3) Concrete meaning and abstract meaning: Concrete meaning refers to the meaning that can be associated with a single, identifiable entity, such as "table", "red", and "run"; whereas abstract meaning pertains to the meaning that cannot be linked to a single, identifiable entity, such as "nature", "stimulus", and "hardship".

II. **The second level**: In terms of the relationship between word meaning and consciousness, as well as thought, the categories can be divided into three groups:

(4) Terminological meaning and general meaning: The terminological meaning of a word refers to its meaning in everyday use, which tends to align with the conceptual meaning in dictionaries, reflecting the essential attributes of things and enhancing people's scientific understanding

of them. In contrast, the general meaning may reflect people's understanding of both essential and non-essential attributes of things (Tian田明明, 2016). Some words have only terminological meanings, such as "toluene" and "logarithm"; others have only general meanings, such as "food" and "lawn". There are also words with both terminological and general meanings, such as "whale", which is a large marine mammal and not a fish (fish are not mammals). As a terminological meaning, "mammal" is its essential attribute. However, many people are not aware of this attribute and mistakenly consider "whale" to be a fish. This erroneous cognition does not affect the word's communicative function as a general term. With the development of society and the popularization of scientific knowledge, many words that originally had only terminological meanings have gradually entered people's daily language communication, thus acquiring general meanings. Terminological meanings embody the pursuit of scientificity and essentiality and are therefore relatively stable. In contrast, general meanings, due to the need for various communicative purposes, will change with the development of society.

(5) Imagery and non-imagery meaning: Imagery meanings are those associated with the tangible characteristics of things, whereas non-imagery meanings solely reflect the essential features of things without any connection to their tangible aspects. For instance, the non-imagery meaning of "flower" is "the sexual reproductive organ of seed plants", while its imagery meaning encompasses attributes such as "beauty" and "fragrance". When we say "the song of birds and the scent of flowers", we convey the imagery meaning of "flower", whereas the statement "flowers are plants" represents its non-imagery meaning.

(6) Sentimental meaning and non-sentimental meaning: Sentimental meaning is associated with human subjective emotions and desires, whereas non-sentimental meaning is not connected with human emotions and desires. For instance, the terms "jiaoshi教师(teacher)" and "xuesheng 学生(student)" carry only non-sentimental meanings, whereas "en shi 恩师(respected teacher)" and "gaozu高足(brilliant disciple)" are imbued with sentimental meanings.

III. **The third level**: according to the semantic relationships within the lexical system between words and words, meanings are divided into four groups:

(7) Synonymy meaning and antonymy meaning: Synonymy meaning refers to the identical or similar meanings shared among synonyms, while antonymy meaning denotes the opposite or contradictory meanings between antonyms.

(8) Polysemy meaning and homophone meaning: Polysemy meaning refers to the multiple meanings of a single word, which are interconnected; homophone meaning pertains to words that share the same phonetic form but differ in meaning. It is important to note that some words are both homophonic and homographic, which can easily lead to confusion with

polysemy. For instance, in English, the word "bank" can refer to a financial institution or a riverbank, while in Chinese, the term "fangdong房东" can mean both the owner of a house or the eastern side of a house. These meanings are unrelated both semantically and etymologically, and they are not synonyms.

(9) Arbitrary meaning and motivated meaning: The arbitrariness of linguistic symbols refers to the initial lack of association between the initial phonetic symbols and the meanings they refer to, making them arbitrary. This kind of meaning is known as arbitrary meaning. The connection between sound and meaning in this case is conventional, and the meaning cannot be understood from the symbol itself or through other semantic components of the symbol. Motivated meaning, on the other hand, refers to meanings that can be understood based on other semantic components of the sign and can be traced back to their origins. For instance, the meaning of "zhuozi桌子table" is arbitrary, as there is no connection between the sound and the meaning, and its meaning cannot be inferred from other parts of the symbol. In contrast, the meaning of "zhuomian桌面tabletop" is motivated, as it can be deduced from its constituent semantic components (morphemes) "zhuo桌table" and "mian面top". Arbitrary meaning and motivated meaning can coexist within the meaning of a single word. For example, some polysemous words have an arbitrary meaning for their first sense, while the other senses have a motivational association with this first sense.

(10) Original meaning and derivative meaning: The original meaning refers to the meaning that can generate new words and meanings, while the derivative meaning is the meaning of derived from the original meaning of a word or another word. For instance, the word "evaporation" has two meanings (pleremes): ❶ the transformation of a liquid into a gas at its surface, and ❷ the quick or sudden disappearance. The former is the original meaning, and the latter is the derivative meaning. The meaning of the word "writer" is derived from the meaning of the word "write".

IV. **The fourth level:** based on the degree of fixity of the words meaning as they are employed, they can be categorized into langue meaning and parole meaning.

(11) Langue meaning refers to the inherent, context-independent meaning of words that can be mutually understood and recognized by the collective members of the language community. Parole meaning, on the other hand, depends on the context and is a temporary meaning that arises within a specific context. For instance, in the sentence "lao wang shige dalaba 老王是个大喇叭Old Wang is a loudspeaker", the linguistic meaning of the word "dalaba大喇叭loudspeaker" is "a device for amplifying sound", which is a fixed langue meaning. However, in this sentence, the meaning conveys that Old Wang cannot keep secrets and enjoys spreading news everywhere. This is the parole meaning, which does not exist outside the context of the sentence.

2.1.4 The Classification by Fomina

The Russian scholar, Fomina (М. И. Фомина), also categorized meanings from various perspectives (Fu符淮青, 1996: 36–39).

I. **Direct meaning and transferred meaning:** This classification is based on the relationship between word meaning and the objective reality of the world. Direct meaning, also known as basic meaning, directly indicates the meaning of things, phenomena, behaviors, and characteristics. Transferred meaning, on the other hand, arises when the direct meaning shifts from indicating one object to indicating another, being constrained by association and comparison. This perspective is similar to that of Gorovin. Compared to other meanings of words, direct meaning is less restricted by combinability, mainly governing the paradigtnatic relationship of words. The direct meaning of a word is synchronic, and can only be determined from the contemporary lexical system; it undergoes evolution in the diachronic dimension. Some transferred meanings may retain the imagery of their original direct meaning, while others may lose it. For instance, the direct meaning of "qiang墙(wall)" is "the perimeter of houses, courtyards, cities, etc., usually made of earth or bricks, perpendicular to the ground". In expressions like "tongqiang tiebi铜墙铁壁(impenetrable fortress)" and "renqiang人墙(crown of people)", "qiang墙(wall)" is used metaphorically, retaining the imagery of its direct meaning; however, in "firewall" (a term in network technology, referring to the protective barrier constructed by hardware and software at the boundary between networks to ensure network security), it loses the original imagery of its direct meaning.

II. **Derivative meaning and non-derivative meaning:** It's similar to Gorovin's "Original and Derivative Meaning", but there is a distinction that Fomina's concept of derivative meaning refers to the semantic relationships between different words, excluding the derivative relationships between different meanings within the same word.

III. **Free meaning and non-free meaning:** This classification is based on the intercombinatorial relationships between different words. Free meaning refers to the meaning of a word that can freely function as a constituent of a sentence according to its word class, which is the case for the basic meanings of most words. Non-free meaning, on the other hand, cannot be used freely and is constrained by various combinatorial conditions. Fomina has summarized three situations:

   (1) The meaning associated with idoms: Certain meanings of some words are exclusively manifested in idioms and cannot be freely used in other contexts. This phenomenon is relatively common in idioms.

   (2) The meaning constrained by syntax: Some words, according to their word class, should be capable of serving as certain sentence components (e.g., nouns can act as subjects and objects), but in actual usage, they are unable to do so.

(3) The meaning constrained by structure: Certain meanings can only appear within specific structural contexts.

IV. **General nominal reference meaning and emotional nominal reference meaning**: General nominal reference meaning refers to the meaning of words that name things and phenomena, while emotional nominal reference meaning refers to the act of naming something accompanied by a certain emotional tone. For instance, "teacher" is a general nominal reference meaning, "laoshi老师(teacher)" is an emotionally charged nominal reference with a positive connotation, and "jiaoshujiang教书匠(pedagogue)" is an nominal reference meaning with a negative connotation.

Fomina research on semantic classification is significantly influenced by Academician Viktor Vladimirovich Vinogradov (Виктор Владимирович Виноградов), a leading lexicologist from Russian. In particular, her distinction between free and non-free meaning is developed on the basis of Vinogradov's concept of "restricted by habitual range, restricted by syntactic function, and restricted by collocational patterns", which was proposed in the 1950s.

2.1.5 The Classifications by Chinese Scholars

Chinese scholars have proposed numerous diverse perspectives on the typology of word meaning, primarily including:

(1) Zhou周祖谟 (1959): Lexical meaning and rhetorical features.
(2) Lü 吕叔湘 (1981): Basic meaning (conceptual meaning) and additional meaning.
(3) Liu刘叔新 (1995): Rational meaning and affective meaning (expressive color), lexical meaning and grammatical meaning, and vague meaning and definite meaning
(4) Fu符淮青 (1996): Conceptual meaning and accessorial meaning (including connotative meaning, affective meaning, and stylistic meaning).
(5) Zhan詹人凤 (1997): Rational meaning, concomitant meaning, emotional tone, stylistic tone, figurative tone, temporal and regional tone, and speech community tone.
(6) Zhang张志毅 and Zhang张庆云 (2001): Focusing on the plereme, they propose four major theories: the theory of plereme structure, the theory of plereme characterization, the theory of plereme context, and the theory of plereme evolution. From these discussions, we can deduce their trisection of meaning: semantic meaning (basic meaning and supplementary meaning), pragmatic meaning (combinational meaning and contextual meaning), and grammatical meaning (categorical meaning, structural meaning, and functional meaning).
(7) Ge葛本仪 (2001): Lexical meaning, grammatical meaning, and connotative meaning.

(8) Xing邢福义 and Wu吴振国 (2002): Conceptual meaning and additional meaning (evaluative meaning, figurative meaning, cultural meaning, stylistic meaning).
(9) Cao曹炜 (2001: 14) Presents a theory of lexical meaning structure and types: He categorizes the structure of modern Chinese lexical semantics into five components of meaning: rational meaning, connotative meaning, structural meaning, cultural meaning, and associative meaning. Furthermore, he classifies the types of meaning into four groups: original and derived meanings, historical and present meanings, basic and general meanings, and stored and used meanings.

In summary, there is a diversity of opinions regarding the study of lexical meaning classification, and to date, there has been no unified understanding. The differences in perspectives reflect discrepancies in the understanding of lexical semantic structure on one hand, and on the other hand, they are beneficial for us to gain a comprehensive understanding of the nature of lexical semantics, providing multi-angle references for our computational description of lexical semantics.

2.2 Lexical Semantics Construction and Component Analysis

2.2.1 The Constituent Units of Lexical Semantics

The study of lexical meaning initially confronts the issue of the composition structure of meaning and the segmentation of semantic units.

As a trinity of phonetics, morphology, and semantics, linguistic symbols and their combinations are integrations of phonetics and semantics (Shi石安石 & Zhan詹人凤, 1988: 62). Morphology refers to the construction of linguistic forms through the arrangement of linguistic building blocks such as words according to certain grammatical relationships (Gao高圣林, 2000). In the study of morphology, the written form of language is generally used as the carrier of expression. Various symbolic units that constitute the language system often carry semantic value. Some units themselves carry semantic content, such as syllables, morphemes, words, and sentences; while others, although lacking explicit semantic content, possess the function of distinguishing meanings, such as phonemes, the tones in Chinese, and the radicals in Chinese characters.

Phonetics and morphology both have specific physical carriers, thus the segmentation of is relatively straightforward. However, the challenge of semantic segmentation lies in the intangible nature of meaning, which is primarily a spiritual construct and lacks a physical form. Consequently, the process of dividing meaning into segments is inherently more complex. Even at the smallest level of phonetic and morphological units, the meaning units they carry may not be the smallest, as they can be further segmented. For instance, the linguistic unit "ren人(person)" is both a word, representing the smallest unit that can be independently used in terms of sound and meaning, and a morpheme that can combine with other morphemes to form new words, such as "nanren男人(man)", "nüren女人(woman)", and "renmin人民(people)". Morphologically, it is already the smallest unit and cannot be further divided. Nevertheless, its semantics is not the smallest. According to the definition in *The Contemporary Chinese Dictionary (7th Edition)*, an analysis of its semantic components would reveal more semantic units.

人: [高等][动物][能制造工具][会使用工具][能劳动].

[Advanced][Animals][Can make tools][Can use tools][Can labor]

Even with such analysis, the semantic units obtained are not the smallest. Some of these units are even larger than the original unit "ren人(person)", with richer semantics, and can be further divided. This can lead to an infinite loop, extending until all the words in a language dictionary are exhausted. This is the tremendous technical challenge faced in semantic segmentation.

In the semantic studies of modern Chinese, the segmentation of semantic units often commences with the lexical semantic units. The following section introduces several major viewpoints.

I. **Plereme and Sememe** (Zhan詹人凤, 1997: 56–64):

A plereme refers to the semantic item extracted from the content of a linguistic unit. It is primarily used for the analysis of word meanings and can also be applied to the semantic analysis of other linguistic units. The content of linguistic units varies in complexity, ranging from a single plereme, such as the meaning of a monosemy, to several interrelated pleremes, such as the various meanings of a polysemy.

A sememe, also known as a semantic constituent or semantic component, is the constituent part of a plereme. It represents the smallest unit that constitutes semantics. The plereme can be further divided, and the smallest unit obtained after the final division is sememe.

Sememes differ from pleremes. Pleremes are the various relatively independent, complementary parts derived from the overall meaning of a word, which together constitute the entire meaning of the word. Each plereme of a word independently explicates the meaning of the word within a specific context. In contrast, sememes cannot be used independently in a context; they are the result of further analysis of the plereme.

II. **Plereme, sememe, plereme cluster, and expression** (Xing邢福义 & Wu吴振国, 2002: 114–117):

(1) Plereme: It is an independent, generalized, and fixed semantic unit represented by lexical forms. Pleremes have the following basic properties:
   A. A plereme is represented by lexical forms, which encompass morphemes, words, and fixed phrases. A single semantic content represented by a lexical form constitutes a plereme. Each distinct meaning of a polysemous word constitutes a plereme. Generally, plereme is predominantly associated with the meanings of words; however, morphemes and the meanings of fixed phrases are also considered as

plereme. It is worth noting that certain phrases can function both as fixed phrases and as free phrases, such as "qiangtoucao墙头草 (fence-sitter)", "tong mafengwo捅马蜂窝(making trouble)", and " cu tanzi 醋坛子(a person of jealous nature)". When functioning as a fixed phrase, it represents a single plereme, whereas when functioning as a free phrase, it is combined by multiple pleremes.

B. A plereme is a semantic unit capable of independent application. A plereme encompasses both the conceptual meaning and various supplementary meanings that are appended to the conceptual meaning. The supplementary meanings are inextricably linked to the conceptual meaning and generally cannot be utilized independently. Consequently, the supplementary meanings appended to the conceptual meaning cannot constitute a plereme on their own. Certain special word classes do not convey specific concepts but are limited to affective or grammatical meanings. For instance, interjections such as "heng哼(ahem)" and "aiya哎呀 (oh)" solely express affective meanings; particles like "zhe着(added to a verb or adjective to indicate a continued action or state)", "le了(used after a verb or an adjective to indicate the completion of an action or a change)", and "guo过(used after a verb or an adjective to indicate the completion of an action or a past action or state)", as well as particles of mood such as "ne呢(used at the end of a question)", "ba吧(used at the end of a sentence,implying solicting, suggestion request or command,ect.)" and "ma吗(used at the end of a question)" exclusively convey grammatical meanings. The affective or grammatical meanings of these words are not appended to other conceptual meanings but exist independently and can be applied independently. Therefore, they are also considered pleremes.

C. A plereme is a generalized and fixed semantic unit. A plereme is a general, inherent, and abstract meaning that is abstracted from the various usages of a word, and does not include the specific referent and temporary contextual meaning within a particular linguistic environment. In a semantic field constructed by hypernyms and hyponyms, the hypernym can be used to refer to the hyponyms in a general sense. For instance, the word "che车(vehicle)" has hyponyms such as "kache卡车(truck)", "keche客车(bus)", "jiaoche轿车(sedan)" and "yueyeche越野车(SUV)", and so on. In specific contexts, they may refer to different objects. For example, "sijiache私家车(private car)" generally refers to "sedan" or "SUV", "xiaoche校车(school bus)" generally refers to "bus", "liangche shuini两车水泥(two trucks of cement)" generally refers to "truck", and "jinzhi jiuhou kaiche禁止酒后开车(prohibition of driving under the influence of alcohol)" includes all types of vehicles. These meanings are not the pleremes of "car"; they can all be attributed to a single plereme, "a wheeled land transportation vehicle".

(2) Sememe: Also named as semantic component, semantic feature, semantic marker, semantic atom, etc., is the semantic components that makes up a plereme. They are distinctive semantic features abstracted from a set of related words. Traditional linguistics generally analyzes the meaning of words up to the pleremes, while modern linguistics further analyzes the plereme as a combination of several sememes. Sememes have the following characteristics:

A. Sememes are derived through the comparative analysis of the meaning of a set of related words, which are semantic features that mark the distinctions between words.
B. Sememes are abstract units of meaning that do not possess a specific phonetic form. There is no particular phonetic connection between sememes and the words they constitute. For instance, the sememes of the word "bi笔(writing tool)" include [Tool], [Writing], and [Drawing], which are not phonetically connected to each other.
C. Sememes do not equate to the meaning of morphemes; the meaning of morphemes is associated with their phonetic forms.

(3) Plereme cluster: A plereme cluster refers to a semantic unit composed of several pleremes, which is represented by a general phrase. Some phrases have multiple meanings, each of which constitutes a distinct plereme cluster. For instance, the phrase "zhaodai hao pengyou招待好朋友" can denote the act of treating friends well or entertaining friends with good relationships, which are two different plereme clusters. The plereme clusters of polysemous phrases are analogous to the pleremes of polysemous words. Plereme clusters possess the following characteristics:

A. The plereme cluster is formed by combining the pleremes according to certain rules, thus the meaning of the plereme cluster is equivalent to semantics reflected by the pleremes of the constituent words that make up the plereme cluster plus the the specific relationships that enable their combination. For instance, the meaning of "kan dianying看电影(watch a movie)" is the combination of the meaning of "watch" and the meaning of "movie", as well as the relational meaning of the "action-patient" combination relationship.
B. The meaning of fixed phrases and idoms is generally not a simple combination of the meanings of their components, but rather an integral meaning. Therefore, the meaning of a fixed phrase or an idom constitutes a single plereme, rather than a plereme cluster. For instance, phrases such as "kai lüdeng开绿灯(give the green light)", "tuo houtui拖后腿(hinder sb.)", "chuan xiaoxie穿小鞋(make things difficult for sb.)", and "wa qiangjiao挖墙脚(poach talents)" are examples of this.
C. Plereme cluster generally refers to the meaning expressed by phrases that do not form sentences, whereas the meaning expressed by sentence forming phrases is considered to be the sentence meaning, and generally not termed as a plereme cluster.

(4) Expression: An expression is a semantic unit represented by a sentence. The meaning conveyed by a sentence constitutes an expression. Similar to a plereme cluster, a sentence with ambiguity represents multiple meanings, each of which is considered an expression. Expressions possess the following characteristics:

A. The meaning of an expression does not equate to the simple summation of the meanings of individual words within the sentence, as it also encompasses various complex syntactic relation semantics.
B. If a sentence becomes a syntactic component of another sentence, it loses its independence in sentence formation, and its meaning accordingly transforms into a plereme cluster, rather than an expression. For instance, "He is coming." is a sentence, with its meaning unit being an expression; however, in the sentence "I heard that he is arrving", "he is arrving" functions as the object clause of the verb "heard", ceasing to stand alone as a sentence. Consequently, its meaning unit becomes a plereme cluster.

III. **Plereme, sememe, morpheme meaning, plereme cluster** (Zhang张志毅 & Zhang张庆云, 2001):

(1) Plereme: The concept of plereme encompasses three types: large, medium, and small. It ① refers to all the pleremes of a word; ②refers to a single plereme of a word; ③ refers to the semantic components of a word, which is equivalent to sememe. Among these, the second type is a middle concept that lies between macro and micro perspectives, and is widely accepted.
(2) The sememe: also known as the distinctive semantic feature, which is the smallest unit of meaning employed in structural semantics for the description of semantics. It constitutes the component of a plereme. A plereme is composed of semantic value and semantic range. The semantic value represents the value of the plereme, which is the qualitative sememe, while the semantic range denotes the quantity of the plereme, which is the quantitative sememe.
(3) Morpheme meaning: It serves as the fundamental unit in word formation. It forms categories, positions, and hierarchies in both the aspects of aggregation and combination with other units of stability and certainty. They are organized into an orderly whole through a network of structural relationships that are interdependent, mutually constrained, and hierarchical. Morpheme meaning can be categorized into free morpheme meaning and non-free morpheme meaning.
(4) Plereme Cluster: A combination of pleremes, analogous to the meaning of a phrase.

Zhang张志毅 and Zhang张庆云 have proposed four units of meaning, yet they have not specifically discussed the other three units apart from "plereme". They point out that among the four units, the "plereme" is predominant, being the most fundamental and the one most easily recognized by common sense as a natural and smaller semantic unit. Therefore, their research is based on the "plereme", and they have put forward four theories: the the theory of plereme structure, the theory of plereme characterization, the theory of plereme pragmatics, and the theory of plereme evolution. Their research focus is on the systematicness of plereme, rather than the individual plereme.

IV. **Plereme, sememe, morpheme meaning, plereme cluster, sentence meaning, meaning of speech works, additional meaning** (Jia贾彦德, 1992: 20–23):

(1) Plereme: It roughly corresponds to the semantic unit of a sense. Semantics primarily focuses on the study of the meanings of content words, which are further divided into monosemy and polysemy. Monosemy refers to a word with a single sense, whereas polysemy involves multiple senses. Therefore, when discussing semantic units, the term "word meaning" is not very convenient to use. Considering that the term "sense" is a lexicographical term, which is constrained by dictionary compilation, the term "plereme" is adopted instead.

(2) Sememe: They are the constituent elements of pleremes, derived from the decomposition of pleremes. Sememes cannot be directly attached to perceptible phonetic forms and are not easily perceived.

(3) Morpheme Meaning: Morpheme meaning refers to the meaning of morphemes (roots, affixes) that constitute content words. Like words, phrases, and sentences, morphemes are both grammatical units and contain certain semantic fragments. Single-morpheme words are formed solely by a root, and their pleremes are equivalent to the morpheme meaning of the root. In the case of compound words and derived words, the pleremes are not constructed by the meanings of the morphemes that compose them. However, these morpheme meanings still play a significant and undeniable role. They either prompt the pleremes or add some additional meanings.

(4) Plereme Cluster: Refers to the meaning aspect of a phrase. The plereme cluster is composed of pleremes, which differs from the relationship between pleremes and sememes, as well as morpheme meanings. Corresponding to the fixed phrases and free phrases, the plereme cluster is also divided into two types: fixed plereme clusters and temporary combination plereme clusters (free plereme clusters).

(5) Sentence Meaning: The meaning aspect of a sentence is also a semantic unit, which is referred to as sentence meaning, and it constitutes the largest unit within the semantic system. It is composed of pleremes and free plereme clusters. The content of sentence meaning is the smallest and most meaningfully complete fragment in communication, and it belongs to speech. Generally, sentence meanings are diverse and distinct from each other, except for coincidences and formulistic expression (such as "Hello!" and "Thank you!" etc.).

(6) The meaning of speech works: refers to the meaning of a specific speech work, such as the meaning of an utterance, an article, a book, or the cumulative meaning of an author's entire works. This unit belongs to the category of parole and is a unit superior to the sentence meaning, as well as the largest semantic unit within speech.

(7) Additional Meaning: Certain pleremes, sentence meanings, and meanings of speech works contain additional elements, which constitute a type of semantic unit known as additional meaning. The additional meanings of a plereme or a sentence can be more than one. For instance, the pleremes of the words "qizi妻子(wife)" and "laopo老婆(wife,oral expression)" are identical, but the latter carries additional meaning. The sentence "How are your family members?" not only conveys the basic meaning of inquiring about the listener's family situation but also carries the additional meaning of expressing friendliness towards the listener.

Compared to the theories of semantic typology, there is less divergence among scholars regarding the recognition of semantic constituent units. Some of the aforementioned discussions transcend the meanings of words and phrases, including what Xing and Wu refer to as "expression" and Jia's concepts of "sentence meaning" and "meaning of speech works", which do not pertain to the study of word meaning. Moreover, Jia's notion of "additional meaning" is subject to debate. Semantic units, which can be employed as a measure for analyzing the components of semantic constitution, essentially belong to the metalanguage system used in semantic analysis. For instance, pleremes can be used to describe the entire meaning constitution of a word, while sememes can be used to describe the components of pleremes. Additional meaning is merely one type of meaning constitution and can be analyzed using other semantic units; however, it cannot be used to describe other semantic components, thus it is not suitable to be treated as a semantic unit.

The concepts of "plereme (or sense)", "sememe" and "plereme cluster" are areas where there is generally a consensus among scholars. However, there are still some subtle disagreements regarding a more specific and microcosmic understanding of these units.

(1) Does the sense equivalent mean the plereme?

Xing邢福义, Wu吴振国 and Jia贾彦德 all hold that they are roughly similar. Zhang张志毅 and Zhang张庆云, although they adopted the intermediate view of defining plereme as "a sense of a word", did not use the term "sense" and argued that "sense" cannot be equated with "plereme". They pointed out that "non-free morpheme meaning, which is considered a sense in dictionaries, cannot be termed a plereme (Zhang张志毅 & Zhang张庆云, 2001: 16)", and analyzed the twelve senses listed for "jia家(home)" in *The Contemporary Chinese Dictionary (7th Edition)*, among which the 4th, 5th, 6th, 8th, 9th, and 10th senses do not belong to pleremes. They are as follows:

❹ Individuals engaged in a particular trade or those holding a specific status: nong jia农家(farmer)|chang jia厂家(manufactor)|yu jia渔家(fisherman)|chuan jia船家(boatman)|hang jia行家(expert).

❺ Individuals who possess specialized knowledge or engage in specialized activities: shuidao zhuanjia水稻专家(rice expert)| zhengzhijia政治家(politician) | kexuejia科学家(scientist)| yishujia艺术家(artist) |she hui huo dong jia社会活动家(Social activist).

❻ School of Thought: rujia儒家(the Confucianists) |fajia法家(the Legalists) |baijia zhengming百家争鸣(all schools of thoughts contending for attention) |yijia zhiyan一家之言(statements of a school).
❽ Self-depreciatory expression used to refer to one's elder relatives in terms of their seniority or age: jiafu家父 (my father)|jiaxiong家兄 (my elder brother).
❾ Domesticated (opposite of 'wild'): jiachu家畜(livestock)| jiaqin家禽(poultry) | jiatu家兔(domesticated rabbits).
❿ Domestication after breeding: zhezhi xiaonian yang jia le这只小鸟养家了(This little bird has been raised and domesticated).

The senses listed here are the compositional meanings of "jia家" as a morpheme, which cannot be used independently and, therefore, cannot be considered as "plereme". Xing邢福义 and Wu吴振国 (2002: 114) explicitly propose that "a sense is a semantic unit that can be used independently", which contradicts the aforementioned linguistic facts.

Most scholars acknowledge that "sense" is a term used in lexicography, while "plereme" is a term employed in semantics. In light of this, we consider it appropriate to treat "plereme" as a semantic unit.

(2) Does the plereme cluster include the meaning of fixed phrases?

Xing邢福义 and Wu吴振国 argue that the term "plereme cluster" refers solely to the meaning of general phrases, while fixed phrases, which are equivalent to a single word, should be categorized under "senses". Jia贾彦德, based on the meanings of general phrases and fixed phrases, distinguishes between "free plereme clusters" and "fixed plereme clusters". Zhang张志毅 and Zhang张庆云 do not provide a detailed discussion of "plereme clusters", merely pointing out that "plereme clusters are combinations of pleremes, equivalent to the meaning of a phrase". Zhan詹人凤 does not mention "plereme clusters". Synthesizing the views of various scholars, we propose that "plereme cluster" can be regarded as the meaning unit of general phrases, while the meaning unit of fixed phrases is a "plereme".

(3) Should morpheme meanings be listed separately?

Zhan詹人凤 and Xing邢福义 and Wu吴振国 have not mentioned the "morpheme meaning". Jia is only concerned with the meaning of morphemes that constitute content words. In fact, morphemes also include delexical morphemes, which can form function words. For instance, "ran然" commonly used as a suffix for adjectives or adverbs, indicates a certain state, such as "huoran豁然(suddenly)", "huangran恍然(suddenly)", "hunran浑然(completely)", "huaran哗然(noisily)", and so on. In conjunction with the discussions of Zhang张志毅 and Zhang张庆云, we believe that "morpheme meaning" is also a semantic unit, and it is not limited to centent words.

The present book describes lexical semantics based on five structural units: sense, plereme, sememe, morpheme meaning, and plereme cluster. It further analyzes the microstructure and computational expressions of lexical semantics.

2.2.2 *Componential Analysis*

2.2.2.1 Early Thoughts on Componential Analysis

The concept and methodology of componential analysis can be traced back to the Western classical philosophy. According to Lyons (1968: 472; 1977: 317–330), the analysis of semantic components has a long history, and the analytical methods are closely related to the multi-level classification approach from the classical philosophy, which categorizes things from the macro to the micro. The theoretical thoughts are also associated with Gottfried Wilhelm Leibniz's theory of "Univeral symbolistic". The earliest and most significant research in the field of linguistics, advocating for componential analysis, was conducted by Louis Hjelmslev, a representative figure of the Copenhagen School (Denmark), and Roman Jakobson (Роман Якобсон), the founder of the Moscow Linguistic Circle. They both advocated for the expansion of the principles and methods of the phonetics led by Nikolay Trubetzkoy (Николай Трубецкой), from the Prague School, into grammar and semantics. Hjelmslev applied the theory of correlation of proportional oppositions from Trubetzkoy's phonological theory to analyze the semantics of a set of English words (Fu 符准青, 1996: 50):

D1=boy|girl=man|woman=bull|cow
D2 =boy|man=girl|woman
D3=boy|bull=girl|cow

The analysis reveals that the oppositional components of meaning between certain word pairs, such as "boy | girl", persist even when they are replaced with other pairs, such as "man | woman" and "bull | cow". Based on this observation, a distinctive feature of meaning can be generalized, denoted as D1. By continuing this analysis, more distinctive features can be identified, such as D2, D3, …, Dn……. The meanings of these distinctive features can also be elucidated: D1 represents "male | female", D2 represents "young | adult", and D3 represents "human | animal".

Hjelmslev divided linguistic components into two planes: "content" and "expression", which are further divided into "form" and "substance" layers. He endorsed Saussure's view that "language is form rather than substance", arguing that linguistics should only study form, i.e., structural relationships. "Form" encompasses both content form and expression form, each with its own minimal elements. The minimal element of content form is semantic features, while the minimal element of expression form is phonemes or phonetic features. The introduction of the contrastive replacement structural analysis into semantic research can be regarded as the earliest germ of the theory of sememe analysis (Hu胡惮, 2014: 16).

2.2.2.2 The Emergence and Development of the Sememe Analysis

The American structuralist also independently developed a similar semantic component analysis, which was initially proposed by the anthropologists Floyd Glenn Lounsbury and Ward Hunt Goodenough as a method for describing and comparing kinship terms in languages. In the 1950s, they examined kinship terms in Indigenous languages, extracting a set of key semantic components that differentiate kinship relationships by analyzing 15 kinship terms. Leech posits that the determination of componential elements is analogous to the application of the complementary principle in phonology when inducting phonemes. If two or more linguistic elements have the same form and do not functionally oppose each other, they are not different components but different varieties of the same constituent (Leech, 1974: 242).

The research conducted by Lounsbury and Goodenough is widely recognized by linguists as the inception of the sememe analysis method. In the early 1960s, American linguists Jerrold Katz and Janet Dean Fodor employed this method to offer semantic features for transformational-generative grammar, which garnered considerable attention from the semantic and grammatical communities of the time (An安华林, 2005a).

The sememe analysis has been highly valued in the linguistic circle since its inception, being incorporated as one of the fundamental methods in modern semantics in Europe and America. It has been rapidly disseminated across linguistic circles worldwide and is widely applied in the study of lexical semantics across various languages. Practical evidence has demonstrated the efficacy of the sememe analysis, not only in its ability to reveal the semantic structure of individual words and provide us with refined means of semantic interpretation, but also in its advantage of illustrating the semantic relationships among words in a vocabulary, which can help us understand and explain various semantic clusters (Liu刘桂芳, 1995).

The concept of "sememe" was first introduced into China by Gao高名凯. In 1963, in his book "On Language", he firstly adopt the terms "plereme" and "sememe". He believed that "the smallest semantic unit in language is called a plereme, and its varieties are called sememes" (Wu伍铁平, 1979). Although this does not correspond to the concept of "sememe" that we commonly use today, it marks the first time that the concept of sememe as a unit of meaning entered the Chinese linguistic study.

The formal introduction of the sememe analysis into China occurred in the 1980s. Jia (1982) explored the program of sememe analysis in Chinese in *On the Issues of the Program of Semantic Component Analysis*. Subsequently, a series of related studies emerged, and Chinese scholars began to widely apply the theory of sememe analysis to Chinese semantics, leading to the gradual rise of sememe analysis in China. After more than 20 years of research, significant progress has been made in the theory of sememe analysis (Hu胡惮, 2014: 45).

2.3 Sememe Analysis

2.3.1 The Procedure and Methodology of Sememe Analysis

Jia贾彦德 (1992: 47) points out that sememe analysis is a type of aggregate analysis. The method of sememe analysis involves identifying how the sememes are contained within different pleremes through the comparison of these pleremes. He proposes four procedures for sememe analysis and further elaborates on the analytical method (Jia贾彦德, 1992: 48–118).

2.3.1.1 Determine the Semantic Field

In the sememe analysis, whether it is for a single plereme or for certain pleremes, it is necessary to conduct comparisons within an appropriate scope, that is, within an appropriate semantic field. Semantic fields are structured hierarchically, and the sememe analysis should commence at the level of the smallest subfield. Failure to do so may result in the oversight of unique differences and commonalities present only within this smallest subfield. Additionally, certain sememes or their variants may not be discernible. Observing pleremes within the smallest semantic field facilitates the segmentation and description of the smallest semantic components. Therefore, a correct analysis should commence from a specific smallest subfield.

2.3.1.2 Make Comparison

By initially defining the semantic field to limit the scope of analysis, sememes are identified through comparison within this field. Subsequently, the structural pattern of a specific plereme, which is formed by a combination of these sememes, is elucidated. There are three methods for comparison:

(1) Present data in tabular form for comparative analysis. Tabular data are convenient for analyzing multiple pleremes within a minimal semantic field; however, the number of sememes contained within these pleremes must be relatively few, and the semantic relationships between the cshould be relatively simple. Otherwise, the table will struggle to clearly represent the complex sememes.
(2) Compare within the context. The context can reveal the meanings of pleremes. By altering the contexts in which pleremes appear, one can examine the similar and different meaning factors between pleremes to determine the complementary distributional relationships among different pleremes, thereby extracting sememes.
(3) Compare with dictionary definitions. By referencing multiple authoritative philological dictionaries, sememes can be extracted from the definitions provided. Through comparison, sememes of nominal pleremes can be extracted,

representing the essential attributes, substance, and categories of things and objects; sememes of adjective pleremes can be extracted, indicating qualities, states, degrees, polarity, imagery, and emotions; and sememes of verbal pleremes can be extracted, representing actions, behaviors, changes, existence, intentions, and movements.

2.3.1.3 Expand the Comparison

The second step of comparison is conducted within the confines of a minimal semantic subfields are sought for further comparative field. After that, the adjacent co-equal subfields are sought for further comparative analysis, with a view to identifying implicit or potentially overlooked sememes. Following the comparison of co-equal subfields, the analysis proceeds to the higher semantic field, and this iterative process continues until the extraction of sememes from the entire semantic field is completed.

2.3.1.4 Verify

When extracting sememes through the above procedures and methods to obtain the plereme structural formulas, it is often inevitable to overlook or make inappropriate judgments. Therefore, necessary verification is a quality assurance measure for the extraction of sememes. There are two approaches to verification:

(1) Contextual verification: Place the pleremes in an appropriate context (including the context of pleremes and sememes). Since a plereme is composed of a set of sememes, statements that indicate whether a particular plereme includes this sememe or that one should be valid. The validity of such statements can then be used to verify whether the sememes derived from a particular plereme are appropriate. This method can only verify the inappropriate sememes but cannot detect the missing ones.
(2) Dictionary definition verification: The sememes obtained through tabular comparison and contextual comparison can be verified by the definitions provided in philological dictionaries. Anyway, as the theories and methods currently employed in compiling dictionaries are rooted in traditional semantics, this has an impact on the definition of terms. Should we identify any shortcomings in the definitions provided by dictionaries, we should critically evaluate and distinguish them. If the verification results show discrepancies between the dictionary's definitions and the corresponding plereme structural formulas, as long as these discrepancies do not indicate any impropriety in the structural formulas, it demonstrates that the patterns are appropriate, and there is no need to accommodate the dictionary.

Since the methods of extracting sememes vary, the verification process should be conducted in an interdisciplinary manner. If the previous analysis of sememe is based on comparisons of dictionary definitions, then further verification using dictionaries would be redundant. In such cases, contextual verification can be employed.

On the basis of Jia's work, other scholars have made some local adjustments according to their respective researches. For instance, some have introduced corpus linguistic methods into the comparison and verification of sememes to quantitatively analyze the results of sememe analysis, aiming to make the outcomes more scientific and rational (Zhou周洋, 2011). On the whole, these methodologies and procedural steps exhibit a high degree of similarity, with only minor distinctions (Hu胡惮, 2014: 46).

2.3.2 The Significance and Value of Sememe Analysis

The theory of sememe analysis has epoch-making significance in the field of linguistics, particularly exerting profound influence on the semantic studies of Chinese. In the era of artificial intelligence, as the requirements for the precision of natural language semantic analysis and computation continue to rise, the theoretical ideas of sememe analysis undoubtedly hold great referential significance for us to reveal and describe the internal micro-symbolic structure of lexical semantics and to construct large-scale lexical semantic knowledge bases oriented towards semantic computation.

2.3.2.1 The Analytic Approach of Atomism

The sememe, as generally defined, is considered the smallest unit of meaning within a word, which indicates the dimensional features of the word within the semantic space.

The pleremes are amenable to an internal atomistic analysis, much like phonemes. The differences in meaning among different pleremes arise due to the differences in their internal constituent elements. These differences in internal constituent elements serve as the signs and characteristics that distinguish one plereme from another (Cao曹炜, 2001: 86). In previous studies, people often treated word meaning as a whole, paying little attention to the micro-structural components within word meaning. Gao高名凯 once mentioned that phonetics and semantics are closely intertwined, interdependent, but this does not prevent us from conducting independent research on semantics and phonetics (Liu刘桂芳, 1995). Traditional Chinese lexical semantic studies, namely the study of exegetics, have always bundled phonetics and semantics together, lacking the concept of distinction and independence. Influenced by this tradition, modern Chinese semantic studies have, for a relatively long time, regarded morphemes as the smallest semantic units. This notion is not conducive to our in-depth examination of the micro-structure within lexical semantics, leading to a description of lexical semantics with an overly coarse granularity.

The proposal of the concept of "sememe" reflects the philosophical thought of "atomism" and marks the shift of research on lexical semantics from macroscopic to microscopic levels. This is essential for the precise semantic computation involved in the processing of natural language by artificial intelligence.

2.3.2.2 Analysis Strategies of the Materialization of Meaning

The sememe analysis materializes the meaning, allowing for a clear revelation of the structure of lexical semantics and a comprehensive description of the feature attributes of words across various dimensions within the semantic space.

Words are the projection of concepts into the linguistic space, serving as the means by which concepts, as units of thought, are symbolized in the material world. A concept possesses multiple-dimensional feature attributes, reflecting the human brain's cognition of objects in the objective world from different levels and perspectives. The words, as the symbolic carrier of concepts, their meanings are composed of different semantic particles that describe these features respectively.

Through sememe analysis, it is possible to unveil the features of concepts across various dimensions, thereby opening up entirely new approaches for semantic computations such as semantic similarity and semantic distance.

2.3.2.3 The Analytical Method of Cluster and Comparison

The sememe analysis employs the method of lexical cluster and comparison to extract and analyse sememes. This approach emphasizes the extraction and analysis of the constituent elements of word meaning by focusing on a group of words or a set of words. It suggests that the meaning of a word becomes more accurate and comprehensive when compared with other related words. Traditional dictionary definitions strive to collect examples within a broad scope, then summarize the meaning of the word based on these examples, without considering the comparison of the meanings of a group of words or a set of words as a necessary condition (Fu符淮青, 1988).

Lexical semantic clustering is a crucial issue in semantic computation, with the results obtained through statistical methods falling short of expectations. However, by conducting semantic clustering computation based on the atomization description of the microstructure of lexical semantics, not only do the algorithms become simpler and more interpretable, but the precision is also effectively enhanced.

2.3.2.4 Descriptive Ability of Lexical Combination Restrictions

The sememe description of lexical semantic structures, not only reveals the regularities of lexical clustering but also, through the comparison of the sememe commonalities between words, uncovers the restrictive conditions for semantic combination.

Formally, linguistic symbols are meaningfully expressed through the linear combination of symbols according to certain rules. From words to phrases, to sentences, and further to paragraphs and essays, this is a process of recursive expansion through linear combinations. The combination of linguistic symbols is not arbitrary; it must adhere to specific grammatical rules and semantic combination constraints. The aggregation and combination of lexical semantics follow a universal axiom: a set of words that can aggregate within a semantic field must share the same semantic components; a set of words that can form a meaningful linear sequence must have compatible semantic components. For instance, one can say "We eat fish for lunch and vegetables for dinner", but one cannot say "We eat a table for lunch and a chair for dinner". Although the grammatical structures of "eat fish", "eat vegetables", "eat a table", and "eat a chair" are the same, in the real world (excluding virtual contexts in fairy tales, myths, etc.), the semantics of "eat a table" and "eat a chair" are not valid. This is because the meanings of "fish" and "vegetables" both contain the sememe of "edible", while the meaning of "eat" includes the sememe "[Swallow][Food]". Therefore, their conceptual meanings are compatible. However, "table" and "chair" do not contain this sememe, and thus, due to semantic combination constraints, they cannot be combined with "eat".

In the field of NLP technology, the analysis of the possibilities of linguistic symbol combinations is primarily conducted by calculating the probabilities of linguistic symbol collocations in large-scale text data, which lacks sufficient linguistic evidence. However, by analyzing the regularities of linear linguistic symbol combinations through the compatibility of semantic components, it is possible to endow semantic computation with linguistic rationality and enhance the interpretability of algorithms. Moreover, through the micro-analysis of the semantic structure components, computers can accurately and efficiently identify incorrect expressions with inappropriate semantic collocations.

2.3.3 Problems and Limitations of the Componential Analysis Method

The theory of sememe analysis is not without its flaws, as the complexity of the semantic system in natural language is not fully captured. During its rapid dissemination, it has faced continuous criticism and skepticism. For instance, the British linguist Lyons raised four critical points: (1) The distinction between sememes and the conceptual meaning of a word is not always clear; the conceptual meaning of one word can serve as a sememe in another, which raises the suspicion of circular argument. (2) Several analyses can be proposed for the same lemma, which contradicts the view that sememes are the smallest units of meaning. (3) The binary approach of affirming or denying the existence of a sememe may not always be effective in explaining the meaning of some words. (4) The sememes that constitute the meaning of a word are not an unstructured sequence (Ye叶斌 & Xie谢国剑, 2007).

The theoretical and methodological approaches of sememe analysis can provide references for the computational processing of semantics; however, they are not inherently designed for semantic computation. As a human-oriented linguistic study, it cannot avoid the numerous confusions caused by the inherent characteristics of natural language, such as ambiguity, redundancy, ellipsis, metaphor, and context dependence. From the perspective of symbolic intelligence, the primary challenge in achieving the computational processing of natural language is the formal description of symbols. The intrinsic connotativeness, ambiguity, and interactivity of natural language semantics pose significant difficulties for its formalization, with the symbolization and formalization of semantics being particularly challenging. From this perspective, we analyze the problems existing in the sememe analysis method in a meticulous and systematic manner, aiming to capitalize on its strengths and circumvent its weaknesses.

2.3.3.1 The Definition of Sememes Is Not Unified

Symbols in a symbolic system should possess simplicity and certainty. The nature and meaning of each symbol should be free from ambiguity, and the compositional structure of symbols can be modeled. However, in the sememe analysis, there is a significant divergence in the identification of the properties of sememes as basic semantic symbols. Zhou周一民 (1995) categorizes sememes into: explicit and implicit sememes, categorical and feature sememes, central and modifying sememes, dominant and subordinate sememes, aggregative and combinational sememes, identical and distinguishing components, fixed and temporary components, and so on. Wang王宁 (1996: 210) divides sememes into type sememes, external sememes, and core components. Liu刘道英 (2002) suggests distinguishing rational sememes from additional sememes. Zhang张双棣et al. (2002: 134) propose the concepts of reference sememes (core sememes), distinguishing sememes (restrictive sememes), and inherited sememes. Su苏宝荣 (2000: 209) introduces the concepts of explicit sememes (real sememes) and implicit sememes (virtual sememes). Wang王军 (2005: 154–161) similarly proposes the concept of implicit sememes, and mainly categorizes sememes into conventional and implicit sememes, as well as marked and unmarked sememes, with marked sememes further divided into real marked sememes, deficiently unmarked sememes, virtually marked sememes, and incorrectly marked sememes. Liu刘桂芳 (2006) divides sememes into lexical and grammatical sememes, with lexical sememes further divided into rational and colored sememes, rational sememes into conceptual and additionanl sememes, and colored sememes into affective, figurative, and stylistic sememes. Zhang张廷远 (2007) mainly categorizes sememes into rational and implicit sememes. Cao曹炜 (2001: 88) believes that sememes can be divided into three major categories: scope sememes, feature sememes, and restriction sememes. The lack of an overall, roughly unified philosophical thought in these different classifications of the nature of sememes leads to a variety of descriptive frameworks in the analysis sememes, making it difficult to convert the analysis results into computable formal descriptions. Additionally, different scholars lack a unified descriptive framework for the internal composite structures of sememes within words, failing to provide standard and universal models of sememe structures, which makes it challenging to achieve formal processing of data.

2.3.3.2 The Extraction of Sememes Is Subjective and Arbitrary

The symbol system requires standardization, objectivity, and stability, whereas sememe analysis is characterized by a significant degree of subjectivity and arbitrariness, lacking unified standards and operational procedures, which makes it difficult to ensure consistency within the system. Analyses of the same word by different schloars may produce results that vary significantly in terms of their interpretations or findings. For example:

父亲: +[有子女]+[成年]+男人].
Father: + [Having children] + [Adulthood] + [Man] (Xu徐思益, 1984)
父亲: +[男性]+[直系亲属]+[长辈].
Father: + [Male] + [Direct Relative] + [Senior] (Wang王德春, 1983: 143)
父亲: [+人+男性+亲属+直系+长辈].
Father: [+Person + Male + Kinship + Direct Line + Senior] (Cen岑运强, 1994)
父亲: (亲属) → (生育关系)+(男性)
Father:
(Kinship) → (Parental relationship) + (Male) (Jia贾彦德, 1992: 98)

This phenomenon is attributed to the differing perspectives on semantic cognition among various analysts. In the interpretation of the semantic components of the word "father", Xu focuses on the presence or absence of offspring, Wang emphasizes the proximity of kinship relationships and generational hierarchy, while Jia focuses on the relationships between individuals. For NLP, this subjectivity, arbitrariness, and instability can lead to confusion in semantic computation programs.

2.3.3.3 The Number of Sememes Is Uncontrolled

The symbol set adopted by the symbol system should possess finiteness and controllability, whereas the sememe set utilized in sememe analysis is open-ended, rendering its quantity uncontrollable. In fact, we cannot even precisely assert the existence of a sememes set that is available for analysis.

The purpose of sememe analysis originally lies in expressing an infinite range of word meanings with a limited set of sememes. Therefore we firstly need to identify a relatively fixed set of sememes to analyze the meanings of the entire lexical system. However, this issue presents two challenges:

(1) There is no definitive answer to how many sememes are needed in a language to fully describe its entire semantic system, as many views are merely assumptions that have not been empirically tested.

(1) For instance, Wang王德春 (1983: 97) proposed that "the number of sememes in a language is generally around a thousand, with common sememes not exceeding two hundred". Yang杨升初 (1982) argued that "the Contemporary Chinese Dictionary contains a total of over 53,000 entries, excluding single characters, idioms, and colloquialisms, the number of compound words is no more than 30,000. Therefore, if the meaning structures of 50,000 compound words can be described, it would be sufficient. The characters that make up these 50,000 compound words amount to only 4,800, so the number of morphemes should not exceed this figure. To leave room for error, if we assume that each morpheme contains an average of nine sememes, the calculated number of sememes would be no more than 40,000. Therefore, considering the number of morphemes involved, sememe analysis of morpheme meanings is feasible and can be considered cost-effective in terms of analytical effort." The discrepancy in the estimated number of sememes between these two views is as vast as heaven and earth. Many people hold a pessimistic view, believing that it is very difficult, if not impossible, to obtain this set of sememes.

(2) Unrestricted extraction of sememes may result in an unmanageable surge in the total count of semantic features. Although most scholars agree with the fundamental assertion that "sememes are the smallest units of meaning", this is far from the case in the actual process of analysis, and there is no strict adherence to this definition. For instance, in the above examples, "having children", "adulthood", "man", "male", "direct relative", "senior", "kinship", and "parental relationship" are not the smallest semantic components, as they can be further decomposed. It is a common occurrence to arbitrarily identify sememes in many work or paper discussing the sememe analysis. If the extraction of sememes follows this methodology, the resultant set of sememes is inherently open-ended, with its quantity being essentially unregulatable. Consequently, the establishment of such a set of sememes becomes unfeasible. Moreover, in the analysis process, the issue of words being interdependent as sememes and circular argument is prevalent.

2.3.3.4 Analysis of the Relationships Between Semantic Components Is Monolithic

The combinations of symbols within the symbol system exhibit a multiplicity of logical properties and computability, rather than being confined to a singular logical "AND" operation. The sememe analysis is generally quite monolithic in its understanding of semantic relationships, failing to differentiate the primary and secondary positions of semantic components within the structure of word meanings, and neglecting the different natures of semantic components and their complex logical relationships with each other.

In the current practice of semantic analysis, two primary methods are employed to represent semantic structures: one-dimensional structural expressions and two-dimensional sememe matrices. For example, the terms "gege哥哥(elder brother)", "jiejie姐姐(elder sister)", "didi弟弟(younger brother)" and "meimei妹妹(younger sister)" can be represented in terms of sememe structural formula as follows (Zhang 张万有, 2001):

哥哥:	[男性、年长、同胞、亲属]或者[+男性 → 年长 ↔ 同胞+亲属].
Elder brother:	[Male, Elder, Sibship, Relative] or [+Male → Elder ↔ Sibship + Relative]
姐姐:	[女性、年长、同胞、亲属]或者[-男性 → 年长 ↔ 同胞+亲属].
Elder sister:	[Female, Elder, Sibship, Relative] or [-Male → Elder ↔ Sibship + Relative]
弟弟:	[男性、年幼、同胞、亲属]或者[+男性 ← 年长 ↔ 同胞+亲属].
Younger brother:	[Male, Young, Sibship, Relative] or [+Male ← Elder ↔ Sibship + Relative]
妹妹:	[女性、年幼、同胞、亲属]或者[-男性 ← 年长 ↔ 同胞+亲属].
Younger sister:	[Female, Young, Sibship, Relative] or [-Male ← Older ↔ Sibship + Relative]

They can also be represented by a sememe matrix, as shown in Table 2.1.

Regardless of the method, the primary means of indicating whether a word possesses a certain sememe or not is through the use of binary (+ or –) notation, sometimes may be supplemented by other symbols to explain the nature, state, or trend of change in the state of certain sememes. However, there is a deficiency in the description of the relationships among sememes and the role of each sememe within the comprehensive semantic structure. Following this approach, each sememe is considered to be in a parallel relationship, which is not the case in reality. For instance, the semantic components "relative" and "sibship" are, in fact, the attributes and values of a word in a certain dimension of the semantic space, representing a functional relationship. "Relative" is an attribute function *f(x)*, where the variable x has several possible values, and "sibship" is just one specific value of x, which

Table 2.1 Sememe matrix

Sememe / Plereme	Male	Elder	Sibship	Relative
哥哥	+	+	+	+
姐姐	–	+	+	+
弟弟	+		+	+
妹妹			+	+

can also take on values such as "eldership", "descendant", or "in-laws". Moreover, for the majority of words, the roles of the semantic components are not identical; some components are central, while others are subordinate, differing in their levels of weights. The sememe analysis failes to distinguish between them, which is disadvantageous for assigning specific weights to individual semantic components in semantic computation.

2.3.3.5 The Description of Lexical Semantics Lacks Universality

The symbol system, as the discipline's metalanguage, exhibits a broad applicability, intended to be suitable for all objects encountered. The sememe analysis avoids the description of abstract concepts and is limited to a small subset of nouns, verbs, and adjectives with relatively clear connotations and extensions. At the inception of the sememe analysis, its research objects were some semantic fields with strong systematicity and strictly arranged internal pleremes, such as the semantic field of kinship terms studied by American anthropologists and the semantic field of military ranks in Chinese studied by Jia. Jia贾彦德 (1992: 47) explicitly pointed out that the sememe analysis is only applicable to content words and does not study function words. It is well known that although the number of function words is not as numerous as that of content words, they are an essential part of the linguistic symbol system. The absence of the description of this part can lead to many issues in semantic computation.

In summary, the sememe analysis, as an innovative endeavor in linguistic research that focuses on the analysis and description of the internal microstructure of lexical semantics, represents a significant milestone in the development of semantics. Although the sememe analysis does encounter certain problems, by addressing these problems and researching reasonable solutions, the atomicist philosophy it upholds and the comparative analytical method it employs undoubtedly provide us with beneficial insights for constructing resources for artificial intelligence-based semantic computation. Sememe analysis, despite its own limitations, offers valuable perspectives. By addressing the challenges it presents with well-researched solutions, the atomistic philosophy and the comparative analytical method it employs have the potential to significantly contribute to the development of resources for artificial intelligence-driven word meaning computation.

2.4 Computational Attributes of Lexical Semantics as the Processing Object of Symbolic Intelligence

2.4.1 Feature Dimensions of the Lexical Semantic Space

In the first chapter, we addressed the issue of simulating human language intelligence through computers. It is important to note that this simulation does not encompass a comprehensive replication of the thinking process by language; rather, it focuses on mimicking the outcomes of such processes. Specifically, it is not a full-scale simulation of the cognitive mechanisms underlying language, but rather an approximation of the final results. The process of processing natural language by the human brain and machines is actually fundamentally different. This characteristic determines that natural language research oriented towards machines requires different theories and methods from that oriented towards humans. The latter demands that the description of linguistic facts should meet the needs of machine computation. From this perspective, we need to observe, define, and describe lexical semantics with a new perspective.

2.4.1.1 The Meaning of a Word Is a Collection of Features Across Various Dimensions Within the Semantic Space

When we discuss the types and nature of word meaning, as well as the analysis of semantic components, it in essence, involves the exploration of the multiple-dimensional features that words manifest in the semantic realm.

Any entity possesses an infinite number of feature dimensions, including both distinctive and non-distinctive features. The semantics of words are no exception. Therefore, the various theories of semantic classification, which scholars have observed and extracted from different perspectives, represent certain aspects of the features of lexical semantics and are of referential value to our research.

For lexical semantic analysis, it is necessary to address four key questions:

(1) How many pleremes can the meaning of a word be divided into?
(2) How many dimensions can a plereme be divided into?
(3) Which aspect of semantic features does each dimension represents?
(4) What are the specific semantic features of each dimension?

Each plereme of a word is an individual analytical object, forming a relatively independent multi-dimensional semantic space. This can be simply illustrated as follows (Fig. 2.1).

Let's analyze several terms following this method (based on the interpretation in *The Contemporary Chinese Dictionary (7th Edition) definitions*):

[Dog]: The dog is a mammal with a keen sense of smell and hearing, characterized by a long and thin tongue that aids in heat dissipation. Its fur

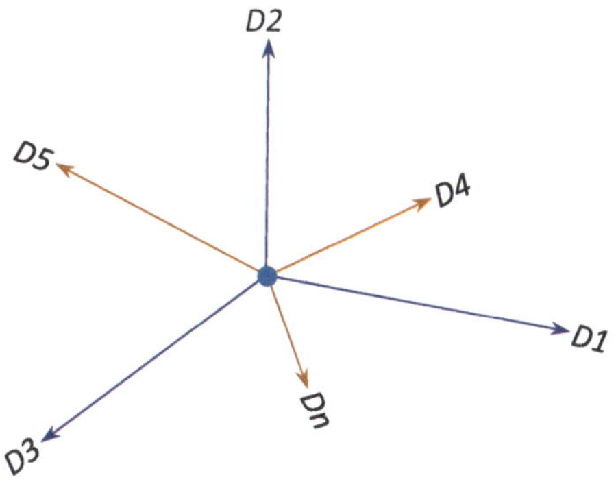

Fig. 2.1 Semantic feature dimension of plereme

comes in various colors such as yellow, white, and black. It is one of the earliest domesticated animals by humans, with a wide variety of breeds. Some can be trained as police dogs, while others are used for hunting, herding, and other purposes. It is also known as the canine.

[Cat]: The cat is a mammal with a slightly rounded face, a long body, small ears, large eyes, and pupil sizes that change with the intensity of light. Its limbs are relatively short, with padded paws, and it is agile in movement, skilled in jumping, and capable of catching mice. The fur is soft and comes in colors such as black, white, yellow, and gray-brown. To crouch; to crouch down. Refers to idling or hiding: mao dong猫冬 (hiding at home for the winter) | mao zai jia猫在家 (hiding at home for the winter).[1]

[Crow]: A bird characterized by a large and straight beak, is predominantly black in plumage with a green sheen on its wings. It tends to form flocks in forests or fields, feeding on grains, fruits, and insects. In some regions, it is referred to as "laogua老鸹" or "lao ya老鸦".

[Flamingo]: A bird resembling a crane in appearance, features a curved beak, a long neck, and white feathers with a faint reddish hue. Its toes are webbed. It feeds on fish, clams, insects, and aquatic plants. They are predominantly found along the Mediterranean coast.

The analysis is as follows:

[Dog]: D1. Categorical Feature Dimension: Mammal.
D2. Physical Feature Dimension (Individualization): Long and thin tongue and tongue can dissipate heat.
D3. Physical Feature Dimension (Color): Yellow or white or black.
D4. Ability Feature Dimension: Olfactory acuity and auditory acuity.
D5. Functional Feature Dimension: Hunting or shepherding or for police use.
D6. Alias Feature Dimension: Canine.

[1] Here we initially focus on the first plereme.

[Cat]: D1. Categorical Feature Dimension: Mammal.
D2. Physical Feature Dimension (Individualization): Round face and long trunk and short limbs and small ears and large eyes and variable pupil size (condition: light intensity) and padded paws and soft fur.
D3. Physical Feature Dimension (Color): Yellow or white or black or gray-brown.
D4. Ability Feature Dimension: Agility in movement and proficiency in Jumping.
D5. Functional Feature Dimension: Mice capture.

[Crow]: D1. Categorical Feature Dimension: Bird.
D2. Physical Feature Dimension (Individualization): Large and straight beak and wings with a green sheen.
D3. Physical Feature Dimension (Color): Black.
D4. Habitat Feature Dimension: Forests or fields.
D5. Food Feature Dimension: Grains and fruits and insects.
D6. Alias Feature Dimension: "lao gua老鸹" or "lao ya老鸦".

[Flamingo]: D1. Categorical Feature Dimension: Bird.
D2. Physical Feature Dimension (Individualization): Appearance resembling a crane and curved beak and long neck and webbed toes.
D3. Physical Feature Dimension (Color): Pink or red.
D4. Habitat Feature Dimension: Mediterranean coastal regions.
D5. Residing Habit Feature Dimension: Group living Characteristics.
D6. Food Characteristic Dimensions: Fishand clams and insects and aquatic plants.

This is a semantic description of dimensions for pleremes according to the dictionary definitions. It can be observed that dictionaries focus on different dimensions for different types of words. For instance, the definitions of "cat" and "dog" include dimensions of functional features, while those of "crow" and "flamingo" encompass dimensions of habitat and food. In the subsequent chapters, we will delve into the specific semantic analysis dimensions and patterns associated with various word classes.

2.4.1.2 The Selection and Weighting of Semantic Dimensions

The definitions provided by authoritative dictionaries serve as the primary basis for our analysis, yet they do not necessarily have to be followed slavishly. The selection of dictionary definitions can be guided by the following two scenarios:

(1) In some respects, the definitions do not possess distinctive features for the majority of similar words. For instance, the concept of biodiversity determines that many animals encompass numerous subspecies. Whether it be "cat", "dog", "crow", or "flamingo", the number of species they include is substantial. However, only the definition of "dog" in the dictionary includes the component

"many species". We believe that this component is not a distinctive feature of "dog", and thus, it is not adopted.

(2) The meaning of words can change with the evolution of society, thus necessitating continuous revision of dictionary definitions. For instance, the definition of "dog" includes the phrase "the earliest domesticated animal by humans". On April 8, 2020, the Ministry of Agriculture and Rural Affairs of the People's Republic of China issued a notice for public comments on the *Catalogue of National Genetic Resources for Livestock and Poultry*. The explanatory attachment to this notice states, "With the advancement of human civilization and the increasing attention and preference for animal protection by the public, dogs have been transformed from traditional domestic animals into companion animals. They are generally not considered livestock internationally, and it is not appropriate for China to classify them as livestock." Therefore, in the semantic description of the word "dog", we have abandoned the related explanations concerning "livestock".

The distinguishing features and non-distinguishing features of word meanings are relative, as is the case with other phenomena. For instance, when comparing "cat" and "bird", "mammal" serves as a distinctive feature, whereas when comparing "cat" and "dog", it becomes a non-distinctive feature. Similarly, "color" is a distinctive feature when comparing "crow" and "flamingo", but not when comparing "crow" and "magpie". Distinctive features carry greater weights, yet it is not advisable to directly assign weights to each feature during analysis. Instead, we should differentiate between different feature dimensions. In specific computational applications, the assignment of weights should be determined based on the purpose and domain of the application.

In the actual process of human language use, the meaning of a word is treated as a general and vague holistic object, without being decomposed into different features. However, for computers, it is necessary to describe the various features of word meaning as comprehensively as possible to accommodate different application scenarios.

Although features are infinite, there is a necessity for selection in their description and application. Even if a comprehensive description of words in the lexical database serving as a computational resource is provided to meet the application requirements of various computational scenarios, it is not feasible to utilize all of them in practical computational applications. This is because in machine learning algorithms, features of data are generally represented as dimensions in a vector space. As the number of dimensions increases, the computational complexity grows exponentially, leading to the "Curse of Dimensionality", where an excessive number of dimensions can introduce data noise, affect the fitting performance, and diminish the generalization ability of the computational model. Therefore, dimensionality reduction is required. In specific computational contexts, different dimensions of the data carry varying weights, with higher-weighted dimensions being prioritized for application.

2.4.2 Functional Representation of the Semantic Feature Dimensions

From the perspective of symbolic computation, we can propose new definitions for lexical semantics and its types.

The different components of meaning represent a feature function of a word at a certain dimension in the semantic space, which can be represented as $f(x)$. Any feature is composed of a feature attribute and a feature value, for instance, the black feature of "crow" and the red feature of "flamingo" belong to the same attribute, namely the "color" attribute, with the feature values being "black" and "red", respectively.

In this context, the function f represents a specific attribute dimension of feature properties, with x being the variable of the function, which can take on different values. For instance, the semantic function C (black) denotes the color feature of "crow", while C (red) represents the color feature of "flamingo". Different semantic functions have varying types of values for the *variable x*. Some are single data, others are arrays, and still others are logical expressions. For example, in the color function C, the semantic color function variable x for "crow" and "flamingo" is a single value ("black" and "red"). However, the color attribute of "silver ring snake" is "black and white mixed", so its value for variable x is a logical expression (black∧white). The meaning of the word "bi笔(pen)" includes "used for writing and drawing", indicating its functional aspect. This aspect is referred to as the "functional dimension" and can be represented by the function F, and the variable x is an array (writing, drawing), so the entire function is represented as: F (writing, drawing).

The semantics of a word is characterized by a complex set of features, often involving multiple dimensions. Consequently, we can further define the semantics of a word as a collection of feature functions across various dimensions within the semantic space, which can be represented by an equation: $S = \{f1, f2, f3, \ldots fn\}$. This is merely a rough model; in reality, the features of a word are not always simply combined. In many cases, there exist various semantic logical relationships among these features, which also require description. Moreover, different word classes exhibit different patterns of semantic structure. Therefore, the word meaning equation may have several varieties.

It is important to clarify that, adopting the perspective of semantic feature dimensions, the construction of word meanings and the representation of their constituent elements are modeled as functions. This approach to knowledge representation exhibits a finer granularity compared to traditional linguistic research on word meaning types. Some semantic types can be represented by a single function, such as color meaning and stylistic connotations. However, some meaning types encompass multiple feature dimensions, such as conceptual meaning, cultural meaning, and associative meaning, which necessitate decomposition into multiple functions. This book does not confine itself to any single theory of lexical semantics. Instead, it draws on a variety of perspectives, synthesizing the viewpoints of various scholars in the field, and endeavors to comprehensively summarize the feature dimensions of lexical semantics.

References

An, H. 安华林 (2005a). *Research on Definition Primitives of Modern Chinese 现代汉语释义基元词研究*. China Social Sciences Press.

An, H. 安华林. (2005b). Forming of Metalanguage Theory and Linguistics Metalanguage View 元语言理论的形成和语言学的元语言观.*Inner Mongolia Social Sciences内蒙古社会科学, 26*(1), 104–108.

Cao, W. 曹炜. (2001). *Lexical Semantics of Modern Chinese 现代汉语词义学*. Xuelin Press.

Cen,Y. 岑运强.(1994).Further Exploration on Semantic Fields and Sememe Analysis 语义场和义素分析再探.Foreign Languages In Fujian福建外语 (Z2), 1–7.

Fu, H. 符淮青. (1988). Componential Analysis and Lexical Definition 构成成分分析和词的释义. *Lexicography Research辞书研究* (1), 48–55.

Fu, H. 符淮青. (1996). *Analysis and Description of Lexical Meaning 词义的分析和描写*. Language & Culture Press.

Fu, H. 符淮青. (2002). Symbolic Meaning: Its Nature and Definition 指号义的性质和释义. *Lexicographical Studies 辞书研究* (5), 1–10.

Gao, S. 高圣林. (2000). The Deconstruction of Linguistic Forms and the Emergence of Semantics—One of the Structural Patterns of Humor 语形的解构与语义的隐现——幽默的结构模式之一. *Contemporary Rhetoric 修辞学习* (Z1), 16–18.

Ge, B. 葛本仪. (2001). *Lexicology of Modern Chinese 现代汉语词汇学*. Shandong People's Publishing House.

Grice, H. P. (1957). Meaning. *Philosophical Review, 66*(3), 377–388.

Grice, H. P. (1968). Utterer's Meaning, Sentence-Meaning, and Word-Meaning. *Foundations of Language, 4*(3), 225–242.

Grice, H. P. (1969). Utterer's Meaning and Intentions. *Philosophical Review, 78*(2), 147–177.

Hu, D. 胡惮. (2014). *Research on Modern Chinese Lexical Primitives for Natural Language Processing 面向自然语言处理的现代汉语词义基元结构研究*. World Publishing Corporation.

Jia, Y. 贾彦德. (1982). On the Issues of the Program of Semantic Component Analysis 语义成分分析法的程序问题. *Journal of Xinjiang University (Philosophy and Social Sciences) 新疆大学学报(哲学社会科学版)*, (03),63–69.

Jia, Y. 贾彦德. (1992). *Chinese Semantics 汉语语义学*. Peking University Press.

Kittay, E. F. (1987). *Metaphor: Its Cognitive Force and Linguistic Structure*. Oxford University Press.

Leech, G. (1974). *Semantics: The Study of Meaning*. Penguin Books.

Liu, D. 刘道英. (2002). Several Thoughts on the Theory of Morpheme in the Cognizance 谈义素理论认知上的几个问题. *Journal of Qinghai Nationalities Institute (Social Sciences) 青海民族学院学报* (3), 100–103.

Liu, G. 刘桂芳. (1995). A Brief Discussion on Sememe Analysis 义素分析略说. *Journal of Shanxi Normal University (Social Sciences) 山西师大学报(社会科学版)* (2), 96–98.

Liu, G. 刘桂芳. (2006). My Opinions on Types of Sememe and Its Analysis 义素类型及分析之我见. *Academic Exchange学术交流* (12), 141–143.

Lü, S. 吕叔湘. (1981). *Preface to the Concise Thesaurus 简明同义词词典.序》*. Shanghai Lexicographical Publishing House.

Lyons, J. (1968). *Introduction to Theoretical Linguistic*. Cambridge University Press.

Lyons, J. (1977). *Semantics*. Cambridge University Press.

Shi, A., 石安石 & Zhan, R. 詹人凤. (1988). *Introduction to Linguistics 语言学概论*. Higher Education Press.

Su, B. 苏宝荣. (2000). *A Study on Lexical Semantics and Lexicographical Interpretation 词义研究与辞书释义*. The Commercial Press.

Tian, M. 田明明. (2016). On the Impact of Cognitive Levels in Different Eras on Lexical Meaning through the Development of Terminological Semantics 从术语义的发展演变看不同时代人

们的认知水平对词义的影响. *Modern Chinese Language (Language Research)* 现代语文(语言研究) (9), 38–39, 40.
Wang, D. 王德春. (1983). *Studies on Lexicology* 词汇学研究. Shandong Education Press.
Wang, J. 王军. (2005). *Research on the Semantic System of Chinese Words* 汉语词义系统研究. Shandong People's Publishing House.
Wang, N. 王宁. (1996). *Principles of Chinese Exegetics* 训诂学原理. China International Broadcasting Press.
Wu, T. 伍铁平. (1979). A Review of the Etic and Emic Theory in Gao Mingkai's *On Language* 评高名凯《语言论》中的位素理论. *Language Teaching and Linguistic Studies*语言教学与研究 (2), 135–151.
Xing, F. 邢福义 & Wu, Z. 吴振国. (2002). *Introduction to Linguistics* 语言学概论. Central China Normal University Press.
Xu, S. 徐思益. (1984). On the Semantic Structure of Sentences 论句子的语义结构. *Journal of Xinjiang University (Philosophy and Social Sciences)* 新疆大学学报(哲学社会科学版) (1), 96–105.
Xu, L. 徐烈炯. (1995). *Semantics* 语义学(修订本). The Education Press.
Yang, S. 杨升初. (1982). Issues in the Sememe Analysis of Modern Chinese 现代汉语的义素分析问题. *Journal of Xiangtan University (Philosophy and Social Sciences)* 湘潭大学学报(哲学社会科学版) (3), 49–57+93.
Ye, B. 叶斌 & Xie, G 谢国剑. (2007). The Summary of Domestic "Sememe Theory" in Recent Twenty Years 20多年来国内义素论综述. *Journal of Hangzhou Teachers College (Social Sciences Edition)* 杭州师范学院学报(社会科学版), *29*(5).
Ye, F. 叶蜚声 & Xu, T. 徐通锵. (1993). *Outline of Linguistics(3rd Edition)* 语言学纲要第3版. Peking University Press.
Zhan, R. 詹人凤. (1997). *Semantics of Modern Chinese* 现代汉语语义学. The Commercial Press.
Zhang, S., 张双棣, Zhang, L., 张联荣, Song, S.宋绍年, et al. (2002). *A Course in Ancient Chinese Language Knowledge* 古代汉语知识教程. Peking University Press.
Zhang, T. 张廷远. (2007). An analysis of the Implied Semantic Components and Their Pragmatic Value 隐含义素的剖析及其语用价值. *Chinese Linguistics*汉语学报 (3), 44–52+96.
Zhang, Z. 张志毅 & Zhang, Q. 张庆云. (2001). *Lexical Semantics* 词汇语义学. The Commercial Press.
Zhang, W. 张万有. (2001). A Brief Talk About Semantic Analysis 义素分析略说. *Language Teaching and Linguistic Studies*语言教学与研究 (1), 61–65.
Zhou, Y. 周洋. (2011). A Review of Semantic Feature Analysis 义素分析法评述. *Journal of Hotan Teachers College*和田师范专科学校学报, *30*(4), 65–67.
Zhou, Y. 周一民. (1995). Types of Sememes and Their Analysis 义素的类型及其分析. *Chinese Language Learning*汉语学习, (6), 34-36.
Zhou, Z. 周祖谟. (1959). *Lectures on Chinese Lexicology* 汉语词汇讲话. People's Education Press.

Chapter 3
Semantic Gene and Metalanguage System for Semantic Computation and Description

3.1 The Metalanguage Thought in Semantic Research

In linguistics, research that seeks to analyze the meaning of lexical systems and even the entire language system using controllable linguistic units, in addition to the sememe analysis of structuralist school, the cognitive linguistics and the semantic primitive research in lexicography belong to the metalinguistic research in linguistics. In the field of linguistics, studies aiming to analyze the meanings of lexical systems, and even the entire linguistic system by using manageable linguistic units encompass more than just sememe analysis of the structuralist school. They also involve the investigation of semantic primitives within the domains of cognitive linguistics and lexicography. They are all part of the metalanguage studies within linguistics.

3.1.1 The Theory of Metalanguage in Language Studies

The concept of metalanguage originates from modern logic philosophy and has been a significant keyword in the humanities and social sciences since the early twentieth century. It has garnered extensive attention in the fields of philosophy, logic, linguistics, literature, art studies, and artificial intelligence research.

In the *Dictionary of Philosophy* it is defined as: "Metalanguage is the language used to study and describe the object language. It is relative to object language. The object language is the language used to discuss the nature and interrelations of external objects, its vocabulary mainly including the names of external objects and predicates referring to the nature and relations of external objects, which constitutes the first-level language. The metalanguage is the language used to discuss the object language, its vocabulary including the names of the object language and predicates referring to the nature of the object (such as 'true' or 'false'), which is at a higher level than the object language" (Feng 冯契, 2001: 1879).

D. Hu, *Lexical Semantic Gene Structure of Modern Chinese*,
https://doi.org/10.1007/978-981-96-6425-2_3

In the discourse of philosophers and logicians when exploring metalanguage, it is inevitable to mention the natural language itself. Natural language is a primary research object shared by philosophy, logic, and linguistics. The concept of metalanguage was proposed as a solution to the dilemmas encountered by philosophers and logicians when using natural language as a tool to discuss philosophical and logical issues related to language. The metalanguage theory has been inherently intertwined with natural language from its nascent stages, evolving in parallel and in contrast to natural language. Influenced by philosophy and logic, linguistic studies inevitably focus on the theory of metalanguage.

The definition of metalanguage cited in the aforementioned *Dictionary of Philosophy* also discusses the metalanguage in linguistic research: "When studying the formal structure of language and proving the grammatical validity in logical calculus, the grammatical metalanguage is employed; whereas, when studying the meaning or interpretation of language, the semantic metalanguage is utilized." (Feng 冯契, 2001: 1879).

Numerous linguistic dictionaries also include the term "metalanguage", such as:

> In *Dictionary of language and linguistics*: METALANGUAGE: The language or set of symbols which is used to analyse and describe another language (the observed or → object language), e.g. the words which paraphrase another word or the native language in foreign language teaching. Alternative term: second-order language. (Hartmann & Stork, 1972: 140)

In *Longman Dictionary of Language Teaching and Applied Linguistics (4th Edition)*: Meta-language: the language used to analyze or describe a language. For example, the sentence:

> *In English, the phoneme /b/ is a voiced bilabial stop* is in metalanguage. It explains that the b-sound in English is made with vibration of the vocal cords and with the two lips stopping the airstream from the lungs. (Richards & Schmidt, 2010: 361)

In *Routledge dictionary of language and linguistics*:

> Metalanguage:Second-level language (also called language of description) by which natural language (object language) is described. (Bussmann, 1996: 742)

In *A Dictionary of Linguistics and Phonetics (6th Edition)*:

> Metalanguage: linguistics, as other sciences, uses this term in the sense of a higher-level language for describing an object of study (or 'object language') – in this case the object of study is itself language, viz. the various language samples, intuitions, etc., which constitute our linguistic experience. (Crystal, 2008: 302)

There are also other various specialized linguistic dictionaries that offer definitions of metalanguage, which are generally similar in nature, and it is not necessary to list them one by one.

The metalanguage employed in linguistic research can be categorized into four main types.

3.1.1.1 The Natural Language Itself

This scenario is commonly encountered in the context of bilingual dictionary compilation. Within bilingual dictionaries, we employ Language A to explain Language B, where Language A serves as the metalanguage and Language B as the object language. In this instance, the Language A used, most of the time, is a natural language.

3.1.1.2 The Blending of Natural Language and Metalanguage

This type is most prevalent and is primarily used in linguistic research and the compilation of dictionaries. This blended form of language employs the grammatical structures of natural language, but it extensively incorporates linguistic terminology, which constitutes the professional metalanguage of linguistics. For instance, terms such as "phoneme", "syllable", "root", "stem", "affix", "monomorphemic word", "compound word", "noun", "verb", "adjective", "subject", "predicate", "object", "simple sentence", "complex sentence", "plereme", "sememe", "agent", "patient", "valency", "dependency", and so on. These terms are generally used in linguistic research and language teaching, and are rarely employed in other communication contexts. There is also another category of terms that are directly borrowed from the general vocabulary of a natural language, such as "negation", "affirmation", "imperative", "disjunction", "category", "focus" etc. These terms carry specific disciplinary connotations within linguistics and also belong to the commonly used professional metalanguage of linguistics. In dictionary compilation, abbreviations are also often used to represent these terms, such as adj. (adjective), v. (verb), prep. (preposition), n. (noun), and other abbreviation symbols, which are also part of the metalanguage of lexicography.

Some scholars have also cited specific symbols in addition to the abbreviations. For instance, in sememe analysis, symbols such as "[](indicating the boundary of a sememe)", " $+$ (indicating that a plereme possesses a certain sememe)", and " $-$ (indicating that a plereme does not possess a certain sememe)" are commonly used. Furthermore, Jia has created a set of analytical symbols, including "x (indicating action, behavior, movement, or change)", "fa (indicating manner)", and "$\uparrow$, $\downarrow$ (indicating that the differences of the objects they refer to are comparative in nature, with $\uparrow$ tending towards stronger and $\downarrow$ towards weaker)", and " $\rightarrow$ (indicating the tendency or the direction of behavior or action)".

3.1.1.3 The Direct Borrowing of the Metalanguage System from Mathematics and Logic

This scenario is commonly employed in the fields of mathematical linguistics, quantitative linguistics, formal syntax, and logical semantics. Unlike the metalanguages of types I) and II), the meta-language systems of mathematics and logic are artificial languages, possessing their own unique, grammatical and lexical systems that are fundamentally different from those of natural languages. For example:

The description of syntactic rules in formal syntax. A fundamental Chinese sentence can be described by the following rules:

① S → NP + VP
② NP → N
③ VP → V + NP
④ N → {cow, grass, water……}
⑤ V → {eat, drink, buy……}"

Among them, S represents a sentence, NP represents a noun phrase, VP represents a verb phrase, N represents a noun, and V represents a verb (Shi 石定栩, 2002: 17).

The description of sentence meaning in formal semantics, for example:

A. A dog runs.
B. Every dog runs.

Their semantics can be described as:

A'. ∃ u[dog'*(u)∧run'*(u)] (the existence of a dog that is running)
B'. ∀u[dog'*(u)→run'*(u)] (all dogs run) (Zhang 张韧弦 & Liu 刘乃实, 2004)

Under the influence of linguistic philosophy and philosophy of logic, and in line with the needs of linguistic research, linguists have also conducted multi-perspective studies on metalanguage. However, in the linguistic circle, scholars have not yet developmed their distinct metalanguage framework. Some scholars have pointed out that "since Tarski and Carnap introduced the concept of metalanguage, it has always served as a handmaid of logic and philosophy. Although the linguistics has borrowed the concept of metalanguage, it has not broken free from the confines of logic. It has neither conducted an independent systematic study of metalanguage from the perspective of linguistics, nor seriously discussed the systematic construction of metalanguage from the height of discipline construction, resulting in mere echoing of others (An安华林, 2005b)." Being conscious of this issue, scholars have attempted to build a metalanguage system for linguistics from the perspective of the discipline. For instance, Li 李葆嘉 (2002) pointed out: "Exploring metalanguage from the perspective of linguistics will inevitably differentiate between logical metalanguage and linguistic metalanguage. The metalanguage of linguistics is an interpretive symbolic system of the object language, which can be either a language system or a part of the linguistic symbols within the same system. Depending on the language level and application function, there exist three types of metalanguages: lexical metalanguage, interpretive metalanguage, and semantic metalanguage." He proposed a theoretical framework and research methods for the construction of the Chinese metalanguage system and conducted a series of theoretical and practical studies.

3.1.2 *Natural Semantic Metalanguage Theory*

Diverging from the approach of sememe analysis within structuralist linguistics that explores the internal composition of semantics, the Natural Semantic Metalanguage (NSM) theory endeavors to identify the most fundamental set of concepts in natural language communication. The aim is to express the entire semantics of natural language through these concepts, with the components that express these basic concepts referred to as semantic primitives. Essentially, these so-called "semantic primitives" are neither specialized terms in semantics nor other artificial languages; their form is inherently a part of the natural language symbol system.

While many scholars have also categorized this type of research under atomistic philosophical thought, incorporating it into "new-structuralism". But in essence, from the perspective of theoretical origins, the Natural Semantic Metalanguage theory draws its roots from the General Component Semantic Theory, as proposed by Igor Mikhailovich Boguslavsky(Игорь Михайлович Богуславский) of the Moscow School of Semantics, and the Semantic Primitive Theory, developed by A.K. Zhukovsky (А.К.Жуковский). The fundamental philosophical ideas of this theory do not belong to structuralism (Qiu 邱雪玫& Li 李葆嘉, 2016).

3.1.2.1 The Proposal of the Natural Semantic Metalanguage Theory

The Natural Semantic Metalanguage Theory was proposed by Anna Wierzbicka, the founder of the Poland Semantic School in the latter half of the twentieth century. It represents a new paradigm in contemporary semantic studies and is grounded in the rationalist philosophical foundation (Li 李炯英, 2011).

In communication, due to the subjectivity and complexity of natural language semantics, it is often difficult for speakers and listeners to ascertain whether they use the same words to express the same ideas. This issue is particularly prominent especially in cross-cultural and cross-linguistic studies due to the unequal values of linguistic symbols and the influence of different cultural factors. So how to analyze the meanings of human cognition, interaction, and culture correctly remains a challenging task for modern linguists. In the 1960s and 1970s, Wierzbick became aware of the importance of this issue through her research on cross-cultural comparisons of cognitive patterns in different languages. She began to attempt to study the determination of meaning, intercommunicable words, and their combination rules in order to explore a universal method for describing the object language. This led to the formulation of the idea of natural semantic metalanguage (Pu 蒲冬梅, 2009).

Wierzbick argues that language originates from thought, and users of different languages think using different conceptual categories, which often do not fully correspond across languages. However, most concepts can be expressed through vocabulary, otherwise communication would be difficult. Concepts are attached to language, and the characteristics of different languages can be reflected through conceptual differences. Semantics can influence ways of thinking, thus the description of semantics must consider the relationship between language and the human brain. Semantics is both a reflection of objective reality and inseparable from subjective cognition, being the product of the interaction between the subjective and objective worlds. From this perspective, the natural semantic metalanguage theory is more in line with the characteristics of "cognitive linguistics" (Li 李炯英 & Li 李葆嘉, 2007).

3.1.2.2 Basic Content of the Natural Semantic Metalanguage Theory

The fundamental perspective of NSM posits that in the process of analyzing and interpreting semantics, words with complex meaning should be described by primitives with simple meaning to the greatest extent. These semantic primitives are difficult to define and, individually, they constitute a mini-language that exhibits equivalent interpretive and expressive capabilities to natural language. To overcome problems such as inaccurate interpretation, ambiguity, and circular interpretation, the only way is to seek a semantic core that can express the simplest meanings and is suitable for all languages (Li 李炯英 & Li 李葆嘉, 2007).

Wierzbicka posits that a thorough analysis of any natural language can reveal its semantic primitives, as these primitives possess a universality in representing fundamental human cognitive concepts, which are manifest in any specific language. Elements that can be used to explain and define the meanings of other words, yet themselves are undefined, are considered semantic primitives (Wierzbicka, 1996: 10). She points out that undefined words are present in the lexical dictionaries of any language, forming a distinct system, albeit in small numbers, and their basic function is to serve as prototypical definitions for other words. These undefined words vary across different languages, yet they can be corresponded to one another, sharing semantic equivalence and can be regarded as "universal vocabulary" (Su 苏新春, 2003). Based on the concept of this universal vocabulary, Wierzbicka initially extracted 14 non-arbitrary universal semantic primitives, which are:

I, YOU, SOMEONE, SOMETHING, PART, LIVE, THIS, SAY, GOOD, HAPPEN, WANT, FEEL, NOT, IMAGINE (Wierzbicka, 1972).

These primitives, also referred to as "Conceptual Primes", are the simplest vocabulary that can be used for interpretation (Wierzbicka, 2004). They can be words, phraseme, bound morphemes, or other linguistic forms. As a metalanguage tool for semantic analysis, semantic primitives possess characteristics such as universality, indefinability, and testability (Li 李炯英, 2005).

Following the relentless efforts of successive researchers in the NSM tradition, this set of primitives has gradually expanded and now encompasses over 60 elements. This has resulted in the development of a set of semantic analysis tools that establish a descriptive framework for the "reductive paraphrase" of words, grammatical structures, and cultural scripts across various languages (Li 李炯英et al., 2014). The following is a list of these primitives:

1) **Substantives:** I, YOU, SOMEBODY/PERSON,PEOPLE
2) **Relational Substantives:** SOMETHING/THING, BODY, KIND, PART
3) **Determiners:** THIS, THE SAME, OTHER
4) **Quantifiers:** ONE, TWO, SOME, ALL, MANY/MUCH
5) **Evaluators:** GOOD, BAD
6) **Descriptors:** BIG, SMALL
7) **Mental/Experiential Predicates:** THINK, KNOW, WANT, FEEL, SEE, HEAR
8) **Speech:** SAY,WORDS,TRUE
9) **Actions & Events:** DO, HAPPEN, MOVE
10) **Existence & Possession:** THERE IS/EXIST, HAVE
11) **Life & Death:** LIVE, DIE
12) **Time:** WHEN/TIME, NOW, BEFORE, AFTER, A LONG TIME, A SHORT TIME, FOR SOME TIME, MOMENT
13) **Space:** WHERE/PLACE, HERE, ABOVE, BELOW, FAR, NEAR, SIDE, INSIDE, TOUCHING/CONTACT
14) **Logical Concepts:** NOT, MAYBE, CAN, BECAUSE, IF
15) **Intensifier & Augmentor:** VERY, MORE
16) **Taxonomy & Partonomy:** KIND OF, PART OF
17) **Similarity:** SIMILARITY, LIKE/WAY (Goddard & Wierzbicka, 2002)

The core propositions of the Natural Semantic Metalanguage theory can be summarized as follows: "Without a set of semantic primitives, it is impossible to describe the meaning of words. Complex and ambiguous meanings must be defined through simple and self-evident meanings. These undefined, simple semantic primitives constitute a mini-language, yet they possess the same expressive and interpretive capabilities as the complete natural language. To overcome problems such as circularity, ambiguity, and inaccuracy in the process of interpretation, the only way is to identify the semantic core that can express the simplest meaning across various languages (Li 李炯英, 2006)."

3.1.3 Semantic Primitives in Conceptual Semantics

Contemporary with Wierzbicka, the American cognitive linguist Ray Jackendoff also proposed the theory of semantic primitives, which originates from conceptual cognition. Jackendoff was one of the earliest (in the 1980s) linguists to examine the cognitive relationship between language meaning and the objective world (Jackendoff, 1983). Subsequently, his discussions expanded further to encompass the cognitive relationships between semantics, grammar, and the world. Based on the fundamental ideas of generative linguistics, he proposed the theory of "Conceptual Semantics", which, grounded in spatial concepts and cognitive research, has become an independent linguistic school.

Conceptual semantics is grounded in the conceptual structure and spatial structure. The conceptual structure is composed of semantic primitives, which are innate and intrinsic to the human brain. These primitives are organized according to certain rules to form the conceptual structure, which is then projected onto the sentence to generate the syntactic structure. All meanings can be represented in the conceptual structure, but they are selectively projected into the syntactic structure (Liu 刘晓林, 2006). For instance: the verb "leave" can be decomposed into two semantic primitives: GO and OUT. GO is a basic semantic primitive in the conceptual structure of the event "leave", while OUT is a PATH primitive.

Jackendoff believes that semantic primitives are finite conceptual components (primitives) that express infinite concepts. He proposes a set of conceptual categories, including THING, EVENT, STATE, PLACE, ACTION, PATH, DIRECTION, PROPERTY, MANNER, and AMOUNT. These conceptual categories can be further refined into specific Function Argument organizations, which are the internal conceptual structures of verbs and prepositions. For example, the category of events can be refined into functions such as GO and STAY, while prepositions like TO, FROM, and AWAY are typical examples of path category. Jackendoff categorizes concepts into five types, which can be represented by the following schema (Jackendoff, 1990: 43):

1) [PLACE] → $[_{\mathrm{Place}}$ PLACE-FUNCTION([THING])]
2) [PATH] → $[_{\mathrm{Path}}$(TO, FROM, TOWARD, AWAY, VIA) ([THING][PLACE])]
3) [EVENT] → $[_{\mathrm{Event}}$GO([THING], [PATH])]
   $[_{\mathrm{Event}}$STAY([THING], [PLACE])]
4) [STATE] → $[_{\mathrm{State}}$BE([THING], [PLACE])]
   [StateORIENT([THING], [PATH])]
   [StateEXIT([THING], [PATH])]
5) [EVENT] → [CAUSE([THING,EVENT], [EVENT])] (Li, 2006; Liu, 2006)

This notion is analogous to the perspective discussed in Chap. 2, where word meaning is conceptualized as a feature function spanning various dimensions within the semantic space of words. The difference lies in that we decompose word meaning into a set of dimension functions, whereas Jackendoff, using the concept as the unit, posits that the overall semantic structure of a concept is a function. For example:

Conceptual prime ① PLACE is a function named PLACE-FUNCTION, with the variable being THING. For instance, the phrase "on the desk" represents a place function, where "desk" is a specific instance of the variable THING, i.e., an argument, and "on" is the functional operator.

Conceptual prime ② PATH can be further divided into five functions: TO, FROM, TOWARD, AWAY, and VIA. The structural framework of these functions is identical, consisting of two variables: THING and PLACE. For instance, the phrase "from Beijing to Wuhan" contains two path functions, $_{\mathrm{Path}}$FROM and $_{\mathrm{Path}}$TO. The variable THING in the first function is empty, while the variable PLACE is assigned the value "Wuhan". Similarly, the variable THING in the first function is also empty, and the variable PLACE is assigned the value "Beijing". This empty variable will be filled in with specific context, such as identifying who or what is traveling from Wuhan to Beijing, where the object will serve as the value of the variable THING.

Conceptual prime ③ EVENT is divided into two sub-functions $_{\text{Event}}$GO and $_{\text{Event}}$STAY, each with two variables: THING, PATH, and THING, PLACE. For instance, the sentence "The birds fly to the south." contains the $_{\text{Event}}$GO function, with the functional term being $_{\text{Event}}$GO(fly). The first variable, THING, takes the value of "bird", and the second variable, PATH, takes the value of "to the south". Here, PATH itself can also be represented as a path function (i.e., a function serving as a variable).

Conceptual prime ⑤ is also defined as an EVENT function with the CAUSE variable, carrying two variables, the first being THING or EVENT, and the second being EVENT. This prime differs from prime ③, although it is defined as an event, it constitutes a composite event, with both of its variables being capable of containing other events.

This approach can be employed to analyze word meaning. For instance, the word "drink" can be dissected into:

Drink = [Event CAUSE([THING]i, Event GO([THING liquid]j, PathTO([PLACE[N([THING mouth of]([THING] i)])])])])]. (Goddard, 1998: 67)

In this semantic structure, the nesting of variables is intricate, which can pose challenges in comprehension and readability. It can be approximately translated into a natural language form as: Drinking is an event in which something *i* causes liquid *j* to go into its it's own mouth.

It can be observed that the semantic primitives research conducted by Jackendoff and Wierzbick differs significantly. Although both studies fall within the scope of cognitive linguistics, their observations and research perspectives on semantic primitives are not identical.

Wierzbicki sought a descriptive framework for the universality of meaning, grammar, and cultural scripts to enhance the translatability between languages by looking for a common core of semantic primitives. Jackendoff, on the other hand, attempted to explore the underlying concepts behind word meanings (Li 李炯英, 2006). He posits that the thoughts expressed by language are constructed by a cognitive mechanism called conceptual structure. The conceptual structure is not part of language but of thought (Jackendoff, 2002: 123). Therefore, word concepts can be decomposed into a finite set of (minimal) metalanguage components. These metalanguage components themselves form concepts with internal structures. The internal structure of a word refers to the conceptual phrases that can be derived from the original components of verbs and prepositions" (Cheng 程琪龙, 1997). What he refers to as semantic primitives are actually conceptual primes.

There are also commonalities between them, which are reflected in the fact that certain semantic primitives discussed can be verified in each other's systems. For instance (Table 3.1) (Li 李炯英, 2006):

Table 3.1 Correspondence of Primitives in Natural Language Meta-Linguistics and Conceptual Semantics

Semantic Primitive by Wierzbick	Conceptual Structure Prime by Jackendoff
DO/HAPPEN	$[_{Event}X]$
THERE IS	$[_{State}BE]$
MOVE	$[_{Event}GO]$
INSIDE	$[_{Place}IN]$

3.1.4 Metalanguage in Dictionary Definitions

3.1.4.1 The Dilemma of Circular Interpretation in Semantic Study

The study of interpreting lexical meaning is a major research content in traditional Chinese lexicology and exegetics. Wang 王宁 (1988) points out: "In ancient China, the explanation of lexical meaning can be divided into two major categories based on the methods of interpretation: zhi xun直训(direct explanation, interpreting a word with another word) and yi jie义界(definition). Direct explanation can be further divided into dan xun单训(unilateral explanation) and hu xun互训(mutual explanation). In mutual explanation, the words being interpreted can interchange positions with each other or do so successively."[1]

The examples of mutual explanation in the "shuowen jiezi说文解字(origin of Chinese Characters)" are abundant and can be found with ease, for instance:

① Zhui, zhu ye; zhu, zhui ye.追,逐也;逐,追也。(Chase, to pursue; Pursue, to chase.)

Ji, xü ye; xü, ji ye.继,续也;续,继也。(Succeed, to continue; Continue, to succeed.)

Gen, muzhu ye; zhu, mugen ye.根,木珠也;株,木根也。(Root, the stem of the tree; Stem, the root of the tree.)

Xiao, shuojin ye; shuo, xiaojin ye.销,铄金也;铄,销金也。(Melt, the fusion of metal; Fusion, the melting of metal.)

Ku, gao ye; gao,muku ye.枯,槁也;槁,木枯也。(Withered, dried out; Dried, the withering of wood.)

Hai, jing ye; jing, ma hai ye;骇,惊也;马骇也。(startled, be frightened; frightened, the horse is startled.)

Traditional exegetics treats word meaning as an integrated entity, explaining the meaning of one word directly with another, which naturally leads to a large number of mutual explanations. This method of interpretation is clearly not

[1] Regarding the methods of explanation, there are various opinions. For instance, Xu 许威汉 (1987: 99) suggests three methods: hu xun 互训 (mutual explanation), tui yuan 推源 (etymological derivation), and yi jie 义界 (definition). Additionally, there are other terms such as tong xun 同训(synonymous explanation) and di xun 递训 (progressive explanation). The relationship between direct explanation and mutual explanation is controversial. This section will only discuss the issue of mutual explanation without elaborating on other aspects.

conducive to the understanding of word meaning. Huang Jianhua, a lexicographer, expounded on several fundamental principles of dictionary lexicography in his work *On Dictionaries*, with the first principle being "avoiding circular mutual explanation" (Huang, 2001: 84). However, this phenomenon is still widely prevalent in modern dictionary compilation. Random access to an authoritative Chinese dictionary reveals that the phenomenon of circular explanation is still ubiquitous. For example, in *The Contemporary Chinese Dictionary (5th Edition)*:

② [Liuxing流行(Popularize)]: guangfan chuanbu 广泛传布,盛行(Widespread dissemination and prevalence)

[Shengxing盛行(Prevail)]: guangfan liuxing 广泛流行(Widely Popularized)

③ [Gongju工具(Tool)]: jinxing shengchan laodong shi suo shiyong de qiju 进行生产劳动时所使用的器具(The implement used in productive labor)

[Qiju器具(Implement)]: yongju用具; gongju工具 (Utensil; tool)

[Yongju用具(Utensil)]: richang shenghuo shengchan suo shiyong de qiju日常生活生产所使用的器具(The implements used in daily life)

If these entries, when involved in circular definitions, the meanings of them can be roughly understood through mutual references among them, then extreme examples like the following become rather troublesome.

④ [Sihu似乎(Seem to)]: fangfu仿佛(as if); haoxiang好像(as though).

[Fangfu仿佛(As if)]: sihu似乎(seem to); haoxiang好像(as though).

[Haoxiang好像(As though)]:sihu 似乎(seem to); fangfu仿佛(as if).

The definitions of these three words are essentially spinning in circles, repeating the same points, and basically fail to achieve the intended definition effect. For beginners who rely on dictionaries to understand word meanings, such as primary school students or non-native speakers, the lack of prior knowledge of these words makes the dictionary's definitions appear confusing and unhelpful. Of course, dictionary compilers are continuously revising their methods of definition. In the 7th edition of this dictionary, the definition of the word "haoxiang 好像" (as if) has been revised to: "indicating an uncertain judgment or feeling".

This phenomenon is widely present in various linguistic dictionaries across languages, and is not exclusive to Chinese dictionaries. For instance, the renowned Oxford Advanced Learner's Dictionary (hereinafter referred to as the *Oxford)* and the Longman Dictionary of Contemporary English (hereinafter referred to as the *Longman*) are no exception.[2]

⑤ **anxious:**feeling anxiety; <u>*worried*</u>; uneasy

worry:be <u>*anxious*</u> (about sb, difficulties, the future, etc.)*(Oxford)*

anxious:<u>*worried*</u> about something

worry:be <u>*anxious(Longman)*</u>

[2] Both of these dictionaries consistently rank among the top in various listings of the "most authoritative dictionaries in the world".

⑥ **correct**:true; <u>*right*</u>; accurate
right:true or <u>*correct (Oxford)*</u>
correct:having no mistakes = <u>*right*</u>
right:true/<u>*correct(Longman)*</u>

Different from Chinese, English exhibits a more complex system of inflection. So during the process of interpretation, the forms of words may vary (e.g., worry and worried), yet they still belong to the same lemma, which constitutes a circular interpretation.

The circular interpretation is a common problem in lexicography, a long-standing dilemma existing in both the lexicographical and linguistic communities. The fundamental cause of this issue is is rooted in the specific characteristics of lexicographical dictionaries. Lexicographical dictionaries are intended for reference by human, providing assistance for language learning and research. Their target audience is human beings, thus they can primarily use natural language that is comprehensible to the general public, supplemented by a limited number of metalanguage symbols for interpretation. In dictionaries, the same natural language serves both as the tool language of expression and the object language of expressed content. From a logical perspective, this mode of interpretation clearly exhibits flaws, as Wittgenstein pointed out in *Tractatus Logico-Philosophicus*: No proposition can express itself, because the symbols that express a proposition cannot contain themselves among these symbols (Wittgenstein, 1922: 23). Algirdas Julien Greimas, a linguist from the Paris Semiotic School, discussed this issue from a linguistic perspective in *Structural Semantics*: "Semantics seeks to compile the necessary and sufficient conceptual tools to describe any natural language which is considered a set of signs, such as French. The main difficulty encountered in this description, as we have seen, arises from the particularity of various natural languages. Generally speaking, the description of a painting can be understood as translating the language of painting into French. However, from the same perspective, the description of French can only be translating French into French. Thus, the object of study becomes confused with the tool of study, much like a defendant being both the defendant and the presiding judge" (Greimas, 1986: 13–14).

If the method of circular interpretation in dictionaries is only passable for human readers, it becomes even more inadequate when it comes to semantic computation. The purpose of establishing machine dictionaries or lexical semantic knowledge bases was originally to formalize the description of lexical meanings in the form of structured data convenient for computer processing, thereby endowing computers with sufficient prior linguistic knowledge to achieve automatic understanding of unstructured natural language texts. However, if the prior knowledge of lexical meanings itself is described in this unstructured natural language, it clearly falls into another logical fallacy of circular reasoning (Hu 胡惮, 2011: 70).

3.1.4.2 Origin and Development of Interpretive Metalanguage Research

Does the meaning of words actually definable? Or how should we scientifically define the meaning of each word?

In the mid-seventeenth century, Antoine Arnauld, a renowned French philosopher and logician proposed a pessimistic thesis:

> It would be impossible to define every word. For in order to define a word it is necessary to use other words designating the idea we want to connect to the word being defined. And if we again wished to define the words used to explain that word, we would need still others, and soon to infinity. Consequently, we necessarily have to stop at primitive terms which are undefined. (Arnauld & Nicole, 1996: 64)

In posing this question, Arnauld had already implied the approach to solving it, which is to trace the meaning back to the "indefinable primitives". This idea, in fact, is what many scholars later engaged in during their studies of semantics and dictionary definition, and it has become a major object of research in the metalanguage of dictionary definition.

The study of the interpretive metalanguage in western countries commenced at an early stage, with the quantitative development of "basic vocabulary lists" and the practical compilation of language teaching dictionaries using limiting words for interpretation beginning as early as the late 1920s.

In 1928, the British linguist and educator Charles Kay Ogden, along with Ivor Armstrong Richards, proposed the Basic English vocabulary list, which contained 850 words. In 1932, they published *The Basic Dictionary*, using these 850 basic words to explain 20,000 English words. This represents the earliest endeavor to employ a collection of quantifiers as the foundational lexical units for lexicographical definitions in dictionaries.

In 1935, Michael West proposed the *Definition Vocabulary* containing 1,490 words, and in collaboration with James Gareth Endicott, they compiled the first English teaching dictionary, The *New Method English Dictionary*. In This dictionary, over 24,000 English words were defined by the 1,490 definition words to explain (An 安华林, 2013).

The first edition of the Longman Dictionary, published in 1978, utilized only 2,000 basic vocabulary items to explain over 56,000 pleremes. Subsequent editions, the second published in 1987 and the third in 1995, made subtle adjustments to these basic interpretive primitive words. The various subsequent editions have continued to undergo adjustments and optimizations, yet the total number of defining primitive words used in the explanations has remained around 2,000, making it a model of dictionary lexicography. The interpretive vocabulary list of the Longman Dictionary is based on West's "List of Defining Words" and is cross-referenced with a list of high-frequency common words extracted from the *British National Corpus*, maintaining over 85% consistency in the root words between the two (Bai 白丽芳, 2006).

The 1995 edition of the Collins *COBUILD English Dictionary* was compiled based on the English Corpus (*The Bank of English*) and utilized over 2,000 common interpretive primitive words to explain 75,000 entries.

The Oxford Dictionary, published in 2000, employs 3,000 basic interpretive primitive words.

The *Macmillan English Dictionary for Advanced Learners*, published in 2002, employs 2,500 basic interpretive primitive words.

The major English language learning dictionaries, including Longman, Oxford, and Collins, among others, have all introduced their own limited-word lists for definitions, which has become a mainstream trend in contemporary lexicography (An 安华林, 2005).

In China, the research on the interpretive primitives of Chinese has only recently begun to gain traction. The linguists, lexicographical scholars, and computational linguists have all started to pay attention to this issue and have conducted research from various perspectives. To date, significant achievements have been made. However, these accomplishments are still at the stage of theoretical research and statistical analysis, and have not been substantially applied in the practice of lexicography. As of now, there is no Chinese dictionary that has been entirely compiled using interpretive primitive words. Even in the *Modern Chinese Dictionary*, widely regarded as the most authoritative dictionary in CHinese, the interpretive primitive words employed for explaining 60,000 characters and words, exceed 36,000 (An Hualin, 2005).

The pioneering systematic research on the extraction of interpretive primitive words in Chinese lexicography within China, which was conducted in 1996, originated not from the linguistic field but from Professor Huang Changning, a computer expert, and his team at Tsinghua University in 1996. They input the text of authoritative Chinese dictionaries into computers and utilized statistical models to calculate the semantic relationships between the defining terms and the terms being defined, resulting in a Chinese interpretive metalanguage set containing 3,857 words. Based on the *Synonymy Thesaurus*, they further conducted an investigation into the distribution of semantic categories and evaluated the statistical results (Zhang 张津 & Huang 黄昌宁, 1997; Su 苏新春, 2003).

Li 李葆嘉 (2002) and other scholars have, while gradually focusing on the exploration of the metalanguage theory of Chinese, also embarked on a rigorous and meticulous task of extracting the basic interpretive primitive words of Chinese.

Su 苏新春 (2005) extracted 4,324 Chinese interpretive primitive words by means of quantitative analysis and a comparative study with the Synonymy Thesaurus. An 安华林 (2005) determined 2,878 Chinese interpretive primitive words through a multi-step process involving various word list comparisons and semantic verification procedures.

The research conducted by Zhang 张津 & Huang 黄昌宁 employs purely statistical methods, lacking in-depth artificial observation and analysis of linguistic facts. Moreover, the classification of semantic categories is based on the *Synonymy Thesaurus*, which contains an excessive number of entries and lacks sufficient selection criteria. Consequently, the results obtained by them are quite distant from the linguistic facts. Many of the words they extract, such as "bankuai xueshuo板块学说plate tectonics theory", "fe xing banjing飞行半径flight radius", "bubian jiage不变价格constant price", "baohu maoyi保护贸易protective trade", "fading renshu法

定人数quorum", "chudeng jiaoyu初等教育primary education", "baogao wenxue报告文学literary reportage", and the "baguo lianjun八国联军Eight-Nation Alliance", among others, are questionable in terms of their qualification as interpretive primitive words. Therefore, it can be said that, as the earliest conducted research on interpretive metalanguage in China, this work has a far greater exemplary role than its actual practical value.

The research by Su and An, based on statistical analysis, pays more attention to the study of linguistic facts and extracts more persuasive primitive words. However, these achievements are primarily confined to theoretical discussions and the extraction of interpretive primitive words, lacking definitions of the phonetic, morphological, and semantic aspects of each interpretive primitive word. Therefore, a larger-scale verification of interpretations is required to test their validity. As for the practical application of interpretive primitive word primitive words in compiling Chinese learning dictionaries or general dictionaries, this work has not yet truly commenced (An 安华林, 2013).

3.1.5 Semantic Primitives in Chinese Information Processing

The Hierarchical Network of Concepts (HNC) theory, developed by Huang 黄曾阳, and the HowNet, created by Dong 董振东, are two prominent approaches in the field of Chinese information processing, which aim to provide a structured and systematic way of understanding and representing semantics in Chinese. They both focus on segmenting and formalizing semantics, with the former emphasizing "Conceptual primitive" and the latter introducing the concept of "Semantic Prime".

3.1.5.1 Description of Conceptual Primitives and Lexical Semantics in HNC

The HNC theory is based on the conceptualization, hierarchization, and networking of semantic expressions, dividing the cognitive structure of the human brain into two types of association venations: local and global. It posits that the expression of association venations is the fundamental issue at the deep level of language (i.e., the semantic level of language). Local association refers to the associative connections at the lexical level, while global association pertains to the associative connections at the sentence and discourse levels. The starting point of the HNC theory is to utilize these two types of association venations to assist computers in understanding natural language (Xiao 萧国政 & Hu 胡惮, 2007).

The HNC theory has designed a four-level digital symbol system for the conceptual space of language: the conceptual primitive expression, the sentence expression, the context unit expression, and the context expression, which correspond to words and phrases, sentences and semantic blocks, clusters of sentences, and discourse in natural language, respectively (Huang 黄曾阳, 2004) Through these expression systems, the HNC theory endeavors to express infinite linguistic units with limited symbols and rules: using a limited set of conceptual primitives to represent infinite concepts, a limited set of sentence types to represent infinite sentences, and a limited set of context units to represent infinite contexts. Moreover, HNC has completely constructed and identified these three finite sets: approximately 20,000 conceptual primitives, 57 types of sentence structures, and about 15,000 types of context units. The conceptual primitives form a hierarchical and networked system, divided from high to low into 18 conceptual categories, 101 conceptual groups, and 456 conceptual trees, which serve as the core and foundation for the HNC theory to establish the conceptual association venations. The metalanguage system of the HNC theory for the semantic expression and formal description of concepts includes (Huang 黄曾阳, 1998: 18–19):

1) **Conceptual Quintuple:** a framework used to describe the typological characteristics of abstract concepts. Each abstract concept possesses five aspects of typological features, namely: dynamics, stasis, attributes, values, and effect expressions, which are represented as a quintet (v, g, u, z, r). This quintuple can also be referred to as the morphology or external characteristics of the abstract linguistic concept.
2) **Conceptual Classification:** Abstract language concepts can be divided into three basic categories: fundamental concepts, primitive concepts, and logical concepts, which are respectively represented as j, φ, and l.
3) **Category Symbol Set:** Abstract concepts with comprehensive features of three major categories of abstract concepts are represented as: s; grammatical concepts are represented as: f, q, h; concrete concepts of objects and individuals are represented as: w, p; material concepts with both abstract and concrete dual characteristics are represented as: x.
4) **Hierarchical Symbol Set:** This set denotes the hierarchical position of a concept node within the conceptual tree, represented by hexadecimal digits ranging from 0 to 13, specifically: 0, 1, 2, 3, 4, 5, 6, 7, 8, 9, a, b, c, d.

In addition to the concept combination structure symbols set, there are also the general expressions of concepts and the hierarchical symbol string expressions.

Through this metalanguage system, we can express the meaning of each word in Chinese, as indicated by (Tang 唐兴全, 2001):

Noun:yeji业绩(achievement)[r30a1], kaimo楷模(role model)[jg737], biaoshuai表率(exemplary role)[jr737], xingwei行为(behaviour)[gd0], weiwang威望(prestige)[rd001]

Verb: wancheng完成(finish)[v930a8], sikao思考(think)[v810], zhaokai召开(convene)[v3959 + va01], qicheng启程(set off)[vlll,v22b], sunhao损耗(lose)[vz3b2]

Multi-category words: chenggong成功(succeed/success)[vg930a1], jingzheng竞争(compete/competition)[gvb30], fazhan发展(develop/development)[gv10a]

Adj/Adv: feifa非法(illegal)[ua59], zhongyao重要(important)[gu725], feichang 非常(very)[juu60c43], wanquan完全(complete)[juu501], meili美丽(beautiful)[u51 + j831]

3.1.5.2 Description of Semantic Primes and Lexical Semantics in HowNet

The HowNet is a common-sense knowledge base that describes concepts represented by words in both Chinese and English, with the fundamental content being the relationships between concepts and their attributes. Unlike other lexical knowledge bases, the HowNet, as a knowledge system, has knowledge nodes that are networked rather than tree-structured. It focuses on reflecting the commonalities and individualities of concepts, as well as the various relationships between concepts and their attributes. The HowNet explicitly teaches the computer the knowledge network system, thereby making knowledge operable for computers. The basic unit of meaning described in the HowNet is the semantic prime. "Generally speaking, a semantic prime is the smallest unit of meaning that is the most fundamental and not easily divisible (Dong 董振东 & Dong 董强, 1998)." For instance, the concept of "man" can be described using the three semantic primitives "human, family, male". Assuming that all concepts can be decomposed into semantic primes, the set of semantic primes is finite, whereas the set of concepts obtained through their combination is infinite. The HowNet employs a finite set of semantic primes to describe all concepts.

The HowNet currently employs a total of 2,196 semantic primes. Based on the role these primes play in conceptual description, they are categorized into three major groups and ten subcategories.

1) **Basic semantic primitives:** Event, Entity, attribute, aValue, quantity, qValue, SecondaryFeature
2) **Grammatical semantic primitives:** Syntax
3) **Relational semantic primitives:** EventRole, EventFeatures

In addition to the semantic primes, HowNet employs a set of symbolic systems to describe conceptual and lexical meaning knowledge, which includes lexical category symbols, boundary symbols, information structure symbols, special semantic primitive symbols, and semantic role symbols. By this system, HowNet is capable of describing the meanings of each word in both Chinese and English, for instance:

[Applause]
No.= 067328
W_C=Applause
G_C=V
E_C=Clap to signal, clap as a signal, approve with a clap
W_E=Clap one's hands
G_E=V

E_E=
DEF={ShowGoodEmotion|表示好情感: means={Beat|打:PartOfTouch={Part|部件:PartPosition={Hand|手}, whole= {Human|人}}}}
[Electrician]
No.= 046908
W_C=Electrician
G_C=N
E_C=He is an electrician, an electrician, to work as an electrician, a first-class electrician, master electrician.
W_E=Electrician
G_E=N
E_E= DEF={Human|人: HostOf={Occupation|职位}, RelateTo= {Electricity|电}}

The research and development of HowNet has been ongoing for nearly three decades, with the scale of its vocabulary continuously expanding. To date, the HowNet knowledge base employs a total of 2,196 semantic primitives, describing 35,202 concepts, and encompasses 229,767 Chinese and English terms.

3.2 Semantic Gene: A New Perspective on the Description of Microstructure of Semantics

In the first chapter, we have elaborated on the law of holographic isomorphism between natural language and biological organisms from the perspective of holographic philosophy. Drawing on the theoretical framework and research methods of life sciences, observing and analyzing the microstructure of word meaning from the perspective of genetic engineering has attracted the attention of some scholars. Li 李葆嘉 (2002) proposed in his discussion of the construction of the Chinese metalanguage system: The study of the modern Chinese metalanguage system is a fundamental research, which can be termed as the "linguistic gene map analysis project". The author of this book has also put forward the preliminary conception of semantic gene analysis respectively in 2009, 2011, and 2014, (Hu 胡惮 & Gao 高精炼, 2009; Hu 胡惮 et al., 2011; Hu 胡惮, 2014).

3.2.1 What is Semantic Gene

3.2.1.1 The Definition of Semantic Gene

This book draws upon the theories and methods of genetic science to conduct a micro-analysis of semantics, treating the semantic gene as the fundamental unit of analysis. In linguistics, when defining a certain basic structural unit of language, the term "minimum" is generally mentioned. Could the semantic gene simply be defined as the "minimum unit of meaning"? Let's first examine the definitions of some "minimum units" of phonetics and vocabulary provided in two linguistic dictionaries[3]:

[Phone]

① The most basic elements that constitute phonetics, they are the **minimum** units of speech sounds, which are differentiated based on timbre (Wang 王今铮 et al., 1985: 401).
② The **minimum** phonetic unit differentiated according to the differences in timbre (Ge 葛本仪, 1992: 26).

[Syllable]

① The **minimum** phonetic structure unit composed of phonemes, also known as yin zhui音缀. A syllable can be formed by a single phone (a vowel or a consonant), or by two or more phones. Most syllables consist of both vowels and consonants (Wang王今铮 et al., 1985: 398).
② The fundamental unit of phonological structure is the naturally produced, **minimum** phonetic segment that occurs spontaneously during speech and is naturally perceived during listening (woconditionGe 葛本仪: 25).

[Phoneme]

① In a specific language, a collection of several similar or related phonemes that do not distinguish meaning internally but externally serve to differentiate meaning (王今铮 et al., 1985: 402).
② The **minimum** phonetic unit capable of distinguishing meaning within a language or dialect (葛本仪, 1992: 26).

[Morpheme]

① Morphemes are the constituent elements of words, representing the **minimum** unity of sound and meaning in language (王今铮 et al., 1985: 60).
② Also known as yu su语素, a unit of sound and meaning combination, it is the **minimum** structural unit of a word that can be independently used (葛本仪, 1992: 77).

[Word]

① The **minimum** unit of syntactic structure, the smallest unit that can be freely used in a language. By "free use", it is meant that a word, as a complete syntactic unit, functions as a part of the syntactic structure; by "**minimum**", it refers to its ultimate nature in the analysis of syntactic structures, being a unit that does not require further analysis (王今铮 et al., 1985: 52).
② A fixed structure of phonetic-semantic combination in language represents the **minimum** unit that can be independently used in constructing sentences (葛本仪, 1992: 72).

---

[3] The *Concise Dictionary of Linguistics* edited by Wang Jingzheng et al., and the *Practical Dictionary of Chinese Linguistics* edited by Ge Benyi.

The definitions of the aforementioned concepts provided in various linguistic monographs and textbooks are generally similar in meaning. These definitions all employ the attributive adjective "minimum", yet each comes with certain limitations:

Phones, syllables, and phonemes are concepts in phonetics, which focus on the physiological, physical, psychological, and social attributes of speech sounds. A phone is the smallest phonetic-physical unit, with the constraint being the division down to the minimum unit based on the phonetic features of the articulatory organs and the physical characteristics of the sounds produced.[4] A syllable is the smallest phonetic psychological unit, with the constraint being the division down to the minimum unit based on the psychological perception of listening and speaking.

Morphemes and words are concepts from morphology and syntax, focusing on the morphological structure of language. Both are the smallest unities combined of sound, form, and meaning, yet they belong to distinct higher linguistic categories. A morpheme is the smallest unity combined of sound, form, and meaning that constitutes a word, while a word is the smallest unity combined of sound, form, and meaning that constructs a sentence. The form of both words and morphemes is a physical aspect, the sound is a psychological aspect, and the meaning is a psychological and socio-functional aspect.

It is evident that in linguistics, when we define a "minimum" structural unit, we should take into account two conditions:

1) **The perspective of definition.** For instance, from the perspective of social function, phonemes are considered the smallest phonetic units, whereas from the physical and psychological perspectives, they are not the smallest. Morphemes, from the psychological and social function perspectives, are regarded as the smallest configurational units; however, from the physical perspective, they are not (for example, morphemes in phonetic writing systems can be further divided into letters, and morphemes in Chinese can be further divided into characters, even to the level of radicals).
2) **The referent of definition, i.e., its superordinate category.** In terms of phonetics, the referent of the syllable is the word; in comparison to the word, the syllable is the smallest natural phonetic construction unit, yet it is not the smallest when compared to the phone; the syllable is composed of phones. In terms of morphology, the referent of the word is the sentence; in comparison to the sentence, the word is the smallest unit of phonetic, morphological, and semantic integration, yet it is not the smallest when compared to the morpheme; the word is composed of morphemes.

When considering the definition of lexical semsntic genes under these two conditions, the problem of defining them remains unresolved. As Dong 董振东 pointed out

[4] Syllables can also be distinguished from physical characteristics, "From an acoustic perspective, a syllable has a process of intensity increase and decrease. When a syllable is pronounced, the intensity of the sound goes from weak to strong and then back to weak, and the number of syllables pronounced corresponds to the number of such processes" (Xing, 2002: 92). However, except for experimental phonetics, when we generally discuss syllables, we start from the perspective of the psychological perception of listening and speaking.

when defining the semantic primes, it is quite challenging to define the fundamental unit of meaning.

The physical form of the semantic gene differs from the concepts discussed above, such as phones, syllables, phonemes, morphemes, and words, which all possess a certain physical form of natural language, including phonetic and written forms, and are part of natural language. Meaning, however, lacks a physical form in natural language. Although the metalanguage systems used in the discussion of semantics can include a part of natural language, they themselves are not the physical form of meaning. The metalanguage symbols specific to semantics, such as agents and patients, are merely referential symbols for semantic relationships and do not represent the physical form of meaning. Without a physical form, it is difficult to accurately segment semantic units. In traditional linguistics, both sememes and pleremes are referred to as semantic units, but they are not the physical form of semantics either. According to the sememe analysis, they can still be infinitely divided.

Furthermore, the referent of semantic genes is not exclusively words, although in most cases the objects processed by semantic genes are words. The superordinate categories they are governed by sometimes extend beyond the scope of words. For instance, the agents and patients of the verb "eat" cannot generally be objects like "table" or "chair". When describing the semantics of "eat", this point cannot be overlooked; however, it already transcends the scope of the word itself, involving the logical constraints of composition.

In classical genetics, "gene" is defined as the basic element of genetic information, the functional unit controlling a specific aspect of phenotype, and the structural unit that cannot be separated from recombination and mutation. From the perspective of molecular biology, modern genetics defines "gene" as: a gene is the basic unit of genetic information, generally referring to a segment of nucleotide sequence located on a chromosome that encodes a specific functional product (such as proteins or RNA molecules, etc.) (Snustad, 2011: 349; Xu 徐晋麟 et al., 2001: 7).

According to these definitions, several key properties of genes can be ascertained:

1) Genes are the fundamental units that control the traits of organisms. Phenotype refers to the observable morphological traits and the molecular traits that are intrinsic to an organism or cell, which require detection through biochemical or molecular biological methods. A gene controls the traits of an organism in a specific aspect.
2) From an angle of controlling biological traits, genes, as the fundamental units of genetic information, cannot be further subdivided. During the process of inheritance, genes may undergo recombination and mutation; however, these recombination and mutation events occur at the level of the gene as the smallest unit, and their physical structures cannot be separated.
3) From the perspective of molecular biology, a gene is a sequence of nucleotides, where a nucleotide is a chemical compound composed of purine or pyrimidine bases, ribose or deoxyribose, and phosphoric acid. Therefore, a gene is in fact not the smallest physical structural unit, as it can be divided into several nucleotides,

and these nucleotides can, in turn, be further dissected into other substances. However, this refers to the intramolecular structure of the gene. Although it can be further divided, it remains the minimum unit of genetic information that controls biological traits.

Referring to the definition of the smallest linguistic unit in linguistics and the definition of genes in genetics, we define the "semantic gene" as: *the fundamental structural unit of meaning that controls a certain semantic feature of a word and can construct new meanings through inheritance and recombination.*

3.2.1.2 The Nature of Semantic Gene

Based on the definition conditions of the phonetic and lexical minimal units and the analysis of the nature of genes in genetics, we can correspondingly analyze the properties of semantic genes.

1) The semantic gene is the unit of information structure in semantics. Unlike the primary units of phonetics and words, the semantic gene lacks a fixed physical form and, therefore, cannot be segmented based on physical structure. It is a unit that is segmented from the perspective of the information structure that constitutes meaning. Information structure involves two aspects: psychological cognition and social function.
2) The number of semantic genes is limited, forming a relatively stable set. The types and quantities of semantic genes vary across different languages, with each language having its own set of semantic genes. Anyway, there are also a certain number of common genes that are suitable for all languages. By extracting the gene sets from various languages and taking their intersection, we can obtain theese common genes. Within the same language, different word classes exhibit distinct semantic feature dimensions and information structures, with their genetic types differing accordingly. For instance, the [Agent] and [Patient] genes exist only within the semantic information structures of verbs describing actions, while the [Speed] and [Direction] genes are only present in the semantic information structures of verbs indicating movement; the [Color] and [Volume] genes are only found in the semantic information structures of nouns referring to things, while the [Age] and [Gender] genes are only present in the semantic information structures of nouns referring to biological entities. The extraction of the semantic gene set is an immense and long-term endeavor. Although we are currently unable to precisely define the size and specific elements of this set, research experiences from various linguistic fields indicate that this set is definable and limited in number. For example, the English dictionary's set of interpretive primitive words contains only 3,500 words, the HowNet defines only over 2,000 semantic primes, and the HNC defines only over 1,200 conceptual primitives. Although the "interpretive primitive words", "semantic primes", and "conceptual primitives" involved in these studies are not identical to the

"semantic genes" we are discussing, the idea of a finite set proposed by them can serve as a reference for us to extract the semantic gene set.

3) The function of the semantic gene targets the entire semantic features of a word, with the semantic meaning itself serving as its superordinate category. Referring to the word meaning as the benchmark, the semantic gene constitutes the smallest unit of semantic information structure. A semantic gene represents the semantic feature information of a word within a specific dimension, embodying a relatively complete minimal concept and generally should not be further divided.
4) The function of semantic genes is to control the semantic features of words. A word typically possesses multiple dimensions of semantic features, each dimension being controlled and represented by one or a group of semantic genes. Semantic genes constitute an independent unit of semantic structure, expressing a simple feature of a word; multiple semantic genes can be combined through some functional relationship to collectively represent a complex feature of a word.
5) The mechanism of neologism generation is analogous to genetic inheritance, where multiple semantic genes can be recombined according to certain rules, and variations may also occur during the recombination process. The emergence of new words is the result of the inheritance, recombination, and variation of semantic genes.
6) The semantic gene also possesses a more microcosmic internal structure, akin to the nucleotide sequence of biological genes. Analyzing the internal structure of semantic genes is conducive to understanding and mastering their nature, thereby enabling us to scientifically and reasonably define and extract a set of semantic genes. However, when it comes to controlling the dimensional features of semantics and constructing new words through inheritance, recombination, and mutation, the semantic gene serves as the smallest structural unit and is no longer further divisible.

For instance, we conventionally refer to "human" as a semantic gene, denoted as [human]. Let us analyze this further:

① The explanation of "Human" as a semantic gene: Let's start with the dictionary definitions. Under the entry for "ren人(human)" in the *The Contemporary Chinese Dictionary*, there are eight pleremes, among which the first one is "a high-level animal capable of manufacturing tools and using tools for labor: nanren男人(man)|nüren女人(woman)|ren men人们(people)|ren lei人类(mankind)" represents the basic semantic information carried by the semantic gene "ren人(human)". These information will play a role in controlling the semantic features of words with this gene. The reason why "ren人(human)" can be considered as a semantic gene and does not (or need not) be further divided is because in our cognitive system, it is a relatively complete smallest concept. Whether in the acquisition of language by children, second/foreign language teaching, or daily language communication, this concept will not be further explained according to the dictionary definition. On the contrary, if it is further

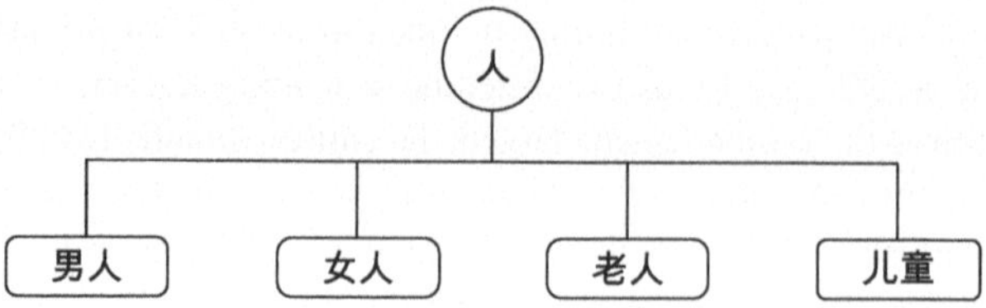

Fig. 3.1 A lexcial Family containg Semantic Gene [Human]

divided using the sememe analysis, it will become more complex and difficult to understand.

② The controlling of semantic gene [ren人(Human)] over the semantic feature dimensions of words: this gene governs the "semantic category" dimension of words. That is to say, all words containing this gene, such as "man", "woman", "child", "adult", and so on, belong to the semantic category of "human".

③ The heredity of the semantic gene [ren人(Human)] in word formation: This gene itself can form a word independently. In the lexical composed of all words possessing this gene, "human" occupies the topmost position, serving as the superordinate term for all other words within the family. For instance, the other five words listed here form the following lexical family (Fig. 3.1).

All the hyponyms within this lexical family have inherited the semantic genes of their superordinate term "human", which encompasses the full semantic information of [human].

④ The semantic gene [ren人(Human)] combines with another semantic gene [nian-ling年龄(Age)] to form the new word "adult", "child"; and combines with the semantic gene [xingbie性别(gender)] to form the new words "man", "woman".

⑤ The genetic variation of the semantic gene [ren人(Human)] in word formation: In the following lexical items containing the semantic gene [ren人(Human)], the semantic information of [Human] undergoes variation.

Ren li人立(stand like a human): Variant to "like a human (in behavior)"
Ren huo人祸(man-made calamities): Variant to "man-made"
Ren jun人均(per person): Variant to "per person"
Chuan ren传人(pass on) (verbal sense): Variant to "others"
Qiu ren求人(seek help from others): Variant to "others"
ji suo bu yu wu shi yu ren己所不欲勿施于人(Do not do unto others what you would not have them do unto you): Variant to "others"
Diu ren丢人(lose face): Variant to "a person's dignity"
Ji qi ren 机器人(robot): Variant to "something like a human"
Ni ren泥人(clay figure): Variant to "something like a human"
Jing se yi ren景色宜人(scenery that makes people happy): Variant to "a person's mood"
Chong xin zuo ren 重新做人(turn over a new leaf): Variant to "an upright person"

These variant semantic information, while still containing the gene [human], have undergone more complex combinations and information reactions with other semantic genes. The original semantic gene [human] is no longer capable of controlling the feature dimensions of these lexical items.

3.2.1.3 Semantic Gene and the Semantic Space Dimension of Words

In the first chapter we have discussed that the meaning of a word is a collection of features across various dimensions within the semantic space. The meaning of a word often encompasses multiple feature dimensions, and the structural dimensions of the semantic space for words of the same category are similar, with the specific features on each dimension differing from word to word. For instance, words that refer to physical objects typically have feature dimensions such as size, shape, color, temperature, weight, composition, and form; words that refer to actions or behaviors have feature dimensions such as time, space, subject, object, cause, effect, purpose, process, tool, method, means, direction, and path; and words that refer to qualities or states have feature dimensions such as object, degree, scope, existence, time, and space.

While each word within the same category may possess distinct overall features, the dimensions along which these features vary are consistent. At the level of perception, people can directly discern the differences in these features to distinguish between different objects without the need for linguistic thought, for instance, through tactile sensation to perceive the temperature's intensity, through visual perception to discern the color's saturation, or through auditory perception to judge the volume of sound. However, If separated from specific objects, words representing different objects need to be distinguished through linguistic thinking to identify the features of their meanings (Hu 胡惮, 2014: 72).

Different words are distinguished from each other due to the presence or absence of certain features across various dimensions, or due to the specific values of these features that they share. These dimension features are governed by semantic genes. Some feature dimensions can be controlled by a mono semantic gene; others require the combination of multiple mono semantic genes into a semantic gene chain based on a certain functional relationship; and still other feature dimensions, which are more complex, necessitate the control by a cluster of genes and gene chains with similar properties, forming a semantic gene cluster.

3.2.1.4 Distinctions and Connections Between the Basic Units of Semantic Analysis in the Semantic Genes and Other Theories

The preceding discussion has explored various theories of semantic analysis within the fields of linguistics and NLP, which all base their descriptive analysis of semantics on a set of fundamental or minimum semantic units. The semantic genes discussed in this book draw upon the research experiences of predecessors, yet they fundamentally differ. The most critical distinction lies in our perspectives and focuses in defining semantic genes. Previous research has been structured from the perspectives of structuralism or conceptual cognition, defining the basic units of semantics with a focus on the explanation or structural description of semantics; whereas, we define semantic genes based on the philosophical thought of holographicism, from the perspective of biological genetics, with a focus on the semantic feature dimensions, the control of semantic genes over the semantic feature dimensions, the genetic operational mechanisms of semantic genes, the genetic structure map of semantics, and its formal description. The specific distinctions and connections between the theory of semantic genes and other theories are briefly analyzed as follows:

1) Differences and Connections with the Theory of Sememe Analysis:

   ① The extraction of sememes is subjective and random, whereas the convention and extraction of semantic genes are strictly standardized.
   ② The sememe set lacks a unified standard, with different words serving as sememes for each other, resulting in a prevalent occurrence of circular definitions; in contrast, the set of semantic genes is relatively stable. By using elements from the gene set to describe word meanings, the phenomenon of circular definitions can be restricted through the dimension of semantic features.
   ③ The sememe structure of words lacks a standardized pattern, making it difficult to express the semantic relationships between sememes; the structural equation of semantic genes is standardized, and the dimensions and structural equations can clearly describe the semantic relationships between all semantic genes.
   ④ The semantic field comparison method adopted in the sememe analysis and a part of semantic roles used in the analysis can provide references for the analysis of semantic genes.

2) Differences and Connections with the Natural Semantic Metalanguage Theory:

   ① The natural semantic metalanguage theory is aimed at extracting universal semantic primitives suitable for multiple languages and cultures across languages; the semantic gene extraction is specific to a particular language, and the gene sets extracted from different languages are different.
   ② The semantic primitives defined in the natural semantic metalanguage theory are insufficient in amount. Since the release of the first batch of over 60 semantic primitives by Wierzbick and her team in 2002, there has been no subsequent continuous update. This is clearly insufficient to describe the semantics of a single language, let alone the majority of vocabulary across languages. Therefore, the value of this theory lies primarily in its methodological significance and is not sufficient to support large-scale engineering applications. The development of the semantic gene bank proposed in this book is a continuous engineering project aimed at semantic computation processing. The construction of the gene bank for a part of the modern

Chinese word classes has already been completed, and the subsequent development will continue.

③ There is a certain gap between the definition of semantic primitives in the natural semantic metalanguage theory and the semantic genes. Among them, some semantic primitives, such as A LONG TIME, A SHORT TIME, and FOR SOME TIME, cannot be considered as the smallest conceptual semantic units in Chinese.

④ Some semantic primitives in the natural semantic metalanguage theory can serve as references for the extraction of semantic genes.

3) Differences and Connections with with Conceptual Semantics: Similar to natural semantic metalanguage, Jackendoff's conceptual semantics primarily lies in its theoretical value, with a limited set of conceptual primitives that are insufficient to describe the majority of vocabulary. Its theoretical approach also holds reference value for the analysis of lexical semantics.
4) Differences and Connections with Dictionary Interpretive Primitive Words:

① In the extraction of primitive words in the study of dictionary interpretive metalanguage, the method of word frequency statistics is generally adopted. This involves using computers to extract high-frequency words from large-scale corpora or to conduct statistical analysis on dictionary definition texts to extract high-frequency explanatory words. These words are then manually selected, merged, and optimized to form a set of explanatory basic words. The extraction of semantic genes is primarily achieved through semantic analysis, and statistical methods are also employed in the verification and optimization stages.

② Dictionary interpretive words are themselves words and have a fixed physical form that belongs to the vocabulary system of natural language. Semantic genes, on the other hand, are not words. Although some genes can be recorded using morphemes and words of natural language, this is merely for the purpose of expression and understanding, and they do not possess a physical form in natural language.

③ Interpretive primitive words are mainly used to explain the meaning of vocabulary, with the target audience being humans. Semantic genes, however, are primarily used to analyze the semantic feature dimensions and semantic information structure of words, mainly for computational semantic processing and can also be read by humans.

④ Interpretive primitive words can provide material for the extraction of semantic genes, and some interpretive primitive words that represent the smallest cognitive concepts can serve as semantic genes.

5) Differences and Connections with the Theory of Hierarchical Network of Concepts:

① The HNC theory constructs a conceptual associative network by simulating the local and global associative patterns of human brain cognition. It treats conceptual primitives as the activating factors for semantic association, and analyzes and extracts conceptual primitives from the top down. The semantic gene, based on the internal microstructure of lexical semantics, acquires the structural genes of semantics through semantic analysis, and generates the conceptual semantic network from the bottom up through the semantic relationships among semantic genes.

② The conceptual primitive system of the HNC theory describes the semantics of concepts using pure mathematical expressions, and then corresponds to the vocabulary of natural language through mapping relationships, which cannot fully and accurately describe all aspects of semantics. In the analysis of semantic genes, the description of word meaning is achieved through semantic structural equations, which precisely describe the features of semantics in various dimensions and the complex semantic relationships among semantic genes.

③ The HNC theory is directly oriented towards computational applications and lacks readability for human readers. The semantic gene functions and the semantic gene structural equations can be directly used for computation and are also convenient for human reading and processing, and can be directly applied to dictionary compilation and language teaching.

④ The conceptual network and conceptual primitives in the HHNC theory can serve as an important reference for the study of semantic genes.

6) Differences and Connections with HowNet:

① The HowNet is oriented towards common-sense knowledge, as knowledge representation necessarily involves semantics, thus necessitating semantic description. Its starting point is world knowledge, and its endpoint is the description of semantic relationships. The semantic gene directly addresses the semantic analysis of natural language, with its starting point being the natural language itself and its endpoint being the computational representation of natural semantic knowledge.

② The HowNet emphasizes the description of relationships, with a coarse granularity in the structural decomposition of semantics, resulting in insufficient explanatory power of sememes. For instance, in the definition of "science" as DEF = {knowledge}, is clearly that "science" is not equivalent to "knowledge", as there is a significant difference between the two. The semantic genes can describe all semantic feature dimensions of a word, with a finer granularity of knowledge.

③ The HowNet employs the same structural description for the meanings of synonyms, such as "hongguang manmian红光满面(glow with health)", "hongpupu红扑扑(flushed)", "hongrun红润(rosy)", "mianse hongrun面色红润(ruddy complexion)", and "qise hao气色好(good complexion)", all represented as DEF = {Red:{mean: descriptive = {sturdy}, relevant = {~}}}. This fails to reflect the differences between word meanings and, in fact, none of these words should imply the meaning of "sturdy". By using the semantic gene function and the semantic information structural equation, we can achieve a more precise description of semantics, effectively avoiding these issues.

④ The semantic role classification in HowNetis very detailed, which can provide beneficial references for the analysis of semantic genes.

3.2.2 *Features and Classification of Semantic Genes*

The morphological and functional diversity of semantic genes allows for their classification from two distinct perspectives.

3.2.2.1 Morphological Categories and Morphological Features of Semantic Genes

Although semantic genes lack a physical form, they possess different information structures internally. These information structures necessitate the employment of corresponding metalanguage systems for their description. According to their information structures, semantic genes can be categorized into the following types:

1) Free semantic genes and bound semantic genes

The free semantic gene does not require the dependence on other semantic genes and can exist independently while performing various functions, such as [shiwu 事物(Thing)], [shijian时间(Time)], [kongjian空间(Space)], [ren人(Human)], [da 大(Large)], [xiao小(Small)], and so on.

The bound semantic gene cannot exist independently; it generally needs to be attached to other genes, forming a semantic gene chain, which collectively exert the functions. This includes suffixes such as [zhe者] ("one" or "someone", often used as a suffix similar to "-er" in English), [men们] ("plural marker", used at the end of a word to indicate plurality), [jia家]("expert" or "specialist"), [chu初] ("initial" or "beginning"), [di第] ("ordinal number prefix", used before numbers to indicate order, similar to "first", "second", etc.), [lao老] (used before a person's name to express familiarity, affection, or respect, similar to the term "old" in English), [a阿] (used before a person's name to indicate intimacy, friendliness, or as a nickname), and superlinear structures that express certain semantic relationships, such as [like…], [a member of…], [a part of…], [for the purpose of…], [driven by…], etc. Chinese is not an inflected language, lacking rich morphological changes. In languages with morphological changes, such as English, there are numerous prefixes like [dis-], [in-], [un-], [-er], [-tion], [-ness], [-ly], etc., which can all represent a bound semantic gene.

The free semantic genes exhibit the following features:

① They correspond to the smallest cognitive concept, capable of independently forming a word, serving as the core component of the semantic gene set, such as: [yanse颜色(Color)], [wendu温度(Temperature)], [you有(Existence)], [wu 无(Non-existence)].

② They play a dominant role in controlling the semantic dimension features, representing the key feature information of the semantic dimensions. For instance, the manner dimension of the verb "ren li人立(Standing like a human)" is composed of two semantic genes [Human] and [Like…], among which the free gene [Human] represents the key feature information of the manner dimension of the word.

③ In semantic inheritance, the overall activity level is high, and during the process of inheritance, it may undergo semantic variation through combination with other semantic genes. However, its internal information structure remains stable and is not disrupted by the variation or recombination of semantic genes. The variation requires the participation of other semantic genes, resulting in the formation of a new semantic gene chain. For instance, in the word-formation from "ren人(Human)" to "ren li人立(standing like a human)" the semantic gene [human] undergoes variation, which is achieved through recombination with another bound gene [like…], forming a gene chain {manner([[like x], x = [Human])]}, which collectively influences the action manner dimensional feature control of the verb"ren li人立(Standing like a human)". The variation and recombination do not alter the internal information structure of the semantic gene [human].

The bound semantic genes exhibit the following features:

① They cannot independently represent concepts nor independently control the dimensional features of lexical semantics. It requires combination with other free genes through certain functional relationships to form a gene chain, which is an indispensable component of the semantic gene chain. Some bound semantic genes can independently constitute words, but they lack concrete meaning and are generally functional particles, such as [zai在(In)], [cong从] (From)], [yu 于(At)], [jiayi加以(By)], [jinxing进行(Conduct)], etc.

② With low activity and stable nature, these genes do not carry genetic information independently for direct inheritance. Instead, they act as novel genetic components, participating in the semantic inheritance process and combining with other genes that are actually involved in inheritance to serve as catalysts for semantic variation. For instance, in the example of "ren li人立(standing like a human)", the gene directly involved in inheritance is the semantic gene [human]…… As an independent word, "human" is represented by only this gene, while [like…] is not a semantic gene of "human". In the new word "ren li人立(standing like a human)", the mechanism of variation for the free gene [Human] is triggered by the involvement of the bound gene [like…], which recombines with it. The bound gene [like…] acts as a catalyst in the semantic information variation reaction.

2) Explicit Semantic Genes and Implicit Semantic Gene

The types of semantic construction in language are diverse, with some being explicit, such as conceptual meaning (rational meaning), which is generally described in detail in dictionary definitions. However, there are also implicit meanings, such as social meaning, cultural meaning, and collocative meaning, which are typically not included in dictionary entries but are crucial components of language use. For instance, the word "snail" carries an implicit meaning of "slow-moving"; "fox" implies "cunning"; and "Xie zhi獬豸" (haetae, a mythical creature) signifies "justice". In many pragmatic contexts, we directly employ the implicit meanings of words, while their explicit meanings are completely overlooked. For example, in the sentence "He is an old fox", the implicit meaning of "fox" is used, and its explicit meaning holds no communicative value in this context.

The semantic genes that control and represent the dimensions of explicit meaning of words are referred to as explicit semantic genes; those that control and represent the dimensions of implicit meaning associated with words are known as implicit semantic genes.

The explicit and implicit semantic genes exhibit the following characteristics:

① The manifestation (explicit or implicit) of the semantic gene is independent of the symbolic form of the wordsymbolic form of the word. For instance, the semantic gene [like…] of the word "ren li人立(standing like a human)" is not reflected at the symbolic level of the word, yet it is a exlicit gene, forming an integral part of the gene chain that controls the rational meaning dimension of the word. The basic rational meaning of the word "catwalk" is "walking steps like a cat", but the primary expression of this word is the walking style of a cat "moving in a straight line", thus it possesses a semantic gene chain {[lujing路径(Path)]([zhixian直线(Straight line)])}. This gene chain is closely related to the semantic gene of the morpheme "cat", but it is not the explicit semantic gene of "cat". Therefore, although the gene chain {[lujing路径(Path)]([zhixian直线(Straight line)]))} has a corresponding symbol in the morphological form of "catwalk", it still belongs to the implicit gene. Similar examples include "shexing蛇行(to move like a snake)", "woju蜗居(to live in a snail-like dwelling)" "longxing hubu龙行虎步(to walk with the grace of a dragon and the stride of a tiger)", "fengchi dianche风驰电掣(to move as fast as the wind and lightning)", and so on.

② The explicit semantic genes and the implicit semantic genes function identically in controlling and representing the feature dimensions of semantics, but with different weights for the dimensions. Generally, the dimensions controlled by the implicit genes are lower. However, in certain specific contexts, such as in the example "He is just an old fox" mentioned above, the weight of the dimension controlled by the implicit gene may be influenced by the context and thus increased.

③ The explicit semantic genes may undergo variation during genetic recombination, yet they generally maintain a relative stability in most cases. Even when recombination and variation occur, the internal information structure of the semantic genes themselves remains unaltered. In contrast, the implicit semantic genes are predominantly the result of recombination and variation, and their nature is unstable during the process of variation. This is because the implicit meanings of words may involve multiple dimensions, each of which can experience variation, leading to a variety of resultant variations. For instance, the implicit semantic genes of the word "shu鼠(rat)" can undergo variation to produce new words with different implicit meanings such as "shubei鼠辈(rat-like individuals, despicable persons)", "shumu cunguang鼠目寸光(short-sighted as a rat, or limited vision)", "shucuan鼠窜(to scurry like a rat)" and "shudu jichang鼠肚鸡肠(a petty and narrow-minded person like a rat)". Similarly, the recessive semantic genes of the word "hu虎(tiger)" can undergo variation to generate new words with different implicit meanings such as "hudan虎胆(courage of a tiger)", "hubu虎步(striding like a tiger)", "huxue虎穴(lair of the tiger)", "hushi虎视(to glare like a tiger)" and "hutou shewei虎头蛇尾(a tiger's head and a snake's tail, a strong start and a weak finish).

3) Family semantic gene and Individual semantic gene

The inheritance of semantic genes is most pronounced in lexical families. In lexical families, the superior parent word inherits all its semantic genes intact to the inferior offspring word. Meanwhile, the various sibling words at a lower generation each possess their own unique genes.

A word's semantic gene inherited from its superordinate term is referred to as a family gene; in addition to the family gene, the other individualized genes possessed by the word are called individual genes. For instance, in the following local lexical family of "Kitchenware" categorized by function (Fig. 3.2).

chuju厨具(kitchenware):
{[工具]:{[功能]({[制作]([饭]∨[菜])})}}
{[Tool]:{[Function]({[Cook]([Staplefood]∨Cuisine])})}}
guo锅(pot):
{[工具]:{[功能]({[制作]([饭]∨[菜])})}} + {[功能]({[[内置]($_{Gs}$[食材])]∧$_{Gs}$[加热])}}}

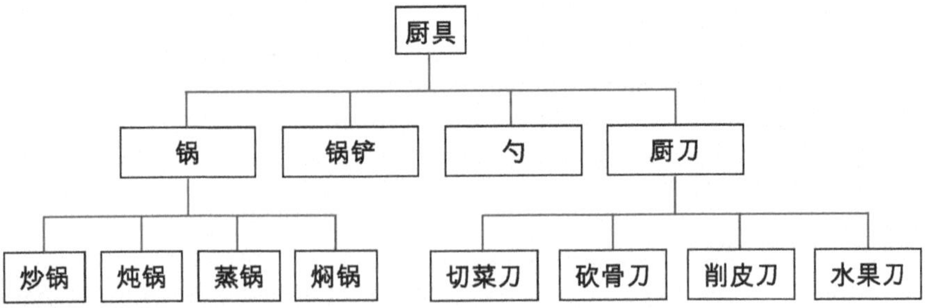

Fig. 3.2 Part of a "Kitchenware" Lexical Family

{[Tool]:{[Function]({[Cook]([Staplefood]∨Cuisine])})}} +
[Function]({[[Contain](Gs[Ingredients])]∧Gs[Heating])}}}.[5]

guochan锅铲(spatula):

{[工具]:{[功能]({[制作]([饭]∨[菜])})}} + {[功能]({[[翻]∨[炒]](Gs[食材])}}}
{[Tool]:{[Function]([Cook]([Staplefood]∨[Cuisine]))}} +
{[Function]([Stir]∨[Fry] (Gs[Ingredients]))}}

shao勺(spoon):

{[工具]:{[功能]({[制作]([饭]∨[菜])})}} + {[功能]({[舀](Gs[食材])}}}
{[Tool]:{[Function]({[Cook]([Staplefood]∨[Cuisine])})}} +
{[Function]({[Scoop](Gs[Ingredients])})}}.

chudao厨刀(kitchen knife):

{[工具]:{[功能]({[制作]([饭]∨[菜])})}} + {[功能]({[分割](Gs[食材])}}}
{[Tool]:{[Function]({[Cook]([Staplefood]∨[Cuisine])})}} +
{[Function]({[Cut](Gs[Ingredients])})}}

The hypernym "kitchenware" inherits all semantic genes{[工具]:{[功能]({[制作]([饭]∨[菜])})}}{[Tool]: {[Function] ({[Cook] ([Staplefood]∨[Cuisine])})}} to its hyponyms "pot", "spatula", "spoon", and "kitchen knife". This set of semantic genes constitutes the family semantic genes of the lexical family. The four hyponyms "pot", "spatula", "spoon", and "kitchen knife" each possess a distinct genetic chain {[功能]({[[内置](Gs[食材])]∧[加热])}}{[Function]({[[Contain](Gs[ingredients])]∧[Heat])}}, {[功能]({[[翻]∨[炒]](Gs[食材])}} {[Function]({[[Stir]∨[Fry]] (Gs[Ingredients])}}},{[功能]({[舀](Gs[食材])}}{[Function]({[Scoop](Gs[Ingredients])}}} and {[功能]({[分割](Gs[食材])}}{[Function]({[Cut](Gs[Ingredients])}}} respectively. This genetic chain represents their individual genes.

The family semantic genes exhibit the following characteristics:

① Within the lexical family, the complete semantic gene cluster of the hypernym is inherited as a family semantic gene from the top down in an integrated manner. All hyponyms acquire the entire family semantic genes of the hypernym, and the structural integrity of the hypernym's semantic gene chain is not altered during the inheritance process.

② In a multi-generational lexical family, each pair of consecutive generations constitutes a smallest family unit, within which the lexical heritage of the parent generation serves as the foundational 'family' genes for the childe generation. For instance, as illustrated in Fig. 3.2, the set {chuju厨具(kitchenware): guo锅(pot), guochan锅铲(spatula), shao勺(spoon), chudao厨刀(kitchen knife)} constitutes a smallest family. The semantic gene cluster of the hypernym "chuju厨具(kitchenware" serves as the family gene for this smallest family, which is completely inherited by the four hyponyms:guo锅(pot), guochan锅铲(spatula), shao勺(spoon) and chudao厨刀(kitchen knife). After inheriting the family gene,

[5] Here, "Ingredients" and "Heating" are words, not semantic genes. They are themselves composed of other semantic genes. The semantic information structure gene cluster composed of these genes for the word is denoted as Gs[shicai食材(Ingredients)], Gs[jiare加热(Heating)]. For the sake of simplicity in expression, the gene chain is not elaborated upon in this context.].

the hyponym "pot" recombines with its own individual genes to form a new gene cluster. In the next smallest lexical family of a lower level {guo锅(pot): chaoguo炒锅(frying pot), dunguo炖锅(stewing pot), zhengguo 蒸锅(steaming pot), menguo焖锅(braising pot)}, having guo锅(pot) as the hypernym, the semantic gene cluster of "pot" continues to act as the family gene for this smallest lexical family, and is inherited as a whole to the lower generation. The same situation applies to the smallest family {chudao厨刀(kitchen knife): qiecaidao切菜刀(chopping knife), kangudao砍骨刀(bone-cutting knife), xiaopidao削皮刀(peeling knife), shuigoudao水果刀(fruit knife)}.

③ In any multi-generational lexical family, the semantic genes of the ancestor word at the top of the family hierarchy represent the most core family genes for the entire family, which are shared among all the lexical members of the family.

The individual semantic genes exhibit the following characteristics:

① In a lexical family, the individual semantic genes control and represent the individualized features dimensions of each word, which serve as the sole basis for distinguishing between sibling words within the family.

② In lexical families strictly aggregated according to a single standard, the semantic feature dimensions controlled and represented by individual gene for sibling words are identical; the differences lie in the varying semantic feature values of each sibling word along this common dimension. This eigenvalue constitutes the individual gene (chain) of each word. For instance, Fig. 3.2 depicts the "kitchenware" lexical family categorized by function, with each generation's evolution being guided by the standard of functional division. Consequently, the sibling words in each generation only exhibit differences in the functional dimension. In some semantic field studies, multiple criteria are adopted for classification, such as the semantic field "pot":{guo锅(pot), tieguo铁锅(iron pot), shaguo砂锅(clay pot), buzhanguo不粘锅(non-stick pot), chaoguo炒锅(frying pot), dunguo炖锅(stewing pot), zhengguo蒸锅(steaming pot), menguo焖锅(braising pot)}, which is a mixture of material and functional classification criteria, and is logically imprecise.

③ The individual semantic gene is relative to the hypernyms and sibling words in the family. In contrast to hyponyms, the individual gene, along with the semantic gene inherited from the preceding generation, recombines to form the family gene of a new minimal family.

4) Semantic gene chain and semantic gene cluster

The function of an individual semantic gene is limited; generally, multiple semantic genes need to be recombined in a certain pattern to form larger genetic units, which can effectively control and represent the feature dimensions of semantic features.

A semantic gene chain refers to a unit of semantic genes that recombines two or more semantic genes according to a certain functional relationship to express a complete piece of semantic information. For instance, the gene chain f(x) = {[颜色]([红])} *f(x)* = {[Color]([Red])} consists of two genes [yanse颜色(Color)] and [hong红(Red)], which form a feature function. Here, [Color] serves as the functional operator, analogous to *f*, while "Red" is the specific value of the variable *x*. Similar examples include: f(x) = {[温度]([高])} *f(x)* = {[Temperature]([High])}, f(x) = {[速度]([大])} *f(x)* = {[Speed] ([Fast])}, and f(x) = {[施事]([人])} *f(x)* = {[Agent]([Person])}, among others.

The semantic genes with multiple feature dimensions and the gene chains continue to combine in more complex relationships, forming a relatively stable structure that expresses a relatively complete and independent concept, which constitutes a gene cluster. For instance, the semantic gene structure of the term "qianbixin铅笔芯(pencil lead)" can be represented as: {[[x的部分], x = [铅笔]]:{[材料]([石墨]∨[$_{Gs}$[黏土]∧$_{Gs}$[颜料]])}} {[[Part of x], x = [Pencil]]:{[Material]([Graphite]∨[$_{Gs}$[Clay] ∧ $_{Gs}$[Pigment]])}}, which is composed of gene chains controlling the "composition" dimension and the "material" dimension, and has a stable structure, expressing the relatively independent and complete concept of "the lead of a pencil". This set of genes forms a gene cluster. The semantic gene chains and gene clusters possess the following characteristics:

① A single semantic gene chain controls and represents a complete semantic feature, but a semantic feature does not necessarily correspond to a semantic dimension. Some semantic dimensions may encompass multiple features, requiring the collaborative control and representation by multiple semantic gene chains. For instance, the semantic gene structure of the term "qianbi 铅笔(pencil)" can be represented as: {[工具]:{[功能]([写]∨[画])} + {[结构]({[芯]:{[材料]([石墨]∨[$_{Gs}$[黏土]∧$_{Gs}$[颜料]])}} + {[壳]:{[材料]([木]∨[纸]∨[塑料]∨[金属])}})}} {[Tool]:{[Function]([Write]∨[Draw])} {[Structure]:{[Lead]:{[Material]([Graphite]∨[$_{Gs}$[Clay]∧$_{Gs}$[Pigment]])}}{[Shell]:{[Material]([Wood]∨[Paper]∨[Plastic]∨[Metal])}}}}, where the "jiegou结构(structure)" dimension includes two features, the core and the shell, which are controlled by two gene chains in collaboration.

② The semantic gene chain can be nested, meaning that a smaller gene chain can serve as a component of a larger chain. For instance, the structural gene chain of "qianbi铅笔(pencil)" is a large chain:{[结构]({[芯]:{[材料]([石墨]∨[$_{Gs}$[黏土]∧$_{Gs}$[颜料]])}} + {[壳]:{[材料]([木]∨[纸]∨[塑料]∨[金属])}})} {[Structure]:{[Lead]:{[Material]:($_{Gs}$[Graphite]∨[$_{Gs}$[Clay]∧$_{Gs}$[Pigment]])}}{[Shell]:{[Material]:([Wood]∨ [Paper]∨[Plastic]∨[Metal])}}}. This larger chain encompasses two smaller chains: {[芯]:{[材料]([石墨]∨[$_{Gs}$[黏土]∧$_{Gs}$[颜料]])}}{[Lead]:{[Material]: ($_{Gs}$[Graphite]∨ [$_{Gs}$[Clay]∧$_{Gs}$[Pigment]])}} and{[壳]:{[材料]([木]∨[纸]∨[塑料]∨[金属])}} {[Shell]: {[Material]: ([Wood]∨[Paper]∨[Plastic]∨[Metal])}}, each of which includes even smaller chains, specifically{[材料]([石墨]∨[$_{Gs}$[黏土]∧$_{Gs}$[颜料]])} {[Material]: ([Graphite]∨[$_{Gs}$Clay]∧$_{Gs}$[Pigment]])} and{[材料]([木]∨[纸]∨[塑料]∨[金属])} {[Material]: ([Wood]∨[Paper]∨[Plastic]∨[Metal])},respectively controlling and represeting the "cailiao材料(material)" dimension of the pencil lead and shell.

③ The semantic gene clusters can also be nested. A gene cluster can contain other gene clusters within it. For instance, the gene cluster "qianbixin铅笔芯(pencil lead)" can encompass other gene clusters. The structural representation of this gene cluster, {[[x的部分],x = [铅笔]]:{[材料]([石墨]∨[$_{Gs}$[黏土]∧$_{Gs}$[颜料]])}} {[[Part of x], x = [Pencil]]:{[Material]([Graphite]∨[$_{Gs}$[Clay]∧$_{Gs}$[Pigment]])}}, includes the gene clusters $_{Gs}$[niantu黏土(Clay)] and $_{Gs}$[yanliao颜料(Pigment)] as well.

④ The concept of "semantic gene chain" and "semantic gene cluster" are not two parallel or hierarchical concepts; rather, they are interrelated and can transform into one another. A group of semantic gene sequence with a basically similar information structure, when representing an independent concept, constitutes a gene cluster. Conversely, when it merely represents a semantic feature dimension value of a word, it forms a gene chain. Sometimes, there are differences in the structural representation of these two concepts. For instance, in the example provided, "qianbixin铅笔芯(pencil lead)" as a gene cluster representing an independent concept requires clarification of its object to which it belongs as a component, denoted by the semantic gene [[x的部分],x = [铅笔]] [[Part of x], x = [Pencil]]. When it is described as a gene chain representing the constituent part of a pencil, it is represented through the "jiegou结构(structure)structure" dimension by[结构]([芯]) [Structure]([Lead]).

⑤ The complete semantic gene chain of a word can serve as a fixed set of gene clusters to describe the semantic gene structure of other words that do not have the relationship of reverse implication. In the case of the words "qianbi铅笔(pencil)" and "qianbixin铅笔芯(pencil lead)", there exists a relationship of reverse implication, as "qianbi铅笔(pencil)" constitutes a part of "qianbi铅笔(pencil)" and entails the semantics of "qianbi铅笔(pencil)". When describing the semantic gene structure of "qianbixin铅笔芯(pencil lead)" individually, it is necessary to refer back to "qianbi铅笔(pencil)". Therefore, we do not use the gene cluster $_{Gs}$[qianbi铅笔(Pencil)] to describe the gene structure of "qianbi铅笔(pencil)". On the other hand, $_{Gs}$[niantu黏土(Clay)] and $_{Gs}$[yanliao颜料(Pigment)] do not have a relationship of reverse implication with pencil lead, and thus can be employed to describe the semantic gene structure of pencil lead.

⑥ In the description of the semantic gene structure, semantic gene chains and semantic gene clusters can be mutually inclusive. That is, a single gene chain can contain multiple gene clusters, and a group of gene clusters can also encompass several gene chains.

3.2.2.2 Functional Categories and Functional Characteristics of Semantic Genes

In the vocabulary system, except for a small portion of primitive words independently composed of single free semantic genes, the meanings of most words are formed by the combination of various semantic genes according to certain functional relationships. This semantic structure function can be roughly represented as: $S = a{:}f_1(x_1)$

$+ f_2(x_2) + f_3(x_3) + \ldots\ldots + f_n(x_n)$[6] Here, S represents the semantic function, a is a constant, x is a variable, and f is a functional operator representing different semantic feature dimensions. Based on the functional roles played by each semantic gene in the above functional expression, they can be categorized into semantic constant genes, semantic dimension genes, and semantic variable assignment genes.

1) Semantic constant gene

When describing the meaning of a word, the first step is to define the most core gene within the rational meaning words. This gene represents the superordinate category to which the referent of the word belongs. This gene is referred to as the semantic constant gene. For example:

ChujU厨具(kitchenware):$S_{厨具} = \{[\text{Tool}]:\{f_1(x_1) + f_2(x_2) + f_3(x_3) + \ldots\ldots + f_n(x_n)\}\}$[7]
Wuya乌鸦(crow):$S_{乌鸦} = \{[\text{Animal}]:\{f_1(x_1) + f_2(x_2) + f_3(x_3) + \ldots\ldots + f_n(x_n)\}\}$
Biaoyan表演(perform):$S_{表演} = \{[\text{Activity}]:\{f_1(x_1) + f_2(x_2) + f_3(x_3) + \ldots\ldots + f_n(x_n)\}\}$
Qiaoda敲打(beat):$S_{敲打} = \{[\text{Action}]:\{f_1(x_1) + f_2(x_2) + f_3(x_3) + \ldots\ldots + f_n(x_n)\}\}$
Fanzui犯罪(crime):$S_{犯罪} = \{[\text{Behavior}]:\{f_1(x_1) + f_2(x_2) + f_3(x_3) + \ldots\ldots + f_n(x_n)\}\}$
Jüsang沮丧(dispirited):$S_{沮丧} = \{[\text{State}]:\{f_1(x_1) + f_2(x_2) + f_3(x_3) + \ldots\ldots + f_n(x_n)\}\}$
Guanyu关于(about):$S_{关于} = \{[\text{Function word}]:\{f_1(x_1) + f_2(x_2) + f_3(x_3) + \ldots\ldots + f_n(x_n)\}\}$
Zhuyu主语(subject):$S_{主语} = \{[\text{Metalanguage}]:\{f_1(x_1) + f_2(x_2) + f_3(x_3) + \ldots\ldots + f_n(x_n)\}\}$

Here, [gongju工具(Tool)], [dongwu动物(Animal)], [huodong活动(Activity)], [dongzuo动作(Action)], [xingwei行为(Behavior)], [zhuangtai状态(State)], [gongnengci功能词(Function word)], [yuanyuyan元语言(Metalanguage)] are semantic constant genes representing the superordinate concepts to which each of these words belongs.

The semantic constant genes exhibit the following properties:

① The constant gene of a word directly represents the most fundamental part of its rational meaning and is also the family semantic gene (or the core part of the family semantic gene) of the lexical family of words. Therefore, within the same lexical family, the constant genes are identical.

[6] In the practical use of language, not all functional dimensions of words are simply added together in parallel; there are also various complex semantic relationships. For the sake of convenience in expression, the plus sign is used here to represent them. The specific structural relationships will be discussed in detail in the following sections of this chapter.

[7] The examples provided here mainly discuss constant genes, while the semantic gene structures of other parts are represented by general functional forms, and are not listed in detail.

② The word and its constant semantic gene exhibit an implication relationship in semantics. Conceptually, the objects they represent exist in a genus-species relationship. This can be tested by the following proposition: "*X is a [Y]*", where X represents a word and [Y] represents the semantic constant gene of that word. The logical value of this proposition is always true. This is an important foundation for computer semantic reasoning.

③ The constant gene serves as the starting point and core for the description of semantics, with other components attaching to the constant gene, controlling and representing various feature dimensions involved in the constant gene.

2) Semantic dimension genes

The semantic genes that control and represent the specific features of various dimensions of meaning reflect the individual differential features of meaning in a certain aspect. For example:

qianbi铅笔(pencil):
{[工具]:{[功能]([写]∨[画])} + {[结构]({[芯]:{[材料]([石墨]∨[$_{Gs}$[黏土]∧$_{Gs}$[颜料]])}} + {[壳]:{[材料]([木]∨[纸]∨[塑料]∨[金属])}})}}
{[Tool]:{[Function]([Write]∨[Draw])} + {[Structure]({[Lead]:{[Material]([Graphite]∨[$_{Gs}$[Clay]∧$_{Gs}$[Pigment]])}} + {[Shell]:{[Material]([Wood]∨[Paper]∨[Plastic]∨[Metal])}})}}.
The semantic dimension genes are: [gongneng功能(Function)], [jiegou结构(Structure)] and [cailiao材料(Material)].
chudao厨刀(kitchen knife):
{[工具]:{[功能]({[制作]([饭]∨[菜])})}} + {[功能]({[分割]($_{Gs}$[食材])})}}
{[Tool]:{[Function]({[Cook]([Rice]∨[Dishes])})}} + {[Function]({[Cut]($_{Gs}$[Ingredients])})}}
The semantic dimension genes are: [gongneng功能(Function)], [zhizuo制作(Cook)] and [fenge分割(Cut)].

The semantic dimension genes possess the following properties:

① Each aspect of semantics is represented as a function $F = f(x)$. The semantic dimension gene is an operator of function, akin to f in functional expressions, which cannot exist independently; it must be accompanied by variables. For example:

The [gongneng功能(Function)] feature of "qianbi铅笔(pencil)":
F = 功能(x), x = [写]∨[画] F = Functional(x), where x = [Writing]∨[Drawing], abbreviated as:{[功能]([写]∨[画])} {[Function]([Writing]∨[Drawing])}.
The [jiegou结构(Structure)] feature of "qianbi铅笔(pencil)":
F = 结构(x), x = $_{Gc}$[芯]∨$_{Gc}$[壳] F = Structure(x),x = $_{Gc}$[Lead]∨$_{Gc}$[Shell], abbreviated as:{[结构]($_{Gc}$[芯] + $_{Gc}$[壳])} {[Structure]($_{Gc}$[Lead] + $_{Gc}$[Shell])}.

The [yanse颜色(Color)] feature of "xueye血液(blood):
F = 颜色(x), x = [红] F = Color(x), x = [Red], abbreviated as:{[颜色]([红])} {[Color]([Red])}.
The[yanse颜色(Color)] feature of "kongqi空气(air)":
F = 颜色(x), x = [φ] F = Color(x), x = [φ], abbreviated as:{[颜色]([φ])} {[Color] ([φ])}.[8]
The [wendu温度(Temperature)] feature of "kaishui开水(boiling water)":
F = 温度(x), x = [热] F = Temperature(x), x = [Hot], abbreviated as{[温度]([热])} {[Temperature]([Hot])}.

② The value of the feature function variable x can be a single semantic gene, such as the "color" feature function of "air" and "blood" and the"temperature" feature function of "boiling water"; or it can be an expression composed of multiple semantic genes, for instance, the "function" function of "pencil"; the variable expression can also include semantic gene chains and clusters, such as the "structure" function value of "pencil" being composed of two gene chains $_{Gc}$[xin芯(Lead)] and $_{Gc}$[ke壳(Shell)], and the "material" function value of "pencil lead" containing two gene clusters $_{Gs}$[niantu黏土(Clay)] and $_{Gs}$[yanliao颜料(Pigment)].
③ In a minimal lexical family, the sibling words, in addition to sharing the same family genes, generally also possess identical dimension genes, often distributed symmetrically or parallelly. However, the semantic differences among them are manifested solely in the different values of a specific feature function variable. For instance, as illustrated in Fig. 3.6, the lexical family of "Kitchenware".
④ According to the range of values of the feature function variables, semantic dimension genes can be categorized into finite valued semantic genes and infinite valued semantic genes.

The values of the variables for the finite valued dimension feature functions are confined to a finite closed set. For instance, the values of the feature function variable for [chengdu程度(Degree)] can only be assigned from the closed set{[da大(Large)], [xiao小(Small)], [gao高(High)], [di低(Low)], [zhong中(Medium)]}, so [chengdu程度(Degree)] falls into a finite valued gene.

The values of the variables for the infinite valued dimension feature functions are an open and productive set. For instance, the values of the feature function variable [cailiao材料(Material)] are derived from the open set {[jinshu金属(Metal)], [suliao塑料(Plastic)], [boli玻璃(Glass)], [zhi纸(Paper)]……}. The size of this set corresponds to the variety of materials found in nature. This set is productive, as with the advancement of technology, new materials are continuously invented and discovered. Therefore, [cailiao材料(Material)] is a infinite valued gene.

[8] Air is colorless; however, this dimension feature cannot be omitted from description, as we generally define "air" as a "colorless, odorless gas", implying that "colorlessness" is an essential feature of air, representing the empty set. The value of the [Color] function is denoted as φ, representing a empty set.

⑤ Based on the distribution structure of the value sets of the feature function variables, the semantic dimension genes can be categorized into five different types: symmetric, opposite, parallel, gradual, and discrete.

The value set of the symmetric feature function includes a pair of semantic genes with antonymic semantics plus a neutral semantic gene, forming a geometric structure that is symmetric with the neutral gene as the axis of symmetry and the two antonymic genes as the symmetric point. For instance, the value set of the variables of the [ganqing secai感情色彩(Sentimental polarity)] feature function is {[bao褒(Positive)], [zhong中(Neutral)], [bian贬(Negative)]}, where the semantic genes [bao褒(Positive)] and [bian贬(Negative)] form a symmetric structure with the gene [zhong中(Neutral)] as the axis of symmetry. Therefore, [ganqing secai感情色彩(Sentimental polarity)] is a dimension gene of symmetric values. Such genes are generally finite valued genes.

The value set of the variable of the opposite feature function includes a pair of semantic genes or gene clusters with antonymic semantics. For instance, the value set of the variable of the feature function [luoji zhenzhi逻辑真值(Logic value)] is {[zhen真(True)], [jia假(False)]}; the value set of the variable of the feature function [xingbie性别(Gender)] is {[nan男(Male)], [nü女(Female)]}. [zhen真 (True)]and [jia假(False)], [nan男(Male)]and [nü女(Female)] are antonymous, thus [luoji zhenzhi逻辑真值(Logic value)] and [xingbie性别(Gender)] are dimension genes of opposite values. These genes are also finite valued genes.

The value set of the variable of the parallel feature function is composed of a set of genes or gene clusters with mutually parallel semantics. For instance, the range of values for the [yanse颜色(Color)] feature function variable is {[hei黑(Black)], [bai白(White)], [hui灰(Gray)], [hong红(Red)], [cheng 橙(Orange)], [huang黄(Yellow)], [lü绿(Green)], [qing青(Cyan)], [lan蓝(Blue)], [zi紫(Purple)], $_{Gs}$[lanhei蓝黑(Blue-black)], $_{Gs}$[fenhong粉红(Light red)], $_{Gs}$[qianlü浅绿(Light green)]… …}; the set of values for the [wuzhi zhuangtai物质状态(Material state)] feature function variable is {[gutai固态(Solid)], [yetai液态(Liquid)], [qitai气态(Gas)]}; and the set of values for the [fangxiang方向(Direction)] feature function variable is {{[dong东(East)], [xi西(West)], [nan南(South)], [bei北(North)], $_{Gs}$[dongnan东南(Southeast)], $_{Gs}$[dongbei东北(Northeast)], $_{Gs}$[xinan 西南(Southwest)], $_{Gs}$[xibei西北(Northwest)]}, {[qian前(Front)], [hou后(Back)], [zuo左(Left)], [you右(Right)]}, {[shang上(Up)], [zhong中(Middle)], [xia下(Down)]}, {[li 里(Inside)], [wai外(Outside)]}}.[9] The semantic genes (or gene clusters) within these sets are all parallel, thus [yanse颜色(Color)], [wuzhi zhuangtai物质状态(Material state)], and [fangxiang方向(Direction)] are dimension genes of parallel values. Such genes can be either finite valued or infinite valued.

The value set of the variable of the gradual type feature function is composed of a set of genes (or gene clusters) that form a certain semantic continuum. For instance, the set of values for the variable of the feature function [wendu温度(Temperature)] is

[9] This is a complex set containing nested structures. That is, the set itself is composed of multiple subsets. The genes within each subset have parallel semantics, and the semantics between different subsets are also parallel.

{[re热(Hot)], [wen温(Warm)], [liang凉(Cool)], [han寒(Chilly)], [leng冷(Cold)]}; the set of values for the the variable of the feature function [nianling年龄(Age)] is {$_{Gs}$[laonian老年(Old-aged)], $_{Gs}$[zhongnian中年(Middle-aged)], $_{Gs}$[qingnian青年(Young)], $_{Gs}$[shaonian少年(Adolescent)], $_{Gs}$[ertong儿童(Child)], $_{Gs}$[ying'er婴儿(Infant)]} and so on. The semantics of the genes (or gene clusters) within these sets form a continuum from large to small in terms of degree or quantity, with the boundaries between quantities being fuzzy, lacking an accurate numerical interval, and only a general grade difference. Therefore, [wendu温度(Temperature)] and [nianling年龄(Age)] belong to the gradual dimension genes. Such genes can be either finite valued or infinite valued.

The value set of discrete feature function variables is composed of a group of genes (or gene clusters) that do not exhibit a clear structural distribution pattern in terms of semantics. These include [gongneng功能(Function)], [xingzhuang形状(Shape)], [cailiao材料(Material)], [zucheng组成(Composition)], and so on. The value bearing genes cannot be predetermined and are generally determined by their constituent objects. These genes are all infinite valued genes.

3) Semantic variable assignment gene

In the semantic feature function $F = f(x)$, the range of values for the variable x is determined by the specific function operator f. Generally, it can be a semantic gene, a gene cluster, or a gene chain. There exists classes of semantic genes that cannot typically be used as constant genes or dimension genes; instead, they are generally employed to assign values to the variable x. Such genes are referred to as semantic variable assignment genes. For instance:[da大(Big)], [xiao小(Small)], [duo多(Many)], [shao少(Few)], [nan男(Male)], [nü女(Female)], etc.

The semantic variable assignment genes possesses the following properties:

① Assignment genes generally cannot be used individually,they cannot exist independently within the structure of semantic genes. They must be combined with semantic dimension genes to form a minimal gene chain, which is necessary for controlling and representing the feature dimensions of semantics.

② Assignment genes exhibit mutual mandatory selectivity towards dimension genes. An individual or a group of assignment genes with similar semantic properties can only assign values to a specific dimension gene. For instance, the set {[nan男(Male)], [nü女(Female)]} can only assign values to the gene [xingbie性别(Gender)], and conversely,the variables of the [xingbie性别(Gender)] feature function can only take its value from the assiggnment gene set {[nan男(Male)], [nü女(Female)]}; similarly, the set {[hong红(Red)], [cheng橙(Orange)], [huang黄(Yellow)], [lü绿(Green)], [qing青(Cyan)], [lan蓝(Blue)], [zi紫(Purple)]…} can only assign values to the gene [yanseyanse(Color)], and the set {[da大(Large)], [xiao小(Small)]} can only assign values to dimension genes such as, [chengdu程度(Degree)], [zhi值(Value)], [shuliang数量(Quantity)], and so on.

③ Although assignment genes cannot control the semantic features of words independently, some assignment genes can form words on their own and possess a highly active syntactic combination ability. In fact, even when used as standalone words in sentences, the essential meaning of assignment genes remains unchanged; it is merely that the dimension features they are associated with are embedded within the contextual setting of the sentence. For example:

(1) Zhe suo fangzi henda这所房子很大。(This house is very large.)
(2) Wo bi ta da我比他大。(I am older than him.)

In Example (1), "da大(large)" refers to the large space of the house. With the expression of semantic gene structure, the semantic structure of this sentence can be represented as:{[房子]:{[空间]:{[度量值]([大])}}} {[House]:{[Space]:{[Measure value]([Large])}}}. It is evident that [Large] serves as the assignment gene of the feature function of the [duliangzhi度量值(Measure value)].

In Example (2), "da大(older)" refers to being older in age. The semantic structure of the sentence can be represented as: {[[我] → [他]]:{[比较]({[年龄]([大])})}} {[[I] → [He]]:{[Comparison]({[Age]([Older])})}}, where [da大(older)] is the assignment gene of the [nianling年龄(Age)] feature function.

④Some combinations of assignment genes and dimension genes form feature functions with active word-formation capabilities, where a simple feature function can itself constitute a word. For instance, the set of assignment genes {[hong红(Red)], [cheng橙(Orange)], [huang黄(Yellow)], [lü绿(Green)],…} combined with the dimension gene [yanse颜色(Color)] can generate the word set {hongse红色(Red), chengse橙色(Orange),huangse黄色(Yellow),lüse绿色(Green),…}.

3.3 The Metalanguage System of Semantic Gene Description

The metalanguage system of semantic gene description employed in this book encompasses three components: semantic gene units extracted from natural languages, descriptive symbols for gene structures of semantic information, and XML language codes. The design of the metalanguage system takes into account both human usability and machine applicability, featuring strong readability for ease of reading and understanding by human readers, as well as serving as a tool for semantic research. Additionally, it possesses characteristics of high formalization and computability, allowing it to be directly accessed by various NLP systems.

3.3.1 Semantic Genes Extracted from Natural Language

The semantic genes extracted from natural language constitute a finite set, which forms the foundation of the entire metalanguage system of semantic gene description. Theoretically, the composition of all the semantics of the entire lexical system of a natural language, as well as the semantics of the entire language system (including the semantics of discourse), are all based on this finite gene set. The specific methods and operational procedures for the extraction of semantic genes are elaborated in Chap. 4, while this section primarily describes the overview of the semantic genes extracted from natural language.

3.3.1.1 I. The Semantic Genes Representing Name of Human or Things

These genes correspond to nouns in traditional linguistics. In the lexical systems of most natural languages, nouns are the most numerous, and thus, this category requires the extraction of the largest number of semantic genes. A selection of examples is provided below:

1) The semantic genes representing names associated with person

① [ren人(Person)], [ziji自己(Self)], [duif对方(The other)], [taren他人(Others)].
② [xingbie性别(Gender)], [nan男(Male)], [nü女(Female)].
③ [nianling年龄(Age)], [lao老(Elderly)], [zhong中(Middle-aged)], [qing青(Youth)], [you幼(Child)], [ying婴(Infant)]…
④ [qinshu亲属(Kinship)], [beifen辈分(Generation)], [shangdai上代(Parent)], [xiadai下代(Child)], [tongdai同代(Sibling)], [muxi母系(Matriarchal)], [fuxi父系(Patrilineal)]…
⑤ [xingge性格(Personality)], [timao体貌(Appearance)], [shenfen身份(Identity)], [zhiye职业(Occupation)]…

2) The semantic genes representing names associated with things

   ① [duixiang对象(Object)], [wu物(Object)], [zhuangzhi装置(Device)], [qiju器具(Instrument)], [shiti实体(Entity)]…
   ② [ziran自然(Nature)], [tian天(Heaven)], [di地(Earth)], [shan山(Mountain)], [he河(River)], [hu湖(Lake)], [hai海(Sea)], [bo波(Wave)], [lang浪(Ripple)]…
   ③ [tianqi天气(Weather)], [feng风(Wind)], [yu雨(Rain)], [yin阴(Overcast)], [qing晴(Sunny)]…
   ④ [wuzhi物质(Matter)], [cailiao材料(Material)], [jinshu金属(Metal)], [jin金(Gold)], [yin银(Silver)], [tie铁(Iron)], [tong铜(Copper)], [lü铝(Aluminum)], [xi锡(Tin)]…
   ⑤ [dongwu动物(Animal)], [niao鸟(Bird)], [shou兽(Beast)], [chong虫(Insect)], [yu鱼(Fish)]…
   ⑥ [zhiwu植物(Plant)], [cao草(Grass)], [mu木(Wood)], [hua花(Flower)], [muben木本(Woody)], [caoben草本(Herbaceous)]…
   ⑦ [xianxiang现象(Phenomena)], [benzhi本质(Essence)], [shijian时间(Time)], [kongjian空间(Space)], [fuhao符号(Symbol)], [jingshen精神(Spirit)], [siwei思维(Mind)], [shehui社会(Society)], [guojia国家(State)],

[zuzhi组织(Organization)], [zhidu制度(System)], [wenhua文化(Culture)], [zhengzhi政治(Politics)]…

⑧ [jiegou结构(Structure)], [zhengti整体(Whole)], [bufen部分(Part)], [bumen部门(Department)], [qiguan器官(Organ)], [chengyuan成员(Member)], [dian点(Point)], [xian线(Line)], [mian面(Area)], [changdu长度(Length)], [mianji面积(Surface)], [tiji体积(Volume)], [gongneng功能(Function)], [shuliang数量(Quantity)], [danwei单位(Unit)]…

3) The semantic genes representing names associated with events

① [shijian事件(Event)], [xingwei行为(Behavior)], [huodong活动(Activity)], [jingli经历(Experience)]…
② [shigu事故(Accident)], [zaihai灾害(Disaster)], [huo祸(Calamity)]…
③ [zhanzheng战争(War)], [geming革命(Revolution)], [fengchao风潮(Upheaval)]…
④ [huiyi会议(Meeting)], [shenghuo生活(Life)]…
⑤ [chengji成绩(Achievement)], [gongxian贡献(Contribution)], [zui罪(Crime)]…
⑥ [yuanyin原因(Cause)], [jieguo结果(Result)], [fangshi方式(Manner)], [shouduan手段(Means)], [mudi目的(Purpose)], [didian地点(Location)], [fangxiang方向(Direction)], [luoji路径(Path)], [fanwei范围(Range)], [guimo规模(Scale)], [guocheng过程(Process)], [sudu速度(Speed)]…

4) The semantic genes representing linguistic concepts

This category of semantic genes constitutes a universal metalanguage for linguistic research and is frequently employed in semantic analysis.

① [mingci名词(Noun)], [dongci动词(Verb)], [xingrongci形容词(Adjective)], [daici代词(Pronoun)], [jieci介词(Preposition)], [fuci副词(Adverb)]…
② [zhuyu主语(Subject)], [weiyu谓语(Predicate)], [binyu宾语(Object)], [dingyu定语(Attribute)], [zhuangyu状语(Adverbial)], [buyu补语(Complement)]…
③ [Agent], [Patient], [Case], [Argument], [Reflexive], [Reference]…
④ [xiuci修辞(Rhetoric)], [yuyan隐喻(Metaphor)], [yinshen引申(Extension)], [zidai指代(Reference)], [niren拟人(Personification)]…
⑤ [jixing极性(Polarity)], [baoyi褒义(Positive)], [bianyi贬义(Negative)]…

3.3.1.2 The Semantic Genes Representing Behavioral Actions

These genes correspond to verbs in traditional linguistics.

① [zhongzhi终止(Terminate)], [weiyi位移(Displace)], [kaishi开始(Start)], [ting停(Stop)], [jinxing进行(Conduct)], [zhuanyi转移(Transfer)]…
② [caozuo操作(Operate)], [yunxing运行(Run)], [juxing举行(Hold)], [bianhua变化(Change)], [fanying反应(React)], [fasheng发生(Occur)]…
③ [fangzhi防止(Prevent)], [baochi保持(Maintain)], [baohu保护(Protect)], [shi…bianhua使……变化(Cause to change)], […hua ……化(……ization)] …

④ [jiechu接触(Touch)], [jiejin接近(Approach)], [jiehe结合(Combine)], [fenli分离(Separate)], [lianjie连接(Connect)]…
⑤ [sikao思考(Think)], [renzhi认知(Cognize)], [zhuyi注意(Pay attention to)], [lijie理解(Understand)], [jiyi记忆(Memory)], [yiwang遗忘(Forget)], [faxian发现(Discover)], [yanshuo言说(Speak)], [ting听(Hear)], [kan看(See)], [wen问(Ask)], [da答(Answer)], [qingqiu请求(Request)]…
⑥ [ganjue感觉(Feel)], [chang尝(Taste)], [xiu嗅(Smell)], [ku哭(Cry)], [xiao笑(Laugh)]…
⑦ [na拿(Take)], [fang放(Put)], [kai开(Open)], [guan关(Close)], [danren担任(Undertake)], [pin聘(Hire)]…
⑧ [zhixing执行(Execute)], [tongyi同意(Agree)], [fandui反对(Oppose)], [jianyi建议(Suggest)], [dizhi抵制(Resist)], [jueding决定(Decide)], [kongzhi控制(Control)], [jiang奖(Reward)], [cheng惩(Punish)]…
⑨ [zhizao制造(Manufacture)], [xiu修(Repair)], [jiejue解决(Solve)], [shixian实现(Realize)], [xiaomie消灭(Eliminate)], [chuli处理(Handle)]…

3.3.1.3 The Semantic Genes Representing the Nature and State of Human or Things

These genes correspond to adjectives and adverbs in traditional linguistics.

1) The semantic genes representing the nature and state of human

① [shan善(Kind)], [e恶(Evil)], [hao好(Good)], [huai坏(Bad)], [mei美(Beautiful)], [chou丑(Ugly)]…
② [jiankang健康(Healthy)], [sheng生(Living)], [lao老(Old)], [bing病(Ill)], [si死(Dead)]…
③ [xi喜(Joyful)], [nu怒(Angry)], [ai哀(Sad)], [le乐(Happy)], [you忧(Worried)], [hen恨(Hateful)]…
④ [xingfu幸福(Happy)], [tongku痛苦(Pain)], [jili吉利(Lucky)], [ganga尴尬(Awkward)], [yuan冤(Wronged)]…
⑤ [ya雅(Elegant)], [su俗(Vulgar)], [congming聪明(Smart)], [jiaohua狡猾(Cunning)], [chun蠢(Foolish)], [chengshi诚实(Honest)], [yansu严肃(Serious)], [wenhe温和(Gentle)]…
⑥ [jianqiang坚强(Strong)], [guoduan果断(Decisive)], [zhengzhi正直(Upright)], [guzhig固执(Stubborn)], [yinxian阴险(Wicked)], [kelian可怜(Pitiful)], [kailang开朗(Outgoing)], [neixiang内向(Introverted)]…
⑦ [qinfen勤奋(Diligent)], [landuo懒惰(Lazy)], [renzhen认真(Serious)], [qianxu谦虚(Modest)], [tan贪(Greedy)], [lian廉(Incorruptible)]…

2) The semantic genes representing the nature and state of things

① [hao好(Good)], [huai坏(Bad)], [mei美(Beautiful)], [chou丑(Ugly)], [dui对(Right)], [cuo错(Wrong)]…
② [anquan安全(Safe)], [weixian危险(Dangerous)], [nan难(Difficult)], [yi易(Easy)]…

③ [luan乱(Messy)], [za杂(Miscellaneous)], [fanrong 繁荣 (Prosperous)], [kong空(Empty)], [man满(Full)], [jiandan简单(Simple)]…
④ [ping平(Flat)], [zhi直(Straight)], [qu曲(Curved)], [zheng 正(Straightforward)], [wai歪(Oblique)], [fengli锋利(Sharp)], [dun 钝(Blunt)]…
⑤ [sheng生(Raw)], [shu熟(Mature)], [nong浓(Dense)], [xi稀(Dilute)], [ming 明(Bright)], [an暗(Dark)]…
⑥ [qingche清澈(Clear)], [hunzhuo浑浊(Turbid)], [qingxi清晰(Clear)], [mohu 模糊 (Blurred)]…
⑦ [gan干(Dry)], [shi湿(Wet)], [cucao 粗糙 (Rough)], [guanghua光滑(Smooth)], [xizhi细致(Delicate)]…
⑧ [suan酸(Sour)], [tian甜(Sweet)], [ku苦(Bitter)], [la辣(Spicy)], [xian 咸(Salty)], [xiang香(Scented)], [chou臭(Stinky)]…

3.3.1.4 The Functional Semantic Genes Representing Linguistic Combinatorial Relations

These genes correspond to the functional words such as prepositions, conjunctions, particles, and words used for logical judgments in traditional linguistics.

① [genju根据(According to)], [yikao依靠(Rely on)], [guanyu关于(About)]…
② [you有(Have)], [wu无(None)], [shi是(Is)], [fou否(No)], [zhen真(True)], [jia 假(False)]…
③ [bijiao比较(Relatively)], [xiangtong相同(Same)], [xiangsi相似(Similar)]…
④ [keneng可能(Probably)], [bixu必须(Must)]…

The examples cited above are merely simple classifications based on the semantic information inherent in the semantic genes, and do not imply that they are exclusively applicable to their respective categories. In the actual use of language,the description of the meaning of a word often requires the use of multiple or even all types of semantic genes.

3.3.2 Descriptive Symbols for Semantic Gene Structure

The descriptive symbols for semantic gene is an important means to represent the nature of semantic genes and the semantic relationships among them. Following the general conventions of metalanguage systems in other disciplines, the symbols used in the structure of semantic gene information are categorized into the following types.

3.3.2.1 Boundary Markers

1) Square bracket []: It represents the semantic gene boundary markers, indicating that the component within the brackets is a single semantic gene. For example: [Tool], [Function], [Large], [φ], etc.
2) Parentheses (): It serve as variable boundary markers, indicating that the components within the parentheses represent specific values of a semantic feature function variable. These values can be either a single gene or an expression of a gene structure. An expression enclosed in parentheses must immediately follow an expression enclosed in square brackets, where the semantic gene component within the square brackets denotes a feature function operator. For example:[颜色]([红]) [Color]([Red]), [材料]([金属]∨[塑料])[Material]([Metal]∨[Plastic]), [吸收]($_{Gs}$[养分])[Absorption] ($_{Gs}$[Nutrient]), [Function]({[Contain]([Liquid])}) and so on.
3) Curly brace { }: It serve as boundary markers for semantic gene chains, indicating that the components within the braces form a semantic gene chain. A minimal gene chain represents a single feature of the meaning of a word, and multiple gene chains can be combined to form a complete gene chain, which signifies the entire semantic structure of a word. For instance, the semantic gene chain of the word "shugui书柜(bookshelf)" is: {[器具]:{[功能]([装]([书]))} + {[形状]([方])} + {[材料]([木]∨[金属])}} {[Instrument]: {[Function]([Contain]([Book]))} + {[Shape]([Square])} + {[Material]([Wood]∨[Metal])}}, which includes three sub-chains: {[功能]([装]([书]))}{[Function]([Contain]([Book]))}, {[形状]([方])}{[Shape]([Square])}, and {[材料]([木]∨[金属])}{[Material]([Wood]∨[Metal])}, respectively representing the function chain, shape chain, and material chain.

To represent the complex semantic relationships between semantic genes, nested boundary markers are generally required. As required, the three types of boundary markers can be nested within each other. In the nesting of curly braces and parentheses, it is generally necessary to include the other two markers, and they cannot be nested solely by themselves. Only square brackets can be nested by themselves without the need for other boundary markers, such as: [$_{Gs}$[黏土]∧$_{Gs}$[颜料]] [$_{Gs}$[Clay]∧$_{Gs}$[Pigment]]、[[翻]∨[炒]] [[Stir]∨[Fry]]. This is because square brackets represent a single semantic gene, and self-nesting indicates the combination of multiple genes, which also functions as a single gene. In the gene chain {[材料]([石墨]∨[$_{Gs}$[黏土]∧$_{Gs}$[颜料]])} {[Material]($_{Gs}$[Graphite]∨[$_{Gs}$[Clay]∧$_{Gs}$[Pigment]])}, $_{Gs}$[shimo石墨(Graphite)] and $_{Gs}$[niantu黏土(Clay)] are two selectable values of the feature function variable "material", and $_{Gs}$[niantu黏土(Clay)] is mixed with $_{Gs}$[yanliao颜料(Pigment)], forming an integral entity, hence represented as [$_{Gs}$[黏土]∧$_{Gs}$[颜料]] [$_{Gs}$[Clay]∧$_{Gs}$[Pigment]]; while in the gene chain {[[翻]∨[炒]]($_{Gs}$[食材])} {[[Stir]∨[Fry]]($_{Gs}$[Ingredients])}, [fan翻(Stir)] and [chao炒(Fry)] are two different function operators of the [gongneng功能(Function)] feature function, but their variable values are the same, both being $_{Gs}$[shicai食材(Ingredients)]. They should be represented as:{{[翻](Gs[食材])}∨{[炒](Gs[食材])}}{{[Stir](Gs[Ingredients])}∨{[Fry](Gs [Ingredients])}}, and after combining, a more concise expression is obtained: {[[翻]∨[炒]](Gs[食材])}{[[Stir]∨[Fry]](Gs[Ingredients])}.

3.3.2.2 Connector Symbols

1) The colon:: It is used to connect constant genes and feature dimension gene chains in the expression of semantic information gene structures. A single gene structure expression can accommodate no more than one constant gene, hence there is only one colon. For instance, the semantic gene expression of "bi笔(pen)" is {[工具]:{[功能] ([写]∨[画])} {[Tool]:{[Function]([Write]∨[Draw])}}. If the gene structure expression of the entire word contains nested gene chains, i.e., the semantic meaning of the entire word is composed of multiple gene chains, where the main chain has exactly one constant gene, the sub-chains can have their own constant genes. For example, the gene structure expression of "qianbi铅笔(pencil)" is {[工具]:{[功能]([写]∨[画])} + {[结构]({[芯]:{[材料]([石墨]∨[Gs[黏土]∧Gs[颜料]])}} + {[壳]:{[材料]([木]∨[纸]∨[塑料]∨[金属])}})}} {[Tool]:{[Function]([Write]∨[Draw])} + {[Structure]({[Lead]:{[Material]([Graphite]∨[Gs [Clay] ∧ Gs[Pigment]])}} + {[Shell]: {[Material]([Wood]∨[Paper]∨[Plastic]∨[Metal])}})}}, where [Tool] is the constant gene of the main chain, and [xin芯(Lead)] and [ke壳(Shell)] are the constant genes of the two sub-chains within the [jiegou结构(Structure)] dimension.
2) The horizontal arrow → : It is used to connect two semantic genes in a contrasting or comparative relationship, indicating a directional nature that represents the primary and secondary relationship of comparison or contrast. For instance, the definition of "ju局(bureau)" in the *The Contemporary Chinese Dictionary* is: "Bureau, a unit in the organizational system of an agency, divided according to business functions (the level is generally lower than that of a ministry and higher than that of a department)." The part within the brackets of this definition can be represented as:{[级别]([比较]([[局] → [部]]([低])∧[[局] → [处]]([高])))} {[Level]([Comparison]([[Bureau] → [Department]]([Low\)∧[[Bureau] → [Ministry]]([High]))).}
3) The vertical arrow ↑: It is used to link two semantic genes that are interrelated through mutual reference; these genes maintain an equitable relationship, devoid of any hierarchical differentiation. For example, the definition of "chuizi锤子(hammer)" in *The Contemporary Chinese Dictionary* is: "A tool for striking things. It has a head made of metal or other materials and a handle perpendicular to the head." The description of the hammer head and handle can be represented as: {[位置]([头]↑[柄] (垂直))} {[Position] ([Head]↑[Handle] ([Perpendicular]))}
4) The plus sign + : it is used to connect two gene chains expressing different feature dimensions in the semantic gene structure expression. For instance, in the semantic gene expression of "chuizi锤子(hammer)" as {[工具]:{[功能]([敲]∨[

打])} + {[结构]({[组成]({[头]:{[材料]([金属]∨[其他])}}∧[柄])} + {[位置]([[头]↑ [柄]](垂直))})}} {[Tool]: [Function]([Knock]∨[Strik])} + {[Structure]({[Composition]({[Head]:{[Material] ([Metal]∨[Other])}}∧[Handle])} + {[Position]([[Head]↑[Handle]]([Perpendicular]))})}}, the first level contains two sub-chains, "Function" and "Structure", while the "Structure" sub-chain at the second level further includes "Composition" and "Position" sub-chains.

5) *Of*: It is used to indicate a possessive, subordinate, or affiliated relationship between two semantic genes, akin to "A's B." For instance, "jiujiu舅舅(mother's brother,uncle)" can be represented as: {[关系]($_{Gs}$[兄弟]of $_{Gs}$[妈妈])} {[Relation] ($_{Gs}$[Brother] of $_{Gs}$[Mother])}.
6) The greater-than sign (>) and the less-than sign (<): These are used to connect two semantic genes that have a temporal relationship. [A] > [B] indicates that A occurs after B, while [A] < [B] indicates that A occurs before B. For example, the term "fanmai贩卖(trafficking)" signifies "buying first and selling later", and the semantic information gene structure expression can be described as:[买] < [卖] [Buy] < [Sell].
7) The equals sign = : It is used to connect a word with its semantic gene structure expression. For the sake of convenience in description, the term on the left of the equals sign is denoted as S_{word}, and the term on the right as the structure expression. For instance, the aforementioned examples can be represented as follows:

   S笔 = {[工具]:{[功能]([写]∨[画])}.
   S笔 = {[Tool]:{[Function]([Write]∨[Draw])} .

3.3.2.3 Logical Symbols

1) Logical AND ∧: Conjunctional relationship, indicating the parallel existence of two or more semantic genes, and both need to exist simultaneously. For example, [头]∧ [柄] [Head]∧[Handle], $_{Gs}$[黏土]∧$_{Gs}$[颜料] $_{Gs}$[Clay]∧$_{Gs}$[Pigment], and the like.
2) Logical OR ∨: It represents a choice relationship, indicating that among two or more possible options of the semantic genes, any one of them can be selected. For instance, [写]∨[画] [Write]∨[Draw], [木]∨[纸]∨[塑料]∨[金属] [Wood]∨[Paper]∨ [Plastic]∨[Metal], [金属]∨[其他] [Metal]∨[Other], and so on.
3) Logica NOT !: It is placed before a bracket signifying the negation of a semantic gene. *The Contemporary Chinese Dictionary* defines "angzang肮脏" as "unclean" and "meimen er没门儿" as "indicating disagreement", which can be represented as ![干净] ![Clean] and ![同意] ![Agreement], respectively.

3.3.2.4 Specialized Semantic Genes

1) Null Value Gene [φ]: It represents the case where the value of a feature variable for a semantic dimension is null. For instance, the [yanse颜色(Color)] dimension of the word "shui水(water)" is expressed as: {[颜色]([φ])} {[Color]([φ])}.
2) Uncertain Value Gene [u]: It signifies the uncertainty of the value of a variable representing a certain dimension of meaning, for instance, "ji几(several)" denotes "an uncertain quantity":{[数量]:[值]([u])} {[Quantity]: [Value]([u])} (means the [zhi值(value)] dimension feature variable of "shuliang数量(quantity)" has an uncertain value); "mou某(a)" indicates "an uncertain person or thing": {[[人]∨[事]∨[物]]:[对象]([u])} {[Person]∨[Event]∨[Thing]]: [Object]([u])} (means the [duixiang对象(object)] dimension feature variable of "ren人(person)", "shi事(event)" or "wu物(thing)" has an uncertain value).
3) Reflexive Gene [i]: When describing the semantic features of a word, it is necessary to involve the reference to the object being described itself, which is referred to as the reflexive gene, denoted by the lowercase letter [i]. For instance, the term "ya mi哑谜(charades)" meaning "a riddle that is hard to figure out" can be expressed as: {{[问题]:[猜]([受事]([i]))} + {[修辞]([比喻])}} {{[Question]:[Guess]([Patient]([i]))} {[Rhetoric]([Metaphor])}}, where the [i] refers to the object being described [wenti问题(Question)] itself.
4) Anaphora Reflexive Gene [I]: When describing the semantic features of a word, it is necessary to involve two objects, or include the reference to both the object being described and another object. These two objects are generally inseparable at the symbolic level and are typically indicated by words such as "each other" or "mutually". This is referred to as the anaphora reflexive gene, denoted by the uppercase letter [I]. For instance, in expressions like "care for each other" or "be adjacent to each other": {[Care]([I])}, {[Adjacent]([I])}.

3.3.2.5 Subscript Symbols

1) Gene cluster Gs: In the semantic gene structure expression, there are instances where, in the description of word A, the descriptive unit is not a semantic gene but the complete semantic content of another word B. For the sake of brevity, this unit can be denoted as $_{Gs}$[B], with Gs being written as the left subscript of the gene boundary symbol. The complete meaning of word B is treated as a gene cluster here. For example, the [cailiao材料(Material)] dimension of "qianbixin铅笔芯(pencil lead)" is represented as $_{Gs}$[黏土]∧$_{Gs}$[颜料] $_{Gs}$[Clay]∧ $_{Gs}$[Pigment]. It should be noted that when describing the meaning of word B, it is not permissible to use $_{Gs}$[A] in reverse, otherwise, it would lead to circular interpretation.
2) Gene chain Gc: Similar to gene clusters, for simplicity, a single semantic gene chain is denoted as $_{Gc}$[X], for instance, the structure dimension of "qianbi铅笔(pencil)" can be represented as $_{Gc}$[芯]∧$_{Gc}$[壳] $_{Gc}$[Lead]∧$_{Gc}$[Shell]. The gene chain and gene cluster differ in meaning; the gene cluster represents the complete

meaning of a word and is stable. Under the premise of avoiding circular interpretation, it can serve as a semantic gene for the description of the semantic information gene structure for multiple different words. While the gene chain is not fixed and is only effective for the word being described at the moment. For example, both "qianbi铅笔(pencil)" and "gangbi钢笔(pen)" have "xin芯(lead)" and "ke壳(shell)" in their structures. The gene chain $_{Gc}$[芯] $_{Gc}$[Lead] and $_{Gc}$[壳] $_{Gc}$[Shell] used to describe "pencil" are not applicable to "pen".

3) The semantic symbol S_{Word}: Placed on the left side of the equals sign, it represents the meaning of a word. S denotes the meaning of a certain word, with the word serving as the right subscript of S.

These three types of subscript symbols, as a representation method for gene clusters, facilitate the expression of semantic gene research and can also be directly employed for computation. Once the entire gene structure bank of the lexical system is established, the data volume is immense. In such cases, this representation method can significantly compress the size of the database, simplify data retrieval, and enhance computational speed. The representation methods for gene chains and semantics are intended not only for the convenience of research expression and also significance for semantic computation.

References

An, H. 安华林. (2005a). *Research on Definition Primitives of Modern Chinese* [现代汉语释义基元词研究]. China Social Sciences Press.

An, H. 安华林.. (2005b). Forming of Metalanguage Theory and Linguistics Metalanguage View [元语言理论的形成和语言学的元语言观]. *Inner Mongolia Social Sciences* [内蒙古社会科学], *26*(01), 104–108.

An, H. 安华林. (2013). On the Definition of Chinese Explanatory Primitive Words [关于汉语释义基元词的界定问题]. *Lexicographical Studies* [辞书研究], (03), 15–20.

Arnauld, A., & Nicole, P. (1996). Foreword. In J. V. Buroker (Ed.), *Antoine Arnauld and Pierre Nicole: Logic or the Art of Thinking*. Cambridge Texts in the History of Philosophy. Cambridge University Press.

Bai, L. 白丽芳. (2006). *A Comparative Study of English and Chinese Metalanguage* [英汉元语言比较研究]. Nanjing Normal University [南京师范大学].

Bussmann, H. (Ed.). (1996). *Routledge Dictionary of Language and Linguistics* (G. P. Trauth & K. Kazzazi, Trans. & Ed.). Routledge.

Cheng, Q. 程琪龙. (1997). Jackendoff's Theory of Conceptual Semantics Jackendoff [的概念语义学理论]. *Foreign Language Teaching and Research* [外语教学与研究], (02), 9–14+81.

Crystal, D. (2008). *A Dictionary of Linguistics and Phonetics* (6th ed.). Blackwell Publishing.

Feng, Q. 冯契. (Ed.). (2001). *Encyclopedia of Philosophy* (Revised Edition) [哲学大辞典(修订本)]. Shanghai Dictionary Press.

Ge, B. 葛本仪. (1992). *Practical Chinese Linguistics Dictionary* [实用中国语言学词典]. Qingdao Publishing House [青岛出版社].

Goddard, C., & Wierzbicka, A. (Eds.). (2002). *Meaning and Universal Grammar: Theory and Empirical Findings* (2 vols.). John Benjamins.

Goddard, C. (1998). *Semantic Analysis: A Practical Introduction*. Oxford University Press.

Greimas, A. J.(1986). *Sémantique structurale*. Presses Universitaires de France.
Hartmann, R. R. K., & Stork, F. C. (1972). *Dictionary of Language and Linguistics*. John Wiley & Sons.
Hu, D., & Gao, J. (2009). Semantic Genes and the Semantic Composition of Adjectives in Modern Chinese. In *2009 International Conference on Asian Language Processing*. IEEE CPS.
Hu, D. 胡惮, Gao, J. 高精炼, & Zhao, L. 赵玲. (2011). Semantic Genes and the Formal Expression of Lexical Semantics [语义基因与词义结构的形式化表达初论]. *Yangtze River Academic* [长江学术], (4), 138–143, 168.
Hu, D. 胡惮. (2011). *Alloconcepts and Their Formalized Description* [概念变体及其形式化描写]. China Social Sciences Press.
Hu, D. 胡惮. (2014). *Research on Modern Chinese Lexical Primitives for Natural Language Processing* [面向自然语言处理的现代汉语词义基元结构研究]. World Publishing Corporation.
Huang, Z. 黄曾阳. (1998). *Hierarchical Network of Concepts - A New Approach to Research on Computer Understanding of Language* HNC [概念层次网络理论—计算机理解语言研究的新思路]. Tsinghua University Press [清华大学出版社].
Huang, Z. 黄曾阳. (2004). *Basic Theorems and Mathematical-Physical Representations of Language Concept Space* [语言概念空间的基本定理和数学物理表示式]. Marine Press [海洋出版社].
Jackendoff, R. (1983). *Semantics and Cognition*. The MIT Press.
Jackendoff, R.(1990). *Semantic Structures*. The MIT Press.
Jackendoff, R. (2002). *Foundations of Language: Brain, Meaning, Grammar, Evolution*. Oxford University Press.
Li, B. 李葆嘉. (2002). The Study of Metalanguage System of Chinese: An Analysis Project of Language Gene Atlas [汉语元语言系统研究的理论建构及应用价值]. *Journal of Nanjing Normal University (Social Science Edition)* [南京师大学报(社会科学版)], (04), 140–147.
Li, J. 李炯英, & Li, B. 李葆嘉. (2007). An Examination of the Objectives, Principles and Methodology of Natural Semantic Metalanguage Approach NSM [理论的研究目标、原则和方法]. *Contemporary Linguistics* [当代语言学], (01), 68–77+94.
Li, J. 李炯英, Liu, P. 刘鹏辉, & Ding, J. 丁洁. (2014). Research Into NSM Theory in China: A Review [国内自然语义元语言理论研究: 现状与思考]. *Journal of Nanjing University of Posts and Telecommunications (Social Science)* [南京邮电大学学报 (社会科学版), *16*(03), 87–93.
Li, J. 李炯英. (2005). The Poland Semantic School: A Review [波兰语义学派概述]. *Foreign Language Teaching and Research* [外语教学与研究], (05), 377–382+401.
Li, J. 李炯英. (2006). A Comparison of the Semantic Theories of Wierzbicka and Jackendoff from Perspective of Semantic Primitives [从语义基元的视角比较] Wierzbicka [与] Jackendoff [的语义学理论——波兰语义学派研究之三]. *Foreign Language Education* [外语教学], *27*(05), 16–18.
Li, J. 李炯英. (2011). The Philosophical Foundation and Six Core Ideas of the Polish Semantic School [波兰语义学派的哲学基础及其六大核心思想——波兰语义学派研究之五]. *Contemporary Foreign Language Studies* [当代外语研究], (11), 8–11+51+60.
Liu, X. 刘晓林. (2006). A Review of Jackendoff's Conceptual Semantics Jackendoff [概念语义学述评]. *Foreign Language Education* [外语教学], *27*(02), 12–15.
Qiu, X. 邱雪玫, & Li, B. 李葆嘉. (2016). The Formation Process and Academic Background of Semantic Analysis Methods—Unveiling the Second Mystery of Structural Semantics [语义解析方法的形成过程及其学术背景—揭开结构主义语义学的第二个谜]. *Jianghai Academic Journal* [江海学刊], (03), 65–73.
Richards, J. C., & Schmidt, R. (2010). *Longman Dictionary of Language Teaching and Applied Linguistics* (4th ed.). Longman.
Shi, D. 石定栩. (2002). *Chomsky's Theory of Syntax* [乔姆斯基的形式句法]. Beijing Language and Culture University Press.
Snustad, D. P., & Simmons, M. J. (2011). *Principles of Genetics* (6th ed.). John Wiley & Sons.

Su, X. 苏新春. (2003). Three Interpretations of Metalanguage and Different Researches on Defining Metalanguage [元语言研究的三种理解及释义型元语言研究评述]. *Journal of Jiangxi Normal University (Philosophy and Social Sciences Edition)* [江西师范大学学报(哲学社会科学版)], (06), 93–102.

Su, X. 苏新春. (2005). *Studies on Chinese Definitional Metalanguage* [汉语释义元语言研究]. Shanghai Education Press [上海教育出版社].

Tang, X. 唐兴全. (2001). The Quintuple of HNC Theory and Part of Speech HNC [理论的五元组与词性]. In *Natural Language Understanding and Machine Translation—Proceedings of the Sixth National Joint Academic Conference on Computational Linguistics* [自然语言理解与机器翻译——全国第六届计算语言学联合学术会议论文集] (pp. 263–268). China Society of Chinese Information Processing [中国中文信息学会].

Wang, N. 王宁. (1988). On the Explanation of Word Meaning [论词义训释]. *Lexicographical Studies* [辞书研究], (01), 2–11.

Wang, J. 王今铮, et al. (1985). *Concise Linguistics Dictionary* [简明语言学词典]. Inner Mongolia People's Publishing House [内蒙古人民出版社].

Wierzbicka, A. (2004). Conceptual Primes in Human Languages and Their Analogues in Animal Communication and Cognition. *Language Sciences, 26*(5), 413–441.

Wierzbicka, A. (1996). *Semantic: Prime and Universals*. Oxford University Press.

Wierzbicka, A. (1972). *Semantic Primitives*. Athenäum-Verl.

Wittgenstein, L. (1922). *Tractatus Logico-Philosophicus*. Routledge & Kegan Paul.

Xiao, G. 萧国政, & Hu, D. 胡惮. (2007). The Constructive State of & Prospective on the Chinese Semantic Resources of Information Processing [信息处理的汉语语义资源建设现状分析与前景展望]. *Yangtze River Academic* [长江学术], (2), 86–91.

Xu, J. 徐晋麟, Xu, Q. 徐沁, & Chen, C. 陈淳. (2001). *Principles of Modern Genetics* [现代遗传学原理]. Science Press.

Xu, W. 许威汉. (1987). *Introduction to Exegetics* [训诂学导论]. Shanghai Education Press.

Zhang, J. 张津, & Huang, C. 黄昌宁. (1997). Method of Deriving Definition Primitives from a Monolingual Dictionary [从单语词典中获取定义原语的一种方法]. *Journal of Tsinghua University (Science and Technology)* [清华大学学报(自然科学版)], (03), 29–34.

Zhang, R. 张韧弦, & Liu, N. 刘乃实. (2004). Towards a Formal Approach to Semantics [语义学的形式化研究]. *Shandong Foreign Languages Teaching Journal*, (2), 18–21.

Chapter 4
Analysis and Extraction of Semantic Genes

Despite the unique genetic structure of each individual, the genome structures of organisms within the same species are typically similar. Individual variations are reflected in the differences of specific genes within their genome structures. There is a degree of genetic similarity and shared gene sequences among different populations of the same species. This similarity extends to certain segments of the gene chains. Moreover, even across different species, there are instances of shared genes and genomes.

The distribution of the semantic genes of natural language also presents a similar pattern. It is hypothesized that across all natural languages, there are a few shared semantic genes and segments of gene chain sequences that represent the structure of semantic information. Within the same language family, a greater number of shared semantic genetic elements are present among different languages. Eventually, within a particular language, each possesses its distinct collection of gene sets and gene chains. Among different language families, there can be overlaps in the sets of semantic genes. Similarly, within the same language family, different languages may share common semantic gene sets.

Wierzbicka's research partially supports this assumption. She suggested that every language has a set of undefinable words, which are fewer in number and form a distinct category. These words are crucial for defining other terms. Undefinable words are countable, and other words in the language can be defined through them. While undefinable words vary across languages, they correspond to each other and are semantically equivalent. Consequently, these words can be regarded as universal vocabulary in various languages. (Su 苏新春, 2003). She extracted more than sixty semantic primitives, which are common semantic primitives obtained on the basis of examining multiple languages, which are shared by all languages being examined.

In addition to the method proposed by Wierzbicka, which involves extracting common semantic primitives across multiple languages through cross-linguistic comparison, it is more beneficial to systematically address issues by initially extracting a set of lexical meaning genes within a single language, followed by

D. Hu, *Lexical Semantic Gene Structure of Modern Chinese*,
https://doi.org/10.1007/978-981-96-6425-2_4

seeking the intersection of gene sets across various languages. This chapter discusses the method of extracting a set of lexical semantic genes within the modern Chinese vocabulary system.

4.1 Research on the Basic Units of Semantic Analysis in Modern Chinese

Chinese semantics researchers and computational linguists have engaged in substantial research on extracting the basic semantic units in Chinese, resulting in a series of remarkable achievements. When discussing the Chinese metalanguage system, Li 李葆嘉 (2002), noted linguistic metalanguage comprises three layers: the minimal set of everyday vocabulary essential for daily communication, the interpretive metalanguage system for dictionary compilation and language teaching, and the semantic metalanguage system for semantic feature analysis. Following this idea, the existing research on the extraction of Chinese metalanguage units can be broadly classified into three categories: common vocabulary (basic vocabulary), interpretive basic units, and analytical basic units.

4.1.1 Research on Basic Vocabulary and Common Vocabulary in Modern Chinese

There exists a basic vocabulary set in every language. The basic vocabulary constitutes an indispensable element of human language, serving to denote the most fundamental objects and ideas encountered in everyday life. It is most closely associated with people's daily lives. Basic vocabulary is characterized by its universality and stability and serves as the foundation for the creation of new words. (Ge 葛本仪, 2001: 3–4). The basic vocabulary is the foundation of the lexicon, having certain relationships with all words in the language. The number of basic vocabulary is limited and possesses universality. In contrast, common words are those used in daily life to express people's thoughts and are words that the general public can master. There are many common words in Chinese that have survived for thousands of years, demonstrating strong word-formation abilities, and are undoubtedly basic words (Zhou 周祖谟, 1959: 11–13).

The development of the Chinese basic vocabulary and common vocabulary has achieved some significant milestones, such as the *The List of Three Thousand Common Words in Putonghua* 普通话三千常用词表 compiled by the State Language Commission and published in 1959; and a revised version by Zheng 郑林曦 and published in 1987; the *Frequency Dictionary in Modern Chinese* 现代汉语频率词典 compiled by Beijing Language and Culture University and published in 1986; the *List of Three Thousand Common Words in Modern Chinese* 现代汉语

三千常用词表 edited by He 何克抗 & Li李大魁 and published in 1987; and the *List of Common Words in Modern Chinese* 现代汉语常用词表 compiled by Li 李行健 & Su苏新春 and published by the Commercial Press in 2021, etc.

The methods for developing these vocabulary are largely similar, with the fundamental methodology involving the integration of a scaled corpus selection process and statistical analysis techniques. The differences lie in the scope of corpus selection and the statistical tools employed.

Basic vocabulary, while generally stable, is not static. Some scholars argue that the basic vocabulary of all languages can only retain approximately 81% after every thousand years. (Zhang 张能甫, 1999). The process of identifying basic vocabulary from the total vocabulary of a language has traditionally relied on subjective human judgment, encompassing methods such as empirical rules, etymological analysis, explanation frequency assessment, word-forming ability assessment, and vocabulary intersection method (Zhang 张志平, 2007). These approaches are inherently subjective and can result in discrepancies. Currently, using computers to statistically identify and extract basic vocabulary from extensive corpora is considered a more reliable method. This involves statistical algorithms such as word frequency calculation, vocabulary circulation calculation, and vocabulary universality calculation.

Han 韩秀娟 et al. (2005) and Zhao 赵小兵 (2007) from Beijing Language and Culture University reported reported a method for modeling on the basis of a small-scale basic vocabulary prior set, and obtaining a basic vocabulary set by machine learning from a large-scale corpus. Such kind of approach of combining linguistic rules with the extraction of basic vocabulary based on statistical features has minimal subjective influence and can also avoid the errors that may arise from the imbalance of corpus in simple word frequency calculations, resulting in better extraction effects and strong representativeness.

4.1.2 Research on the Basic Interpretive Units of Modern Chinese

(1) Extraction of Defining Primitive in Chinese

As mentioned in Chapter 3.1.4, as a pioneering study of extracting defining Primitives in Chinese, Huang 黄昌宁 and his team designed an algorithmic model based on graph theory and ultimately extracted 3857 defining primitives from the *Modern Chinese Dictionary* in 1995. Although their work hold significant landmark significance, due to its excessive reliance on mathematical methods and the neglect of linguistic facts to accommodate algorithmic axioms, many unreasonable defining primitives exist in the extracted results. For instance, proper nouns such as "diyi yuzhou sudu第一宇宙速度(first cosmic speed)", "chuji zhongxue初级中学(junior middle school)", "a'erfa shexian阿尔法射线(alpha rays)", account for nearly a third of the entire set of defining primitives. These phrases are obviously inappropriate for serving as metalanguage in the context of term definition.

(2) Extraction of Explanatory Basic Words in Modern Chinese

In 2005, An 安华林, based on the *The Contemporary Chinese Dictionary (3rd edition)*, *The Frequency Dictionary in Modern Chinese* and the *List of Common Words in Modern Chinese*, extracted over 2800 interpretive basic words for Chinese which are categorized into 3 major categories, 8 middle categories, and 50 minor categories. His research mainly focuses on corpus analysis with statistical methods as a supplement, which holds significant linguistic implications.

While Su 苏新春 extracted 4324 high-frequency Chinese defining words as the interpretive metalanguage set for Chinese in 2005 also based on *The Contemporary Chinese Dictionary (3rd edition).*

Compared to An's study, Su utilized a more limited corpus source. The statistical methods employed include absolute word frequency, cumulative word frequency, relative frequency, median, mode, and weighted methods, which are somewhat cumbersome. The resulting set of interpretive metalanguage is significantly larger than that of the former.

4.1.3 Research on the Basic Semantic Analysis Units of Modern Chinese

The research of the basic units for semantic analysis in early times is typically represented by sememe analysis. Jia 贾彦德 (1992) actively advocated the sememe analysis method, proposing a set of methods and principles for it, and conducting fruitful practices in the sememe analysis of Chinese vocabulary.

Li 李葆嘉 (2003) conducted a systematic study on the interpretation and semantic analysis of vocabulary, proposing the theory of "Semantic Analyzing Matalanguage". The semantic analyzing matalanguage system is a semantic feature set designed to analyze the object language, with its primary function being the discrimination of semantic features and the construction of semantic fields. The research content of the semantic analyzing matalanguage mainly includes semantic features and semantic association. The extraction of semantic features is the key to establishthe semantic analyzing matalanguage system, and the criterion for success is whether it can meet the functions of semantic analysis. To date, they have extracted over 2,800 semantic analyzing features of Chinese.

One of this research values is to serve language information processing, which is an innovative endeavor that is bound to leave a profound mark on the Chinese semantic processing project. Of course, due to its pioneering nature, there are still some areas that require improvement:

1) They distinguished interpretive metalanguage form semantic analyzing matalanguage, treating them as two sub-projects of a serial engineering tasks. However, there is no further differentiation provided for the final outcomes of these two sub-projects, namely, the interpretive basic word set and the semantic analyzing

feature set. Thus, some doubts arise: Whether these two sets can be used interchangeably? Can the interpretive basic words be applied in semantic analysis? Can the semantic analyzing features be used for interpreting? What is the size of the intersection between the two sets? Since the elements in both sub-sets are lexical items of natural language, theoretically, the semantic analyzing features should also be applicable for interpreting.

2) From the perspective of semantic computation, the smaller the semantic connotation of the unit of semantic analysis, the greater its extension, and thus it performs better in terms of the precision of semantic representation and the efficiency of semantic computation. Wierzbicka pointed out that semantic primitives are undefinable in language, and the traditional theory of sememe analysis also considers sememes to be the smallest units in the semantic system, which means they cannot be further decomposed.[1] However, in the published semantic analyzing feature set, there are quite a number of components that can still be further decomposed. For example: "yiyuan医院 (hospital)","xuexiao学校(school)","bingren病人(patient)","tinei体内(invivo)","yingshi影视(film and television)","chuanmei传媒(media)","tushi土石(soil-stone)","tielu铁路(railway)","shuangzhang双掌(two hands)","zhongzhi种植(grow plants)","dongfa懂法(understand the law)","sifa司法administration of justice)","shuochang说唱(rap)","yanzou演奏(play a musical instrument)","caifang采访(interview)","gaizhu盖住(cover)","taigao抬高(raise)","zhiliao治疗(treat)","tanpai摊派(apportion)","tiaoyue跳跃(jump)","licai理财(manage money matters)","tingche停车(park the car)","tianhei天黑(get dark)","tianliang天亮(day break)", and so on. The meanings described by these units are still not sufficiently fine-grained in terms of knowledge granularity, and are far from meeting the needs of semantic computation.

We have previously elucidated that the distribution of semantic components of words is not linear; there exist various complex semantic relationships among these components, forming a feature dimension space that characterizes the entire semantics of a word. The sememe analysis employs a simple notation of " + " and "-" to describe whether a word or a group of words possesses or lacks a certain feature, depicting the semantics in a linear manner, which fails to accurately reflect the multiple semantic relationships among the components. Although the semantic feature analysis emphasizes the importance of the relationships between semantic components, it is not fully reflected in the specific structural formulas of lexical semantic analysis. The method of semantic analysis still resembles that of the sememe analysis, primarily using the presence or absence of semantic features as the main descriptive approach. For instance: (Sun孙道功 & Li李葆嘉, 2008).

[1] In fact, the sememe analysis has not achieved this in practice. In many of the published studies on the sememe analysis conducted by scholars, the so-called "sememe" they use for semantic analysis are far from being the smallest semantic units. The theory and practice of sememe analysis are seriously disconnected, which is one of the fatal problems of this theory.

tuo托(support from under):
[+动作][+手掌][+向上][+承受][+物体][-传递].
[+Action][+Palm][+Upward][+Bear][+Object][-Pass]
jie接(catch)
[+动作][+手掌][-向前][+接受][+物体][+传递].
[+Action][+Palm][-Forward][+Accept][+Object][+Pass]

This describes the semantic features of two words in the semantic field related to "hand gestures of humans".

There are several problems here:

① The semantic features [xiangshang向上(Upward)] and [xiangqian向前(Forward)] is ambiguous, as it is unclear whether they refer to the direction of the action or the direction of the palm. There is a semantic feature [chuandi传递(Pass)], and "Pass" is an action with a clear directional nature. However, in this context, [xiangshang向上(Upward)] and [xiangqian向前(Forward)] refer to the orientation of the palm. This ambiguity can be discerned by humans but poses difficulties for computers.

② The word "jie接" has the semantic feature [chuandi传递(Pass)], whereas "tuo托" has not. To maintain the symmetry of the semantic field, the description of "tuo托" uses [-Pass]. This arrangement appears neat within the semantic field, but when describing "tuo托" alone, it seems redundant. In the computational representation of semantic computation, this is redundant data.

③ Similarly, to ensure the neatness of the semantic field representation, the description of "jie接" includes [-Forward], indicating that the direction cannot be [Forward]. However, can it be [xianghou向后(Backward)], [xiangshang向上(Upward)], [xiangxia向下(Downward)], [xiangzuo向左(Leftward)] or [xiangyou向右(Rightward)]? This could also cause confusion in semantic computation.

④ There is a semantic implication between the semantic features [jieshou接受(Accept)] and [chuandi传递(Pass)]. The current description appears redundant and does not fully reflect the directionality of [chuandi传递(Pass)].

More examples (Sun 孙道功, 2011):
cu簇(Cluster):
[+丛状][+聚集][+密][+多][+植物][+毛发][+人类][-口语].
[+Tuft][+Gather][+Dense][+Multiple][+Plants][+Hair][+Human][-Spoken]
cong丛(Clump):
[+丛状][+聚集][+密][+多][+植物][-毛发][-人类][-口语]
[+Tuft][+Gather][+Dense][+Multiple][+Plants][-Hair][-Human][-Spoken]

The semantic features [maofa毛发(Hair)] and [renlei人类(Human)] of "cu簇" exhibit a "modification" or "attachment" relationship, as in "the hair of humans" or "hair attached to humans", which is not reflected here; the two semantic features [zhiwu植物(Plant)] and [maofa毛发(Hair)] have a "logical OR" relationship, i.e., "either [zhiwu植物(Plant)] or [maofa毛发(Hair)]", which is also not demonstrated. To be strictly, the semantic feature analysis method merely lists the semantic features contained in each analyzed word without describing the semantic relationships between the features. Theoretically, when conducting large-scale semantic analysis and description of words, it is possible to encounter a set of identical semantic features being combined in different semantic relationships, resulting in words with different meanings.

4) The phenomenon of semantic feature redundancy not only occurs in the context of symmetric semantic field descriptions but can also be observed in other situations, for instance (li 李葆嘉，2013: 319):
   piaoliang漂亮(Beautiful):
   漂亮:[+人类][+性质][+外貌][+长相∨装束][+好看]
   [+Human][+Nature][+Appearance][+Looks∨Costume][+Good looks]
   choulou 丑陋 (Ugly):
   丑陋: [+人类][+性质][+外貌][+长相∨装束][-好看]
   [+Human][+Nature][+Appearance][+Looks∨Costume][-Good looks]

Actually, the words "beautiful" and "ugly" can not only be employed to describe human beings but also extend to things, such as "a beautiful car" or "an ugly toad". Moreover, they can refer not only to appearance but also to content, as in "beautiful language" or "ugly soul". Therefore, the semantic features [renlei人类(Human)], [waimao外貌(Appearance)], and [zhangxiang长相(Looks)] here need to be further examinated.

5) On the contrary to the redundancy of semantic features, there are instances where the absence of semantic features is observed. For instance (Li 李葆嘉, 2013: 182):
   laoban 老板 (Boss):
   [+人类][+称谓][+社会][±男性][+成年][+声望][±敬称]
   [+Human][+Title] [+Society] [±Male] [+Adult] [+Reputation] [±Respectful Title]
   shifu 师傅 (Master worker):
   [+人类][+称谓][+社会][±男性][+成年][+声望][±敬称].
   [+Human][+Title] [+Society] [±Male] [+Adult] [+Reputation] [±Respectful Title]

This is the semantic feature expressions of "laoban老板(Boss)" and "shifu师傅(Master worker)" in the "social title" semantic field, they are indistinguishable from one another. It is evident that there is a pragmatic distinction between these two words, and there should be corresponding semantic features to reflect this semantic difference. Furthermore, the two semantic features [nanxing男性(Male)] and [jingcheng敬称(Respectful Title)] both carry the symbol " ± ", indicating that either of the two situations is acceptable. So they are redundant elements, which are unnecessary to use.

6) Without the formal representation processing suitable for computer semantic computation, it is difficult to achieve effective application in NLP engineering.

The analysis above is merely from the perspective of meeting the needs of semantic computation, and does not negate the linguistic value of the interpretive metalanguage theory.

4.1.4 Research on Concept Primitives in Chinese Information Processing

In Chapter 3 we have already discussed the most representative conceptual semantic primitive resources in Chinese information processing: the Hierarchical Network of Concepts (HNC) and HowNet. Both approaches start from the representation of concepts and each extracts a finite set of "Conceptual Primes" and "Semantic Primes", respectively. Their research methodologies combine introspection with statistics, filtering out basic conceptual units from Chinese characters and words.

4.1.4.1 Extraction of Concept Primitive in HNC

The HNC system achieves the representation of semantics through the mapping from the conceptual space to the linguistic space. A hierarchical and networked system of concepts is established firstly from the top down, where each node in the network represents a concept. Subsequently, specific words are mapped onto the nodes within the network, thereby expressing the meaning of the words. Within the HNC system, there are four conceptual networks: the primitive concept semantic network, the basic concept semantic network, the linguistic logic concept network, and the grammatical concept network. These networks collectively define approximately 20,000 elements, which constitute the set of conceptual primitives. These conceptual primitives form a rigorous, hierarchical, and networked conceptual semantic system, consisting of 18 conceptual categories, 101 conceptual groups, and 456 conceptual trees from the highest to the lowest level (Miao苗传江 & Liu刘智颖, 2010).

4.1.4.2 Extraction of Semantic Prime in HOWNET

The extraction and assessment of semantic primes are one of the key projects in the construction of HOWNET, and they are interactive with the construction of other parts of HOWNET, running throughout the entire process of its development. The fundamental method for semantic prime extraction is an inductive approach starting from the bottom up. Based on Chinese characters, they have examined and analyzed approximately six thousand characters, preliminarily extracting a limited set of semantic primitives, and continuously engaging in merging, organizing, supplementing, adjusting, and assessing these primitives (Dong董振东 & Dong董强, 1999).

The construction of the HowNet has been ongoing. With the continuous expansion of content, the semantic primitive set undergoes continuous revisions and enhancement. The latest version (open version) of this set employs a total of 2,540 semantic primitives.

4.2 Extraction Strategy of Semantic Genes in Modern Chinese

Chomsky (1987) pointed out that it is an extremely difficult task to define vocabulary, because it involves complex linguistic features. The definitions offered by ordinary dictionaries are significantly distant from the features of lexical meaning.. Although the task is challenging, we cannot shy away from it. Especially in the era of artificial intelligence, the requirements for semantic processing in NLP are increasingly stringent, and the construction of beneficial semantic resources for computation cannot be avoided. The extraction of semantic genes is a meticulous and arduous project that requires a significant investment of labor forces and finances. It is not a task that can be completed in a short span of time. Many scholars have already done a great deal of beneficial works. We can progressively realize this grand objective in stages.

The various strategies for semantic (conceptual) primitive extraction in the fields of linguistics and computational linguistics can be summarized into the following categories:

I. The conceptual prime extraction of pure rationalism

This approach does not originate from the vocabulary itself and does not aim for precise description of meanings. Instead, it entirely proceeds from the philosophical and cognitive perspectives, inductively generalizing a cognitive conceptual system shared by humans, and extracts conceptual primes from it to explain the semantic structure of language. For instance, the conceptual categories proposed by Jackendoff and the conceptual primes of the HNC theory proposed by Huang Zengyang. In fact, concepts do not equate to words, and the connotation of concepts is not entirely identical to the meanings of words. Even for concepts expressing the same object, different variants exist in different contexts, requiring the expression of different words with slightly different semantic nuances (Hu 胡惮, 2011). Therefore, it is questionable whether such pure conceptual-level primes can accurately represent word meanings. The mapping from conceptual primes to semantic primitives necessitates practical operations based on linguistic facts (Xiao萧国政 et al., 2011).

II. The extraction of semantic primitives based on cultural commonality

This approach involves examining the common basic concepts across different language and culture, and extracts semantic primitives through induction. For instance, Wierzbicka, based on English and several other European languages, combined with other languages, has selected over 60 semantic primitives that are common across these languages. Although Wierzbicka employs the term "semantic primitive", her research is essentially conceptual primes. She argues that the meaning of semantics is equivalent to concept, where semantic elements represent simple conceptual elements that can be combined according to compositional rules to form complex concepts. Despite the differences in people's cognition of the world due to cultural variations, there exists certain cultural commonality in human society, which validates the universality of the NSM theory and semantic primitives (Pu蒲冬

梅, 2012). They attempt to describe facts objectively and neutrally by such kind of simplified metalanguage, expressing complex cultural concepts and ideas with the most basic manner (Pu蒲冬梅, 2008). This aspiration is commendable, but in reality, semantics and concepts cannot be equated, especially when it comes to different languages and cultures. The concepts they believe to be culturally shared often exhibit significant semantic differences in the corresponding words when mapped onto different languages. Moreover, even within the same language, the semantic primitives extracted by them show semantic overlap. Leibniz, who first proposed the idea of the "alphabet of human thought", believed that each initial element is independent, and if two elements share a common component, their meaning is not simple and cannot be considered as an initial element. Some of the primitives listed by NSM researchers clearly contradict this principle, and the simplicity of their meanings requires further scrutiny. For example, the words "want" and "wish" in English share semantic components, but their meanings are not inclusive; they are overlapping. "Want" carries meanings beyond "desire", including "need", "lack", and "insufficiency", as in "Which one do you want?" and "The rearrangement is wanted." There is no single lexical item that reflects their common semantic part (Zhang张喆, 2007).

III. Rationalist primitive extraction based on linguistic facts

This approach fully respects linguistic facts and starts from the structural rules of language. By deconstructing the semantic microstructure of a portion of sample vocabulary, it derives a basic set of semantic primitives. On this basis, the scope of observation is expanded for verification. Adjustments and optimizations are made to the set of primitives according to the verification results, as exemplified by the semantic analyzing matalanguage studies of Li Baojia and others.

IV. Purely empirical primitive extraction from data

This approach disregards linguistic facts and does not attach importance to semantics, relying on the probability of combinations of linguistic symbols as the basis for statistical computations. For instance, the interpretive primitives extracted by Huang Changning et al. They basically do not consider language rules, treating vocabulary merely as a data node for statistical processing, thus resulting in a high level of noise in the outcome.

V. Extraction of primitives through the combination of empiricism and rationalism

This approach is based on frequency statistics, where words are sorted according to their usage frequency, and high-frequency words are selected for further manual screening and optimization. For instance, the research on the limited set of definition words in English dictionaries, as well as the studies of Chinese interpretive metalanguage by researchers such as Su Xinchun and An Hualin, etc.

Building upon the existing theories of semantic primitives and engineering practices, we propose the theory of semantic gene, explore strategies for formal description of lexical meanings and summarize a set of extraction methods and operational procedures for semantic genes through engineering practice.

4.2.1 *Principles for Extracting Semantic Genes*

In the process of extracting semantic genes, it is essential to be grounded in linguistic facts while fully respecting the needs of semantic data computation and processing. Consequently, the extraction of semantic genes and the description of the semantic gene structure of words adhere to the following principles:

I. The Principle of the Minimum Unit

To ensure the universality, relative minimality, and indivisibility of semantic genes. By definition and minimized segmentation, we aim to guarantee that each element within the gene set constitutes a relatively complete, smallest semantic unit of cognition. While certain free semantic genes can function independently as words, being explained by other terms in dictionaries and potentially represented as combinations of multiple semantic components through sememe analysis, they remain the fundamental units in semantic cognition and should not be further dissected. For instance, terms like [ren人(Person)], [shijian时间(Time)], and [yeti液体(Liquid)].

II. The Principle of Semantic Universality

To ensure the connotative monotonicity and extensional breadth of semantic genes. Semantic genes extracted should be characterized by singular meanings and broad applicability, thus exhibiting both internal accuracy and external universality in semantic description. In other words, they can accurately express the semantic dimensional features of a certain word, with clear and unambiguous meanings; when used to describe the common semantic dimensional features, they are suitable for various words For instance, [xingzhuang形状(Shape)], [yanseyanse(Color)], and [fangxiang 方向(Direction)].

III. The Principle of Minimum Quantity

To ensure uniqueness of semantic genes. Semantically equivalent genes are merged to the greatest extent to ensure non-repetition within the gene set. On the premise of ensuring the accuracy of semantic description, the number of elements within the gene cluster is minimized. For semantic units with identical or similar meanings, only the simplest one is retained as a semantic gene, with other words described through this gene. For instance, "chuzhi处置(dispose)" and "chuli处理(handle)" may appear as synonyms, and their interpretations in *The Contemporary Chinese Dictionary (7th Edition)* are as follows:

[chuzhi处置]: ① Handling, e.g. mishandled, handled appropriately. ② Deal with, punish, e.g. punish in accordance with the law.

[chuli处理]: ① Arrange (things); Solve (problems), e.g. handle daily affairs. ② Treatment; Punishment, e.g. handle in accordance with the law; ③ Selling at a discounted or variable price, e.g. All these stockpiled goods are handled at a discounted price. ④ Process workpieces or products using specific methods to obtain the required performance.

Comparison shows that the meaning of "chuzhi处置" is simpler, and its first plereme is chosen as the semantic gene, represented as [chuzhi处置(Dispose)]. This gene can describe the second plereme of "chuzhi处置" as well as the four pleremes of "chuli处理".

IV. The Principle of Stability and Completeness

To ensure the stability, completeness, and finiteness of the semantic gene set. It is ensured that the gene set possesses the capability to fully describe the entire vocabulary system while maintaining the most concise data structure.

V. Principle of Logical Rigor

In the semantic description, it is crucial to ensure that members of the semantic gene set possess logical rigor. It guarantees that the various semantic relationships and logical relationships among semantic components can be accurately expressed, and it avoids falling into the trap of circular interpretation.

VI. Principle of Precise Description

Ensure that the semantic description of each word is accurate, complete, and unique (except for absolute equivalent words), the semantic expression must be clear, unambiguous, and the scope of meaning should not be expanded or reduced.

4.2.2 Methods for Extracting Semantic Genes

To guarantee the quality of the project, the extraction of semantic genes is predominantly conducted through manual means. In the most critical phases, statistical analysis is selectively applied to enhance the process. However, machine learning techniques are not utilized throughout the entire procedure. The methods employed during the extraction are as follows:

I. Combining resource reuse with independent extraction

The extraction of semantic genes is somewhat related to the predecessors' research on basic vocabulary and semantic (conceptual) primitives. During the extraction process, various resources such as commonly used word lists, frequency lists, semantic primitive word lists, analyzing primitive word lists, and conceptual prime sets, as well as relevant research findings in the fields of lexicology and semantics, are selectively referenced and reused. The work is primarily rely on independent extraction, with resource reuse serving as a supplementary method.

II. Combining Linguistic analysis with statistical optimization

Our research begins with linguistic facts, focusing on the semantics itself, primarily employing a rationalist analysis of semantic features, supplemented by an empiricist statistical optimization. Through in-depth examination, observation, and analysis of the dimensional structure of semantic features, we classify and extract multiple subsets of semantic genes. Subsequently, we further validate, supplement, and merge these subsets through linguistic facts, thereby obtaining an initial set of semantic genes. Then, employing statistical methods, we calculate the frequency and coverage of the extracted primitives, following the principle of survival of the fittest to further optimize the results. Finally, after verification over a broader range of linguistic facts, we determine the final set of semantic genes.

III. Combining top-down and bottom-up Approaches

The terms "up" and "down" refer to the relative hierarchical positions of analyzed words within a semantic classification tree or conceptual tree. "Top-down" analysis originates from the topmost node of the tree and extends downwards, progressively deducing each node at each level until reaching every specific word (or concept), such as the conceptual tree of HNC. Conversely, "bottom-up" analysis starts directly from the specific word (or concept) and, through a series of minimal semantic fields, gradually inducts upwards to the topmost node, such as the semantic analysis of HowNet. We employ a hybrid approach, integrating this two distinct methods.

1) Firstly, from the top down, by integrating various existing resources, we establish the middle and upper level nodes of the modern Chinese semantic classification tree, and build the upper-level general vocabulary ontology of modern Chinese. The upper-level nodes often themselves serve as semantic genes, such as "time", "space", "object", "abstract", and "concrete". When analyzing the specific word meanings at the lower level, these genes are directly utilized.
2) The specific analysis begins with the fundamental minimal semantic field. The extraction of semantic genes essentially follows the structuralist approach. An ideal method would be to adopt a strategy similar to that used in phonological analysis, where minimal pairs are employed to identify phonemes. Initially, several minimal semantic fields with individual differences in semantic genes are established. By analyzing these differences, semantic genes are extracted one by one.
3) Identifying and targeting the superordinate node words of the underlying semantic fields, this study then employs these words to broaden the analysis of the higher-level adjacent subfields, thereby facilitating a more detailed extraction and examination. This process is repeated level by level upwards until it meets with the upper-level general vocabulary ontology. During the analysis of a specific minimal lexical field, it is essential to continuously refer to the peripheral branches and nodes of the semantic tree where the lexical field is located, taking into account its superordinate, subordinate, and adjacent subfields, to ensure the consistency and systematicity of the entire extraction process.

VII. Combining Predefinition and Structural Analysis

The semantic genes can be categorized into two major types based on the functional roles they play in the description of semantic features: natural semantic genes and instrumental genes. Natural semantic genes are the semantic units that inherently exist in natural languages, some of which are words themselves, such as "color", "area", "large", and "small". Instrumental genes are not directly used in natural language communication but serve as adhesive components for natural semantic genes. The instrumental genes further include argument role genes like "agent" and "patient", and logical relation genes like "yes", "no", "and", and "or".

The majority of nodes in the upper-level general vocabulary ontology belong to natural semantic genes. These genes do not require the semantic analysis for extraction and can be predefined as core members of the semantic gene set, such as "time", "space", "human", and "thing". Instrumental genes can also be predefined; however, the convention of instrumental genes needs to be continuously adjusted and optimized in conjunction with specific word example analysis. Other specific semantic genes generally require extraction through the analysis of each word.

VIII. Combining the Linguistic knowledge and encyclopedic knowledge

The encyclopedic knowledge constitutes one of the most challenging aspects in the processing of lexical meaning, as it encompasses a vast and diverse range of content. Language serves as the primary vehicle for the transmission and dissemination of human thought, culture, and knowledge. As the fundamental building materials of language, vocabulary inevitably carries a substantial amount of encyclopedic knowledge. In semantics, the handling of encyclopedic knowledge has been a focus of discussion. The views on meaning proposed by Bloomfield and those of cognitive linguistics can be seen as representing two extreme attitudes towards the processing of encyclopedic knowledge within lexical meaning.

Bloomfield (1933: 139, 145) fell into the quagmire of what is so-called "scientism" in his attitude towards the study of meaning. He stated, "*In order to give a scientifically accurate definition of meaning for every form of a language, we should have to have a scientifically accurate knowledge of everything in the speakers' world. The actual extent of human knowledge is very small, compared to this. We can define the meaning of a speech-form accurately when this meaning has to do with some matter of which we possess scientific knowledge.*" Therefore, the elucidation of meaning in linguistic research is a weak link, and this situation will persist until human knowledge far exceeds its current state. "*linguist cannot define meanings, but must appeal for this to students of other sciences or to common knowledge*".Undoubtedly, the meaning of language must be inseparable from encyclopedic knowledge, but this cannot be a reason for linguistics to reject the study of meaning. While cognitive linguists posit that semantic research must be conducted within the framework of encyclopedic knowledge. Semantic structures are essentially encyclopedic in nature; linguistic units (such as words) do not "carry" pre-packaged meanings but rather provide access points to encyclopedic knowledge (conceptual systems). The semantics of natural language cannot be isolated from other forms of knowledge, and thus there is no strict distinction between semantic knowledge and pragmatic knowledge; both are essentially semantic knowledge (Evans & Melanie, 2006). Lakoff (1987: 70) illustrated this with the example of "bachelor": The term 'bachelor' cannot be defined solely by the three conditions of 'male', 'adult', and 'unmarried'; it must also take into account social and cultural factors such as marriage systems, marriage customs, and religious institutions. Merely by these three criteria, it is not sufficient to explain why the Pope and the fictional character Tarzan cannot be classified as "bachelors".

The so-called "Dictionary View" in traditional linguistics takes a moderate stance, positing that meaning can be divided into two parts: the "dictionary" part and the "encyclopedic knowledge" part. According to this view, lexical semantics should focus on the "dictionary" part, while encyclopedic knowledge is considered extraneous to linguistic knowledge. It belongs to a type of world knowledge and should not be the object of concern for semantics (Wang 王红卫, 2010).

Our analysis of semantic gene primarily focuses on linguistic knowledge, while appropriately considering some encyclopedic knowledge that has a significant impact on language understanding and generation. This knowledge is incorporated into the semantic scope and described using a unified expression method of semantic gene structures. In the process of analyzing specific semantic structures to extract semantic genes, one cannot rely on personal linguistic intuition but should take authoritative dictionary definitions as the basis. Due to differences in linguistic perspectives, different dictionary definitions may emphasize different aspects, thus requiring reference to various dictionaries during the extraction process. For instance, taking "fish" as an example, *The Contemporary Chinese Dictionary (7th Edition)* defines it as: "A vertebrate animal that lives in water, with body temperature varying with the external temperature, generally having a flattened body, scales, and fins, and breathing through gills. There are many species, most of which are edible or used to make fish gelatin." This definition contains a considerable amount of encyclopedic knowledge: "vertebrate", "body temperature varying with the external temperature", "scales and fins", "breathing through gills", and "fish gelatin". However, these encyclopedic knowledge, for the ordinary people's cognition of the concept "fish", are not all necessary, and may even increase the cognitive burden.

In contrast, the *Longman Dictionary of Contemporary English* defines fish as: "An animal that lives in water, and uses its fins and tail to swim." Here, except for fin, which is biological knowledge, the rest are ordinary linguistic knowledge. Therefore, we believe that, in terms of the definition of this word, the *Longman Dictionary of Contemporary English* is more suitable for the extraction of semantic genes than the Contemporary Chinese Dictionary.

4.2.3 Operating Flow for Extracting Semantic Genes

Following the principles and methods discussed above, we have established a standardized operational process for semantic gene extraction. This process is carried out step by step according to the following sequence: "Establishing an upper-level general vocabulary ontology → Predefining a core gene set → Selecting a semantic class → Establishing a minimal semantic field → Semantic analysis → Extraction within the semantic field → Comparison with adjacent fields → Merging and optimization → Establishing an initial set of semantic genes → Expanding the analysis data sample → Verification and optimization → Statistical optimization → Establishing a semantic gene set." The work of semantic gene extraction is conducted on computers through manual analysis. For this purpose, we have specifically developed two tool software: the "Event Ontology" for constructing a general vocabulary ontology and the "Semantic Gene Editor" for editing semantic genes, as shown in the figures below (Figs. 4.1 and 4.2).

I. Constructing an upper-level general vocabulary Ontology

Ontology is a formalized knowledge base widely utilized in the field of artificial intelligence. It is closely related to lexical semantics and has increasingly garnered attention from the linguistic community in recent years (Qiu 邱庆山, 2018).

In short, if we abstract each knowledge domain into a conceptual system and then employ a vocabulary list to represent this system, within which the meanings of words and the relationships between words are explicitly described, and the consensus among experts in the field is reached, enabling everyone to share this vocabulary list, then this list constitutes a ontology within that domain (Hu胡惮, 2009). Ontologies, according to their different applications, can be categorized into upper Ontologies, general common-sense Ontologies, and domain Ontologies. Upper Ontologies describe the common knowledge of human cognition, while domain Ontologies describe the knowledge of specific applied domains, such as agriculture, medicine, and automotive manufacturing. General common-sense Ontologies lie between these two, primarily describing linguistic knowledge in everyday life and are also known as linguistic Ontologies. The general vocabulary Ontology we are discussing here belongs to the category of linguistic Ontologies, which is constructed using the common vocabulary of modern Chinese and describes the various semantic

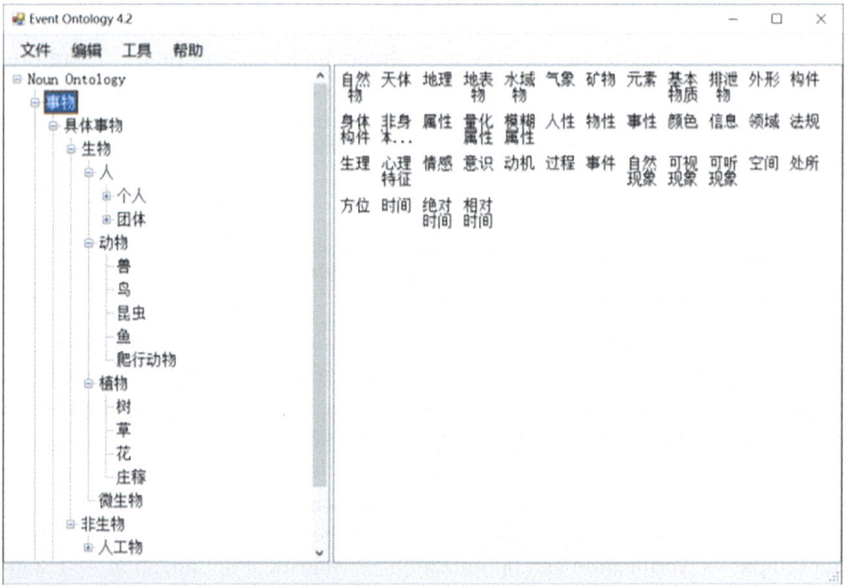

Fig. 4.1 Interface for the General Vocabulary Ontology Construction Tool

Fig. 4.2 Interface for the Semantic Gene Editing Tool

relationships between words according to the theoretical framework of knowledge ontology construction. It can be used for research in lexical semantics and can also directly contribute to semantic computation in artificial intelligence. We initiate the semantic gene extraction project from the upper general vocabulary ontology for the following reasons:

Firstly, the upper general vocabulary Ontology can govern the semantic classification system of the entire vocabulary system, ensuring the systematicity and completeness of the entire semantic gene extraction process.

Secondly, the nodes in the upper general vocabulary Ontology are predominantly fundamental concepts simple in meaning and difficult to dissect, which can be directly predefined as core semantic genes. These serve as the initial units for further analysis of word meanings and extraction of semantic genes.

Furthermore, compared to the construction of domain Ontologies, the development of the middle and lower levels of linguistic Ontologies is extremely challenging. Most concepts in domain Ontologies have single and clear relationships, which can be explicitly and stably arranged in the Ontology, with nodes positioned distinctly. For instance, in the automotive domain Ontology, concepts such as "wheels" and "steering wheel" have stable "part-whole" relationships with "car", forming clear hierarchical relationships. However, the middle and lower-level concepts in linguistic Ontologies are mostly complex in nature, making it difficult to determine node positions within the ontology. For example, the hypernym of "wife" can be either "woman" or "kinship relationship", and if a fixed Ontology is established, logical conflicts are inevitable. Our approach is to only fix only the upper-level general vocabulary Ontology. After the semantic structure description of the entire vocabulary system is completed through semantic gene analysis, the various semantic relationships between words can be extracted automatically by computer. Thus a variety of dynamic Ontologies with different logical structures can be flexibly generated depending on different application needs.

By comprehensively comparing and referencing a variety of resources including the Suggested Upper Merged Ontology (SUMO), the HNC conceptual nodes, the HowNet information structure database, the classification system of Synonym Thesaurus, and the Modern Chinese Classification Dictionary, we have established an upper-level general vocabulary ontology for modern Chinese. Part of the content of the ontology is presented as follows:

1) The semantic classification system of ontology (only a few nodes are displayed)

A [shiti实体(Entity)]
A01 [jutiwu具体物(Concrete object)]
A0101[shengwu生物(Living beings)]
A010101 [ren人(Human)]
A010102 [dongwu动物(Animal)]
A010103 [zhiwu植物(Plant)]
A010102 [weishengwu微生物(Microorganism)]
A0102[fei shengwu非生物(Non-living things)]
A010201 [ziranwu自然物(Natural objects)]
A01020101 [wuzhi物质(Substance)]
A01020102 [ziran ti自然体(Natural body)]
A010202 [renzaowu人造物(Artifacts)]
A01020201 [cailiao材料(Material)]
A01020202 [qiju器具(Utensil)]
A01020203 [yongpin用品(Utility)]
A01020204 [jianzhuwu建筑物(Building)]
A01020205 [shipin食品(Food)]
A01020206 [yaopin药品(Medicine)]
A01020207 [dupin毒品(Drug)]
A01020208 [chuandaiwu穿戴物(Clothing)]
A01020209 [jingshen chanwu精神产物(Mental product)]
A01020210 [piaozheng票证(Ticket)]
A01020211 [daixie yu fenmiwu代谢与分泌物(Metabolism and secretions)]
A02 [chouxiangwu抽象物(Abstract object]
A0201 [ziran chouxiangwu自然抽象物(Natural abstract object)]
A020101 [xinxi信息(Information)]
A020102 [nengliang能量(Energy)]
A020103 [ziran xianxiang chanwu自然现象产物(Product of natural phenomena)]
A020101 [sheng声(Sound)]
A020102 [guang光(Light)]
A020103 [dian电(Electricity)]

A020104 [huo火(Fire)]
A020105 [yan烟(Smoke)]
A020106 [wu雾(Fog)]
A020107 [feng风(Wind)]
A020108 [lang浪(Wave)]
A020104 [shengming生命(Life)]
A020105 [jibing疾病(Disease)]
A0202 [renzao chouxiangwu人造抽象物(Artificial abstract object)]
A020201 [zuzhijigou组织机构(Organization)]
A02020101 [guojia国家(Country)]
A02020102 [zhengdang政党(Political party)]
A02020103 [xingzhengquhua行政区划(Administrative division)]
A02020104 [zuzhituanti组织团体(Organizational group)]
A02020105 [qiye企业(Enterprise)]
A02020106 [xuexiao学校(School)]
A02020107 [yiyuan医院(Hospital)]
A02020108 [chengxiang城乡(Urban and rural)]
A02020109 [shehui社会(Society)]
A02020110 [bumen部门(Department)]
A020202 [jingshen chanwu精神产物(Mental product)]
A02020201 [kexue科学(Science)]
A02020202 [zhishi知识(Knowledge)]
A02020203 [sixiang思想(Thought)]
A02020204 [qinggan情感(Emotion)]
A02020205 [zhidu制度(System)]
A02020206 [zuopin作品(Work)]
A02020207 [xunniwu虚拟物(Virtual object)]
B [shijian事件(Event)]
B01 [ziran xianxiang自然现象(Natural phenomenon)]
B0101 [tianqi xianxiang天气现象(Weather phenomenon)]
B010101 [yin阴(Overcast)]
B010102 [qing晴(Sunny)]
B010103 [yu雨(Rainy)]
B010104 [xue雪(Snowy)]
B010105 [shandian闪电(Lightning)]
B010106 [dalei打雷(Thunder)]
B010107 [fengbao风暴(Storm)]
B010108 [chaoxi潮汐(Tide)]
B0102 [zhouye jiaoti昼夜交替(Alternation of day and night)]
B010201 [tianliang天亮(Daybreak)]
B010202 [tianhei天黑(Dusk)]
B010203 [riyue qiluo日月起落(Rise and set of sun and moon)]
B01020301 [richu日出(Sunrise)]
B01020302 [riluo日落(Sunset)]
B01020303 [yuechu月出(Moonrise)]

B01020304 [yueluo月落(Moonset)]
B0103 [wulixianxiang物理现象(Physical phenomenon)]
B010301 [guangxianxiang光现象(Phenomenon of light)]
B01030101 [fangguang发光(Luminescence)]
B01030102 [zhaoshe照射(Irradiation)]
B01030103 [tuishe褪色(Colour fading)]
B010302 [rexianxiang热现象(Thermal phenomenon)]
B01030201 [fare发热(Heat generation)]
B01030202 [feiteng沸腾(Boiling)]
B01030207 [jiangwen降温(Cooling)]
B010303 [shengxianxiang声现象(Acoustic phenomenon)]
B01030301 [fasheng发声(Sound production)]
B01030302 [gongming共鸣(Resonance)]
B010304 [wutaigaibian物态改变(State change)]
B01030401 [zhengfa蒸发(Evaporation)]
B01030402 [shenghua升华(Sublimation)]
B01030403 [qihua汽化(Vaporization)]
B01030404 [jiedong解冻(Thawing)]
B01030405 [ronghua融化(Melting)]
B01030206 [ningjie凝结(Coagulation)]
B01030207 [jiebing结冰(Freezing)]
B01030208 [ninghua凝华(Desublimation)]
B01030209 [wuhua雾化(Nebulization)]
B01030210 [rongjie溶解(Dissolution)]
B010305 [dianci xianxiang电磁现象(Electromagnetic phenomenon)]
B0104 [huaxue xianxiang化学现象(Chemical phenomenon)]
B010401 [ranshao燃烧(Burning)]
B010402 [baozha爆炸(Explosion)]
B010403 [fenjie分解(Decomposition)]
B010404 [fulan腐烂(Rotting)]
B010405 [fuhsi腐蚀(Corrosion)]
B0105 [shengli xianxiang生理现象(Physiological phenomenon)]
B010501 [sheng生(Birth)]
B010502 [lao老(Aging)]
B010503 [bing病(Illness)]
B010504 [si死(Death)]
B010505 [shengzhang fayu生长发育(Growth and development)]
B02 [shehui xianxiang社会现象(Social phenomenon)]
B03 [huodong活动(Activity)]
B0301 [shenghuo huodong生活活动(Daily life activity)]
B030101 [yi衣(Clothing)]
B030102 [shi食(Feeding)]
B030103 [zhu住(Housing)]
B030104 [xing行(Movement)]
B0302 [shehui huodong社会活动(Social activity)]

B030201 [zhengzhi huodong政治活动(Political activity)]
B03020101 [tongzhi统治(Rule)]
B03020102 [geming革命(Revolution)]
B03020103 [panluan叛乱(Rebellion)]
B03020104 [dongluan动乱(Upheaval)]
B03020105 [pingpan平叛(Counterinsurgency)]
B03020106 [xuanju选举(Election)]
B03020107 [kangyi抗议(Protest)]
B03020108 [gaige改革(Reform)]
B030202 [jingji huodong经济活动(Economic activity)]
B03020201 [shengchan生产(Production)]
B03020102 [maoyi贸易(Trade)]
B03020103 [jinrong huodong金融活动(Financial activity)]
B030203 [junshi huodong军事活动(Military activity)]
B03020301 [zhanzheng战争(War)]
B03020302 [fankong反恐(Anti-terrorism)]
B03020303 [baowei保卫(Defense)]
B03020304 [beizhan备战(Preparation for war)]
B03020305 [yuebing阅兵(Parade)]
B03020306 [qinlue侵略(Aggression)]
B030204 [guanli huodong管理活动(Management activity)]
B03020401 [zhili治理(Governance)]
B03020402 [bushu部署(Deployment)]
B03020403 [anzhi安置(Settlement)]
B03020404 [shezhi设立(Establishment)]
B03020405 [chexiao撤销(Revocation)]
B03020406 [renmian任免(Appointment and removal)]
B03020407 [jiangcheng奖惩(Reward and punishment)]
B03020408 [zhuchi主持(Hosting)]
B03020409 [xuanchuan宣传(Publicity)]
B03020410 [haozhao号召(Call)]
B03020411 [paiqian派遣(Dispatch)]
B03020412 [jiandu监督(Supervision)]
B03020413 [kao ping考评(Evaluation)]
B030205 [wentihuodong文体活动(Recreational and physical activities)]
B03020501 [biaoyan表演(Performance)]
B03020502 [zhanlan展览(Exhibition)]
B03020503 [fangying放映(Projection)]
B03020504 [pianlian排练(Rehearsal)]
B03020505 [luzhi录制(Recording)]
B03020506 [guankan观看(Watching)]
B03020507 [pinjian品鉴(Tasting)]
B03020508 [pailian排练(Rehearsal)]
B03020509[tiyundong体育运动(Sports)]
B03020510 [bisai比赛(Competition)]

B030206 [jiaoyu huodong教育活动(Educational activity)]
B030207 [keyan huodong科研活动(Scientific research activity)]
B030208 [yiliao huodong医疗活动(Medical activity)]
B030209 [shejiao huodong社交活动(Social activity)]
B030210 [sifa huodong司法活动(Judicial activity)]
B030211 [feifa huodong非法活动(Illegal activity)]
B030212 [zongjiao huodong宗教活动(Religious activity)]
B030213 [xinli huodong心理活动(Psychological activity)]
B04 [xingwei yu bianhua行为与变化(Behavior and change)]
B0401 [jiechu接触(Contact)]
B0402 [weiyi位移(Displacement)]
B0403 [fenli分离(Separation)]
B0404 [lingshu guanxi zhuanyi领属关系转移(Transfer of ownership)]
B040401 [shiqu失去(Lose)]
B040402 [dedao得到(Obtain)]
B0405 [guocheng过程(Process)]
B0406 [shenti dongzuo身体动作(Body action)]
B040601 [shangzhi dongzuo上肢动作(Upper limb action)]
B040602 [xiazhi dongzuo下肢动作(Lower limb action)]
B040603 [toubu dongzuo头部动作(Head action)]
B040601 [quanshen dongzuo全身动作(Full-body action)]
B0407 [ganzhi感知(Perception)]
B040701 [shijue ganzhi视觉感知(Visual perception)]
B040701 [tingjue ganzhi听觉感知(Auditory perception)]
B040701 [xiujue ganzhi嗅觉感知(Olfactory perception)]
B040701 [weijue ganzhi味觉感知(Gustatory perception)]
B0408 [xinxi jiaoliu信息交流(Information exchange)]
B040801 [xinxi fasong信息发送(Information sending)]
B040802 [xinxi chuanbo信息传播(Information dissemination)]
B040803 [xinxi jieshou信息接收(Information receiving)]
B040804 [xinxi jiagong信息加工(Information processing)]
C [shikong时空(Space and time)]
C01 [shijian时间(Time)]
C0101 [shidian时点(Time point)]
C0102 [shiduan时段(Time period)]
C0103 [shixu时序(Time sequence)]
C0104 [shiliang时量(Time quantity)]
C02 [kongjian空间(Space)]
C0201 [chusuo处所(Place)]
C0202 [fangwei方位(Direction)]
C0203 [lujing路径(Path)]
C0204 [fanwei范围(Range)]
C0205 [kongjianliang空间量(Spatial quantity)]
D [zhuangtai状态(State)]
D01 [wuli zhuangtai物理状态(Physical state)]

D02 [shenti zhuangtai身体状态(Healthy condition)]
D03 [xinli zhuangtai心理状态(Psychological state)]
E [shuxing属性(Attribute)]
E01 [wuxing物性(Material property)]
E0101 [xingzhuang形状(Shape)]
E0102 [yanse颜色(Color)]
E0103 [weidao味道(Flavor)]
E0104 [waibiao外表(Outward appearance)]
E0105 [neirong内容(Content)]
E0106 [chugan触感(Touch sensation)]
E0107 [yinzhi音质(Tone quality)]
E0108 [zhongliang重量(Weight)]
E0109 [kongjianliang空间量(Spatial quantity)]
E010901 [changdu长度(Length)]
E010902 [kuandu宽度(Width)]
E010903 [gaodu高度(Height)]
E010904 [shendu深度(Depth)]
E010904 [mianji面积(Area)]
E010904 [tiji体积(Volume)]
E0110 [shijianliang时间量(Time quantity)]
E011001 [xin新(New)]
E011002 [jiu旧(Old)]
E0111 [wuli liang物理量(Physical quantity)]
E011101 [nongdu浓度(Concentration)]
E011102 [midu密度(Density)]
E011103 [yingdu硬度(Hardness)]
E011104 [shidu湿度(Humidity)]
E011105 [wendu温度(Temperature)]
E011106 [liangdu亮度(Brightness)]
E0112 [jiazhi价值(Value)]
E02 [renxing人性(Human nature)]
E0201 [nianling年龄(Age)]
E0202 [waimao外貌(Appearance)]
E0203 [xingge性格(Personality)]
E0204 [pinde品德(Moral character)]
E0205 [caigan才干(Talent)]
E0206 [jingkuang境况(Situation)]
F [guanxi关系(Relationship)]
F01 [goucheng构成(Composition)]
F02 [lingshu领属(Possession)]
F03 [bijiao比较(Comparison)]
F04 [biaozheng表征(Representation)]
F05 [guanlian关联(Relation)]

2) The Ontological Axiom

The semantic relationships within an Ontology are insufficiently represented only by semantic categorization system, as the system can only denote categorical relationships, while non-categorical relationships require definition through ontological axioms. The nodes within a semantic tree exhibit a complex array of semantic relationships, such as: [ziran xianxiang chanwu自然现象产物(Product of natural phenomena)] being the result of B01[ziran xianxiang自然现象(Natural phenomenon)], A010202[renzaowu人造物(Artifacts)] being the outcome or material of [shengchan生产(Production)], [ren人(Human)] being the agent of [huodong 活动(Activity)], [yiyuan医院(Hospital)] being the locations of [yiliao huodong医疗活动(Medical activity)], and so on. These relationships can all be described through the axiom of the Ontology.

Manually predefining Ontological axioms is a relatively common approach in the construction of domain Ontologies. For the linguistic common-sense Ontology, the definition of the Ontology is a very complex task, as the semantic relationships involved in linguistic common-sense are much more complex than those in the domain Ontologies. In the subsequent studies, we intend to explore a method for automatically extracting axioms of semantic relationships in the linguistic common-sense Ontology, based on the semantic gene structure description database and through the use of machine learning techniques.

II. Predefine Core Semantic Genes

The predefined set of semantic genes serves as the starting point for the extraction of semantic genes. Without this predefined set, the tasks of semantic analysis and gene extraction cannot be initiated. The entire set of semantic genes is gradually finitely expanded and optimized during the process of word-by-word analysis, based on this predefined set.

1) The primary semantic gene members predefined in the set originate from the aforementioned upper-level general vocabulary ontology. For instance: {[ren人(Human)], [wu物(Thing)], [shengwu生物(Organism)], [dongwu动物(Animal)], [zhiwu植物(Plant)], [weishengwu微生物(Microorganism)], [ziran自然(Nature)], [wuzhi物质(Substance)], [wuti物体(Object)], [cailiao材料(Material)], [qi ju器具(Utensil)], [jingshen精神(Spirit)], [daixie代谢(Metabolism)], [fenmi分泌(Secretion)], [chouxiang抽象(Abstract)], [xinxi信息(Information)], [nengliang能量(Energy)], [xianxiang现象(Phenomenon)], [sheng声(Sound)], [guang光(Light)], [dian电(Electricity)], [huo火(Fire)], [yan烟(Smoke)], [wu雾(Fog)], [feng风(Wind)], [lang浪(Wave)], [shengming生命(Life)], [bing病(Disease)], [zuzhi组织(Organization)], [guojia国家(Country)], [zhengdang政党(Political party)], [xingzheng行政(Administration)], [shehui社会(Society)], [bumen部门(Department)], [jingshen精神(Spirit)], [kexue科学(Science)], [zhishi知识(Knowledge)], [sixiang思想(Thought)], [qinggan情感(Emotion)], [zhidu制度(System)], [zuopin作品(Work)], [xuni虚拟(Virtual)], [zhuangtai状态(State)], [fenjie分解(Decomposition)], [shengzhang生长(Growth)], [shehui社会(Society)], [huodong活动(Activity)], [shi事(Event)], [yin阴(Cloudy)], [qing晴(Sunny)],

[yu雨(Rain)], [xue雪(Snow)], [dian电(Electricity)], [lei雷(Thunder)], [feng风(Wind)], [zhou昼(Day)], [ye夜(Night)], [wuli物理(Physics)], [guang光(Light)], [zhao照(Illuminate)], [sheng声(Sound)], [shenghuo生活(Life)], [zhengzhi政治(Politics)], [tongzhi统治(Rule)], [geming革命(Revolution)], [jingji经济(Economy)], [shengchan生产(Production)], [chuzhi处置(Dispose)], [she li设立(Establish)], [xiaoguo效果(Effect)], [jiang奖(Reward)], [cheng惩(Punish)], [danren担任(Undertake)], [xuanchuan宣传(Propaganda)], [haozhao号召(Call)], [pai派(Send)], [jian du监督(Supervise)], [pingjia评价(Evaluate)], [wenhua文化(Culture)], [biaoyan表演(Performance)], [lianxi练习(Practice)], [kan看(See)], [xinshang欣赏(Appreciate)], [zongjiao宗教(Religion)], [xinli心理(Psychology)], [xingwei行为(Behavior)], [bianhua变化(Change)], [jiechu接触(Contact)], [weiyi位移(Displacement)], [jiechu接触(Contact)], [lingshu领属(Possession)], [guanxi关系(Relationship)], [zhuan yi转移(Transfer)], [guocheng过程(Process)], [shenti身体(Body)], [ganzhi感知(Perception)], [shijian时间(Time)], [dian点(Point)], [duan段(Segment)], [xu序(Sequence)], [liang量(Quantity)], [wendu温度(Temperature)], [kongjian空间(Space)], [chusu处所(Place)], [fangwei方位(Direction)], [lujing路径(Path)], [fanwei范围(Scope)], [zhuangtai状态(State)], [shuxing属性(Attribute)], [goucheng构成(Composition)], [lingshu领属(Possession)], [jiazhi价值(Value)], [xingzhuang形状(Shape)], [yanse颜色(Color)], [weidao味道(Taste)], [waibiao外表(Appearance)], [neirong内容(Content)], [zhi质(Quality)], [liang量(Quantity)], [xin新(New)], [jiu旧(Old)], [nong浓(Thick)], [mi密(Dense)], [ying硬(Hard)], [nianling年龄(Age)], [xingge性格(Character)], [pinde品德(Virtue)], [caigan才干(Ability)], [jingkuang境况(Situation)], [guanxi关系(Relationship)], [bijiao比较(Comparison)], [biaozheng表征(Representation)], [guanlian关联(Correlation)]…} Some of these genes belong to dimension feature function operators, while others are function assignment genes.

2) In addition to extraction from the ontology, a portion of function operators are also predefined during the analysis of word meanings, according to the semantic features of their respective lexical categories. For instance, when analyzing verbs, predefined sets such as {[shishi施事(Agent)], [shoushi受事(Patient)], [fangshi方式(Manner)], [shouduan手段(Means)], [mudi目的(Purpose)], [jieguo结果(Result)], [fangxiang方向(Direction)], [lujing路径(Path)], [sudu速度(Speed)], [lingyu领域(Field)]} and so on can be defined. In addition to these genes, some assignment genes can also be defined based on specific conditions or criteria. Definition and analysis are interwoven, mutually verifying, and conducted in an iterative manner. Anyway, it is difficult to completely define all the initial genes before the analysis of the entire vocabulary system is completed.Therefore, the definition of the initial gene set is also progressive.

III. Selection of Semantic Classes and Semantic Fields

The analysis of semantic genes is an extensive project that requires more than a single effort. We adopt a strategy of segmenting the smallest semantic fields based on semantic categories, progressing step by step in a gradual manner. The classification of semantic categories and semantic fields is extensively referenced from various research literature on lexicology, word lists, semantic classification dictionaries, and database resources, with an approach of top-down segmentation to ensure comprehensive coverage. For instance, following the steps of "Referential word → specific referential words → nouns referring to people → appellation word → occupational appellation word → farmer", we identify a minimal semantic field with "farmer" as the clustering core, which includes {nong min农民(farmer): liangnong粮农(grain farmer), chanong茶农(tea farmer), cainong菜农(vegetable farmer), zhenong蔗农(sugarcane farmer), yannong烟农(tobacco farmer), huanong花农(flower farmer), linnong林农(forestry farmer), miannong棉农(cotton farmer), yaonong药农(medicinal herb farmer)}.

IV. Analysis and Extraction

The first step is to examine whether the clustering core word of the minimal subfield (i.e., the hypernym of the minimal semantic field) is composed of an independent free semantic gene. If it is, the gene can be directly utilized. Otherwise, the core word should be analyzed first and packaged into a gene cluster, which can then be invoked in other semantic analyses. In the above example of the minimal semantic field "nong min农民(farmer)", the word "nong min农民(farmer)" cannot be used as a semantic gene in isolation; thus, it requires analysis.

The term "nong min农民" in *The Contemporary Chinese Dictionary (7th Edition)* is defined as:

A laborer engaged in agricultural production in rural areas.

In the "cihai辞海(*The Grand Dictionary of Chinese Language*)", it is defined as:

A laborer directly engaged in agricultural production (excluding serfs and agricultural workers).

Integrating both interpretations, the semantic genetic structure of the term "farmer" can be described as:

$S_{农民}$ = {[人]:{[职业]([生产])} + {[领域]([农业])} + {[地点]([农村])} + {[方式]([直接])}}

$S_{农民}$ = {[Human]:{[Occupation]([Produce])} + {[Field]([Agriculture])} + {[Location]([Rural area])} + {[Me-thod]([Direct])}}

Through the semantic analysis of this word, we extract a group of semantic genes: [ren人(Human)], [zhiye职业(Occupation)], [shengchan生产(Produce)], [lingyu领域(Field)], [didian地点(Location)], [nongye农业(Agriculture)], [nongcun农村(Rural area)], [fangshi方式(Method)], [zhijie直接(Direct)]. Additionally, we obtain the semantic gene cluster $_{GS}$[Farmer] for further analysis of other words within the semantic field.

According to the definition of *The Contemporary Chinese Dictionary (7th Edition)*, let us proceed to analyze other terms:

chanong茶农(Tea farmer): Farmers primarily engaged in the planting of tea trees.

$S_{茶农}$ = {$_{GS}$[农民]:{[生产]($_{GS}$[茶叶])}}

$S_{茶农}$ = {$_{GS}$[Farmer]:{[Produce]($_{GS}$[Tea])}}

cainong菜农(Vegetable farmer): Farmers primarily engaged in the planting of vegetables.

$S_{\text{菜农}} = \{{}_{GS}[\text{农民}]:\{[\text{生产}]({}_{GS}[\text{蔬菜}])\}\}$

$S_{\text{菜农}} = \{{}_{GS}[\text{Farmer}]:\{[\text{Produce}]({}_{GS}[\text{Vegetable}])\}\}$

huanong花农(Flower farmer): Farmers primarily engaged in the planting of flowers.

$S_{\text{花农}} = \{{}_{GS}[\text{农民}]:\{[\text{生产}]({}_{GS}[\text{花木}])\}\}$

$S_{\text{花农}} = \{{}_{GS}[\text{Farmer}]:\{[\text{Produce}]({}_{GS}[\text{Flower}])\}\}$

liangnong粮农(Grain farmer): Farmers primarily engaged in the planting of grain.

$S_{\text{粮农}} = \{{}_{GS}[\text{农民}]:\{[\text{生产}]({}_{GS}[\text{粮食}])\}\}$

$S_{\text{粮农}} = \{{}_{GS}[\text{Farmer}]:\{[\text{Produce}]({}_{GS}[\text{Grain}])\}\}$

linnong林农(Forestry farmer): Farmers engaged in the breeding, management, and protection of forests.

$S_{\text{林农}} = \{{}_{GS}[\text{农民}]:\{[[\text{生产}]\wedge[\text{管理}]\wedge[\text{保护}]]({}_{GS}[\text{森林}])\}\}$

$S_{\text{林农}} = \{{}_{GS}[\text{Farmer}]:\{[[\text{Produce}]\wedge[\text{Manage}]\wedge[\text{Protect}]]({}_{GS}[\text{Forest}])\}\}$

miannong棉农(Cotton farmer): Farmers primarily engaged in the planting of cotton.

$S_{\text{棉农}} = \{{}_{GS}[\text{农民}]:\{[\text{生产}]({}_{GS}[\text{棉花}])\}\}$

$S_{\text{棉农}} = \{{}_{GS}[\text{Farmer}]:\{[\text{Produce}]({}_{GS}[\text{cotton}])\}\}$

yannong烟农(Tobacco farmer): Farmers primarily engaged in the planting of tobacco.

$S_{\text{烟农}} = \{{}_{GS}[\text{农民}]:\{[\text{生产}]({}_{GS}[\text{烟草}])\}\}$

$S_{\text{烟农}} = \{{}_{GS}[\text{Farmer}]:\{[\text{Produce}]({}_{GS}[\text{Tobacoo}])\}\}$

yaonong药农(Medicinal herb farmer): Farmers who primarily engage in the planting and collection of medicinal plants or the breeding and hunting of medicinal animals.

$S_{\text{药农}} = \{{}_{GS}[\text{农民}]:\{[\text{生产}](\{[[\text{植物}]\vee[\text{动物}]]:\{[\text{功能}]([\text{药用}])\}\}\}$

$S_{\text{药农}} = \{{}_{GS}[\text{Farmer}]:\{[\text{Produce}](\{[[\text{Plant}]\vee[\text{Animal}]]:\{[\text{Function}]([\text{Medical}])\}\}\}$

zhenong蔗农(Sugarcane farmer): Farmers primarily engaged in the planting of sugarcane.

$S_{\text{蔗农}} = \{{}_{GS}[\text{农民}]:\{[\text{生产}]({}_{GS}[\text{甘蔗}])\}\}$

$S_{\text{蔗农}} = \{{}_{GS}[\text{Farmer}]:\{[\text{Produce}]({}_{GS}[\text{Sugarcane}])\}\}$

In the analysis of these terms, five new semantic genes have been added. Consequently, we have obtained the set of semantic genes for this semantic field: [ren人(Human)], [zhiye职业(Occupation)], [shengchan生产(Produce)], [lingyu领域(Field)], [didian地点(Location)], [nongye农业(Agriculture)], [nongcun农村(Rural area)], [fangshi方式(Method)], [zhijie直接(Direct)], [guanli管理(Manage)], [baohu保护(Protect)], [dongwu动物(Animal)], [zhiwu植物(Plant)], [yongyao药用(Medicinal)]}, which are added to the primary semantic gene set for further examination. Among these genes, there are some that overlap with the members of the predefined core gene set. These overlapping members, including any potential duplicate genes that may arise in subsequent analyses, can be processed in one go through computer deduplication during the final summary.

In our analysis, we also employed a set of semantic gene clusters, including ${}_{Gs}$[chaye茶叶(Tea)], ${}_{Gs}$[shucai蔬菜(Vegetable)], ${}_{Gs}$[huamu花木(Flower)],

$_{Gs}$[liangshi粮食(Grain)], $_{Gs}$[senlin森林(Forest)], $_{Gs}$[mianhua棉花(Cotton)], $_{Gs}$[yancao烟草(Tobacco)], and $_{Gs}$[ganzhe甘蔗(Sugarcane)]. These gene clusters are temporarily stored in a semantic gene cluster database. To ensure the logicality and systematicity of the work, they are not processed at this stage but are reserved for further analysis when the semantic fields they belong to are reached. After the analysis of all words is completed, two computer-based checks will be conducted: ① to verify whether the analysis of the gene clusters is complete; if not, the analysis will continue until all gene clusters are fully analyzed and extracted; ② to check for circular interpretation issues; if any are found, the semantic gene structure expressions of the relevant words will be optimized and adjusted to eliminate circular interpretation.

In the process of semantic analysis and gene extraction, we refer to the dictionary definitions, yet we do not merely copy them; instead, we optimize the dictionary definitions as follows:

1) *The Contemporary Chinese Dictionary (7th Edition)* exhibits a highly similar pattern in the definitions of these terms, which are predominantly phrased as "farmers mainly engaged in the planting of XX." There are two issues to be addressed here:

① The definition of "plant" is inadequate. "Plant" is merely a single stage in agricultural production. The dictionary defines "planting" as "burying plant seeds in the soil; transplanting plant seedlings into the soil", which clearly does not align with reality. Breeding, field management, crop harvesting, drying, and storage are all important stages of agricultural production. The definition of "forest farmer" in the dictionary uses terms such as "breeding" and "management", but omits "planting". In fact, when we recognize and differentiate these "farmers" associated with different production fields, the processes and details of their production stages are not the primary basis for our understanding of these concepts; this factor can even be overlooked. Therefore, we replace "plant" with a more extensive and broad-spectrum term "produce", and extract the semantic gene [shengchan生产(Produce)].

② The interpretive term "mainly" imposes an unnecessary and even incorrect restriction on the meanings of these words. As previously mentioned, "planting" is not the sole primary aspect of agricultural production, and thus, we discard this interpretive component. In contrast, the interpretation of "sugarcane farmer" as "farmers engaged in sugarcane production" is the most appropriate. The analysis of the semantic genetic structure of this group of words basically aligns with the interpretation pattern of the word.

2) The substitution of "produce" for "plant" appears to expand the semantic scope, potentially leading to ambiguity. For instance, "producing tea" may be ambiguous, as it could refer to tea farmers planting, managing tea trees, harvesting, and initially processing the raw tea leaves, or it could also refer to tea processing factories engaging in deep processing of the raw tea leaves to produce the final tea products. However, in our expression of semantic genetic structure, this ambiguity does not arise, because the semantic gene [nongmin农

民(Farmer)] already possesses the function of disambiguation, and will not be confused with the workers in tea factories during semantic computation.

3) The semantic analysis and description of "forest farmer" retains the meaning of "management" and extracts the semantic gene [guanli管理(Manage)]. This is because the term "management" in this context differs from "field management" in other agricultural production, as it also encompasses the management of the rational utilization of forest resources. Therefore, it cannot be encompassed by the term "produce".
4) The interpretation of "medicinal herb farmer" has been merged, with the four terms "planting", "collecting", "breeding", and "hunting" being consolidated under the term "produce". Firstly, these are part of the production activities of medicinal herb farmers, but not the entirety, thus necessitating a merger to expand the scope of the interpretation. Secondly, as discussed in point 3) above, the merger does not lead to ambiguity with pharmaceutical factory workers, hence it can be merged to simplify the interpretation.

V. Adjacent Fields Comparison and Optimization

1) Select the smallest semantic field adjacent to the one analyzed in step IV, for instance, the set {gongjiang工匠(craftsman): mujiang木匠(carpenter), wajiang瓦匠(bricklayer), niwajiang泥瓦匠(plasterer), nishuijiang泥水匠(mason), shijiang石匠(stonecutter), pijiang皮匠(tanner), huajiang画匠(artisan-painter), tiejiang铁匠(blacksmith), yinjiang银匠(silversmith), tongjiang铜匠(coppersmith), xijiang锡匠(tinsmith), qijiang漆匠(lacquerer), youqijiang油漆匠(painter), xiejiang鞋匠(cobbler), miejiang篾匠(bamboo craftsman)}. Repeat step IV to analyze the semantic structure of each word and extract the semantic genes.
2) Compare the extracted semantic genes with the genes extracted in step IV. Similar items are eliminated, items with close proximity are merged, and conflicting items are optimized.
3) The process is iteratively repeated until the analysis of all the smallest adjacent semantic fields at the same level under the same node on the classification semantic tree is completed, and the merging and optimization of the semantic gene sets are achieved.

VI. Expansion of Semantic Field Analysis by Induction and Deduction

1) The analysis shifts to a higher level of hierarchy, the superordinate concepts of "occupational titles" are induced from all the minimal semantic fields at the same level within steps IV and V.
2) Induce the same level concepts and higher-level concepts of this concept to form a new upper-level semantic field, such as: {chengwei称谓(title): qinshu chengwei亲属称谓(kinship title), zhiye chengwei职业称谓(occupational title), guanxian chengwei官衔称谓(official title), xueshu chengwei学术称谓(academic title), xingming chengwei姓名称

谓(personal name title), jingcheng敬称(respectful title), qiancheng谦称(humble title), echeng恶称(derogatory title)}.

3) The other concepts within the semantic field, excluding"occupational title" that has already been analyzed, are individually deduced downwards, thereby forming several new sub-minimal semantic fields.
4) Repeat the procedure in step IV, and analyze each of the minimal semantic fields. Extract and merge the sets of semantic genes.

VII. Categorize and merge to establish a primary semantic gene set

At different levels of the semantic classification tree, the steps IV, V, and VI are repeatedly performed until the analysis of all words within the slected scope is completed. This scope can be divided into blocks based on the progress of the project, carried out in stages, and gradually advanced in a manner akin to laying out a carpet.

VIII. Expand the scope of analysis to validate and refine

Analyze more words with the genes from the primary gene set to test their coverage and effectiveness. This process involves identifying gaps and deficiencies, thereby facilitating the optimization of the primary gene set.

IX Establish the final semantic gene set by statistically analysis and optimization

Merge the primary gene set and the predefined core gene set, perform computer -assisted duplication and statistics, eliminate duplicate genes, merge rare frequency genes, eliminate cycle interpretation, and obtain the final modern Chinese semantic gene set.

References

Bloomfield, L. (1933). *Language*. George Allen & Unwin Ltd.

Chomsky, N. (1987). Language in a psychological setting. *Sophia Linguistica, 1987*(22), 1–73.

Dong, Z. 董振东, & Dong, Q. 董强. (1999). An Introduction to HowNet [知网导论]. http://www.keenage.com/Theory-and-practice-of-HowNet/03.pdf

Evans, V., & Melanie, G. (2006). *Cognitive Linguistics: An Introduction*. Lawrence Erlbaum Associates.

Ge, B. 葛本仪. (2001). *Lexicology of Modern Chinese* [现代汉语词汇学]. Shandong People's Publishing House.

Han, X. 韩秀娟. (2005). *The Research Report of the Prior Set of Modern Chinese Basic Words* [现代汉语基本词汇先验集的考察分析研究]. In *Proceedings of the Eighth National Joint Conference on Computational Linguistics* (JSCL-2005) (pp. 219–225).

Hu, D. 胡惮. (2009). On Category Hierarchy and Ontology [略论范畴层次与知识本体]. *Journal of Shenyang Normal University (Social Science Edition)* [沈阳师范大学学报 (社会科学版)], *33*(06), 32–34.

Hu, D. 胡惮. (2011). *Alloconcepts and Their Formalized Description* [概念变体及其形式化描写]. China Social Sciences Press.

Jia, Y. 贾彦德. (1992). *Chinese Semantics* [汉语语义学]. Peking University Press.

Lakoff, G. (1987). *Women, Fire, and Dangerous Things: What Categories Reveal about the Mind*. Chicago University Press.

Li, B. 李葆嘉. (2002). The Study of Metalanguage System of Chinese: An Analysis Project of Language Gene Atlas [汉语元语言系统研究的理论建构及应用价值]. *Journal of Nanjing Normal University (Social Science Edition)* [南京师大学报(社会科学版)], (04), 140–147.

Li, B 李葆嘉. (2013). *A Study on the Interpretive Metalanguage of modern Chinese* 现代汉语析义元语言研究. Beijing:World Publishing Corporation 北京:世界图书出版公司.

Li, B. 李葆嘉. (2003). Theories of Semantic Grammar and Meta-language System: Their Researche [语义语法学理论和元语言系统研究]. *Journal of Shenzhen University (Humanities and Social Sciences)* [深圳大学学报(人文社会科学版)], (02), 105–110.

Miao, C. 苗传江, & Liu, Z. 刘智颖. (2010).The Lexical Knowledge Base of Modern Chinese Based on HNC Theory [基于HNC的现代汉语词语知识库建设]. *Journal of Yunan Normal University(Humanities and Social Sciences)* [云南师范大学学报(哲学社会科学版)], *42*(4), 15–18.

Pu, D. 蒲冬梅. (2008). Analysis on Validity of Natural Semantic Metalanguage [自然语义元语言有效性评析]. *Foreign Language Research* [外语学刊], (4), 55–59.

Pu, D. 蒲冬梅. (2012). Natural Semantic Metalanguage: Rationales and Prospects [自然语义元语言的理论基础及研究前景]. *Foreign Language Research* [外语学刊], (04), 45–49.

Qiu, Q. 邱庆山. (2018). Description and Construction of the Attribute Sense Ontology of Chinese Nouns of “bi” Class [汉语笔类名词的属性义知识本体描写与构建]. *Journal of Hubei University (Philosophy and Social Science)* [湖北大学学报(哲学社会科学版)], *45*(05), 152–159.

Su, X. 苏新春. (2003). Three Interpretations of Metalanguage and Different Researches on Defining Metalanguage [元语言研究的三种理解及释义型元语言研究评述]. *Journal of Jiangxi Normal University (Philosophy and Social Sciences Edition)* [江西师范大学学报(哲学社会科学版)], (06), 93–102.

Sun, D. 孙道功, & Li, B. 李葆嘉. (2008). On Marker Set Construction of Analysis Metalanguage [试论析义元语言标记集的建构]. *Applied Linguistics* [语言文字应用], (02), 132–138.

Wang, H. 王红卫. (2010). The Semantic View of Encyclopedia Knowledge and Its Enlightenment for English Vocabulary Teaching [百科知识语义观及其对英语词汇教学的启示]. *Journal of Liaoning University of Technology (Social Science Edition)* [辽宁工业大学学报(社会科学版)], *12*(3), 124–126, 135.

Xiao, G. 萧国政, Xiao 肖珊, & Guo, T. 郭婷婷. (2011). The Mapping from Space of Concept Primitives to Space of Word Meaning Primitives [从概念基元空间到语义基元空间的映射——HNC联想脉络与词汇语义结构表述研究]. *Journal of East China Normal University (Philosophy and Social Sciences)* [华东师范大学学报(哲学社会科学版), *43*(01), 139–143+156.

Zhang, N. 张能甫. (1999). Review and Prospect of Research on Chinese Basic Vocabulary [汉语基本词汇研究的回顾与展望]. *Journal of Sichuan Normal University (Social Sciences Edition)* [四川师范大学学报(社会科学版)], (02), 90–95.

Zhang, Z. 张喆. (2007). *Natural Semantic Metalanguage: Theory and Practice* [自然语义元语言:理论与实践]. Science Press 科学出版社.

Zhang, Z. 张志平. (2007). *Research on Automatic Extraction of Chinese Basic Vocabulary Based on Genetic Algorithm* [基于遗传算法的汉语基本词汇自动提取研究]. Inner Mongolia Normal University [内蒙古师范大学].

Zhou, Z. 周祖谟. (1959). *Lectures on Chinese Lexicology* [汉语词汇讲话]. People’s Education Press.

Chapter 5
Description of Semantic Gene Structure of Basic Word Classes in Modern Chinese

Nouns and verbs are the most fundamental and important categories of word classes in language, holding the most significant position in the lexical system. Based on the semantic gene extraction process discussed in Chapter 4, we have selected some typical representatives from modern Chinese nouns, verbs, and adjectives as examples to elaborate on the operational process of semantic gene extraction. Taking collection of representative components from these three main word classes as examples to demonstrate the analysis process of semantic gene extraction can reflect the overview of our project.

The selection of analysis objects is based on the word classes rather than the classification tree in the Ontology. This approach is adopted for two reasons: first, it adheres to the general conventions of lexical research in the linguistic community; second, it facilitates practical engineering needs during the operational process. By categorizing the analysis objects into word classes and their internal subclasses, we can comprehensively cover all words, avoiding any omissions. After the analysis is completed, the attachment of each word to the Ontology can be automatically processed and flexibly attached through computer analysis, generating a dynamic general vocabulary Ontology based on the semantic gene structure of words.

5.1 Dictionary Interpretation and Feature Dimensions of Word Meaning

5.1.1 The Interpretation Mode of Language Dictionary

Dictionaries serve as the primary basis for people to learn, understand, and utilize word meanings. The compilation of language dictionaries, particularly authoritative ones, often necessitates the intensive research and verification by a large group of

D. Hu, *Lexical Semantic Gene Structure of Modern Chinese*,
https://doi.org/10.1007/978-981-96-6425-2_5

linguistic and lexicographical experts, which, in a sense, represents a factual standard for the cognitive understanding of vocabulary semantics. Therefore dictionary definitions often serve as the main basis for the study of vocabulary semantics. In the practical process of extracting word meaning genes, dictionary definitions also act as significant reference resources.

5.1.1.1 The Discrepancy Between Dictionary Definitions and Lexical Semantic Computing

The manner in which the human brain and computers process semantics differs significantly, and the methods of word inclusion and definition in philological dictionaries cannot be directly transposed into the field of lexical semantic computation. There are several reasons for this:

(1) For the complexity and ambiguity of word meanings themselves, the human brain's fuzzy cognition and fault tolerance ability far exceed that of computers. In the process of defining words, the dictionaries have less stringent requirements than those of semantic computing engineering for dealing with some special issues, such as the segmentation of pleremes and circular interpretation. For instance, Li 李强 and Yuan 袁毓林 (2016) investigated from the perspective of generative lexicon theory and found, "nouns can be divided into three types based on the content of the meaning they represent: natural, artificial, and synthetic." Words that belong to the synthetic semantic type should be segmented into separate meanings.

For example, in *The Contemporary Chinese Dictionary (7th Edition),* some definitions of "event-material" nouns distinguish between pleremes of event and material meanings, such as:

Yumaoqiu羽毛球(badminton): ❶ *One of the ball games, with its rules and equipment largely resembling those of tennis.* ❷ *The shuttlecock used in badminton is typically made by enclosing a soft wooden core with sheepskin and feathers, although there are also versions made of plastic.*

The term "yumaoqiu羽毛球(badminton)" has been segmented into two pleremes, corresponding to the event meaning and the material meaning of the word. Similarly, terms such as "lanqiu篮球(basketball)", "zuqiu足球(soccer)", and "pingpangqiu乒乓球(table tennis)" also exhibit a similar segmentation, which is quite appropriate.

And some are not distinguished, for example:

Weiqi围棋(Go): *A type of chess game. On the chessboard, there are nineteen lines running vertically and horizontally, intersecting into 361 positions. Two sides respectively use black and white chess pieces to face off against each other, engaging in encirclement and capturing the opponent's chess pieces. The one who occupies the most positions on the board wins.*

The explanation only includes the event meaning plereme of the term "weiqi围棋(Go)", while omitting its material meaning, which fails to account for the meaning of "weiqi围棋(Go)" in sentences such as "wo maile yifu weiqi我买了

一副围棋(I bought a set of Go pieces)." and "ta ba yiguan weiqi dafanle他把一罐围棋打翻了(He knocked over a jar of Go pieces)." Therefore, it is necessary to add an additional plereme to the term, specifying "weiqi yundong zhong yongde qizi huo qipan 围棋运动中用的棋子或棋盘 (Go pieces or the Go board used in the game of Go)." Similarly, the definitions of some other terms such as "xiangqi象棋(Chinese chess)", "junqi军棋(military chess)", "tiaoqi跳棋(Chinese draughts)" and "wuziqi 五子棋(GoBang)" also suffer from the same issue.

Yu雨(rain): *The water that descends from the clouds towards the earth's surface. When the tiny water droplets within the clouds increase in volume to a point where they can no longer remain suspended in the air, they fall as rain.*

The material meaning plereme of the word "yu雨(rain)" has been included here, while its event meaning plereme, "the weather phenomenon of rain", has been omitted. A similar issue is present in the definitions of other words such as "xue 雪(snow)", "bingbao冰雹(hail)", "zaocan早餐(breakfast)", "wucan午餐(lunch)", and "wancan晚餐(dinner)".

Similarly, the explanations of "material-information" nouns such as "changpian 唱片(record)", "shu书(book)", and "pingmu屏幕(screen)", predominantly encompass only plereme of material meaning, lacking the plereme of informational meaning. That is, "the information recorded on records", "the information written in books", and "the information displayed on screens". On the other hand, "event-information" nouns like "yanjiang演讲(speech)", "diaocha调查(survey)", and "fenxi分析(analysis)" primarily carry only the plereme of event meaning, omitting the information aspect. That is, "the content of speech", "the content of investigation", and the "content or conclusion of analysis".

Wang 王惠 (2004: 123) points out: "Due to the significant semantic differences between verb transferred-reference and expressing an action or behavior, we generally consider them as different pleremes, and dictionaries also establish difference plareme for them." Nevertheless, some authoritative dictionaries still lack enough attention in these aspects. For language dictionaries primarily intended for human readers, these omissions may not pose a significant problem. Owing to the holistic nature of cognition, the human brain may automatically complete these informations by referencing the schema structure of existing knowledge. However, for computational processing of semantics, there are evident deficiencies. Unless we prepare an adequately extensive common-sense knowledge base for computers, we cannot base the computation and analysis of semantics on the assumption that computers possess sufficient prior knowledge. The semantic analysis required for semantic computing engineering demands a more nuanced and precise approach. Although achieving absolute objectivity and accuracy is impossible, we still strive to achieve as much objectivity and precision as possible. As Li 李强 (2018) states, "Semantics are characterized by complexity and uncertainty, and disagreements in analysis are inevitable. However, this does not mean that semantics cannot or should not be dissected and examined in detail; seeking certainty amidst uncertainty is the inevitable path and eternal driving force of scientific research."

(2) Because dictionaries also bear the responsibility of disseminating ideas, culture, and scientific and technological knowledge, the definitions of some entries often incorporate domain-specific knowledge. For instance, in the definitions of certain proper nouns and scientific and technical terms in *The Contemporary Chinese Dictionary (7th Edition)*:

Xiangsu像素(pixel): *The fundamental unit of a digital image, representing the portion of the image scanned by the electron beam or light beam at each instant within the photoelectric conversion system. The higher the number of pixels in an image, the clearer the picture quality.*

Xiangwei相位(phase): *The physical quantity undergoing cosine (or sine) variation. The state of this quantity at a specific moment (or position) can be determined by a numerical value, which is termed as the phase.*

Chaoshengbo超声波(ultrasound): *Sound waves with frequencies exceeding the highest audible limit for humans (20,000 Hz). These waves propagate approximately in a straight line and experience less attenuation in solids and liquids, allowing for the easy concentration of energy. Consequently, they can produce a variety of special effects. Ultrasound is widely applied in various technical fields.*

Such concepts, when treated as ordinary vocabulary, are laden with considerable and complex disciplinary domain knowledge, which makes their semantic description in computation engineering quite cumbersome. On the other hand, treating them as domain-specific concepts is challenging in terms of forming a systematic framework and fully expressing the knowledge system of the domain. We believe that a more appropriate approach is to describe these concepts using domain-specific ontologies. If they need to be described in a lexical semantic database, they can be simplified by removing the additional information, as:

Xiangsu像素(pixel): The fundamental unit of a digital image.

Chaoshengbo超声波(ultrasound): Sound waves with frequencies exceeding the highest audible limit for humans (20,000 Hz).

The domain knowledge contained in these word meanings is solved in the domain knowledge base.

(3) The definitions of many entries in the dictionary not only explain connotative meaning of the word, but also list some of its members, that is, the partial extension of the word, such as:

Shuichan水产(aquatic product): *The general term for animals, algae, and other organisms produced in the ocean, rivers, and lakes. It typically encompasses those with economic value, such as various types of fish, shrimp, crabs, shellfish, kelp, and gelidium, among others.*

Kuangchan矿产(minerals): *Substances within the earth's crust that have economic value for extraction, such as copper, iron, mica, natural gas, petroleum, and coal.*

Enumerating these extensions is beneficial for human readers as it aids in quickly categorizing the concepts represented by the explained words, thereby facilitating an understanding of word meanings. However, for semantic computation processing, these extensions are rather information noise. If all extensions cannot be enumerated exhaustively, not only will they fail to assist computers in understanding semantics, but they may also create interference.

(4) In dictionaries, certain words that denote abstract concepts are often explained through illustrative descriptions rather than definitions, for instance:

Xian咸(salty): A taste resembling that of salt, eg.salted fish; the dish is too salty.
Danqing蛋青(pale blue): A color resembling the shell of a cyan duck egg.
Shan膻(smell of mutton): An odor similar to that of mutton.
Tong痛(Ache): *Discomfort caused by diseases, injuries, and other factors.*

This interpretation is based on the assumption that humans possess some form of direct objective experience, and the meaning of the word being interpreted is understood by activating the perceptual memory of this assumed experience. For individuals who lack such experience, the meaning of these word is uncomprehensible. It is evident that machines do not possess such experiences, rendering this approach ineffective for them. In fact, it is extremely difficult to provide an objective and accurate explanation for such words using other methods; we tend to define them as semantic genes.

5.1.1.2 Implications of the Structured Pattern of Dictionary Definitions for the Semantic Computational Representation

The definition patterns in dictionaries are generally standardized, adhering to certain structural rules in most cases. They feature both a unified structure for definitions and a categorized approach for different word classes.

Feng 冯海霞 & Zhang 张志毅 (2006) summarized the definition system of the *Contemporary Chinese Dictionary* from three perspectives: base meaning, supplementary meaning, and semantic range. The plereme is decomposed into two aspects: quality and quantity. The quality aspect is the semantic value, which has qualitative prescriptive nature and serves as the distinguishing feature among pleremes. The quantity aspect is the semantic field, which encompasses the meaning and usage range of the plereme. The semantic value is further decomposed into base meaning and supplementary meaning.

(1) Basic meaning: This refers to the rational meaning or conceptual meaning as discussed in lexical semantics. The basic meaning encompasses not only categorical features but also referential features and expressive features; it includes not only mental forms but also intuitive forms and emotional forms; it not only has reference values but also system values. This is the core concept of the semantic view in modern lexicography. For words of the same lexical category, the pattern of interpretation for their basic meaning is generally similar:

① The definition-type structural formula for noun definitions: [个性义素]+[共性义素] [Individual sememe]+[Common sememe]

② The explanation-type structural formula for verb definitions: [个性义素]+[核心义素] [Individual sememe]+[Core sememe]
③ The description-type structural formula for adjective definitions: [个性义素]+[核心义素] [Individual sememe]+[Core sememe]

These are the universal core interpretation patterns of the three basic word classes. Based on these core structural patterns, several variations can be derived.

(2) Supplementary meaning: It is a secondary component of the semantic value, often referred to asaccessorial meaning. Supplementary meaning is analogous to the connotative meaning in lexical semantics, but it is not entirely equivalent. It also includes some rational meaning components, which are, however, subordinate and secondary. Most of these rational meanings are implicit, while only a small portion are explicit. The *Contemporary Chinese Dictionary* lists six types of supplementary meaning in its definitions.

① Modal supplementary meaning, which is further divided into sixteen subclasses: commendatory, derogatory, euphemistic, polite, respectful, humble, proud, affectionate, regretful, intimate, repulsive, disdainful, sarcastic, teasing, reproachful, and abusive.
② Stylistic supplementary meanings, which primarily includes written and spoken language, denoted as < shu 书 (written) > and < kou 口 (spoken) > respectively. Additionally, it encompasses genres such as academic, official documents, and letters.
③ Temporal supplementary meaning, which encompasses ancient terminology (before the Tang and Song dynasties),early vernacular (from the Tang and Song dynasties to the May Fourth Movement), and old-time terminology (from 1900 to 1940).
④ Register supplementary meaning, which encompasses various fields such as politics, diplomacy, military affairs, commerce, law, literature and arts, and religion.
⑤ Dialectal supplementary meaning, which is denoted as < fang 方 (dialect) >.
⑥ Loan supplementary meaning, which is marked with the original language and the original word form.

Indeed, there are more supplementary meaning types than the six mentioned above. Zhang 张志毅 & Zhang 张庆云 (2001: 42–63) have summarized ten types, namely: attributive supplementary meaning, figurative supplementary meaning, modal supplementary meaning, register supplementary meaning, tone supplementary meaning, stylistic supplementary meaning, regional supplementary meaning, temporal supplementary meaning, cultural supplementary meaning, and loan supplementary meaning.

(3) Semantic range: Refers to the meaning range of a plereme and the extent of its application. This includes:

① Size range: Refers to the size of the objects designated by the plereme.
② Quantity range: Refers to the quantity of the objects designated by the plereme.
③ Partner range: Refers to the scope of plereme application, which is the range of other pleremes that can be paired with the plereme to be defined. In essence, it is a semantic constraint on the combination of pleremes. For instance:

Chuban出版(publication): *The compilation or production of books, periodicals, illustrations, audio-visual products,* etc.

Here, "books", "periodicals", "illustrations" and "audio-visual products" belong to the partner range.

Fu 符淮青 (1992) discussed the interpretive principles for words of different semantic types in dictionaries.

(1) The words for naming often employ the definitional pattern of "specific difference+category", which can also be applied to words referring to actions, behaviors, and qualities. In interpretive language, the words indicating "category" serve as the central term, used to indicate the category of the superordinate concept to which the explained word belongs. The components indicating "specific difference" function as modifiers, used to specify the specific characteristics of the individual or variety of the explained word in terms of its appearance, state, nature, structure, habits, material, and function. For example:

Tuanzi团子(dumpling): *A spherical food made from rice or flour.* Here the central term "food" denotes the object category to which the explained word "tuanzi团子" belongs, while the modifier "spherical made from rice or flour" indicates the specific difference features of the material and shape of the explained word "dumpling".

Paocai泡菜(pickled vegetable): *A type of sour vegetable made by soaking cabbage, radish, and other vegetables in cold water mixed with salt, wine, zanthoxylums, and other ingredients.* Here the center word "vegetable" denotes the category to which the explained word "paocai泡菜" belongs, while the modifier "made by soaking cabbage, radish, and other vegetables in cold water mixed with salt, wine, zanthoxylums, and other ingredients", "sour" specifies the specific difference features of the material, method, and taste of the explained word.

(2) The interpretation of words expressing actions, act or behaviors often employs descriptive and explanatory patterns, which can be categorized into the following types:

① It indicates that the word meaning contains a certain action or behavior, and it imposes restrictions on various aspects of the action and behavior, such as the tool, part, degree, manner, time, direction, location, quantity, and scope involved. For instance:

Xingjin行进(march): *Move forward, typically used in the context of a team.* ("Xingjin 行进" denotes an action, "forward" indicates the direction of this action, and "typically used in the context of a team" specifies the scope of application for this action).

Maiji迈进(stride forward): *Step forward with great strides.* ("Maiji 迈进" denotes an act of movement and "stride" characterizes the manner of that movement).

② It indicates that the word meaning contains a certain action or behavior and its relational object (the patient), and it describes the various constraints that may apply to both the action and the relational object, such as time, place, manner, and tools, among others. For instance:

Taojin淘金(gold panning): *Select alluvial gold from sand by using the method of water separation.* ("Selection" denotes an action, "alluvial gold" is the patient of this action, "water separation" is the method of the action, and "from sand" indicates the location of the action).

Yajing压惊(help sb. get over a shock): *Reassure a person who has been frightened by means such as treating him/her to meals.* ("Reassuring" denotes the action, with "person" serving as the patient of this action. The act of "inviting him/her to meals" constitutes the manner of the action, while "frightened" characterizes the state or condition of the patient).

③ It indicates that the word meaning contains a certain action or behavior and its agent, and describes the various constraints that may exist for the action or behavior and its agent. The patient may or may not be present. For instance:

Qifei起飞(takeoff): *The aircraft begins to fly.* ("Fly" denotes an action, "begins" indicates the stage of the action, and "aircraft" refers to the agent performing the action).

Huanyuan还愿(fulfill a vow): *People who pray for a diety's blessings practice the rewards promised to the diety.* ("Practice" denotes an action, "people" is the agent, "pray for a diety"s blessings" characterizes the nature of the agent, "rewards" is the patient, and "promised to the diety" is the nature of the patient).

④ It indicates that the word meaning contains multiple actions or behaviors, and it describes the various constraints that may apply to each of these actions or behaviors. The agent and the patient may or may not be present. For instance:

Jiaoban搅拌(stir): *Use a stick or other object to rotate and mix a mixture, in order to achieve uniformity.* (This involves two actions, "rotating" and "mixing", with "stick" serving as the tool for the action, "mixture" as the object of the action, and "uniformity" as the purpose of the action).

Jianchi坚持(persist): *Firmly maintain, preserve, or conduct.* (The word encompasses three actions: maintaining, preserving, and conducting, with "firmly" denoting the manner in which these actions are carried out).

⑤ It indicates that the word meaning contains a certain action or behavior, along with the reasons or conditions that give rise to such an action or behavior. It also describes the various constraints that may exist for the action or behavior. The agent and the patient may or may not be present. For instance:

Bianbie辨别(distinguish): *Discriminate in recognition based on the characteristics of different things.* ("Discriminate" refers to the action, "based on the characteristics of different things" is the condition for the action, and "in recognition" is the scope of the action).

⑥ It indicates that the word meaning contains a certain action or behavior, along with its purpose or outcome, and involves the description of various constraints that may exist for such an action or behavior. The agent and the patient may or may not be present. For instance:

Jintou浸透(soak): *Immerse in liquid until thoroughly wet.* ("Immerse in" denotes the action, "thoroughly wet" represents the result of the action, and "in the liquid" indicates the location where the action takes place).

(3) The descriptive and explanatory interpretation patterns employed for words expressing properties are categorized into the following types:

① "适用对象+性状Applicable object+quality": The applicable objects can be objects of one type or multiple types, or they may not appear. For instance:

Liqi离奇(bizarre): *(plot) being unusual or unexpected.* ("Plot" serves as the object of application, while "unusual" and "unexpected" are quality descriptions that pertain to this object).

Yazhi雅致(elegant): *(clothing, utensils, and houses,* etc.*) Beautiful and free from vulgarity.* ("Clothing, utensils, and houses, etc." are applicable objects, while "free from vulgarity" is the quality description).

② "形容...... Used to describe...": The component following "describe" denotes a certain state of affairs itself. The addition of the word "describe" signifies a depiction of such a state. For instance:

Yixian一线(a gleam of): Used to describe something extremely minute. ("Extremely minute" denotes a state, and the meaning of "a gleam" is a depiction of this state).

③ "...de的": The particle "de" serves as a marker for the modifier of the modifying construction, indicating that the modified word typically functions as an attributive (modifier) within the structure and cannot act as a predicate. For instance:

Zhuyao主要(main): 有关事物中最重要的The most significant; 起决定作用的decisive.

Jiandan简单(simple): 简单而容易的Plain and easy.

From the interpretation methods in dictionary definition discussed above, we can derive a wealth of information regarding the semantic computational representation, which primarily encompasses two aspects:

(1) Feature Dimensions of the Lexical Semantic description by referring to the various aspects of lexical meanings involved in dictionary definitions, we can

analyze the universal feature dimensions of different types of lexical meanings, thereby extracting dimension feature function operators.

(2) Description of semantic gene structure Dictionaries typically employ similar patterns of definitions for different types of words. By summarizing the general definition patterns of different word categories within dictionaries, it can provide reference for designing equations of semantic?gene structure description.

5.1.2 Analyzing Semantic Dimension Features and Extracting Semantic Dimension Genes from Dictionary Definitions

5.1.2.1 The Divide of the Three Fundamental Word Classes

The classification of parts of speech in Chinese is a rather complex issue, involving multiple aspects such as semantics, grammar, and morphology. This chapter discusses the analysis and extraction of semantic genes under the category of parts of speech, solely for the convenience of engineering data processing and does not delve into theoretical debates regarding the divide of parts of speech. Based on the basic consensus in the academic community, we provide a rough distinction for the three fundamental parts of speech—nouns, verbs, and adjectives—according to the following definitions:

Noun: Words that express the meaning of a naming something, i.e., words that represent the name of a person or thing.

Verbs: Words that express the meaning of action, i.e., words that describe the actions, situations, or changes of people or things.

Adjectives: Words that express the nature or state, i.e., words that represent the qualities or conditions of people or things.

5.1.2.2 Analysis of the Semantic Feature Dimensions of Nouns

Zhao 赵元任 (1970: 505) once pointed out that "*Nouns form an open class which occupies the major portion of the lexicon of the language. There are not only more nouns than any other part of speech, but more nouns than all the other parts of speech put together.*" So the analysis and extraction of the semantic genes of nouns constitute the main part of the entire project.

In the description of the semantic gene structure of nouns, according to the "individual sememe+common sememe" or the "specific difference+category" pattern, the first step is to identify a semantic gene corresponding to the "common sememe" or "category". This gene is a constant gene, also serving as the family gene within the minimal semantic family (minimal semantic field), representing the superordinate category to which the word belongs. Such genes are not easily extracted from dictionary definitions and their predefined core sets can be selected from other data resources such as general upper vocabulary Ontologies and word frequency lists. Apart from the constant genes, other parts of the word meaning are represented by a feature function, with the function operators being the dimension feature gene. The objects denoted by nouns are characterized by a complex array of features, involving numerous dimensions. By synthesizing references from dictionary definitions and research literature on lexicography, it is possible to generalize the various dimension features of nouns used in dictionary definitions.

(1) Finite Valued Feature: This refers to the situation where the values of the feature function within this dimension are confined to a specified range, forming a small value set, which can be enumerated exhaustively and are not numerous. For instance, the feature function of the "xingbie性别(gender)" dimension can only take the values "male" or "female". This dimension feature and its values can be directly extracted as semantic genes, denoted as {[性别]:[男],[女]} {[Gender]: [Male], [Female]}. The finite valued dimension features and their value genes for nouns include the following types:

① {[xingbie性别(Gender)]: [nan男(Male)], [nü女(Female)]}
② {[jixing极性(Polarity)]: [bao褒(Positive)], [zhong中(Neutral)], [bian贬(Negative)]}
③ {[yuti语体(Register)]: [kou口(Spoken)], [shumian书面(Written)], [fangyan方言(Dialect)], [yiyu译语(Translated Language)]}
④ {[fangwei方位(Orientation)]: [shang上(Up)], [xia下(Down)], [zuo左(Left)], [you右(Right)], [qian前(Front)], [hou后(Back)], [nei内(Inside)], [wai外(Outside)], [dong东(East)], [nan南(South)], [xi西(West)], [bei北(North)], [dongbei东北(Northeast)], [xibei西北(Northwest)], [dongnan东南(Southeast)], [xinan西南 (Southwest)]}
⑤ {[luoji逻辑(Logic)]: [zhen真(True)], [jia假(False)]}
⑥ {[panduan判断(Judgment)]: [dui对(Right)], [cuo错(Wrong)], [shi是(Yes)], [fou否(No)]}
⑦ {[motai模态(Modallity)]: [keneng可能(Possible)], [bukeneng不可能(Impossible)], [bixu必须(Must)], [bubi不必(Need not)], [nan难(Difficult)], [yi易(Easy)]}
⑧ {[chenghu称呼(Address)]: $_{Gs}$[miancheng面称(Direct Address)], $_{Gs}$[beicheng背称(Indirect Address)], $_{Gs}$[jingcheng敬称(Respectful Address)], $_{Gs}$[qiancheng谦称(Humble Address)], $_{Gs}$[zicheng自称(Self-Address)], $_{Gs}$[tacheng他称(Third-person Address)], $_{Gs}$[bizhong鄙称(Despising Address)], $_{Gs}$[aicheng爱称(Affectionate Address)], $_{Gs}$[zhuancheng专称(Specific Address)], $_{Gs}$[daicheng代称(Alternative Address)], $_{Gs}$[tongcheng通称(General Address)]}
⑨ {[qingtai情态(Mood)]: $_{Gs}$[weiwan委婉(Euphemistic)], $_{Gs}$[ketao客套(Courteous)], $_{Gs}$[jingci敬辞(Respectful)], $_{Gs}$[qianci谦辞(Humble)], $_{Gs}$[jiaoao骄傲(Proud)], $_{Gs}$[xiai喜爱(Affectionate)], $_{Gs}$[wanxi惋惜 (Regretful)], $_{Gs}$[qinni亲昵(Intimate)], $_{Gs}$[yanwu厌恶(Disgusted)], $_{Gs}$[jifeng讥讽(Ironical)], $_{Gs}$[qingmie

轻蔑(Contemptuous)], $_{Gs}$[xixue 戏谑(Mocking)], $_{Gs}$[cheze斥责(Reproachful)], $_{Gs}$[lima詈骂(Abusive)]}[1]

(2) Infinite Valued Feature: These refer to the values of a dimension feature function that can be confined to a certain range, creating a value set. However, the members of this set exhibit a degree of productivity and cannot be fully enumerated.[2]For instance, the dimension feature function for the "material" is restricted to "specific substances", yet the vast array of specific substances in nature cannot be fully listed. The infinite valued features and their corresponding value genes for nouns include the following types:

{[cailiao材料(Material)]: [jinshu金属(Metal)], [jin金(Gold)], [yin银(Silver)], [tong铜(Copper)], [tie铁(Iron)], [xi锡(Tin)], $_{Gs}$[boli玻璃(Glass)], $_{Gs}$[mucai木材(Wood)], $_{Gs}$[suliao塑料(Plastic)], $_{Gs}$[xianwei纤维(Fiber)], $_{Gs}$[mian棉(Cotton)], $_{Gs}$[bu布(Cloth)], $_{Gs}$[nilong尼龙(Nylon)]…}

{[yanse颜色(Color)]: [hong红(Red)], [cheng橙(Orange)], [huang黄(Yellow)], [lü绿(Green)], [qing青(Cyan)], [lan蓝(Blue)], [zi紫(Purple)], [shenhong深红(Dark Red)], [huibai灰白(Light Grey)], [qingzi青紫(Cyan Purple])]…}

{[waiguan外观(Appearance)]: [mei美(Beautiful)], [chou丑(Ugly)], [putong普通(Ordinary)], [guanghua光滑(Smooth)], [cucao粗糙(Rough)], [pingzheng平整(Flat)], [tu凸(Convex)], [ao凹(Concave)], [qi起(Rising)], [fu伏(Falling)]…}

{[waimao外貌(Looks)]: [mei美(Beautiful)], [chou丑(Ugly)], [putong普通(Average)], [pang胖(Fat)], [shou瘦(Slim)], [gao高(Tall)], [ai矮(Short)], [miaotiao苗条(Slender)], [cukuang粗犷(Rough)], [qiangzhuang强壮(Strong)], [xianruo纤弱(Delicate)], [kuiwu魁梧(Burly)], [qiaocui憔悴(Emaciated)]…}[3]

{[wulishuxing物理属性(Physical Properties)]: [ruan软(Soft)], [ying硬(Hard)], [nong浓(Concentrated)], [dan淡(Sparse)], [xi稀(Dilute)], [chou稠(Thick)], [mi密(Dense)], [qing轻(Light)], [zhong重(Heavy)], [gao高(Tall)], [ai矮(Short)], [da大(Large)], [xiao小(Small)], [chang长(Long)], [duan短(Short)] …}

[xingge性格(Personality)]: $_{Gs}$[jianqiang坚强(Resilient)], $_{Gs}$[cuiruo脆弱(Fragile)], $_{Gs}$[yonggan勇敢(Brave)], $_{Gs}$[danxiao胆小(Timid)], $_{Gs}$[qinqie亲切(Amiable)], $_{Gs}$[wenrou温柔(Gentle)], $_{Gs}$[cubao粗暴(Rude)], $_{Gs}$[zhishuang直爽(Frank)], $_{Gs}$[cixiang慈祥(Kindly)], $_{Gs}$[reqing热情(Warmly)], $_{Gs}$[lengmo冷漠(Indifferent)], $_{Gs}$[shenchen深沉(Deep)], $_{Gs}$[suihe随和(Easygoing)], $_{Gs}$[baoshou保守(Conservative)], $_{Gs}$[jijin激进(Radical)], $_{Gs}$[huopo活泼(Vivacious)], $_{Gs}$[sanman散漫(Casual)], $_{Gs}$[tianzhen天真(Naive)] …}

[1] $_{Gs}$ marked as a gene cluster, which can be treated as a gene in the semantic gene analysis. However, further analysis is required to identify it as a semantic gene. The analysis is not elaborated here].

[2] This concept of "cannot be fully enumerated" pertains to the values of the feature function, which does not conflict with the assumption that "the set of semantic genes in a language is finite". This is because the values of the feature function may not be single semantic genes but could also be gene clusters or gene chains. While individual semantic genes are finite, the combinations they form into gene clusters are not exhaustive.

[3] [Appearance] and [Looks] are used for different categories of meanings. The former is used to describe nouns of things, while the latter is used for nouns referring to people.

{[pinxing品行(Moral character)]: [shan善(Good)], [e恶(Evil)], [zhong忠(Loyal)], [jian奸(Traitorous)], [zha诈(Crafty)], $_{Gs}$[chengshi诚实(Honest)], $_{Gs}$[xuwei虚伪(Hypocritical)], $_{Gs}$[jiaohua狡猾(Cunning)], [xiong凶(Fierce)], $_{Gs}$[canren残忍(Cruel)], [hen狠(Merciless)], [du毒(Sinister)], [qian谦(Modest)], [ao傲(Arrogant)], $_{Gs}$[zhengzhi正直(Upright)], [lian廉(Incorruptible)], [tanlan贪婪(Greedy)], [qin勤(Industrious)], [lan懒(Lazy)], $_{Gs}$[gaoshang高尚(Noble)], $_{Gs}$[beibi卑鄙(Mean)], [ya雅(Elegant)], [su俗(Vulgar)], $_{Gs}$[yuanhua圆滑(Tactful)], $_{Gs}$[zisi自私(Selfish)], $_{Gs}$[diaoman刁蛮(Unruly)], $_{Gs}$[kechi可耻(Shameful)]...}

{[caigan才干(Talent)]: $_{Gs}$[congming聪明(Intelligent)], $_{Gs}$[chun蠢(Stupid)], $_{Gs}$[youzhi幼稚(Immature)], $_{Gs}$[zhuoyue卓越(Outstanding)], $_{Gs}$[pingyong平庸(Ordinary)], $_{Gs}$[jiechu杰出(Exemplary)], $_{Gs}$[boxue博学(Erudite)], $_{Gs}$[zhuming著名(Famous)]...}

{[qingxu情绪(Emotion)]: [xi喜(Happy)], [nu怒(Angry)], [ai哀(Sad)], [le乐(Joyful)], [fan烦(Annoyed)], [you忧(Worried)], [an安(Calm)], [kong恐(Fearful)], [huang慌(Panicked)], [yumen郁闷(Dejected)], [jusang沮丧(Depressed)], [xiaochen消沉(Despondent)], [tongku痛苦(Miserable)], [cankui惭愧(Ashamed)], [neijiu内疚(Guilty)], [chenzhong沉重(Heavy-hearted)], [gudu孤独(Lonely)], [jimo寂寞(Desolate)], [mimang迷茫(Bewildered)]...}

{[xiangduiweizhi相对位置(Relative position)]: [chuizhi垂直(Vertical)], [shuiping水平(Horizontal)], [pingxing平行(Parallel)], [jiaocha交叉(Crossing)]...}

{[yuyu语域(Regster)]: $_{Gs}$[shuxin书信(Letter)], $_{Gs}$[gongwen公文(Official document)], $_{Gs}$[zhengzhi政治(Politics)], $_{Gs}$[kexue科学(Science)], $_{Gs}$[wenyi文艺(Art)], $_{Gs}$[tiyu体育(Sports)], $_{Gs}$[junshi军事(Military)], $_{Gs}$[jingji经济(Economy)], $_{Gs}$[falü法律(Law)]......}

(3) Discrete Value Feature: It refers to the values of the dimension feature function being discrete, presenting a challenge in defining a consistent range. Generally, such discrete values cannot be adequately represented by a single semantic gene or a gene cluster, necessitating the use of a gene chain. For instance, in the "structure" dimension, nouns refer to things with complex structures, the description of semantics may sometimes refer to the internal structure and at other times to the external structure. The values of the feature function for this dimension typically involve nested other feature functions, with feature values that may include one or more gene chains. For such semantic dimensions, we can only predefine the genes of the feature function; the value genes cannot be pre-defined and must be treated on a case-by-case basis for each specific word. Examples of such dimension genes include:

{[jiegou结构(Structure)], [zucheng组成(Composition)], [xixing习性(Habit)], [diwei地位(Status)], [jingkuang境况(Situation)], [chusuo处所(Location)], [fangshi方式(Method)], [yuanyin原因(Cause)], [jieguo结果(Result)], [gongju工具(Tool)], [yingxiang影响(Impact)]...}

(4) Mixed Valued Feature: It refers to the value range of the dimension feature function, which is composed of a mixture of two or three types of data, including finite, infinite, and discrete. For example, in the "smell' dimension,

the feature values can befinite such as {[xiang香(Fragrant)], [chou臭(Stench)]}, or infinite, such as {$_{\mathrm{Gs}}$[haowen好闻(Good-smelling)], $_{\mathrm{Gs}}$[nanwen难闻(Bad-smelling)], $_{\mathrm{Gs}}$[cibi刺鼻(Pungent)] ...}. Such dimension features and their value genes include:

{[weidao味道(Taste)]: [suan酸(Sour)], [tian甜(Sweet)], [ku苦(Bitter)], [la辣(Spicy)], [xian咸(Salty)], [hao好(Good)], [huai坏(Bad)], [zhong重(Heavy)], $_{\mathrm{Gs}}$[chunhou醇厚(Mellow)], $_{\mathrm{Gs}}$[chunzheng纯正(Pure)], $_{\mathrm{Gs}}$[qingdan清淡(Light)], $_{\mathrm{Gc}}$[nanyijieshou难以接受(Unbearable)], $_{\mathrm{Gc}}$[henshouhuanying很受欢迎(Very popular)][4]...}

{[qiwei气味(Smell)]: [xiang香(Fragrant)], [chou臭(Stench)], $_{\mathrm{Gs}}$[haowen好闻(Good-smelling)], $_{\mathrm{Gs}}$[nanwen难闻(Bad-smelling)], $_{\mathrm{Gs}}$[cibi刺鼻(Pungent)], $_{\mathrm{Gs}}$[nonglie浓烈(Strong)], [zhong重(Heavy)], [teshu特殊(Special)], $_{\mathrm{Gs}}$[qingdan清淡(Light)], $_{\mathrm{Gs}}$[cijixing刺激性(Irritating)], $_{\mathrm{Gc}}$[xiangXde象 X的(Like X)]...}

{[shijian时间(Time)]: [shiji世纪(Century)], [chaodai朝代(Dynasty)], [nian年(Year)], [yue月(Month)], [ri日(Day)], [zhou周(Week)], [shi时(Hour)], [fen分(Minute)], [miao秒(Second)], [qi起(Start)], [zhong终(End)], $_{\mathrm{Gs}}$[qiantian前天(The day before yesterday)], $_{\mathrm{Gs}}$[zuotian昨天(Yesterday)], $_{\mathrm{Gs}}$[jintian今天(Today)], $_{\mathrm{Gs}}$[mingtian明天(Tomorrow)], $_{\mathrm{Gs}}$[houtian后天(The day after tomorrow)], $_{\mathrm{Gs}}$[qiannian前年(The year before last)], $_{\mathrm{Gs}}$[qunian去年(Last year)], $_{\mathrm{Gs}}$[jinnian今年(This year)], $_{\mathrm{Gs}}$[mingnian明年(Next year)], $_{\mathrm{Gs}}$[hounian后年(The year after next)], $_{\mathrm{Gs}}$[congqian从前(Past)], $_{\mathrm{Gs}}$[xianzai现在(Now)], $_{\mathrm{Gs}}$ [jinhou今后(Future)], $_{\mathrm{Gs}}$[shangzhou上周(Last week)], $_{\mathrm{Gs}}$[xiazhou下周(Next week)], $_{\mathrm{Gc}}$[shidianliangzhi时点量值(Time point value)], $_{\mathrm{Gc}}$[shiduanliangzhi时段量值(Time period value)]...}

{[nianling年龄(Age)]:[da大(Old)], [xiao小(Young)], $_{\mathrm{Gs}}$[laonian老年(Elderly)], $_{\mathrm{Gs}}$[zhongnian中年(Middle-aged)], $_{\mathrm{Gs}}$[zhuangnian壮年(Prime of life)], $_{\mathrm{Gs}}$[qingnian青年(Youth)], $_{\mathrm{Gs}}$[shaonian少年(Teenage)], $_{\mathrm{Gs}}$[younian幼年(Infancy)], $_{\mathrm{Gs}}$[tongnian童年(Childhood)], $_{\mathrm{Gc}}$[nianlingliangzhi年龄量值(Age value)]......}

{[changdu长度(Length)]: [chang长(Long)], [duan短(Short)], $_{\mathrm{Gc}}$[changduliangzhi长度量值(Length value)]......}

{[gaodu高度(Height)]: [gao高(Tall)], [ai矮(Low)], $_{\mathrm{Gc}}$[gaoduliangzhi高度量值(Height value)]......}

{[mianji面积(Area)]∨[tiji体积(Volume)]∨[rongji容积(Capacity)]∨[midu密度(Density)]: [da大(Large)], [xiao小(Small)], $_{\mathrm{Gc}}$[jutiliangzhi具体量值(Specific value)]......}

{[zhongliang重量(Weight)]: [da大(Large)], [xiao小(Small)], [qing轻(Light)], [zhong重(Heavy)], $_{\mathrm{Gc}}$[zhongliangliangzhi重量量值(Weight value)]......}

{[nongdu浓度(Concentration)]: [nong浓(Concentrated)], [dan淡(Sparse)], $_{\mathrm{Gc}}$[nongduliangzhi浓度 量值(Dense value)]...}

---

[4] $_{\mathrm{Gc}}$[nayijieshou 难以接受 (Unbearable)] and $_{\mathrm{Gc}}$[henhuanying 很受欢迎 (Very popular)] are discrete values, which need to be represented by the gene chains {[Accept([Patient]([i]))]} {[Modality]([Difficult])} and {[Welcome([Patient]([i]))]} {[Degree]([Very])}, respectively. These two gene chains cannot constitute a relatively stable semantic unit (i.e., a word) because they cannot be represented as a gene cluster].

{{[wendu温度(Temperature)]: [gao高(High)], [di低(Low)], $_{Gs}$[re热(Hot)],$_{Gs}$ [nuan暖(Warm)], $_{Gs}$[wen温(Tepid)], $_{Gs}$[liang凉(Cool)], $_{Gs}$[bing冰(Frozen)], $_{Gs}$[leng冷(Cold)], $_{Gs}$[han寒(Frigid)],$_{Gc}$[wenduliangzhi温度量值(Temperature value)]……}

{[xingzhuang形状(Shape)]:[fang方(Square)], [yuan圆(Round)], [changfang长方(Rectangle)], [sanjiao三角(Triangle)], [tuoyuan椭圆(Oval)], [zhi直(Straight)], [wan弯(Curved)], $_{Gs}$[tixing梯形(Trapezoid)], $_{Gs}$[yuanzhui圆锥(Conical)], $_{Gc}$[X zhuang X 状(X-shaped)]…}

5.1.2.3 Analysis of the Semantic Feature Dimensions of Verbs and Adjectives

Verbs and adjectives in dictionaries often adopt a descriptive interpretation pattern, which can also be expressed in the "specific difference+category" model. The basic rule is still [Individual sememe]+[Core sememe]. Similar to the description of nouns, in the analysis of semantic genes, both of these word classes need to firstly determine a constant gene to define the superordinate semantic category of the action or behavior of verbs or the nature and state of adjectives. Their other dimension genes are more structurally and systematically stronger than nouns. From the definition, verbs represent actions, behaviors, and changes of people or things, while adjectives represent the nature and state of people or things. The meanings of these two word classes are based on nouns. Therefore, for the description of the semantic genes of verbs and adjectives, it only needs to add the dimension genes determined by their respective semantic properties to the semantic gene set of nouns.

(1) Dimension genes of verbs

The description of the semantic genes of verbs generally centers on the semantic roles of verbs. Including:

① {[shishi施事(Agent)], [zhushi主事(Theme)], [shoushi受事(Patient)], [yushi与事([Dative)]…},feature value genes for them are all related nominal terms, which can be analyzed according to the method of nominal part.
② {[shijian时间(Time)], [chusuo处所(Location)]}, the feature values are discrete or mixed, identical to those associated with nouns.
③ {[fangxiang方向(Direction)]:$_{Gc}$[chaoxiang朝向(Toward)]([fangwei方位(Orientation)] ∨(n)]}, the feature values are discrete, where [n] refers to a specific noun.
④ {[lujing路径(Path)]:$_{Gs}$[[qidian起点(Startpoint)]([n])], $_{Gs}$[[zhongdian终点(Endpoint)]([n])], $_{Gs}$[[tujing途经(Via)]([n])]……}, the feature values are discrete, where [n] generally refers to place names.
⑤ {[liang量(Classifier)]: [ci次(Time)], [xia下(Time)], [hui回(Occasion)], [bian遍(Time)], [tang趟(Trip)], [dun顿(Meal)], [fan番(Round)], [zhen阵(Spell)], [chang场(Bout)], [n]…}, the feature values are discrete, generally composed of words indicating "specific quantity" or "general quantity", which the above verb

classifiers. The specific quantity is a numeral and is not included in the gene set as a semantic gene. [n] is a verb classifier expressed by borrowing relevant nouns.
⑥ {[xuci序次(Sequence)]: [qian前(Before)], [zhong中(Middle)], [hou后(After)], [n]……}, the feature values are infinite, where [n] is a numeral, which is not included in the semantic gene set.
⑦ {[yuanyin原因(Cause)], [jieguo结果(Result)], [tiaojian条件(Condition)], [mudi目的(Purpose)], [fanwei范围(Scope)], [yiju依据(Basis)], [gongju工具(Tool)], [fangshi方式(Method)], [shouduan手段(Means)], [yingxiang影响(Influence)]}, the feature values are mostly discrete, and they need to be represented by one or more gene chains.
Dimension genes of adjectives

The fixed dimension genes of adjectives are relatively simple, only a few categories:

① {[duixiang对象(Object)], [fangmian方面(Aspect)], [xingzhuang性状(Attribute)], [qingzhuang情状(Situation)]…}, the feature values are discrete, where the value of [Object] is a noun, and the adjective has semantic constraints on the object or objects it can describe, for example, "handsome" can only be paired with nouns representing persons, while "solid" can only be paired with nouns representing objects. [fangmian方面(Aspect)] is not a specific gene but represents a feature dimension of the object described by the adjective. "Handsome" describes the "appearance" dimension of a person, here [Aspect] = [Appearance]; "Solid" describes the structural dimension of an object, here [Aspect] = [Structure]. For dimensions that are difficult to define clearly, [fangmian方面(Aspect)] and [qingzhuang情状(Situation)] are used as general terms.
② {[chengdu程度(Degree)], [fanwei范围(Scope)]}, the feature values are discrete.

In addition to these, the semantic gene description of adjectives mostly relies on the gene sets of nouns and verbs.

5.1.3 Analyzing Semantic Dimension Features and Extracting Semantic Dimension Genes from Semantic Research Literature

In the literature of semantic description in semantics, particularly in lexical semantics, there are also numerous theories and practical works that can serve as references for us to analyze the semantic dimension features and extract the semantic dimension genes.

5.1.3.1 The Case System of Nouns

The semantic case was originally not an independent semantic feature of nouns, but referred to a semantic relationship feature that arises when nouns are paired with verbs. Since Fillmore (1968) proposed the case theory, research on semantic cases has been continuously developing. Liu 刘顺 (2003: 141) pointed out that "case is the semantic role that a noun assumes when it forms a semantic structure with a verb. In a semantic structure, the appearance of some semantic roles is mandatory, while the others non-mandatory. The mandatory semantic roles are called mandatory cases, and the non-mandatory ones are free cases". The description of lexical semantics appears to be a task within the internal workings of the lexical system, whereas the process of word combination seems to be associated with syntactic-semantic aspects. However, in fact, when we interpret or describe the semantics of nouns or verbs, we often cannot avoid their combination relationships. Therefore, whether it is the definition in dictionaries or our description of the semantic gene structure of words, a considerable part of the content involves semantic cases.

5.1.3.2 The Qualia Role of Nouns

Based on the theory of generative lexicon, Yuan 袁毓林 (2014) designed a system for describing the qualia properties of nouns in modern Chinese, which defined ten types of qualia roles of nouns by a large-scale corpus survey.

(1) Form: The classification properties, semantic type, and ontological hierarchical features of nouns.
(2) Constitute: The structural attributes of entities denoted by nouns, including the state of composition, constituent elements, relationships with other things, and composing or forming other things. It also includes the size, shape, dimensions, color, and orientation of objects.
(3) Unit: The measurement unit for the object referred to by a noun, i.e., the classfier word corresponding to the noun.
(4) Evaluation: The subjective evaluation and emotional tone associated with the thing referred to by a noun.

(5) Agentive: How the thing referred to by a noun is formed.
(6) Material: The material used in the production of the object referred to by a noun.
(7) Function: The usage and function of the object referred to by a noun.
(8) Behavior: The habitual actions, behaviors, or activities of the object referred to by a noun.
(9) Disposal: The habitual actions, behaviors,or influences exerted by a person or other entities on the thing referred to by a noun.
(10) Position: The spatial and temporal relationship between a person or other entity and the place or direction indicated by a noun.

The discussions on semantic roles and qualia structures both address the issue of how the semantic roles are assigned roles in the semantic composition of nouns with other words. The difference lies in that semantic roles focus on examining the role of nouns in the semantic composition with verbs, centered around the verb, while qualia roles examine the semantic roles of other words in the semantic composition with nouns, centered around the noun. Both of these semantic roles reflect the semantic features of nouns on a certain dimension, with most of them matching the semantic genes extracted based on dictionary definitions in our previous work. Although not all of them are suitable for internal semantic gene description of a word, there is still a portion that can be supplemented to our semantic gene system.

5.2 Extraction of Semantic Genes for Nouns in Modern Chinese

5.2.1 Classification of Nouns and Selection of Analysis Samples

5.2.1.1 The Subclassification of Chinese Nouns

Linguists have always been in dispute over the subclassification of Chinese nouns. Approaching the issue from various research perspectives, some scholars categorize them based on semantics, others based on grammatical functions, and still others combine semantic and grammatical categories for classification. In summary, the following viewpoints can be identified:

(1) Ma 马建忠 (1898) proposed the idea of further classify nouns in his work “mashi wentong《马氏文通》(Ma’s Grammar of the Chinese Language)”.

① Public Noun and Proper Noun: Public nouns are those used to name a group of objects, while proper nouns are those used to name a specific person or thing. Public nouns and proper nouns roughly correspond to what is now referred to as common nouns and proper nouns respectively.

② General Nouns and Group Nouns: Within the public nouns, there are further divisions into general nouns and group nouns. General names, which are used to express the appearance or essence of things, referring to descriptions in terms of being separated from the substance. While group nouns are used to denote gatherings of persons or things. These concepts roughly correspond to what is now referred to as abstract nouns and collective nouns.

(2) Li 黎锦熙 (1924: 102–111) classified nouns into three subclasses:

① Unique Noun: The specific name of a person or thing, which cannot be universally used even among persons or objects of the same category. It is further subdivided into six categories: personal names, names of special groups, place names, names of nations and ethnic groups, names of eras, and names of books and articles.
② Common Nouns: These are names for objects of the same category, where any member of the category can be referred to by the same name, while they differ from other categories in other respects. They can be further subdivided into three subcategories: those denoting individuals, materials, and collectives.
③ Abstract Nouns: They ate names of things that are intangible or countless. They are are called virtual nouns which leave the physical properties of things and abstract their nature, attributes, or functions. It can be further divided into three subcategories: intangible objects, the nature and state of things, and human actions.

(3) Lü 吕叔湘 (1942:17) classified nouns into four subclasses based on the principle of "grouping those with similar meanings and functions together."

① Representations of individuals, such as Confucius, father, son, official, soldier, friend, and enemy, etc.
② Representations of objects, such as: cat, dog, peache, plum, ear, eye, book, painting, mountain, river, and so on.
③ Representations of substances, such as water, fire, rice, cloth, iron, air, and the like.
④ Representations of intangible entities, such as: thought, hardship, war, sleep, economy, morality, law, etc.

(4) Wang 王力 (1985: 11) classified nouns into three subclasses based on the nature of their referents.

① General nouns: Referring to the names of a category of things.
② Proper nouns: Referring to nouns that specifically denote a person or a place.
③ Unit Nouns: Referring to nouns that denote units of persons or things.

(5) Zhao 赵元任 (1970: 507) classified nouns into four subclasses based on the nature of the differentiating words and classifiers associated with them: ① individual nouns, ② mass nouns, ③ collective nouns, and ④ abstract nouns.
(6) Zhu 朱德熙 (1982: 41–42) classified nouns into five subclasses based on their relationship with classifiers: ① countable nouns, ② uncountable nouns, ③ collective nouns, ④ abstract nouns, and ⑤ proper nouns.
(7) Peng 彭睿 (1996: 93–103) classified nouns into five subclasses based on the criterion of function, while also taking meaning into consideration. Each type is further subdivided into several subcategories.

① Individual nouns: entities, natural landscapes, groups and organizations, geographical areas, symbols, actions and events, time points and periods, and audio-visual arts.
② Abstract Nouns: conceptual, qualitative, knowledge domain, measure, disease, strategy and rule, rights and interests, and other categories.
③ Material Nouns: inorganic substances, organic substances, weather-related terms, light, sound, electricity, and color-related terms, monetary and financial terms.
④ Collective Nouns: parallel collective nouns composed of morphemes that share semantic relatedness (e.g., newspapers, teachers and students, food and drinks, etc.), and those formed by combining noun morphemes with quantifier morphemes (e.g., shuben书本(books), qiangzhi枪支(firearms), etc.).
⑤ Proper nouns.

(8) Fan 范晓 (2001) initiated a classification of nouns from the perspective of the three-plane theory, dividing them into eight subclasses: ① nouns referring to people, ② nouns referring to objects, ③ institutional nouns, ④ place nouns, ⑤ temporal nouns, ⑥ directional nouns, ⑦ proper nouns, and ⑧ pronouns.
(9) Wang 王珏 (2001: 83) discussed the eight subclasses of nouns from a semantic perspective: ① appellation nouns, ② organ nouns, ③ plant nouns, ④ abstract nouns, ⑤ collective nouns, ⑥ life nouns, ⑦ ambiguous nouns, and ⑧ synonymous nouns. Strictly speaking, what Wang discusses is not a comprehensive classification system of nouns, but rather a selective analysis of several typical noun classes that are aggregated according to different criteria, which falls under categorization rather than classification.

The complexity of the classification of nouns arises from the lack of uniformity in the criteria. To ensure logical rigor in any classification of objects, it is essential to adhere to a single standard throughout the process. When classifying nouns, one must consider both semantics, that is, the natural categorization of the objects referred to by the nouns, and syntax, that is, the constraints on the combination of nouns with other parts of speech. Among these various classification methods mentioned above, the more detailed they are, the more likely they are to encounter the problem of overlapping categories. Therefore, to prevent cross-classification, this monograph employs a classification criterion based exclusively on semantics, specifically the referents designated by nouns.

5.2.1.2 Selection of Analysis Samples for Semantic Gene Information of Nouns

Based on semantics as the primary criterion, the following categories of nouns are selected for analysis as representative examples:

(1) Nouns referring to people: according to the conventions of address, they can be divided into several subcategories.
(2) Nouns referring to objects: they can be categorized into concrete and abstract types, each with several subcategories.
(3) Event Nouns.

Two to three minimal semantic fields are selected for analysis in each subclass, and the universal semantic dimension genes and some assignment genes of the field are extracted.

5.2.2 Semantic Analysis and Semantic Gene Extraction of Nouns Referring to People

5.2.2.1 General Nouns Referring to People

① {dazhong大众(the masses), wanzhong万众(the multitude), gongzhong公众(the public), minzhong民众(the populace), zhongren众人(the crowd), qunzhong群众(the people)}

Dictionary definitions[5]:
Dazhong大众(the masses): *The working people.*
Wanzhong万众(the multitude): *The general public.*
Gongzhong公众(the public): *The majority of individuals in society; the general public.*
Minzhong民众(the populace): *The general people.*
Zhongren众人(the crowd): *Many people.*
Qunzhong群众(the people): *The general masses.*
Analysis:

[5] The dictionary interpretations in this book are primarily based on: The Contemporary Chinese Dictionary (7th Edition, The Commercial Press, 2016),Grand Chinese Dictionary (2nd Edition, Shanghai Lexicographic Publishing House, 2018),Grand Modern Chinese Dictionary (The Commercial Press International, 2015), The Modern Standard Chinese Dictionary (3rd Edition, Foreign Language Teaching and Research Press, 2014).

The core definition words in this group all converge on the word "dazhong大众(the masses)." We can first analyze the semantic gene structure of this word and then use the gene cluster ${}_{\text{Gs}}$[dazhong大众(The masses)] as a basis to examine other terms. However, there are two problems with the definition of "dazhong大众":

Firstly, it points back to "qunzhong群众" which constitutes a circular interpretation that is not advisable; secondly, it introduces the sememe of "work", which is subject to debate. This is because individuals who have lost the ability of work for various reasons or those who do not participate in social labor, such as students and the elderly, should not be excluded from the category of "the masses".

By analyzing the definitions in the dictionary we can find out the semantic distinctions among these words:

Firstly, the scope of the referential objects of word meanings is different. The meaning scopes of "dazhong大众", "wanzhong万众", and "gongzhong公众" all encompass "the whole society", while the interpretation of "zhongren众人" is "many people", the scope of its meaning is not the whole society; instead, it is determined by the utterance context at the time, making it dynamic and uncertain. The scope of "minzhong民众" and "qunzhong群众" is "the people". The scope of the meaning of "people人民" will be further analyzed later, and it can be treated as the gene cluster ${}_{\text{Gs}}$[dazhong大众(The masses)] here. In Chinese, "The people" is contrasted with "cadres", meaning it does not include "cadres".

Secondly, there exists pragmatic differences. The term "wanzhong万众" emphasizes the meaning of "a large number", and if it is replaced by other words in the example "wanzong huanteng万众欢腾(Millions of people are rejoiced)" the meaning would be altered. Similarly, the word "gongzhong公众" emphasizes the concepts of "public consciousness" and "public interest", and it is also not appropriate to substitute it with other words in context.

Based on the analysis above, the semantic gene structure of this group of words can be described as follows:

$S_{\text{大众}}$ = {[人]:{[范围]([社会])}+{[比例]([大])}}
$S_{\text{大众}}$ = {[Person]:{[Scope]([Society])}+{[Proportion]([Large])}}
$S_{\text{万众}}$ = {${}_{\text{Gs}}$[大众]:{[强调]([数量]([多]))}}
$S_{\text{万众}}$ = {${}_{\text{Gs}}$[The masses]:{[Emphasis]([Quantity]([Many]))}}
$S_{\text{公众}}$ = {${}_{\text{Gs}}$[大众]:{[强调](${}_{\text{Gs}}$[公共])}}
$S_{\text{公众}}$ = {${}_{\text{Gs}}$[The masses]:{[Emphasis](Gs[Public])}}
$S_{\text{民众}}$ = {${}_{\text{Gs}}$[大众]:{[范围](${}_{\text{Gs}}$[人民])}}
$S_{\text{民众}}$ = {${}_{\text{Gs}}$[The masses]:{[Scope](Gs[The people])}}
$S_{\text{群众}}$ = {${}_{\text{Gs}}$[大众]:{[范围](${}_{\text{Gs}}$[人民]∧!${}_{\text{Gs}}$[干部])}}
$S_{\text{群众}}$ = {${}_{\text{Gs}}$[The masses]:{[Scope](Gs[The people]∧!Gs[Cadre])}}
$S_{\text{众人}}$ = {${}_{\text{Gs}}$[大众]:{[范围]([u])}}
$S_{\text{众人}}$ = {${}_{\text{Gs}}$[The masses]:{[Scope]([u])}}

From this semantic field, we extract all the semantic genes {[fanwei范围(Scope)], [bili比例(Proportion)], [qiangdiao强调(Emphasis)], [shuliang数量(Quantity)], [ren人(Person)], [shehui社会(Society)], [da大(Large)], [duo多(Many)]} and retain the three gene clusters $_{Gs}$[gonggong公共(Public)], $_{Gs}$[renmin人民(The people)] and $_{Gs}$[ganbu干部(Cadre)] for further analysis.

② {renmin人民(the people), gongmin公民(citizen), guomin国民(national), jumin居民(resident), baixing百姓(common people)}

Dictionary definition:

Renmin人民(the people): *The fundamental members of the society, primarily composed of the laboring masses.*

Gongmin公民(citizen): *Persons who have obtained nationality in a specific country and are entitled to its rights and obligated to fulfill its legal duties.*

Guomin国民(national): *Persons possessing the nationality of a certain country are considered the nationals of that country.*

Jumin居民(resident): *Persons who are settled and habitually resides in a specific location.*

Baixing百姓(common people): *The general populace (formerly distinguished from "officers").*

Analysis:

The differences among these words are primarily manifested in the distinct political connotations they carry. Apart from "jumin居民", the semantic scopes of the others are defined through the additional political implications. "Jumin居民" does not carry any political connotation and its semantic scope is defined by the place of residence. "Baixing百姓" is in contrast to "officers", implying that it does not include "officers".

Description of semantic gene structure:

$S_{人民}$ = {[人]:{[构成]({[社会]:{[成员]([i])+{[比例]([大])}}})}+{[劳动]([施事]([i]))}}

$S_{人民}$ = {[Person]:{[Composition]({[Society]:{[Member]([i])+{[Proportion]([Large])}}})}+{[Labour]([Agent]([i]))}}

$S_{公民}$ = {[人]:{[拥有]([[国籍]([u])]∧$_{Gs}$[权利])}+{[承担]($_{Gs}$[义务])}}

$S_{公民}$ = {[Person]:{[Possess]([[Nationality]([u])]∧$_{Gs}$[Right])}+{[Undertake]($_{Gs}$[Obligation])}}

$S_{国民}$ = {[人]:{[拥有]([国籍]([u])}}

$S_{国民}$ = {[Person]:{[Possess]([Nationality]([u])}}

$S_{居民}$ = {[人]:{[居住]([[处所]([u])]∧[固定])}}

$S_{居民}$ = {[Person]:{[Residence]([[Location]([u])]∧[Fixed])}}

$S_{百姓}$ = {$_{Gs}$[人民]:{[范围](!$_{Gs}$[官吏])}}

$S_{百姓}$ = {$_{Gs}$[The people]:{[Scope](!$_{Gs}$[Officer])}}

From this semantic field, we extract all the semantic genes {[fanwei范围(Scope)], [goucheng构成(Composition)], [chengyuan成员(Member)], [bili比例(Proportion)], [laodong劳动(Labour)], [shishi施事(Agent)], [yongyou拥有(Ownership)], [guoji国籍(Nationality)], [chengdan承担(Undertake)], [juzhu居住(Residence)], [chusuo处所(Location)], [guding固定(Fixed)], [ren人(Person)], [shehui社会(Society)], [da大(Large)]}, and three gene clusters awaiting further analysis, namely $_{\text{Gs}}$[quanli权利(Right)], $_{\text{Gs}}$[yiwu义务(Obligation)] and $_{\text{Gs}}$[guanli官吏(Officer)].

The semantic field composed of this group is an adjacent subfield to the previous one. By merging and deduplicating the genes from both groups, we obtain the set {[fanwei范围(Scope)], [bili比例(Proportion)], [qiangdiao强调(Emphasis)], [shuliang数量(Quantity)], [goucheng构成(Composition)], [chengyuan成员(Member)], [shishi施事(Agent)], [chengdan承担(Undertake)], [yongyou拥有(Own)], [juzhu居住(Residence)], [chusuo处所(Location)], [ren人(Person)], [shehui社会(Society)], [da大(Large)], [duo多(Many)], [laodong劳动(Labor)], [guoji国籍(Nationality)], [guding固定(Fixed)]}.

The residual gene cluster $_{\text{Gs}}$[renmin人民(The people)]from the previous group has been analyzed in this group and can be temporarily stored in a separate database for direct access during subsequent analysis. Among the remaining gene clusters, the $_{\text{Gs}}$[ganbu干部(Cadre)] from the previous group and the $_{\text{Gs}}$[guanli官吏(Officer)] from this group can be merged.

The dictionary definition of "baixing百姓" includes a note indicating that it was used to distinguish from "guanli官吏" in ancient times, only specifying the usage in the past without mentioning the contemporary usage. In fact, similar to "qunzhong群众", "baixing百姓" is also used in contemporary contexts in contrast to "ganbu干部". The concepts of "ganbu干部" and "guanli官吏" are similar in conceptual meaning, differing only in their temporal connotations. If these two gene clusters are unified and merged into $_{\text{Gs}}$[Offical], then the semantic genes within these adjacent semantic fields are merged, leaving only four gene clusters for further analysis: $_{\text{Gs}}$[gonggong公共(Public)], $_{\text{Gs}}$[quanli权利(Right)], $_{\text{Gs}}$[yiwu义务(Obligation)], and $_{\text{Gs}}$[guanyuan官员(Offical)]. Correspondingly, the semantic gene structure of "qunzhong群众" and "baixing百姓" is adjusted as follows:

$S_{\text{群众}}$ = {$_{\text{Gs}}$[The masses]:{[Scope]($_{\text{Gs}}$[The people]∧!$_{\text{Gs}}$[Offical])}}
S百姓 = {$_{\text{Gs}}$[The people]:{[Scope](!$_{\text{Gs}}$[Offical])}}

③ {zijia自家(oneself), ziji自己(one's own), benren本人(self), bieren别人(other people), taren他人(others), mouren某人(someone), pangren旁人(the others)}

Dictionary definition:

Zijia自家(oneself): *Personal pronoun, one's own.*

Ziji自己(one's own): *Personal pronoun, referring back to the preceding noun or pronoun, and emphasizing that something related to the mentioned person is not due to external force.*

Beneren本人(self): *Personal pronoun,* ❶*denoting the speaker,* ❷*or referring to the erson who is speaking or to a person previously mentioned in the text.*

Bieren别人(other people): ❶*Noun,the other person.* ❷*Personal pronoun, denoting oneself or someone other than the speaker or the person being addressed.*

Taren他人(others): *Personal pronoun,other people.*

Mouren某人(someone): ❶*The unknown person.* ❷*A person who is certain and does not need to be named or cannot be named.*

Pangren旁人(the others): *Personal pronoun, referring to others or the other people.*

Analysis: This group of words is not entirely identical to the typical personal pronouns "you", "I", and "he", as they lie between nouns and pronouns, exhibiting partial grammatical functions of both. Semantically, these words are more representative in general words referring to people, for the sake of analysis, we temporarily put them within the category of nouns referring to people.

The antithetical semantic components of words in this group are primarily manifested in two aspects: personal sequence (first, second, or third) and the presence or absence of definiteness. "ziji自己" and "zijia自家" refer to the speaker, thus indicating definiteness; "benren本人" can be used in the first, second, or third person, referring to the speaker, the listener, or a third party whose identity is clear to both, also indicating definiteness. "bieren别人", "mouren某人", and "pangren旁人" can only be used in the second or third person, while "taren他人" can only be used in the third person. Among them, "bieren别人" and "pangren旁人" cannot determine the referent, indicating indefiniteness, whereas "mouren某人" has two senses, representing indefinite and definite referents respectively. When used in the third person, "bieren别人" and "taren他人" also exhibit stylistic differences, with the former commonly used in colloquial speech and the latter in written language (Ji 吉文玉, 2003: 75).

Based on the analysis above, the semantic gene structure of this group of words is described as:

$S_{\text{自己}}$ = {[称代]:{[人称]([1])}+[定指]([T])}
$S_{\text{自己}}$ = {[Address]:{[Person]([1])}+[Definiteness]([T])}
$S_{\text{自家}}$ = {[称代]:{[人称]([1])}+[定指]([T])+[语体]([方])}
$S_{\text{自家}}$ = {[Address]:{[Person]([1])} [Definiteness]([T])+[Style]([Dialect])}
$S_{\text{本人}}$ = {[称代]:{[人称]([1]∨[2]∨[3])}+[定指]([T])}
$S_{\text{本人}}$ = {[Address]:{[Person]([1]∨[2]∨[3])}+[Definiteness]([T])}
$S_{\text{别人}}$ = {[称代]:{[人称]([2]∨[3])}+[定指]([F])+[语体]([口])}
$S_{\text{别人}}$ = {[Address]:{[Person]([2]∨[3])}+[Definiteness]([F])+[Style
]([Spoken])}
$S_{\text{他人}}$ = {[称代]:{[人称]([3])}+[定指]([F])+[语体]([书])}
$S_{\text{他人}}$ = {[Address]:{[Person]([3])}+[Definiteness]([F])+[Style]([Written])}
$S_{\text{旁人}}$ = {[称代]:{[人称]([2]∨[3])}+[定指]([F])}
$S_{\text{旁人}}$ = {[Address]:{[Person]([2]∨[3])}+[Definiteness]([F])}.
$S_{\text{某人}}$ = {[称代]:{[人称]([2]∨[3])}+[定指]([T]∨[T])}
$S_{\text{某人}}$ = {[Address]:{[Person]([2]∨[3])} [Definiteness]([T]∨[F])}

Accordingly, extract the semantic genes of the semantic field {[chengdai 称代(Address)], [rencheng人称(Person)], [dingzhi定指(Definiteness)], [yuti语体(Style)], [fang方(Dialect)], [kou口(Spoken)], [shu书(Written)]}. The dimension feature values of [rencheng人称(Person)] and [dingzhi定指 (Definiteness)] are represented by numbers and boolean value respectively, which are not included in the set of semantic genes.

5.2.2.2 Kinship Appellation Nouns

① {xiongdi兄弟(brothers), xiong兄(elder brother), ge哥(elder brother), gege哥哥(elder brother), di弟(younger brother), didi弟弟(younger brother), jiemei姐妹(sisters), zimei姊妹(sisters), jie姐(elder sister), jiejie姐姐(elder sister), zi姊(elder sister), zizi姊姊(elder sister), mei妹(younger sister), meimei妹妹(younger sister), tangxiongdi堂兄弟(paternal male cousin), tangxiong堂兄(paternal elder brother), tangdi堂弟(paternal younger brother), tangjiemei堂姐妹(paternal female cousin), tangjie堂姐(paternal elder sister), tangmei堂妹(paternal younger sister), biaoxiongdi表兄弟(maternal male cousin), biaoxiong表兄(maternal elder brother), biaodi表弟(maternal younger brother), biaojiemei表姐妹(maternal female cousin), biaojie表姐(maternal elder sister), biaomei表妹(maternal younger sister)}

Dictionary definition:

Xiongdi兄弟: *The elder brother and the younger brother.*

Xiong兄 ❶*Elder brother.* ❷*The male relative who is of the same generation but older in age than oneself.*

Ge哥 ❶*Elder brother.* ❷*The male relative who is of the same generation but older in age than oneself.*

Gege哥哥: ❶*The male who is older than oneself and shares parents (or only the same father or mother).* ❷A *male relative who is of the same generation and lineage but older in age than oneself.*

Di弟: ❶*Younger brother.* ❷*The male relative who is of the same generation and lineage but younger in age than oneself.*

Gege哥哥: ❶*The male who is older than oneself and shares parents (or only the same father or mother).* ❷*A male relative who is of the same generation and lineage but older in age than oneself.*

Jiemei姐妹: *The elder sister and the younger sister.*

Zimei姊妹: *The elder sister and the younger sister.*

Zizi姊姊: *Elder sister.*

Zi姊: *Elder sister.*

Jie姐: ❶*Elder sister.* ❷*The female relative who is of the same generation but older in age than oneself (usually excluding those who can be addressed as sister-in-law).*

Jiejie姐姐: ❶*The female who is older than oneself and shares parents (or only the same father or mother).* ❷*The female of the same generation and lineage who is older than oneself (usually excluding those who can be addressed as sister-in-law).*

Mei妹: ❶*Younger sister.* ❷*The female relative who is of the same generation but younger in age than oneself.*

Meimei妹妹: ❶*The female relative who is younger than oneself and shares the same parents (or only the same father or mother).* ❷*The female relative who is of the same generation and lineage but younger in age than oneself.*

Tangxiongdi堂兄弟: *Brothers who share the same ancestor on the paternal side.*

Tangxiong堂兄: *The son of a paternal uncle who is older than oneself.*

Tangdi堂弟: *The son of a paternal uncle who is younger than the speaker.*

Tangjiemei堂姐妹: *The collective term for one's female cousins on the paternal side.*

Tangjie堂姐: *The daughter of a paternal uncle who is older than oneself.*

Tangmei堂妹: *The daughter of a paternal uncle who is younger than oneself.*

Biaoxiongdi表兄弟: *The kinship relationship between male cousins on the maternal side.*

Biaoxiong表兄: *The son of one's father's sister, mother's brother, or mother's sister, those who are older than oneself are addressed as one's maternal elder brothers.*

Biaoge表哥: *The maternal elder brother.*

Biaodi表弟: *Maternal younger brother, the son of one's father's sister, mother's brother, or mother's sister, those who are younger than oneself are addressed as one's maternal younger brother.*

Biaojie表姐: *Maternal elder sister, the daughter of one's father's sister, mother's brother, or mother's sister, those who are older than oneself are addressed as one's maternal elder sister.*

Biaomei表妹: *Maternal younger sister, the daughter of one's father's sister, mother's brother, or mother's sister, those who are younger than oneself are addressed as one's maternal younger sister.*

Analysis: Kinship terms have been a subject of interest for many anthropologists and linguists, and they are often cited as examples in semantic field analysis and sememe analysis within lexicology and semantics. The semantic analysis of kinship relations and kinship terms may appear complex, but in fact, there is a strong systemic nature within them, with a relatively orderly structure. As long as the dimensions of analysis are designed reasonably, the semantic description of kinship terms can be quite simple.

In contrast to the discussion of the previous groups, where the semantic genes were extracted individually through the analysis of semantic structure, for this group we adopt a method of first defining the semantic genes and then describing them individually. Based on the characteristics of kinship terms in Chinese culture, we predefine a set of semantic dimension genes and their corresponding value genes:

{[qinshuchengwei亲属称谓 (Kinship)]}, a semantic category gene, is constant.

{[beifen辈分(Generation)]:[Numeric Value]}. For persons of the same generation, the value is 0. The value is set to 1 for the preceding generation (parents), 2 for the generation two levels above (grandparents), (1) for the subsequent generation (children), and (2) for the generation two levels below (grandchildren). This pattern is applied recursively.

{[zhangyou长幼(Age Order)]: [da大(Older)], [xiao小(Younger)]}, the [Age Order] semantic gene denotes the age differences among peers, typically with values of [Older] or [Younger]. Theoretically, [Age Order] follows an ordinal structure, such as "eldest brother", "second sister", "third brother", and so on. However, these titles are generally not considered as lexical items and are therefore not included in the semantic gene description. If there is a need to represent them, it can be easily done by altering the dimension's value from a fixed to a mixed type.

{[zuxi族系(Clan)]: [zhixi直系(Lineal)], [jinxi近系(Close)], [pangxi旁系(Collateral)], [fuxi父系(Paternal)], [muxi母系(Maternal)]}: In the Chinese cultural context, the [Clan] dimension typically involves compound values, necessitating the use of one or more assignment genes. For example, "yeye爷爷(grandfather)" and "waigong外公(maternal grandfather)" are assigned the value with [Lineal]∧[Paternal] and [Lineal]∧ [Maternal] respectively on this dimension. It is important to note that, biologically, [Lineal] refers exclusively to ancestors and descendants with direct reproductive relationships, excluding siblings. To differentiate between siblings and cousins, we introduce the [Close] category, which denotes close relatives, i.e., siblings. It should be emphasized that within the [Clan] feature dimension, it is also crucial to distinguish the [Gender] feature, which refers to the gender of the person's ancestors, not the person addressed. For instance, "tang xiong di堂兄弟" refers to the son of the father's brother, while "biao xiong di 表兄弟" refers to the son of the father's sister (the son of the mother's siblings is also known as "biao xiong di表兄弟"). To represent these relationships, a compound variable is required within the [Clan] feature dimension, such as [[Paternal]:[Gender]([Male])] to denote the clan feature of the descendants of father's brother, and [[Paternal]:[Gender]([Female])] for the descendants of father's sister.

{[xueyuan血缘(Blood relationship)]: [xueqin血亲(Consanguinity)], [yinqin姻亲(Affinity)], [yangqin养亲(Adoptive)], [jiqin继亲(Step)]}

{[xingbie性别(Gender)]: [nan男(Male)], [nv女(Female)]}

By employing this specific gene set, the semantic gene structures of words in this group are described as:

$S_{兄弟}$ = {[亲属称谓]:{[辈分]([0])}+{[长幼]([大]∨[小])}+{[族系]([近系])}+{[血缘]([血亲])}+{[性别]([男])}}

$S_{兄弟}$ = {[Kinship]:{[Generation]([0])}+{[Age Order]([Older]∨[Younger])}+{[Clan]([Close])}+{[Blood relationship]([Consanguinity])}+{[Gender]([Male])}}

$S_{兄}$ = {[亲属称谓]:{[辈分]([0])}+{[长幼]([大])}+{[族系]([近系])}+{[血缘]([血亲])}+{[性别]([男])}}

$S_{兄}$ = {[Kinship]:{[Generation]([0])}+{[Age Order]([Older])}+{[Clan]([Close])}+{[Blood relationship]([Consanguinity])}+{[Gender]([Male])}}

$S_{哥}$ = {[亲属称谓]:{[辈分]([0])}+{[长幼]([大])}+{[族系]([近系])}+{[血缘]([血亲])}+{[性别]([男])}}

$S_{哥}$ = {[Kinship]:{[Generation]([0])}+{[Age Order]([Older])}+{[Clan]([Close])}+{[Blood relationship]([Consanguinity])}+{[Gender]([Male])}}

$S_{哥哥}$ = {[亲属称谓]:{[辈分]([0])}+{[长幼]([大])}+{[族系]([近系])}+{[血缘]([血亲])}+{[性别]([男])}}

$S_{哥哥}$ = {[Kinship]:{[Generation]([0])}+{[Age Order]([Older])}+{[Clan]([Close])}+{[Blood relationship]([Consanguinity])}+{[Gender]([Male])}}

$S_{\text{弟}}$ = {[亲属称谓]:{[辈分]([0])}+{[长幼]([小])}+{[族系]([近系])}+{[血缘]([血亲])}+{[性别]([男])}}

$S_{\text{弟}}$ = {[Kinship]:{[Generation]([0])}+{[Age Order]([Younger])}+{[Clan]([Close])}+{[Blood relationship]([Consanguinity])}+{[Gender]([Male])}}

$S_{\text{弟弟}}$ = {[亲属称谓]:{[辈分]([0])}+{[长幼]([小])}+{[族系]([近系])}+{[血缘]([血亲])}+{[性别]([男])}}

$S_{\text{弟弟}}$ = {[Kinship]:{[Generation]([0])}+{[Age Order]([Younger])}+{[Clan]([Close])}+{[Blood relationship]([Consanguinity])}+{[Gender]([Male])}}

$S_{\text{姐妹}}$ = {[亲属称谓]:{[辈分]([0])}+{[长幼]([大]∨[小])}+{[族系]([近系])}+{[血缘]([血亲])}+{[性别]([女])}}

$S_{\text{姐妹}}$ = {[Kinship]:{[Generation]([0])}+{[Age Order]([Older]∨[Younger])}+{[Clan]([Close])}+{[Blood relationship]([Consanguinity])}+{[Gender]([Female])}}

$S_{\text{姊妹}}$ = {[亲属称谓]:{[辈分]([0])}+{[长幼]([大]∨[小])}+{[族系]([近系])}+{[血缘]([血亲])}+{[性别]([女])}}

$S_{\text{姊妹}}$ = {[Kinship]:{[Generation]([0])}+{[Age Order]([Older]∨[Younger])}+{[Clan]([Close])}+{[Blood relationship]([Consanguinity])}+{[Gender]([Female])}}

$S_{\text{姐}}$ = {[亲属称谓]:{[辈分]([0])}+{[长幼]([大])}+{[族系]([近系])}+{[血缘]([血亲])}+{[性别]([女])}}

$S_{\text{姐}}$ = {[Kinship]:{[Generation]([0])}+{[Age Order]([Older])}+{[Clan]([Close])}+{[Blood relationship]([Consanguinity])}+{[Gender]([Female])}}

$S_{\text{姐姐}}$ = {[亲属称谓]:{[辈分]([0])}+{[长幼]([大])}+{[族系]([近系])}+{[血缘]([血亲])}+{[性别]([女])}}

$S_{\text{姐姐}}$ = {[Kinship]:{[Generation]([0])}+{[Age Order]([Older])}+{[Clan]([Close])}+{[Blood relationship]([Consanguinity])}+{[Gender]([Female])}}

$S_{\text{姊}}$ = {[亲属称谓]:{[辈分]([0])}+{[长幼]([大])}+{[族系]([近系])}+{[血缘]([血亲])}+{[性别]([女])}}

$S_{\text{姊}}$ = {[Kinship]:{[Generation]([0])}+{[Age Order]([Older])}+{[Clan]([Close])}+{[Blood relationship]([Consanguinity])}+{[Gender]([Female])}}

$S_{\text{姊姊}}$ = {[亲属称谓]:{[辈分]([0])}+{[长幼]([大])}+{[族系]([近系])}+{[血缘]([血亲])}+{[性别]([女])}}

$S_{\text{姊姊}}$ Elder sister = {[Kinship]:{[Generation]([0])}+{[Age Order]([Older])}+{[Clan]([Close])}+{[Blood relationship]([Consanguinity])}+{[Gender]([Female])}}

$S_{\text{妹}}$ = {[亲属称谓]:{[辈分]([0])}+{[长幼]([小])}+{[族系]([近系])}+{[血缘]([血亲])}+{[性别]([女])}}

$S_{\text{妹}}$ = {[Kinship]:{[Generation]([0])}+{[Age Order]([Younger])}+{[Clan]([Close])}+{[Blood relationship]([Consanguinity])}+{[Gender]([Female])}}

$S_{\text{妹妹}}$ = {[亲属称谓]:{[辈分]([0])}+{[长幼]([小])}+{[族系]([近系])}+{[血缘]([血亲])}+{[性别]([女])}}

$S_{\text{妹妹}}$ = {[Kinship]:{[Generation]([0])}+{[Age Order]([Younger])}+{[Clan]([Close])}+{[Blood relationship]([Consanguinity])}+{[Gender]([Female])}}

$S_{\text{堂兄弟}}$ = {[亲属称谓]:{[辈分]([0])}+{[长幼]([大]∨[小])}+{[族系]([旁系]∧{[父系]:[性别]([男])})}+{[血缘]([血亲])}+{[性别]([男])}}

$S_{\text{堂兄弟}}$ = {[Kinship]:{[Generation]([0])}+{[Age Order]([Older]∨[Younger])}+{[Clan]([Collateral]∧{[Paternal]:[Gender]([Male])})}+{[Blood relationship]([Consanguinity])}+{[Gender]([Male])}}

$S_{\text{堂兄}}$ = {[亲属称谓]:{[辈分]([0])}+{[长幼]([大])}+{[族系]([旁系]∧{[父系]:[性别]([男])})}+{[血缘]([血亲])}+{[性别]([男])}}

$S_{\text{堂兄}}$ = {[Kinship]:{[Generation]([0])}+{[Age Order]([Older])}+{[Clan]([Collateral]∧{ [Paternal]: [Gender]([Male])})}+{[Blood relationship]([Consanguinity])}+{[Gender]([Male])}}

$S_{\text{堂弟}}$ = {[亲属称谓]:{[辈分]([0])}+{[长幼]([小])}+{[族系]([旁系]∧{[父系]:[性别]([男])})}+{[血缘]([血亲])}+{[性别]([男])}}

$S_{\text{堂弟}}$ = {[Kinship]:{[Generation]([0])}+{[Age Order]([Younger])}+{[Clan]([Collateral]∧ {[Paternal]: [Gender]([Male])})}+{[Blood relationship]([Consanguinity])}+{[Gender]([Male])}}

$S_{\text{堂姐妹}}$ = {[亲属称谓]:{[辈分]([0])}+{[长幼]([大]∨[小])}+{[族系]([旁系]∧{[父系]:[性别]([男])})}+{[血缘]([血亲])}+{[性别]([女])}}

$S_{\text{堂姐妹}}$ = {[Kinship]:{[Generation]([0])}+{[Age Order]([Older]∨[Younger])}+{[Clan]([Collateral]∧{[Paternal]:[Gender]([Male])})}+{[Blood relationship]([Consanguinity])}+{[Gender]([Female])}}

$S_{\text{堂姐}}$ = {[亲属称谓]:{[辈分]([0])}+{[长幼]([大])}+{[族系]([旁系]∧{[父系]:[性别]([男])})}+{[血缘]([血亲])}+{[性别]([女])}}

$S_{\text{堂姐}}$ = {[Kinship]:{[Generation]([0])}+{[Age Order]([Older])}+{[Clan]([Collateral]∧{ [Paternal]:[Gender]([Male])})}+{[Blood relationship]([Consanguinity])}+{[Gender]([Female])}}

$S_{\text{堂妹}}$ = {[亲属称谓]:{[辈分]([0])}+{[长幼]([小])}+{[族系]([旁系]∧{[父系]:[性别]([男])})}+{[血缘]([血亲])}+{[性别]([女])}}

$S_{\text{堂妹}}$ = {[Kinship]:{[Generation]([0])}+{[Age Order]([Younger])}+{[Clan]([Collateral]∧ { [Paternal]:[Gender]([Male])})}+{[Blood relationship]([Consanguinity])}+{[Gender]([Female])}}

$S_{\text{表兄弟}}$ = {[亲属称谓]:{[辈分]([0])}+{[长幼]([大]∨[小])}+{[族系]([旁系]∧[{[父系]:[性别]([女])}∨[母系]])}+{[血缘]([血亲])}+{[性别]([男])}}

$S_{\text{表兄弟}}$ = {[Kinship]:{[Generation]([0])}+{[Age Order]([Older]∨[Younger])}+{[Clan]([Collateral]∧[{[Paternal]:[Gender]([Female])}∨[Maternal]])}+{[Blood relationship]([Consanguinity])}+{[Gender]([Male])}}

$S_{\text{表兄}}$ = {[亲属称谓]:{[辈分]([0])}+{[长幼]([大])}+{[族系]([旁系]∧[{[父系]:[性别]([女])}∨[母系]])}+{[血缘]([血亲])}+{[性别]([男])}}

$S_{表兄}$ = {[Kinship]:{[Generation]([0])}+{[Age Order]([Older])}+{[Clan]([Collateral]∧[{[Paternal]: [Gender]([Female])}∨[Maternal]])}+{[Blood relationship]([Consanguinity])}+{[Gender]([Male])}}
$S_{表弟}$ = {[亲属称谓]:{[辈分]([0])}+{[长幼]([小])}+{[族系]([旁系]∧[{[父系]:[性别]([女])}∨[母系]])}+{[血缘]([血亲])}+{[性别]([男])}}
$S_{表弟}$ = {[Kinship]:{[Generation]([0])}+{[Age Order]([Younger])}+{[Clan]([Collateral]∧[{[Paternal]: [Gender]([Female])}∨[Maternal]])}+{[Blood relationship]([Consanguinity])}+{[Gender]([Male])}}
$S_{表姐妹}$ = {[亲属称谓]:{[辈分]([0])}+{[长幼]([大]∨[小])}+{[族系]([旁系]∧[{[父系]:[性别]([女])}∨[母系]])}+{[血缘]([血亲])}+{[性别]([女])}}
$S_{表姐妹}$ = {[Kinship]:{[Generation]([0])}+{[Age Order]([Older]∨[Younger])}+{[Clan]([Collateral]∧[{[Paternal]:[Gender]([Female])}∨[Maternal]])}+{[Blood relationship]([Consanguinity])}+{[Gender]([Male])}}
$S_{表姐}$ = {[亲属称谓]:{[辈分]([0])}+{[长幼]([大])}+{[族系]([旁系]∧[{[父系]:[性别]([女])}∨[母系]])}+{[血缘]([血亲])}+{[性别]([女])}}
$S_{表姐}$ = {[Kinship]:{[Generation]([0])}+{[Age Order]([Older])}+{[Clan]([Collateral]∧[{[Paternal]: [Gender]([Female])}∨[Maternal]])}+{[Blood relationship]([Consanguinity])}+{[Gender]([Male])}}
$S_{表妹}$ = {[亲属称谓]:{[辈分]([0])}+{[长幼]([小])}+{[族系]([旁系]∧[{[父系]:[性别]([女])}∨[母系]])}+{[血缘]([血亲])}+{[性别]([女])}}
$S_{表妹}$ = {[Kinship]:{[Generation]([0])}+{[Age Order]([Younger])}+{[Clan]([Collateral]∧[{[Paternal]: [Gender]([Female])}∨[Maternal]])}+{[Blood relationship]([Consanguinity])}+{[Gender]([Male])}}

② {fuqin父亲(father), ba爸(dad), die爹(dad), baba爸爸(daddy), shushu叔叔(father's younger brother), shufu叔父(father's younger brother), bobo伯伯(father's elder brother), bofu伯父(father's elder brother), jiujiu舅舅(mother's brother), niangjiu娘舅(mother's brother), jiufu舅父(mother's brother), yifu姨夫(husband of mother's sister), yifu姨父(husband of mother's sister), yizhang姨丈(husband of mother's sister), gufu姑夫(husband of father's sister), gufu姑父(husband of father's sister), guzhang姑丈(husband of father's sister)}

Dictionary definition:
Fuqin父亲: *A man who has children is their father.*
Ba爸: *(spoken) Father.*
Die爹: *(spoken) Father.*
Shushu叔叔: *Father's younger brother.*
Shufu叔父: *Father's younger brother.*
Bobo伯伯: *(spoken)Father's elder brother.*
Bofu伯父: *Father's elder brother.*
Jiujiu舅舅: *(spoken)Mother's brother.*
Niangjiu娘舅: *(dialect) Mother's brother.*
Jiufu舅父: *Mother's brother.*
Yifu姨夫: *Husband of mother's sister.*

Yifu姨父: *Husband of mother's sister.*

Yizhang姨丈: *Husband of mother's sister.*

Gufu姑夫: *Husband of father's sister.*

Gufu姑父: *Husband of father's sister.*

Guzhang姑丈: *Husband of father's sister.*

By directly employing the predefined semantic genes in the above set, we describe the group of words as follows:

$S_{\text{父亲}}$ = {[亲属称谓]:{[辈分]([1])}+{[族系]([直系])}+{[血缘]([血亲])}+{[性别]([男])}}

$S_{\text{父亲}}$ = {[Kinship]:{[Generation]([1])}+{[Clan]([Lineal])}+{[Blood relationship]([Consanguinity])}+{[Gender]([Male])}}

$S_{\text{爸}}$ = {[亲属称谓]:{[辈分]([1])}+{[族系]([直系])}+{[血缘]([血亲])}+{[性别]([男])+{[语体]([口])}}

$S_{\text{爸}}$ = {[Kinship]:{[Generation]([1])}+{[Clan]([Lineal])}+{[Blood relationship]([Consanguinity])}+{[Gender]([Male])}}+{[Style]([Spoken])}}

$S_{\text{爹}}$ = {[亲属称谓]:{[辈分]([1])}+{[族系]([直系])}+{[血缘]([血亲])}+{[性别]([男])}+{[语体]([口])}}

$S_{\text{爹}}$ = {[Kinship]:{[Generation]([1])}+{[Clan]([Lineal])}+{[Blood relationship]([Consanguinity])}+{[Gender]([Male])}}+{[Style]([Spoken])}}

$S_{\text{爸爸}}$ = {[亲属称谓]:{[辈分]([1])}+{[族系]([直系])}+{[血缘]([血亲])}+{[性别]([男])}}

$S_{\text{爸爸}}$ Dad = {[Kinship]:{[Generation]([1])}+{[Clan]([Lineal])}+{[Blood relationship]([Consanguinity])}+{[Gender]([Male])}}

$S_{\text{叔叔}}$ = {[亲属称谓]:{[辈分]([1])}+{[族系]([旁系]∧{[父系]:[长幼]([小])})}+{[血缘]([血亲])}+{[性别]([男])}+{[语体]([口])}}

$S_{\text{叔叔}}$ = {[Kinship]:{[Generation]([1])}+{[Clan]([Collateral]∧{[Paternal]:[Age Order]([Younger])})}+{[Blood relationship]([Consanguinity])}+{[Gender]([Male])}+{[Style]([Spoken])}}

$S_{\text{叔父}}$ = {[亲属称谓]:{[辈分]([1])}+{[族系]([旁系]∧{[父系]:[长幼]([小])})}+{[血缘]([血亲])}+{[性别]([男])}}

$S_{\text{叔父}}$ = {[Kinship]:{[Generation]([1])}+{[Clan]([Collateral]∧{[Paternal]:[Age Order]([Younger])})}+{[Blood relationship]([Consanguinity])}+{[Gender]([Male])}

$S_{\text{伯伯}}$ = {[亲属称谓]:{[辈分]([1])}+{[族系]([旁系]∧{[父系]:[长幼]([大])})}+{[血缘]([血亲])}+{[性别]([男])}+{[语体]([口])}}

$S_{\text{伯伯}}$ = {[Kinship]:{[Generation]([1])}+{[Clan]([Collateral]∧{[Paternal]:[Age Order]([Older])})}+{[Blood relationship]([Consanguinity])}+{[Gender]([Male])}+{[Style]([Spoken])}}

$S_{\text{伯父}}$ = {[亲属称谓]:{[辈分]([1])}+{[族系]([旁系]∧{[父系]:[长幼]([大])})}+{[血缘]([血亲])}+{[性别]([男])}}

$S_{\text{伯父}}$ = {[Kinship]:{[Generation]([1])}+{[Clan]([Collateral]∧{[Paternal]:[Age Order]([Older])})}+{[Blood relationship]([Consanguinity])}+{[Gender]([Male])}

$S_{舅舅}$ = {[亲属称谓]:{[辈分]([1])}+{[族系]([旁系]∧{[母系]:[性别]([男])})}+{[血缘]([血亲])}+{[性别]([男])}+{[语体]([口])}}
$S_{舅舅}$ = {[Kinship]:{[Generation]([1])}+{[Clan]([Collateral]∧{[Maternal]:[Gender]([Male])})}+{[Blood relationship]([Consanguinity])}+{[Gender]([Male])}+{[Style]([Spoken])}}
$S_{娘舅}$ = {[亲属称谓]:{[辈分]([1])}+{[族系]([旁系]∧{[母系]:[性别]([男])})}+{[血缘]([血亲])}+{[性别]([男])}+{[语体]([方])}}
$S_{娘舅}$ = {[Kinship]:{[Generation]([1])}+{[Clan]([Collateral]∧{[Maternal]:[Gender]([Male])})}+{[Blood relationship]([Consanguinity])}+{[Gender]([Male])}+{[Style]([Dialect])}}
$S_{舅父}$ = {[亲属称谓]:{[辈分]([1])}+{[族系]([旁系]∧{[母系]:[性别]([男])})}+{[血缘]([血亲])}+{[性别]([男])}}
$S_{舅父}$ = {[Kinship]:{[Generation]([1])}+{[Clan]([Collateral]∧{[Maternal]:[Gender]([Male])})}+{[Blood relationship]([Consanguinity])}+{[Gender]([Male])}
$S_{姨父}$ = {[亲属称谓]:{[辈分]([1])}+{[族系]([旁系]∧{[母系]:[性别]([男])})}+{[血缘]([姻亲])}+{[性别]([男])}}
$S_{姨父}$ = {[Kinship]:{[Generation]([1])}+{[Clan]([Collateral]∧{[Maternal]:[Gender]([Male])})}+{[Blood relationship]([Affinity])}+{[Gender]([Male])}}
$S_{姨丈}$ = {[亲属称谓]:{[辈分]([1])}+{[族系]([旁系]∧{[母系]:[性别]([男])})}+{[血缘]([姻亲])}+{[性别]([男])}}
$S_{姨丈}$ = {[Kinship]:{[Generation]([1])}+{[Clan]([Collateral]∧{[Maternal]:[Gender]([Male])})}+{[Blood relationship]([Affinity])}+{[Gender]([Male])}}
$S_{姨夫}$ = {[亲属称谓]:{[辈分]([1])}+{[族系]([旁系]∧{[母系]:[性别]([男])})}+{[血缘]([姻亲])}+{[性别]([男])}}
$S_{姨夫}$ = {[Kinship]:{[Generation]([1])}+{[Clan]([Collateral]∧{[Maternal]:[Gender]([Male])})}+{[Blood relationship]([Affinity])}+{[Gender]([Male])}}
$S_{姑父}$ = {[亲属称谓]:{[辈分]([1])}+{[族系]([旁系]∧[父系])}+{[血缘]([姻亲])}+{[性别]([男])}}
$S_{姑父}$ = {[Kinship]:{[Generation]([1])}+{[Clan]([Collateral]∧[Maternal])}+{[Blood relationship]([Affinity])}+{[Gender]([Male])}}
$S_{姑丈}$ = {[亲属称谓]:{[辈分]([1])}+{[族系]([旁系]∧[父系])}+{[血缘]([姻亲])}+{[性别]([男])}}
$S_{姑丈}$ = {[Kinship]:{[Generation]([1])}+{[Clan]([Collateral]∧[Maternal])}+{[Blood relationship]([Affinity])}+{[Gender]([Male])}}
$S_{姑夫}$ = {[亲属称谓]:{[辈分]([1])}+{[族系]([旁系]∧[父系])}+{[血缘]([姻亲])}+{[性别]([男])}}
$S_{姑夫}$ = {[Kinship]:{[Generation]([1])}+{[Clan]([Collateral]∧[Maternal])}+{[Blood relationship]([Affinity])}+{[Gender]([Male])}}

It is evident that this descriptive method is rather cumbersome. An alternative approach is to treat the basic terms that have been described as gene clusters, and then connect them using the possessive relationship symbol "*of*".

③ {muqin母亲(mother), ma妈(mom), mama妈妈(mommy), niang娘(mom), shenmu婶母(father's brother's wife), shenniang婶娘(father's brother's wife), shenshen婶婶(father's brother's wife), shenzi婶子(father's brother's wife), jiumu舅母(mother's brother's wife), jiuma舅妈(mother's brother's wife), yi姨(mother's sister), yimu姨母(mother's sister), gu姑(father's sister), gugu姑姑(father's sister), gumu姑母(father's sister), guma姑妈(father's sister)}

Muqin母亲: *A woman who has children is their mother.*
Ma妈: *(spoken) Mother.*
Mama妈妈: *(spoken) Mother.*
Niang娘: *(spoken) Mother.*
Shenmu婶母: *Father's brother's wife.*
Shenniang婶娘: *(dialect) Father's brother's wife.*
Shenshen婶婶: *(dialect) Father's brother's wife.*
Shenzi婶子: *(spoken) Father's brother's wife.*
Jiuma舅妈: *(spoken) Mother's brother's wife.*
Jiumu舅母: *Mother's brother's wife.*
Yi姨: *Mother's sister.*
Yima姨妈: *(spoken)Mother's sister(married).*
Yimu姨母: *Mother's sister.*
Gu姑: *Father's sister.*
Gugu姑姑: *(spoken)Father's sister.*
Guma姑妈: *(spoken)Father's sister.*
Gumu姑母: *Father's sister.*

We adopt the second descriptive approach for this group. We need to introduce a new gene cluster $_{Gs}$[peiou配偶(Spouse)]. Let's first describe this gene cluster according to the dictionary definition.

Peiou配偶: *The object of a marital relationship.*

S配偶 = {[对象]:{[关系]([婚姻])}} $S_{配偶}$ = {[Object]:{[Relationship]([marriage])}}. Among them, [Marriage] is extracted as a semantic gene and should not be further analyzed.

"muqin母亲", "mama妈妈", and "niang娘" are core kinship terms, serving as fundamental designations in familial relationships, so they are described in detail. The other words are described through a combination of "gene cluster plus possessive relationship".

$S_{母亲}$ = {[亲属称谓]:{[辈分]([1])}+{[族系]([直系])}+{[血缘]([血亲])}+{[性别]([女])}}
$S_{母亲}$ = {[Kinship]:{[Generation]([1])}+{[Clan]([Lineal])}+{[Blood relationship]([Consanguinity])}+{[Gender]([Female])}}
$S_{妈}$ = {[亲属称谓]:{[辈分]([1])}+{[族系]([直系])}+{[血缘]([血亲])}+{[性别]([女])}+{[语体]([口])}}

$S_{\text{妈}}$ = {[Kinship]:{[Generation]([1])}+{[Clan]([Lineal])}+{[Blood relationship]([Consanguinity])}+{[Gender]([Female])}}+{[Style]([Spoken])}}

$S_{\text{妈妈}}$ = {[亲属称谓]:{[辈分]([1])}+{[族系]([直系])}+{[血缘]([血亲])}+{[性别]([女])}+{[语体]([口])}}

$S_{\text{妈妈}}$ = {[Kinship]:{[Generation]([1])}+{[Clan]([Lineal])}+{[Blood relationship]([Consanguinity])}+{[Gender]([Female])}}+{[Style]([Spoken])}}

$S_{\text{娘}}$ = {[亲属称谓]:{[辈分]([1])}+{[族系]([直系])}+{[血缘]([血亲])}+{[性别]([女])}+{[语体]([口])}}

$S_{\text{娘}}$ = {[Kinship]:{[Generation]([1])}+{[Clan]([Lineal])}+{[Blood relationship]([Consanguinity])}+{[Gender]([Female])}}+{[Style]([Spoken])}}

$S_{\text{婶母}}$ = {[亲属称谓]:{[关系](Gs[配偶]*of* Gs[叔父])}}

$S_{\text{婶母}}$ = {[Kinship]:{[Relationship](Gs[Spouse]*of* Gs[shu fu叔父])}}

$S_{\text{婶娘}}$ = {[亲属称谓]:{[关系](Gs[配偶]*of* Gs[叔父])}+{[语体]([方])}}

$S_{\text{婶娘}}$ = {[Kinship]:{[Relationship](Gs[Spouse]*of* Gs[shu fu叔父])}+{[Style]([Dialect])}}

$S_{\text{婶婶}}$ = {[亲属称谓]:{[关系](Gs[配偶]*of* Gs[叔父])}+{[语体]([方])}}

$S_{\text{婶婶}}$ = {[Kinship]:{[Relationship](Gs[Spouse]of Gs[shu fu叔父])}+{[Style]([Dialect])}}

$S_{\text{婶子}}$ = {[亲属称谓]:{[关系](Gs[配偶]*of* Gs[叔父])}+{[语体]([口])}}

$S_{\text{婶子}}$ = {[Kinship]:{[Relationship](Gs[Spouse]of Gs[shu fu叔父])}+{[Style]([Spoken])}}

$S_{\text{舅母}}$ = {[亲属称谓]:{[关系](Gs[配偶]*of* Gs[舅父])}}

$S_{\text{舅母}}$ = {[Kinship]:{[Relationship](Gs[Spouse]of Gs[jiu fu舅父])}}

$S_{\text{舅妈}}$ = {[亲属称谓]:{[关系](Gs[配偶]*of* Gs[舅父])}+{[语体]([口])}}

$S_{\text{舅妈}}$ = {[Kinship]:{[Relationship](Gs[Spouse]of Gs[jiu fu舅父])}}+{[Style]([Spoken])}}

$S_{\text{姨}}$ = {[亲属称谓]:{[关系](Gs[姐妹]*of* Gs[母亲])}}

$S_{\text{姨}}$ = {[Kinship]:{[Relationship](Gs[Sister]of Gs[Mother])}}

$S_{\text{姨母}}$ = {[亲属称谓]:{[关系](Gs[姐妹]*of* Gs[母亲])}}

$S_{\text{姨母}}$ = {[Kinship]:{[Relationship](Gs[Sister]of Gs[Mother])}}

$S_{\text{姨妈}}$ = {[亲属称谓]:{[关系](Gs[姐妹]*of* Gs[母亲])}+{[语体]([口])}+{[[状况]([婚姻])]([已婚])]}}

$S_{\text{姨妈}}$ = {[Kinship]:{[Relationship](Gs[Sister]of Gs[Mother])}+{[Style]([Spoken])}+{[[Status]([Marriage])]([Married])]}}

$S_{\text{姑}}$ = {[亲属称谓]:{[关系](Gs[姐妹]*of* Gs[父亲])}}

$S_{\text{姑}}$ = {[Kinship]:{[Relationship](Gs[Sister]of Gs[Father])}}

$S_{\text{姑姑}}$ = {[亲属称谓]:{[关系](Gs[姐妹]*of* Gs[父亲])}+{[语体]([口])}}

$S_{\text{姑姑}}$ = {[Kinship]:{[Relationship](Gs[Sister]of Gs[Father])}}+{[Style]([Spoken])}

$S_{\text{姑母}}$ = {[亲属称谓]:{[关系](Gs[姐妹]*of* Gs[父亲])}}

$S_{\text{姑母}}$ = {[Kinship]:{[Relationship](Gs[Sister]of Gs[Father])}}

$S_{\text{姑妈}}$ = {[亲属称谓]:{[关系](Gs[姐妹]*of* Gs[父亲])}+{[语体]([口])}+{[[状况]([婚姻])]([已婚])]}}

$S_{\text{姑妈}}$ = {[Kinship]:{[Relationship](Gs[Sister]of Gs[Father])}+{[Style]([Spoken])}+{[[Status]([Marriage])]([Married])]}}

By combining the three sets of genes, we obtain a semantic gene set for kinship words: {[qinshuchengwei亲属称谓(Kinship)], [beifen辈分(Generation)], [zhangyou长幼(Age Order)], [da大(Older)], [xiao小(Younger)], [zuxi族系(Clan)], [zhixi直系(Lineal)], [jinxi近系(Close)], [pangxi旁系(Collateral)], [fuxi父系(Paternal)], [muxi母系(Maternal)]}, [xueyuan血缘(Blood relation)], [xueqin血亲(Consanguinity)], [yinqin姻亲(Affinity)], [yangqin养亲(Adoptive)], [jiqin继亲(Step)], [xingbie性别(Gender)], [nan男(Male)], [nü女(Female)], [guanxi关系(Relationship)], [hunyin婚姻(Marriage)], [zhuangkuang状况(Status)], [yihun已婚(Married)], [weihun未婚(Unmarried)], [lihun离婚(Divorced)]}.

5.2.2.3 Occupational Appellation Nouns

① {nongmin农民(peasant), nongfu农夫(farmer), nongfu农妇(woman peasant), zhuangjiaren庄稼人(peasant), zhuangjiahan庄稼汉(peasant)}

Dictionary definition:

Nongmin农民: *A laborer engaged in agricultural production in rural areas.*

Nongfu农夫: *Historically referred to a male individual engaged in agricultural production.*

Nongfu农妇: *A female peasant.*

Zhuangjiahan庄稼汉: *(spoken) A man engaged in farming.*

Zhuangjiaren庄稼人: *(spoken) One engaged in agricultural cultivation; a farmer.*

Analysis: The interpretive patterns of this group of words exhibit significant diversity, which is challenging machines to conduct semantic reasoning. In knowledge engineering, it is a common practice to describe a knowledge domain within a unified framework. If we could represent the meanings of words within the same semantic class as a knowledge domain of a unified framework in meaning description, it would undoubtedly be highly beneficial for the computational processing of semantics. For instance, a unified descriptive framework for the knowledge domain of occupations could be formulated as follows:

{[职业]([a])}+{[领域]([b])}+{[内容]([c])}+{[地点]([d])}+{[方式]([e])}
{[Occupation]([a])}+{[Field]([b])}+{[Content]([c])}+{[Location]([d])}+{[Way]([e])}

This domain framework is composed of five functional expressions, which are not necessarily required to be present in full, and can be selected or omitted based on the specific context. Following this idea, words in this group can be described as follows: (where the term "nongmin农民 (farmer)" has been analyzed in the examples provided in Chapter 4):

$S_{农民}$ = {[人]:{[职业]([生产])}+{[领域]([农业])}+{[地点]([农村])}+{[方式]([直接])}}
$S_{农民}$ = {[Person]:{[Occupation]([Producing])}+{[Field]([Agriculture])}+{[Location]([Rural area])}+{[Way]([Direct])}}

$S_{\text{农夫}}$ = {[人]:{[职业]([生产])}+{[领域]([农业])}+{[地点]([农村])}+{[方式]([直接])}+{[性别]([男])}+{[语体]([旧])}}
$S_{\text{农夫}}$ = {[Person]:{[Occupation]([Producing])}+{[Field]([Agriculture])}+{[Location]([Rural area])}+{[Way]([Direct])}+{[Gender]([Male])}+{[Style]([Old])}}
$S_{\text{农妇}}$ = {[人]:{[职业]([生产])}+{[领域]([农业])}+{[地点]([农村])}+{[性别]([女])}}
$S_{\text{农妇}}$ = {[Person]:{[Occupation]([Producing])}+{[Field]([Agriculture])}+{[Location]([Rural area])}+{[Gender]([Female])}}
$S_{\text{庄稼汉}}$ = {[人]:{[职业]([生产])}+{[领域]([农业])}+{[地点]([农村])}+{[内容]([种植]([庄稼]))}+{[性别]([男])}}
$S_{\text{庄稼汉}}$ = {[Person]:{[Occupation]([Producing])}+{[Field]([Agriculture])}+{[Location]([Rural area])}+{[Content]([Planting]([Crops]))}+{[Gender]([Male])}}
$S_{\text{庄稼人}}$ = {[人]:{[职业]([生产])}+{[领域]([农业])}+{[地点]([农村])}+{[内容]([种植]([庄稼]))}
$S_{\text{庄稼人}}$ = {[Individual]:{[Occupation]([Producing])}+{[Field]([Agriculture])}+{[Location]([Rural area])}+{[Content]([Planting]([Crops]))}

② {yumin渔民(fisherman), yufu渔夫(fisherman), yuweng渔翁(old fisherman)}

Dictionary definition:
Yumin渔民: *individuals engaged in the occupation of fishing.*
Yufu渔夫: *a male engaged in the profession of fishing.*
Yuweng渔翁: *old fisherman.*
By using the knowledge domain framework mentioned above, the description is as follows:

$S_{\text{渔民}}$ = {[人]:{[职业]([生产])}+{[领域]([渔业])}+{[内容]([捕]([鱼]))}
$S_{\text{渔民}}$ = {[Person]:{[Occupation]([Producing])}+{[Field]([Fishing industry])}+{[Content]([Catching]([Fish]))}
$S_{\text{渔夫}}$ = {[人]:{[职业]([生产])}+{[领域]([渔业])}+{[内容]([捕]([鱼]))}+{[性别]([男])}}
$S_{\text{渔夫}}$ = {[Person]:{[Occupation]([Producing])}+{[Field]([Fishing industry])}+{[Content]([Catching]([Fish]))}+{[Gender]([Male])}}
$S_{\text{渔翁}}$ = {[人]:{[职业]([生产])}+{[领域]([渔业])}+{[内容]([捕]([鱼]))}+{[年龄]([老])}}
$S_{\text{渔翁}}$ = {[Person]:{[Occupation]([Producing])}+{[Field]([Fishing industry])}+{[Content]([Catching]([Fish]))}+{[Age]([Old])}}

③ {shangren商人(merchant), shangfan商贩(peddler), xingshang行商(itinerant vendor), zuoshang坐商(shopkeeper), huolang货郎(hawker), fanzi贩子(dealer), xiaofan小贩(small vendor), tanfan摊贩(street vendor)}

Dictionary definition:

Shangren商人: *The person who sells goods to obtain profit.*

Shangfan商贩: *Refers to small merchants who buy and sell goods on the spot.*

Xingshang行商: *Merchants who engage in the buying and selling of goods, without a fixed place of business (distinguishing from 'shopkeeper').*

Zuoshang坐商: *Merchant with a fixed business location (distinguishing from 'itinerant vendor' peddlers).*

Huolang货郎: *The person who sells daily necessities on the move in rural areas, mountainous regions, or urban backstreets, some of whom also engage in the business of purchasing goods.*

Fanzi贩子: *Individuals engaged in the trade of goods across different regions (generally derogatory).*

Xiaofan小贩: *Denotes merchants operating with minimal capital.*

Tanfan摊贩: *A person who sets up a stall to engage in small-scale trading.*

Continue to employ the occupational knowledge domain framework for description:

$S_{\text{商人}}$ = {[人]:{[职业]($_{Gs}$[经营])}+{[领域]([商业])}+{[内容]($_{Gs}$[贩卖]([商品]))+{[目的]([获得]([利润]))}}

$S_{\text{商人}}$ = {[Person]:{[Occupation]($_{Gs}$[Operating])}+{[Field]([Business])}+{[Content]($_{Gs}$[Trading]([Goods]))+{[Purpose]([Obtaining]([Profit]))}}

$S_{\text{商贩}}$ = {[人]:{[职业]($_{Gs}$[经营])}+{[领域]([商业])}+{[内容]($_{Gs}$[贩卖]([商品]))+{[规模]([小])}+{[方式]([即时])}}

$S_{\text{商贩}}$ = {[Person]:{[Occupation]($_{Gs}$[Operating])}+{[Field]([Business])}+{[Content]($_{Gs}$[Trading]([Goods]))+{[scale]([Small])}+{[Way]([Instant])}}

$S_{\text{行商}}$ = {[人]:{[职业]($_{Gs}$[经营])}+{[领域]([商业])}+{[内容]($_{Gs}$[贩卖]([商品]))+{[地点](![固定])}}}

$S_{\text{行商}}$ = {[Person]:{[Occupation]($_{Gs}$[Operating])}+{[Field]([Business])}+{[Content]($_{Gs}$[Trading]([Goods]))+{[Location](![Fixed])}}}

$S_{\text{坐商}}$ = {[人]:{[职业]($_{Gs}$[经营])}+{[领域]([商业])}+{[内容]($_{Gs}$[贩卖]([商品]))+{[地点]([固定])}}}

$S_{\text{坐商}}$ = {[Person]:{[Occupation]($_{Gs}$[Operating])}+{[Field]([Business])}+{[Content]($_{Gs}$[Trading]([Goods]))+{[Location]([Fixed])}}}

$S_{\text{货郎}}$ = {[人]:{[职业]($_{Gs}$[经营])}+{[领域]([商业])}+{[内容]([$_{Gs}$[贩卖]∨[收购]]([商品]))+{[地点]([农村]∨[山区]∨[巷])}}}

$S_{\text{货郎}}$ = {[Person]:{[Occupation]($_{Gs}$[Operating])}+{[Field]([Business])}+{[Content]($_{Gs}$[Trading]∨ [Purchasing]([Goods]))+{[Location]([Rrual Area]∨[Mountain area]∨[Alley])}}}

$S_{\text{贩子}}$ = {[人]:{[职业]($_{Gs}$[经营])}+{[领域]([商业])}+{[内容]($_{Gs}$[贩卖]([商品]))+{[地点]([u])}+{[极性]([贬])}}

$S_{\text{贩子}}$ = {[Person]:{[Occupation]($_{Gs}$[Operating])}+{[Field]([Business])}+{[Content]($_{Gs}$[Trading]([Goods]))+{[Location]([u])}+{[Polarity]([Positive])}}

$S_{\text{小贩}}$ = {[人]:{[职业]($_{Gs}$[经营])}+{[领域]([商业])}+{[内容]($_{Gs}$[贩卖]([商品]))+{[地点](![固定])}}+{[规模]([小])}}

$S_{小贩}$ = {[Person]:{[Occupation]($_{Gs}$[Operating])}+{[Field]([Business])}+{[Content]($_{Gs}$[Trading]([Goods]))+{[Location](![Fixed])}}+{[Scale]([Small])}}
$S_{摊贩}$ = {[人]:{[职业]($_{Gs}$[经营])}+{[领域]([商业])}+{[内容]($_{Gs}$[贩卖]([商品]))+{[地点]($_{Gs}$[摊子])}}}
$S_{摊贩}$ = {[Person]:{[Occupation]($_{Gs}$[Operating])}+{[Field]([Business])}+{[Content]($_{Gs}$[Trading]([Goods]))+{[Location]($_{Gs}$[Stall])}}}

Here, the gene clusters $_{Gs}$[Operating] and $_{Gs}$[Trading] are high-frequency gene clusters, and they are semantically closely related to the semantic field. Firstly, based on the dictionary definitions, an analysis will be conducted.

Jingying经营(Operating): *Refers to the sale of certain types of goods or the provision of services in commerce and the service industry.*

$S_{经营}$ = {[行为]:{[卖]([商品]∨[服务])}}
$S_{经营}$ = {[Behavior]:{[Selling]([Goods]∨[Service])}}

Fanmai贩卖(Trading): *(merchants) buy goods and then sell them to make a profit.*

$S_{贩卖}$ = {[行为]:{[[买]<[卖]]([商品])}+{[目的]([获得]([利润]))}}
$S_{贩卖}$ = {[Behavior]:{[[Buying]<[Selling]]([Goods])}+{[Purpose]([Obtaining]([Profit]))}}

By merging these gene groups, we obtain a partial set of semantic genes for occupational terms:

{[zhiye职业(Occupation)], [lingyu领域(Field)], [neirong内容(Content)], [didian地点(Location)], [fangshi方式(Way)], [mudi目的(Purpose)], [shengchan生产(Producing)], [nongye农业(Agriculture)], [nongcun农村(Rural area)], [zhijie直接(Direct)], [zhongzhi种植(Planting)], [zhuangjia庄稼(Crops)], [yuye渔业(Fishing industry)], [buzhuo捕捉(Catching)], [yu鱼(Fish)], [shangye商业(Business)], [shangpin商品(Goods)], [huode获得(Obtaining)], [lirun利润(Profit)], [guimo规模(Scale)], [xiao小(Small)], [jishi 即时(Instant)], [guding固定(Fixed)], [shougou收购(Purchasing)], [shanqu山区(Mountain Area)], [xiang巷(Alley)], [xingwei行为(Behavior)], [mai买(Buying)], [mai卖(Selling)], [fuwu服务(Service)]},and a gene cluster $_{Gs}$[tanzi摊子(Stall)] for subsequent analysis.

5.2.2.4 Appellation Nouns of Post and Rank

① {shengzhang省长(provincial governor), xianzhang县长(county chief), zhenzhang镇长(town mayor), xiangzhang乡长(township head), cunzhang村长(village chief), cunzhuren村主任(village director)}

Dictionary definition:
Shengzhang省长: *The highest-ranking official of a provincial government.*
Xianzhang县长: *The highest administrative official responsible for managing a county.*

Xiangzhang乡长: *The administrative leader of a township, ranking below the county chief and at the same level as the town mayor.*

Zhenzhang镇长: *The administrative leader of a town, ranking below the county chief and at the same level as the township head.*

Cunzhang村长: ❶*The primary leader of a village.* ❷*The colloquial name for the village director.*

Cunzhuren村主任: *The main leader of a village-level administrative organization.*

Zhang长: *Leader.*

Analysis: The semantic structure in this group is also relatively regular and standardized, which can be analyzed through a description framework. These words belong to official titles, and the knowledge domain framework can be defined as:

{[身份]($_{Gs}$[官员])}+{[职位]([领导者])}+{[等级]([x])}+{[单位]([y])}
{[Identity]($_{Gs}$[Official])}+{[Position]([Leader])}+{[Rank]([x])}+{[Work unit]([y])}

This framework consists of four functions, among which the [Rank] function takes values of [Principal] or [Deputy], and the [Unit] is a generic function. According to the nature of the unit, this function can be differentiated into several sub-functions such as [dangwei党委(Party Committee)], [zhengfu政府(Government)], [jigou机构(Institution)], [bumen部门(Department)], [weiyuanhui委员会(Committee)], [zuzhi组织(Organization)], etc., with the values being the names of the units.

Gene cluster $_{Gs}$[Official] is the semantic unit left over from the previous analysis, which is a high-frequency analysis unit here. So we will firstly analyze its gene structure based on the dictionary definitions.

Guanyuan官员(Official): *Officially appointed government staff of a certain rank; A government employee with a certain level.*

$S_{\text{官员}}$ = {[人]:{[工作]([处所]([政府]))}+{[身份]:{[等级]([u])}}
$S_{\text{官员}}$ = {[Person]:{[Working]([Location]([Government]))}+{[Identity]:{[Rank]([u])}}

Based on the above discussion, the semantic genes structure of words in this group of are described as follows:

$S_{\text{省长}}$ = {[人]:{[身份]($_{Gs}$[官员])}+{[职位]([领导者])}+{[级别]([正])}+{[政府]([省])}}
$S_{\text{省长}}$ = {[Person]:{[Identity]($_{Gs}$[Official])}+{[Position]([Leader])}+{[Rank]([Principal])}+{[Government]([Province])}}
$S_{\text{县长}}$ = {[人]:{[身份]($_{Gs}$[官员])}+{[职位]([领导者])}+{[级别]([正])}+{[政府]([县])}}
$S_{\text{县长}}$ = {[Person]:{[Identity]($_{Gs}$[Official])}+{[Position]([Leader])}+{[Rank]([Principal])}+{[Government]([County])}}
$S_{\text{乡长}}$ = {[人]:{[身份]($_{Gs}$[官员])}+{[职位]([领导者])}+{[级别]([正])}+{[政府]([乡])}}

$S_{乡长}$ = {[Person]:{[Identity]($_{Gs}$[Official])}+{[Position]([Leader])}+{[Rank]([Principal])}+{[Government]([Town])}}
$S_{镇长}$ = {[人]:{[身份]($_{Gs}$[官员])}+{[职位]([领导者])}+{[级别]([正])}+{[政府]([镇])}}
$S_{镇长}$ = {[Person]:{[Identity]($_{Gs}$[Official])}+{[Position]([Leader])}+{[Rank]([Principal])}+{[Government]([Town])}}
$S_{村长}$ = {[人]:{[身份]($_{Gs}$[官员])}+{[职位]([领导者])}+{[级别]([正])}+{[委员会]([村])}}
$S_{村长}$ = {[Person]:{[Identity]($_{Gs}$[Official])}+{[Position]([Leader])}+{[Rank]([Principal])}+{[Committee]([Village])}}

② {jiaoshou教授(professor), fujiaoshou副教授(associate professor), jiangshi讲师(lecturer), zhujiao助教(teaching assistant), boshi博士(doctor), shuoshi硕士(master), xueshi学士(bachelor)}

Dictionary definition:
Jiaoshou教授: *The highest-ranking teacher in a higher education institution.*
Fujiaoshou副教授: *The position in a university ranking second only to professor.*
Jiangshi讲师: *A teacher in a higher education institution who ranks below an associate professor.*
Zhujiao助教: *The lowest-ranking teacher in a college or university.*
Boshi博士: *The highest level of degree.*
Shuoshi硕士*(master): One level of degree. University graduates who have studied in research institutions for one to two years and have achieved satisfactory academic performance are eligible for the award.*
Xueshi学士: *The lowest level of degree, awarded by the school upon graduation from university.*

Analysis: The semantic structure of titles and degrees is also regular and orderly. Unlike official titles, these titles are characterized by a clear hierarchical sequence that can be quantified. Similar terms include military ranks, military positions, and police ranks, etc. These terms can refer to individuals, indicating those who hold a certain title or degree, or they can refer to the names of the titles or degrees themselves. For example:

(1) Xiao Zhang has obtained his doctor degree this year. (Referring to thing)
(2) Our institution has introduced two doctors this year. (Referring to person)

The framework for describing this knowledge domain can be uniformly represented as:

(1) Referring to ting:

{[衔名]:{[级别]([x])}+{[领域]([y])}
{[Title]:{[Rank]([x])}+{[Field]([y])}

The structure is composed of a constant gene [xianming衔名(Title)] and two functions. The constant gene [Title] serves as a generic gene, which can differentiate into specific genes such as [zhicheng职称(Position)], [xuewei学位(Degree)], [junxian军衔(Military rank)] and [jingxian警衔(Police rank)] based on the specific context. The [jibie级别(Rank)] function assigns a numerical value [x], which is not included in the semantic gene set. The [lingyu领域(Field)] function assumes specific field names as its values.

(2) Referring to person:

{[人]:{[身份]([a])}+{[衔名]:{[级别]([x])}+{[领域]([y])}}
{[Person]:{[Identity]([a])}+{[Title]:{[Rank]([x])}+{[Field]([y])}}

When referring to persons, a constant gene [ren人(Person)] and a function [shenfen身份(Identity)] are added. The purpose of adding the [Identity] gene is to ensure the integrity of the knowledge domain framework, facilitating semantic reasoning by computers. The value [*a*] of this function represents the specific occupational identity name, such as the [Identity] value of "Professor" being Gs[jiaoshi教师(Teacher)], and the identity of "Marshal" being Gs[junren军人(Military)]. It should be noted that when the term "Doctor" and other academic titles refer to individuals, the identity is not fixed, as individuals with a certain degree do not correspond to a fixed industry. Therefore, the value [a] is a generalized value [u], and similarly, the value [y] of the [Field] function is also a generalized value [u].

Based on the above analysis, the gene structure of this group (referring to persons) is described as follows:

$S_{\text{教授}}$ = {[人]:{[身份](Gs[教师])}+{[职称]:{[级别]([1])}+{[领域](Gs[教育])}}
$S_{\text{教授}}$ = {[Person]:{[Identity](Gs[Teacher])}+{[Title]:{[Rank]([1])}+{[Field](Gs[Education])}}
$S_{\text{副教授}}$ = {[人]:{[身份](Gs[教师])}+{[职称]:{[级别]([2])}+{[领域](Gs[教育])}}
$S_{\text{副教授}}$ = {[Person]:{[Identity](Gs[Teacher])}+{[Title]:{[Rank]([2])}+{[Field](Gs[Education])}}
$S_{\text{讲师}}$ = {[人]:{[身份](Gs[教师])}+{[职称]:{[级别]([3])}+{[领域](Gs[教育])}}
$S_{\text{讲师}}$ = {[Person]:{[Identity](Gs[Teacher])}+{[Title]:{[Rank]([3])}+{[Field](Gs[Education])}}
$S_{\text{助教}}$ = {[人]:{[身份](Gs[教师])}+{[职称]:{[级别]([4])}+{[领域](Gs[教育])}}
$S_{\text{助教}}$ = {[Person]:{[Identity](Gs[Teacher])}+{[Title]:{[Rank]([4])}+{[Field](Gs[Education])}}
$S_{\text{博士}}$ = {[人]:{[身份]([u])}+{[学位]:{[级别]([1])}+{[领域]([u])}}
$S_{\text{博士}}$ = {[Person]:{[Identity]([u])}+{[Degree]:{[Rank]([1])}+{[Field]([u])}}
$S_{\text{硕士}}$ = {[人]:{[身份]([u])}+{[学位]:{[级别]([2])}+{[领域]([u])}}
$S_{\text{硕士}}$ = {[Person]:{[Identity]([u])}+{[Degree]:{[Rank]([2])}+{[Field]([u])}}
$S_{\text{学士}}$ = {[人]:{[身份]([u])}+{[学位]:{[级别]([3])}+{[领域]([u])}}
$S_{\text{学士}}$ = {[Person]:{[Identity]([u])}+{[Degree]:{[Rank]([3])}+{[Field]([u])}}

Combining these groups, we obtain a subset of lexical genes pertaining to titles and positions: {[shenfen身份(Identity)], [zhiwei职位(Position)], [lingdaozhe领导者(Leader)], [dengji等级(Rank)], [danwei单位(Unit)], [dangwei党委(Party Committee)], [zhengfu政府(Government)], [jigou机构(Institution)], [bumen部门(Department)], [weiyuanhui委员会(Committee)], [zuzhi组织(Organization)], [gongzuo工作(Working)], [chusuo处所(Location)], [zheng正(Principal)], [fu副(Deputy)], [sheng省(Province)], [xian县(County)], [xiang乡(Town)], [zhen镇(Village)], [cun村(Village)], [lingyu领域(Field)], [zhicheng职称(Title)], [xuewei学位(Degree)], [junxian军衔(Military Rank)], [jingxian警衔(Police Rank)], [junzhi军职(Military Position)]}, along with two gene clusters, $_{Gs}$[jiaoshi教师(Teacher)] and $_{Gs}$[jiaoyu教育(Education)], which are reserved for subsequent analysis.

5.2.2.5 Appellation Nouns of Identity Title

① {laoban老板(boss), zhanggui掌柜(shopkeeper), dianzhu店主(store owner), guzhu雇主(employer), yezhu业主(proprietor)}

Dictionary definition:

Laoban老板: *The owner of private industrial and commercial property, also referred to as a shopkeeper.*

Zhanggui掌柜: *Historically known as the owner or manager of a store in ancient China.*

Dianzhu店主: *The proprietor of a store.*

Guzhu雇主: *An individual or entity that hires others for work and compensates them.*

Yezhu业主: *The owner of an enterprise or property in a society with private ownership.*

The owner of assets such as land and houses.

The owner of industries and enterprises (usually referring to private ones).

Analysis: The group of words can be categorized into two types of definitions: "laoban老板", "dianzhu店主", and "yezhu业主" refer to the "owner of something", while "zhanggui掌柜" and "guzhu雇主" refer to the "individuals doing something", with different semantic gene structures.

The knowledge domain framework of "the owner of something" can be described as:

{[人]:{[身份]([x] of [i])}
{[Person]:{[Identity]([x] of [i])}

It is composed of a constant gene [Person] and an [Identity] feature function. The function assigns a value where [x] represents a specific entity, and [i] denotes the reflexive gene, referring to the entity itself that the described word points to.

The knowledge domain framework of "individuals doing something", can be described as:

{[人]:{[行为]([施事]([i])∧[受事]([x])}
{[Person]:{[Behavior]([Agent]([i])∧[Patient]([x])}

This is composed of a constant gene [Person] and an [Behavior] feature function, which is a generic function that can be replaced with a specific behavioral gene or gene cluster according to the context. This is a nested function, with its value determined by the [Agent] function and the [Patient] function. The [Agent] function takes the value of the reflexive gene [i], indicating that the agent is the referent itself described by the word. The [Patient] function takes the value of gene [x], representing the specific object of the behavioral action.

Based on the aforementioned analysis, the semantic gene structure of words in this group is described as:

$S_{\text{老板}}$ = {[人]:{[身份]({Gs[企业]:{[性质]([私有])}}*of* [*i*])}}
$S_{\text{老板}}$ = {[Person]:{[Identity]({Gs[Enterprise]:{[Nature]([Private])}}of [i])}}
$S_{\text{店主}}$ = {[人]:{[身份](Gs[店铺]*of* [*i*])}}
$S_{\text{店主}}$ = {[Person]:{[Identity](Gs[Store]of [i])}}
$S_{\text{业主}}$ = {[人]:{[身份]([[土地]∨Gs[房屋]∨Gs[企业]]*of* [*i*])}}
$S_{\text{业主}}$ = {[Person]:{[Identity]([[Land]∨Gs[House]∨Gs[Enterprise]]of [i])}}
$S_{\text{掌柜}}$ = {[人]:{[管理]([施事]([*i*])∧[受事](Gs[店铺])}∨{[身份](Gs[店铺]*of* [*i*])}}
$S_{\text{掌柜}}$ = {[Person]:{[Manage]([Agent]([i])∧[Patient](Gs[Store])}∨{[Identity](Gs[Store]of [i])}}
$S_{\text{雇主}}$ = {[人]:{[雇]([施事]([*i*])∧[受事](Gs[他人])}∧{[雇](Gs[支付]([i]) ∧[受事](Gs[薪酬])}}
$S_{\text{雇主}}$ = {[Person]:{[Employ]([Agent]([i])∧[Patient](Gs[Others])}∧{[Employ](Gs[Pay]([i])∧[Patient](Gs[Salary])}}

② {xuesheng学生(student), mensheng门生(pupil), tudi徒弟(apprentice), dizi弟子(follower), mentu门徒(disciple), xuetu学徒(trainee)}

Dictionary definition:
Xuesheng学生: *individuals studying in academic institutions.*
Mensheng门生: *in the past referred to individuals who followed a teacher or a senior in their learning.*
Tudi徒弟: *An individual who follows a master to learn a skill, broadly encompassing anyone learning from an expert in a particular field.*
Dizi弟子: *refers to a student or apprentice.*
Mentu门徒: *Disciple, apprentice.*
Xuetu学徒: *An individual who commits to learning a skill under the mentorship of an experienced craftsman.*

Analysis: The meanings of this group of words still belong to the domain of "individuals doing something". However, the verb "learn" in this context differs in domain framework from the preceding verbs. Learning is a process of acquiring knowledge, involving three basic arguments: "the knowledge acquirer", "the content of knowledge", and "the source of knowledge acquisition", as well as optional arguments including "time", "location", and "field". The basic framework of the "learn" domain can be described as follows:

{[行为]:{([施事]([x])∧[受事]([y])∧[来源]([z]))}}
{[Behavior]:{([Agent]([x])∧[Patient]([y])∧[Source]([z]))}}

Here the [Agent] is a necessary gene. In specific contexts, the [Patient] and [Source] may not be present, emerging only when it is necessary to emphasize or clearly identify a particular object.

According to analysis above, the semantic gene structure of words in this group is described as:

$S_{\text{学生}}$ = {[人]:{[学习]([施事]([*i*])}}
$S_{\text{学生}}$ = {[Person]:{[Learning]([Agent]([i])}}
$S_{\text{门生}}$ = {[人]:{[学习]([施事]([i])∧[来源]($_{Gs}$[老师]∨$_{Gs}$[前辈])}+{[语体]([旧])}}
$S_{\text{门生}}$ = {[Person]:{[Learning]([Agent]([i])∧[Source](Gs[Teacher]∨Gs[Senior])}+{[Style]([Old])}}.
$S_{\text{徒弟}}$ = {[人]:{[学习]([施事]([i])∧[来源]($_{Gs}$[师傅])}}
$S_{\text{徒弟}}$ = {[Person]:{[Learning]([Agent]([i])∧[Source](Gs[Master])}}
$S_{\text{弟子}}$ = {[人]:{[学习]([施事]([i])}∧[{[来源]($_{Gs}$[师傅])}∨{[处所]($_{Gs}$[学校])}]}}
$S_{\text{弟子}}$ = {[Person]:{[Learning]([Agent]([i])}∧[{[Source](Gs[Master])}∨{[Location](Gs[School])}]}}.
$S_{\text{门徒}}$ = {[人]:{[学习]([施事]([i])∧[来源]($_{Gs}$[师傅])}+{[语体]([书])}}
$S_{\text{门徒}}$ = {[Person]:{[Learning]([Agent]([i])∧[Source](Gs[Master])}+{[Style]([Written])}}
$S_{\text{学徒}}$ = {[人]:{[学习]([施事]([i])∧[受事]($_{Gs}$[技艺])}}
$S_{\text{学徒}}$ = {[Person]:{[Learning]([Agent]([i])∧[Patient](Gs[Skill])}}

Here "$_{Gs}$[laoshi老师(Teacher)]" and "$_{Gs}$[shifu师傅(Master)]" are two gene clusters that are highly associated with the "learning" domain. They are analyzed together as follows:

Laoshi老师: *The respectful title for those who impart knowledge, skills, or life philosophies.*

Shifu师傅: *One who imparts a specific skill or craft.*

$S_{\text{老师}}$ = {[人]:{[传授]([施事]([*i*])∧[受事]([知识]∨$_{Gs}$[技艺]∨[道理])}+{[语气]([尊重])}}
$S_{\text{老师}}$ = {[Person]:{[Teaching]([Agent]([i])∧[Patient]([Knowledge]∨Gs[Skill]∨[Principle])}+{[Tone]([Respect])}}
$S_{\text{师傅}}$ = {[人]:{[传授]([施事]([*i*])∧[受事]([技术]∨$_{Gs}$[技艺])}}
$S_{\text{师傅}}$ = {[Person]:{[Teaching]([Agent]([i])∧[Patient]([Technique]∨Gs[Skill])}}

③ {mingren名人(personage), mingliu名流(socialite), mingshi名士(celebrity), mingsu名宿(senior celebrity), wenren闻人(well-known figure)}

Dictionary definition:

Mingren名人: *Notable individuals.*

Mingliu名流: *Individuals who were renowned in their time, particularly those from the academic and political spheres.*

Mingshi名士: *Individuals who are renowned but have not held official positions; those who are distinguished by their literary and poetic accomplishments.*

Mingsu名宿: *Individuals who have gained a reputation for distinction or eminence.*

Wenren闻人: *Individuals with fame.*

Analysis: The conceptual meanings of this group of words all refer to individuals who are renowned or well-known. To facilitate a comprehensive understanding, let us first examine a related set of terms:

Mingsheng名声(reputation): *The evaluation that circulates within society.*

Mingqi名气(fame): *(spoken) Reputation.*

Mingwang名望*(Renown): Good reputation, prestige.*

$S_{名声}$ = {[评价]:{[范围]([社会]∧[广])}}
$S_{名声}$ = {[Evaluation]:{[Scope]([Society]∧[Wide])}}
$S_{名气}$ = {[评价]:{[范围]([社会]∧[广])}+{[语体]([口])}}
$S_{名气}$ = {[Evaluation]:{[Scope]([Society]∧[Wide]))}+{[Style]([Spoken])}}
$S_{名望}$ = {[评价]:{[范围]([社会]∧[广])}+{[性质]([好])}}
$S_{名望}$ = {[Evaluation]:{[Scope]([Society]∧[Wide])}+{[Nature]([Good])}}

The analysis yields gene clusters $_{\text{Gs}}$[mingsheng名声(Reputation)], $_{\text{Gs}}$[mingqi名气(Fame)], and $_{\text{Gs}}$[mingwang名望(Renown)]. These gene clusters are then employed to analyze the aforementioned identity titles.

$S_{名人}$ = {[人]:{$_{\text{Gs}}$[名气]([大])}}
$S_{名人}$ = {[Person]:{Gs[Fame]([Great])}}
$S_{名流}$ = {[人]:{$_{\text{Gs}}$[名气]([大])}+{[领域]([学术]∨[政治])}+{[语体]([旧])}}
$S_{名流}$ = {[Person]:{Gs[Fame]([Great])}+{[Field]([Scholarship]∨[Politics])}+{[Style]([Old])}}
$S_{名士}$ = {[人]:{$_{\text{Gs}}$[名望]([高])}+{[领域]($_{\text{Gs}}$[文学])+{[身份](!$_{\text{Gs}}$[官员])}+{[语体]([旧])}}
$S_{名士}$ = {[Person]:{Gs[Renown]([High])}+{[Field](Gs[Literature])+{[Identity](!Gs[Official])}+{[Style]([Old])}}
$S_{名宿}$ = {[人]:{$_{\text{Gs}}$[名望]([高])}
$S_{名宿}$ = {[Person]:{Gs[Renown]([High])}
$S_{闻人}$ = {[人]:{$_{\text{Gs}}$[名气]([大])}
$S_{闻人}$ = {[Person]:{Gs[Fame]([Great])}

The merged set of identity titles, derived from the combination of the above groups, includes: {[guanli管理(Management)], [shishi施事(Agent)], [shoushi受事(Patient)], [xingzhi性质(Nature)], [siyou私有(Private)], [tudi土

地(Land)], [gu雇(Employing)], [laiyuan来源(Source)], [xuexi学习(Learning)], [chuanshou传授(Teaching)], [zhishi知识(Knowledge)], [daoli道理(Principle)], [jishu技术(Technique)], [yuqi语气(Tone)], [zunzhong尊重(Respect)], [pingjia评价(Evaluation)], [fanwei范围(Scope)], [shehui社会(Society)], [guang广(Wide)], [xingzhi性质(Nature)], [hao好(Good)], [lingyu领域(Field)], [xueshu学术(Scholarship)], [zhengzhi政治(Politics)], [wenxue文学 (Literature)]}. Additionally, the gene clusters Gs[fangwu房屋(Housing)], Gs[qiye企业(Enterprise)], Gs[dianpu店铺(Shop)], Gs[xinchou薪酬(Compensation)], Gs[zhifu支付(Payment)], Gs[jiyi技艺(Art)] and Gs[xuexiao学校(School)] are reserved for subsequent analysis.

5.2.2.6 Nouns Expressing Interpersonal Relationships

① {[tongshi同事(co-worker)], [tongren同仁(colleague)], [tongren同人(Colleague)], [tongliao同僚(fellow official)], [tongban同伴(companion)], [tongxue同学 (schoolmate)], [tongchuang同窗(classmate)], [tongmen同门(pupils of the same teacher)]}

Dictionary definition:

Tongshi同事: *An individual who works within the same organization or unit.*

Tongren同人: *In the past it referred to individuals who worked in the same organization or within the same industry.*

Tongren同仁: *Synonym of "tongren同人".*

Tongliao同僚: *Historically, government officials or civil servants who were employed within the same administrative unit were referred to as such.*

Tongban同伴: *Individuals who work or live together with somebody.*

Tongxue同学: *Individuals studying within the same educational institution.*

Tongchuang同窗: *Individuals who study in the same educational institution.*

Tongmen同门: *individuals who have been tutored by the same teacher.*

Analysis: "tong同" denotes a comparative relationship, indicating that two or more individuals or entities are being contrasted, sharing identical values on a specific feature dimension. Words in this group signifie a comparison between two individuals. The contrast is between the individual referred to by the target word and a definite implicit object, which is typically the speaker, or possibly a third one known to both the speaker and the listener. The dimension of comparison is not fixed, the one on which identical values are shared constitutes the distinguishing feature among the words within this semantic field. The knowledge domain framework of "tong同" can be represented as follows:

The domain {[关系]:{[同]([x])}} {[Relation]:{[Common]([x])}} is defined by a constant gene [Relation] and a function [Common], where the function value [x] represents either a dimension feature gene or a dimension feature function. Therefore, this function tends to be complex, featuring multiple nesting. The comparison is based on default values, which are not prominently featured within the domain framework. With this domain framework, the semantic structures can be described as follows:

$S_{\text{同事}}$ = {[人]:{[关系]:{[同]([处所]([单位])}}
$S_{\text{同事}}$ = {[Person]:{[Relation]:{[Common]([Location]([Unit])}}
$S_{\text{同人}}$ = $S_{\text{同仁}}$ = {[人]:{[关系]:{[同]([处所]([单位]∨[行业]))}}+{[语体]([旧])}}
$S_{\text{同人}}$ = $S_{\text{同仁}}$ = {[Person]:{[Relation]:{[Common]([Location]([Unit]∨[Industry]))}}+{[Style]([Old])}}
$S_{\text{同僚}}$ = {[人]:{[关系]:{[同]([处所]([单位])}}+{[身份]($_{Gs}$[官员])}+{[语体]([旧])}}
$S_{\text{同僚}}$ = {[Person]:{[Relation]:{[Common]([Location]([Unit])}}+{[Identity]($_{Gs}$[Official])}+{[Style]([Old])}}
$S_{\text{同伴}}$ = {[人]:{[关系]:{[同]([行为]([工作]∨[生活]))}}}
$S_{\text{同伴}}$ = {[Person]:{[Relation]:{[Common]([Behavior]([Working]∨[Living]))}}}
$S_{\text{同学}}$ = {[人]:{[关系]:[同]{([[行为]($_{Gs}$[学习])]∧[[处所]($_{Gs}$[学校])])}}}
$S_{\text{同学}}$ = {[Person]:{[Relation]:[Common]{([[Behavior]($_{Gs}$[Studying])]∧ [Location](Gs[School])])}}}
$S_{\text{同窗}}$ = {[人]:{[关系]:[同]{([[行为]($_{Gs}$[学习])]∧[[处所]($_{Gs}$[学校])])}}+{[语体]([书])}}
$S_{\text{同窗}}$ = {[Person]:{[Relation]:[Common]{([[Behavior]($_{Gs}$[Studying])]∧[Location]($_{Gs}$[School])])}}}+{[Style]([Written])}}
$S_{\text{同门}}$ = {[人]:{[关系]:{[同]($_{Gs}$[老师]*of* [*i*])}}
$S_{\text{同门}}$ = {[Person]:{[Relation]:{[Common](Gs[Teacher]of [i])}}

② {pengyou朋友(friend), youren友人(chum), haoyou好友(good friend), zhiyou挚友(intimate friend), zhijiao至交 (confidant), zhiji知己(soulmate), sidang死党(bestie)}

Dictionary definition:

Pengyou 朋友: *Individual who lack kinship or teacher-student relationships but is acquainted with and understands each other, capable of showing concern and providing assistance.*

Youren 友人: *Friends.*

Haoyou 好友: *Friends with a deep friendship.*

Zhiji 知己: *Individuals who possess a profound mutual understanding and a deep sense of camaraderie.*

Zhiyou 挚友: *Friends with intimate relationship.*

Zhijiao 至交: *The closest friend.*

Sidang 死党: ❶*Individuals who are willing to offer unwavering support and assistance to one another.* ❷*A rigid and inflexible clique, often carrying a pejorative connotation.* ❸*Metaphorically, it signifies a friend who is willing to go to great lengths, even to the point of risking their own life, in times of difficulty.*

Analysis: The core conceptual meaning of this group of words is "friend", with varying additional meanings primarily reflected in the depth of their emotional connection, which can be roughly arranged in a hierarchy: pengyou朋友 (youren

友人) < haoyou好友 < zhiji知己 < zhiyou挚友 < zhijiao至交 < sidang死党. To facilitate semantic reasoning by computers, we employ a [Emotion grade] feature function to describe this, with values ranging from [1] to [6]. In describing the concept of "mutual understanding and care", we resort to the anaphora reflexive gene [I]. "Care" and "understand" are typical behavioral verbs, whose semantic knowledge domain cannot be devoid of [Agent] and [Patient]. However, due to the semantic constraint imposed by the word "mutual", the [Agent] and [Patient] in this context cannot be distinguished; the two participants involved in the verb are mutually both the agent and the patient. The anaphora reflexive gene [I] is specifically designed for such situations.

According to the analysis, the semantic structures can be described as follows:

$S_{\text{朋友}}$ = {[人]:{[关系]([好])}+{[了解]([I])}+{[关心]([I])}+{[包含](![[亲属]∨Gs[师生]])}+{[感情等级]([1])}}

$S_{\text{朋友}}$ = {[Person]:{[Relation]([Good])}+{[Understanding]([I])}+{[Caring]([I])}+{[Contain](![[kinship]∨ Gs[Teacher-student relationship]])}+{[Emotion grade]([1])}}

$S_{\text{友人}}$ = {[人]:{[关系]([好])}+{[了解]([I])}+{[关心]([I])}+{[包含](![[亲属]∨Gs[师生]])}+{[感情等级]([1])}+{[语体]([书])}}

$S_{\text{友人}}$ = {[Person]:{[Relation]([Good])}+{[Understanding]([I])}+{[Caring]([I])}+{[Contain](![[kinship]∨ Gs[Teacher-student relationship]])}+{[Emotion grade]([1])}}+{[Style]([Written])}}

$S_{\text{好友}}$ = {[人]:{[关系]([好])}+{[了解]([I])}+{[关心]([I])}+{[包含](![[亲属]∨Gs[师生]])}+{[感情等级]([2])}}

$S_{\text{好友}}$ = {[Person]:{[Relation]([Good])}+{[Understanding]([I])}+{[Caring]([I])}+{[Contain](![[kinship]∨ Gs[Teacher-student relationship]])}+{[Emotion grade]([2])}}

$S_{\text{知己}}$ = {[人]:{[关系]([好])}+{[了解]([I])}+{[关心]([I])}+{[包含](![[亲属]∨Gs[师生]])}+{[感情等级]([3])}}

$S_{\text{知己}}$ = {[Person]:{[Relation]([Good])}+{[Understanding]([I])}+{[Caring]([I])}+{[Contain](![[kinship]∨ Gs[Teacher-student relationship]])}+{[Emotion grade]([3])}}

$S_{\text{挚友}}$ = {[人]:{[关系]([好])}+{[了解]([I])}+{[关心]([I])}+{[包含](![[亲属]∨Gs[师生]])}+{[感情等级]([4])}}

$S_{\text{挚友}}$ = {[Person]:{[Relation]([Good])}+{[Understanding]([I])}+{[Caring]([I])}+{[Contain](![[kinship]∨ Gs[Teacher-student relationship]])}+{[Emotion grade]([4])}}

$S_{\text{至交}}$ = {[人]:{[关系]([好])}+{[了解]([I])}+{[关心]([I])}+{[包含](![[亲属]∨Gs[师生]])}+{[感情等级]([5])}}

$S_{\text{至交}}$ = {[Person]:{[Relation]([Good])}+{[Understanding]([I])}+{[Caring]([I])}+{[Contain](![[kinship]∨ Gs[Teacher-student relationship]])}+{[Emotion grade]([5])}}

$S_{\text{死党}}$ = {[人]:{[关系]([好])}+{[了解]([I])}+{[关心]([I])}+{[包含](![[亲属]∨Gs[师生]])}+{[感情等级]([6])}+{[语气]([亲昵])}}

$S_{死党}$ = {[Person]:{[Relation]([Good])}+{[Understanding]([I])}+{[Caring]([I])}+{[Contain](![[kinship]∨ $_{Gs}$[Teacher-student relationship]])}+{[Emotion grade]([6])}+{[Tone]([Intimate])}}

③ {diren敌人(enemy), dikou敌寇(invader), waidi外敌(foreign enemy), waikou外寇(foreign invader), qiongkou穷寇(tottering foe), zhengdi政敌(political opponent), gongdi公敌(public enemy), qingdi情敌(rival in love)}

Dictionary definition:

Diren敌人: *Adversary or opposing party.*

Dikou敌寇: *An enemy invaded by armed forces from abroad.*

Waidi外敌: *An enemy from outside.*

Waikou外寇: *Invading armed forces;an invader from outside; foreign aggression or predatory invasion.*

Qiongkou穷寇: *Desperate bandits,a general term for enemies in a state of ultimate decline.*

Zhengdi政敌: *Individuals who are politically in opposition to oneself.*

Gongdi公敌: *An adversary that is collectively recognized and opposed by a group or society.*

Qingdi情敌: I*ndividuals who have conflicts with each other due to pursuing the same opposite sex.*

Analysis: The core conceptual meaning shared by these words is "diren敌人(enemy)". There are two problems with the explanations provided in dictionaries: (1) The use of "didui敌对(adversary)" to explain "enemy" still leaves the meaning unclear; (2) "didui de ren敌对的人(adversary person)" and "didui de fangmian敌对的方面(opposing party)" can be distinguished into two senses, one referring to a person and the other to a thing, the latter being an extension of the former. While dictionaries may not differentiate between these senses, computational semantic descriptions cannot mix them together.

In addressing the first question, we continue to trace the etymology of the morpheme "di敌". For the second question, we divide it into two pleremes for description. When dealing with multiple pleremes of a single word or homographs, the semantic gene structure differs during the description. In the semantic gene database, each plereme is assigned a unique identity code to ensure that there is no confusion during computation.

Di敌: *Incompatible with conflicts of interest.*

By adhering to the definition provided, the depiction of 'enemy' will not fall into the trap of circular interpretation.

$S_{敌人}$ = {[人]:[冲突]([I])∧!$_{Gs}$[相容]([I])}

$S_{敌人}$ = {[Person]:[Conflict]([I])∧!Gs[Compatible]([I])}

$S_{敌人}$ = {[事物]:[冲突]([I])∧!$_{Gs}$[相容]([I])}

$S_{敌人}$ = {[Thing]:[Conflict]([I])∧!Gs[Compatible]([I])}

$S_{敌寇}$ = {[人]:{[冲突]([I])∧!$_{Gs}$[相容]([I])}+{[行为]($_{Gs}$[侵略])}+{[方式]($_{Gs}$[武力])}+{[来源]($_{Gs}$[国外])}}

$S_{敌寇}$ = {[Person]:{[Conflict]([I])∧!Gs[Compatible]([I])}+{[Behavior](Gs[Invading])}+{[Way]($_{Gs}$[Military force])}+{[Source](Gs[Abroad])}}
$S_{外敌}$ = {[人]:{[冲突]([I])∧!$_{Gs}$[相容]([I])}+{[来源]([外部])}}
$S_{外敌}$ = {[Person]:{[Conflict]([I])∧!Gs[Compatible]([I])}+{[Source]([External])}}
$S_{外寇}$ = {[人]:{[冲突]([I])∧!$_{Gs}$[相容]([I])}+{[行为]($_{Gs}$[侵略])}+{[方式]($_{Gs}$[武力])}+{[来源]($_{Gs}$[国外])}}
$S_{外寇}$ = {[Person]:{[Conflict]([I])∧!Gs[Compatible]([I])}+{[Behavior](Gs[Invading])}+{[Way]($_{Gs}$[Military force])}}
$S_{穷寇}$ = {[人]:{[冲突]([I])∧!$_{Gs}$[相容]([I])}+{[方式]($_{Gs}$[武力])}+{[状态]($_{Gs}$[残败])}}
$S_{穷寇}$ = {[Person]:{[Conflict]([I])∧!Gs[Compatible]([I])}+{[Way]($_{Gs}$[Military force])}+{[State]($_{Gs}$[Defeated])}}
$S_{政敌}$ = {[人]:[冲突]([I])∧!$_{Gs}$[相容]([I])}+{[领域]([政治])}}
$S_{政敌}$ = {[Person]:[Conflict]([I])∧!$_{Gs}$[Compatible]([I])}+{[Field]([Politics])}}
$S_{情敌}$ = {[人]:[冲突]([I])∧!$_{Gs}$[相容]([I])}+{[方面]([爱情])}}
$S_{情敌}$ = {[Person]:[Conflict]([I])∧!$_{Gs}$[Compatible]([I])}+{[Aspect]([Love])}}
$S_{公敌}$ = {[人]:[冲突]([I])∧!$_{Gs}$[相容]([I])}+{[性质]([共同])}}
$S_{公敌}$ = {[Person]:[Conflict]([I])∧!$_{Gs}$[Compatible]([I])}+{[Nature]([Common])}}

The merging of the above sets yields a subset of semantic genes for interpersonal relationship nouns: {[guanxi关系(Relation)], [tong同(Common)], [danwei单位(Unit)], [hangye行业(Industry)], [jiu旧(Old)], [gongzuo工作(Working)], [shenghuo生活(Living)], [liaojie了解(Understanding)], [guanxin关心(Caring)], [baohan包含(Contain)], [ganqing dengji感情等级(Emotion grade)], [yuqi语气(Tone)], [qinni亲昵(Intimate)], [chongtu冲突(Conflict)], [laiyuan来源(Source)], [fangshi方式(Way)], [zhuangtai状态(State)], [fangmian方面(Aspect)], [zhengzhi政治(Politics)], [aiqing爱情(Love)]}. Additionally, gene clusters Gs[shisheng师生(Teacher-student relationship)], Gs[xiangrong相容(Compatible)], Gs[qinlue侵略(Invading)], Gs[wuli武力(Military force)], Gs[guowai国外(Abroad)], Gs[canbai残败(Defeated)]} are reserved for subsequent analysis.

5.2.2.7 Nouns Expressing Situational Conditions

① {bingren病人(patient), bingyuan病员(sick personnel), binghao病号(person on the sick list), shangyuan伤员(wounded personnel), shanghao伤号(the wounded), shangbing伤兵(wounded soldier)}

Dictionary definition:
Bingren病人: *An individual who is suffering from illness or is receiving treatment.*
Bingyuan病员: *Individuals who are ill within a collective unit.*
Binghao病号: *Patient (referring to a collective unit).*

Shangyuan伤员: *Injured individuals, commonly used in military contexts.*
Shanghao伤号: *An injured individual, commonly used in military contexts.*
Shangbing伤兵: *Soldiers injured in the war.*

Analysis: The semantic structure of this group of words is relatively simple, with the distinguishing feature being the state of health. This is described by a dimension gene [Health], with the feature function taking values [illness] and [Injury]. The term [Injury] involves the object of the injury (here, the object referred to by the described word), i.e., the patient. It can be represented as [Injury]([Patient]([i])).

$S_{病人}$ = {[人]:[健康]([病])}
$S_{病人}$ = {[Person]:[Health]([llness])}
$S_{病员}$ = {[人]:{[健康]([病])}+{[处所]([单位])}}
$S_{病员}$ = {[Person]:{[Health]([llness])}+{[Location]([Unit])}}
$S_{病号}$ = {[人]:{[健康]([病])}+{[处所]([单位])}}
$S_{病号}$ = {[Person]:{[Health]([llness])}+{[Location]([Unit])}}
$S_{伤员}$ = {[人]:{[健康]([伤]([受事]([i])))}+{[处所](Gs[军队])}}
$S_{伤员}$ = {[Person]:{[Health]([Injury]([Patient]([i])))}+{[Location](Gs[Army])}}
$S_{伤号}$ = {[人]:{[健康]([伤]([受事]([i])))}+{[处所](Gs[军队])}}
$S_{伤号}$ = {[Person]:{[Health]([Injury]([Patient]([i])))}+{[Location](Gs[Army])}}
$S_{伤兵}$ = {[人]:{[健康]([伤]([受事]([i])))}+{[身份](Gs[士兵])}+{[原因]([战争])}}
$S_{伤兵}$ = {[Person]:{[Health]([Injury]([Patient]([i])))}+{[Identity](Gs[Soldier])}+{[Cause]([War])}}

② {xiazi瞎子(blind person), mangren盲人(the blind), longzi聋子(deaf person), yaba哑巴(dumb person)}

Dictionary definition:
Xiazi瞎子: *A disrespectful name for the blind.*
Mangren盲人: *Individuals who have lost their vision.*
Longzi聋子: *A disrespectful name for individuals who have lost their hearing.*
Yaba哑巴: *Individuals who have lost the physiological ability to speak.*

Analysis: This group of words shares the common conceptual meaning of "a person who has lost some ability", and the knowledge domain framework can be represented as:

{[人]:[丧失]([主体]([i])∧[受事([能力]([x]))])}
{[Person]: [Lose]([Subject]([i])∧[Patient]([Ability]([x]))])}.

This framework describes two dimensions features, namely [Subject] and [Object], which are implicitly implied in the meaning of the words. Explicitly describing these features is conducive to semantic inference.

According to analysis above, the semantic gene structure of words in this group is described as:

$S_{\text{瞎子}}$ = {[人]:{[丧失]([主体]([i])∧[受事([能力]([看]))])}+{[语气](![尊重])}}
$S_{\text{瞎子}}$ = {[Person]:{[Losing]([Subject]([i])∧[Patient([Ability]([See]))])}+{[Tone](![Respectful])}}
$S_{\text{盲人}}$ = {[人]:[丧失]([主体]([i])∧[受事([能力]([看]))])}
$S_{\text{盲人}}$ = {[Person]:[Losing]([Subject]([i])∧[Patient([Ability]([See]))])}
$S_{\text{聋子}}$ = {[人]:{[丧失]([主体]([i])∧[受事([能力]([听]))])}+{[语气](![尊重])}}
$S_{\text{聋子}}$ = {[Person]:{[Losing]([Subject]([i])∧[Patient([Ability]([Hear]))])}+{[Tone](![Respectful])}}
$S_{\text{哑巴}}$ = {[人]:{[丧失]([主体]([i])∧[受事([能力]([说]))])}+{[语气](![尊重])}}
$S_{\text{哑巴}}$ = {[Person]:{[Losing]([Subject]([i])∧[Patient([Ability]([Speak]))])}+{[Tone](![Respectful])}}

③ {guafu寡妇(widow), yishuang遗孀(relict), guanfu鳏夫(widower), gu'er孤儿(orphan)}

Dictionary definition:
Guafu寡妇: *A woman who has lost her husband.*
Yishuang遗孀: *A woman who is living in widowhood after the death of her husband, used for back-appellation.*
Guanfu鳏夫: *An adult male who is either unmarried or has lost his wife.*
Gu'er孤儿: ❶*Children who have lost their fathers.* ❷*Children who have lost both parents.*

Analysis: This group of words constitutes a special appellation for individuals who have experienced the death of their immediate relatives, carrying with it additional social meanings regarding the survival circumstances of the referent. The knowledge domain framework can be represented as:

{[人]:{[境况]([状态]([死亡]([x]of[i])))}+{[性别]([y])}+{[年龄]([z])}}
{[Person]: {[Situation]([State]([Death]([x]of[i])))}+{[Gender]([y])}+{[Age]([z])}}

Here the variable of the [Death] feature function takes the value of the composite gene [x]of [i], with [x] representing the deceased relative and the reflexive gene [i] indicating the referent themselves. Based on this domain framework, the semantic gene structure of words in this group can be described as:

$S_{\text{寡妇}}$ = {[人]:{[境况]([状态]([死亡]([配偶]of[i])))}+{[性别]([女])}+{[年龄]([成年])}}
$S_{\text{寡妇}}$ = {[Person]:{[Situation]([State]([Death]([Spouse]of[i])))}+{[Gender]([Female])}+{[Age]([Adult])}}
$S_{\text{遗孀}}$ = {[人]:{[境况]([状态]([死亡]([配偶]of[i])))}+{[性别]([女])}+{[年龄]([成年])}+{[语用]([背称])}+{[语体]([书])}+{[语气]([庄重])}}
$S_{\text{遗孀}}$ = {[Person]:{[Situation]([State]([Death]([Spouse]of[i])))}+{[Gender]([Female])}+{[Age]([Adult])}+{[Pragmatic]([Back-appellation])}+{[Style]([Written])}+{[Tone]([Solemn])}}

$S_{鳏夫}$ = {[人]:{[境况]([状态]([[死亡]∨[φ]]([配偶]of[i])))}+{[性别]([男])}+{[年龄]([成年])}}[6]
$S_{鳏夫}$ {[Person]:{[Situation]([State]([[Death]∨[φ]]([Spouse]of[i])))}+{[Gender]([Male])}+{[Age]([Adult])}}[7]
$S_{孤儿}$ = {[人]:{[境况]([状态]([死亡]([[父]∨[[父]∧[母]]of[i])))}+{[年龄](![成年])}}
$S_{孤儿}$ = {[Person]:{[Situation]([State]([Death]([[Father]∨[[Father]∧[Mother]]of[i])))}+{[Age](![Adult])}}

④ {fuweng富翁(rich man), fuhao富豪(magnate), kuolao阔佬(jet-set)

Dictionary definition:
Fuweng富翁: *Individuals who possess a large amount of private wealth.*
Fuhao富豪: *Individuals who possess both wealth and power.*
Kuolao阔佬: *Individuals who possess both wealth and power.*
Analysis: The core conceptual meaning of this group is "a person who is very wealthy or powerful", with the knowledge domain framework being "a person who possesses…", which can be represented as:

{[人]:[拥有]([主体]([i])∧[客体](x))}
{[Person]: [Possessing]([Subject]([i]) ∧[Object](x))}.

The semantic gene structures of this group of words can be described within this framework as follows:

$S_{富翁}$ = {[人]:[拥有]([主体]([i])∧[客体]([财产]:{[数量]([多])}))}
$S_{富翁}$ = {[Person]:[Possessing]([Subject]([i])∧[Object]([Property]:{[Quantity]([Large])}))}
$S_{富豪}$ = {[人]:[拥有]([主体]([i])∧[客体]([财产]∧[权势]))}
$S_{富豪}$ = {[Person]:[Possessing]([Subject]([i])∧[Object]([Property]∧[Power]))}
$S_{阔佬}$ = {[人]:[拥有]([主体]([i])∧[客体]([财产]∧[权势]))+{[语体]([口])}}
$S_{阔佬}$ = {[Person]:[Possessing]([Subject]([i])∧[Object]([Property]∧[Power]))+{[Style]([Spoken])}}

The partial semantic gene set for situational nouns is obtained by merging the above groups, which includes:{[jiankang健康(Health)], [chusuo处所(Location)], [jingkuang境况(Situation)], [yuyong语用(Pragmatic)], [shuliang数量(Quantity)], [yuanyin原因(Cause)], [bing病(Illness)], [shang伤(Injury)], [siwang死亡(Death)], [zhanzheng战争(War)], [sangshi丧失(Losing)], [nengli能力(Ability)], [kan看(See)], [zunzhong尊重(Respect)], [ting听(Hear)], [shuo说(Speak)], [beicheng背称(Back-appellation)], [zhuangzhong庄重(Solemn)], [caichan财产(Property)], [duo多(Large)], [quanshi权势(Power)]}, as well as the gene clusters Gs[jundui

6 "鳏夫"不仅指死了妻子的男人，也指年纪大而没有结婚的男人。 "无妻"的状态用虚值基因[φ]表示。

7 The term "widower" encompasses not only men who have lost their wives but also those who are of advanced age and have never marriedThe state of being "unmarried" is represented by the modal gene [φ].

军队(Army)] and Gs[shibing士兵(Soldier)] which are reserved for subsequent analysis.

5.2.2.8 Respect and Humble Appellation

① {lingzun令尊(your beloved father), lingtang令堂(your beloved mother), linglang令郎(your son), ling'ai令爱(your beloved daughter), ling'ai令媛(your beloved daughter), lingxiong令兄(your elder brother), lingdi令弟(your younger brother)}

Dictionary definition:
Lingzun令尊: *A respectful address for the addressee's father.*
Lingtang令堂: *A respectful address for the addressee's mother.*
Linglang令郎: *A respectful address for the addressee's son.*
ling'ai令爱*: A respectful address for the addressee's daughter. It can also be referred to as "ling ai 令媛".*
Lingxiong令兄: *A respectful address for the addressee's to elder brother.*
Lingdi令弟: *A respectful address for the addressee's younger brother.*

Analysis: The respectful, humble, contemptuous, harsh, and euphemistic appellatives can be described by a feature gene [yuqi语气(Tone)]. The set of value genes is {[jing敬(Respectful)], [zun尊(Honorific)], [qian谦(Humble)], [bi鄙(Contemptuous)], [e恶(Harsh)], [ni昵(Intimate)], [xi戏(Playful)], [wan婉(Euphemistic)] …}.

$S_{令尊}$ = {[人]:{[称谓]($_{Gs}$[父亲]of[对方])}+{[语气]([尊])}}
$S_{令尊}$ = {[Person]:{[Address](Gs[Father] of $_{Gs}$[Addressee])}+{[Tone]([Honorific])}}
$S_{令堂}$ = {[人]:{[称谓]($_{Gs}$[母亲]of[对方])}+{[语气]([尊])}}
$S_{令堂}$ = {[Person]:{[Address](Gs[Mother] of $_{Gs}$[Addressee])}+{[Tone]([Honorific])}}
$S_{令郎}$ = {[人]:{[称谓]($_{Gs}$[儿子]of[对方])}+{[语气]([尊])}}
$S_{令郎}$ = {[Person]:{[Address](Gs[Son] of $_{Gs}$[Addressee])}+{[Tone]([Honorific])}}
$S_{令爱}$ = $S_{令媛}$ = {[人]:{[称谓]($_{Gs}$[女儿]of[对方])}+{[语气]([尊])}}
$S_{令爱}$ = $S_{令媛}$ = {[Person]:{[Address]($_{Gs}$[Daughter] of $_{Gs}$[Addressee])}+{[Tone]([Honorific])}}
$S_{令兄}$ = {[人]:{[称谓]($_{Gs}$[兄]of[对方])}+{[语气]([尊])}}
$S_{令兄}$ = {[Person]:{[Address]($_{Gs}$[Elder brother] of $_{Gs}$[Addressee])}+{[Tone]([Honorific])}}
$S_{令弟}$ = {[人]:{[称谓]($_{Gs}$[弟]of[对方])}+{[语气]([尊])}}
$S_{令弟}$ = {[Person]:{[Address]($_{Gs}$[Younger brother] of $_{Gs}$[Addressee])}+{[Tone]([Honorific])}}

② {zunjia尊驾(your excellency), zunfuren尊夫人(your wife), zunshi尊师(your honored teacher)}

Dictionary definition:
Zunjia尊驾: *A respectful address to the addressee.*
Zunfuren尊夫人: *A respectful address for the addressee's wife.*
Zunshi尊师: *A respectful address for the addressee's teacher or master.*

$S_{\text{尊驾}}$ = {[人]:{[称谓]([对方])}+{[语气]([敬])}}
$S_{\text{尊驾}}$ = {[Person]:{[Address]($_{Gs}$[Addressee])}+{[Tone]([Respectful])}}
$S_{\text{尊夫人}}$ = {[人]:{[称谓]($_{Gs}$[妻子]of[对方])}+{[语气]([敬])}}
$S_{\text{尊夫人}}$ = {[Person]:{[Address]($_{Gs}$[Wife] of $_{Gs}$[Addressee])}+
{[Tone]([Respectful])}}
$S_{\text{尊师}}$ = {[人]:{[称谓]($_{Gs}$[老师]of[对方])}+{[语气]([敬])}}
$S_{\text{尊师}}$ = {[Person]:{[Address]($_{Gs}$[Teacher] of $_{Gs}$[Addressee])}+
{[Tone]([Respectful])}}

③ {jiafu家父(my father), jiayan家严(my father), jiamu家母(my mother), jiaci家慈(my mother)}

Dictionary definition:
Jiafu家父: *One's own father, a self-humbling expression.*
Jiayan家严: < *written* > *One's own father, a self-humbling expression.*
Jiamu家母: *One's own mother, a self-humbling expression.*
Jiaci家慈: < *written* > *One's own mother, a self-humbling expression.*

$S_{\text{家父}}$ = {[人]:{[称谓]($_{Gs}$[父亲]of$_{Gs}$[自己])}+{[语气]([谦])}}
$S_{\text{家父}}$ = {[Person]:{[Address]($_{Gs}$[Father] of $_{Gs}$[Own])}+{[Tone]([Humble])}}
$S_{\text{家严}}$ = {[人]:{[称谓]($_{Gs}$[父亲]of$_{Gs}$[自己])}+{[语气]([谦])}+{[语体]([书])}}
$S_{\text{家严}}$ = {[Person]:{[Address]($_{Gs}$[Father] of $_{Gs}$[Own])}+{[Tone]([Humble])}+
{[Style]([Written])}}
$S_{\text{家母}}$ = {[人]:{[称谓]($_{Gs}$[母亲]of$_{Gs}$[自己])}+{[语气]([谦])}}
$S_{\text{家母}}$ = {[Person]:{[Address]($_{Gs}$[Mother] of $_{Gs}$[Own])}+{[Tone]([Humble])}}
$S_{\text{家慈}}$ = {[人]:{[称谓]($_{Gs}$[母亲]of$_{Gs}$[自己])}+{[语气]([谦])}+{[语体]([书])}}
$S_{\text{家慈}}$ = {[Person]:{[Address]($_{Gs}$[Mother] of [Own])}+{[Tone]([Humble])}+
{[Style]([Written])}}

④ {biren鄙人(my humble self), zhuojing拙荆(my humble wife)}

Dictionary definition:
Biren鄙人: *A self-humbling expression, an old-fashioned address used for self-reference.*
Zhuojing拙荆: *A self-humbling expression in the old times, used to refer to one's own wife.*

$S_{\text{鄙人}}$ = {[人]:{[称谓]([i])}+{[语气]([谦])}}
$S_{\text{鄙人}}$ = {[Person]:{[Address]([i])}+{[Tone]([Humble])}}

$S_{拙荆}$ = {[人]:{[称谓](Gs[妻子]of[i])}+{[语气]([谦])}}
$S_{拙荆}$ = {[Person]:{[Address](Gs[Wife] of [i])}+{[Tone]([Humble])}}

The semantic gene set of respect and humble appellation primarily consists of the values of the feature functions of the tone dimension, represented by the genes {[jing敬(Respectful)], [zun尊(Honorific)], [qian谦(Humble)], [bi鄙(Contemptuous)], [e恶(Harsh)], [ni昵(Intimate)], [xi戏(Playful)], [wan婉(Euphemistic)] …}, among which the other gene clusters mentioned in the analysis above have been discussed.

5.2.3 *Semantic Analysis and Semantic Gene Extraction of Nouns Referring to Objects*

5.2.3.1 Nouns Referring Natural Objects

① {ludi陆地(land), haiyang海洋(ocean), he河(river), shan山(mountain)}

Dictionary definition:
Ludi陆地: *To the portion of the Earth's surface that is not covered by the oceans.*
Lu陆: *Land.*
Haiyang海洋: *The vast, saline bodies of water covering the Earth's surface, encompassing both seas and oceans.*
Yang洋: *The vast expanse of water on the Earth's surface that is larger than the sea.*
Hai海: *Oceanic region adjacent to the landmass.*
He河: *A natural or artificial large watercourse.*
Shan山: *The massive and towering portion formed on the ground by soil and rocks.*

Analysis: Geographical and geomorphological features are typical components of the natural world. Since the birth of humanity, the most frequent and direct contact with nature has been with elements such as rivers, seas, mountains, and streams. Therefore, in human language, there is a vast number of words expressing this part of things, with complex meanings, and the meanings of words are intertwined with each other, with subtle and nuanced differences between them of words in many cases. From a comprehensive examination of the definitions in multiple authoritative Chinese dictionaries, it is noted that some elemental words such as "lu陆(land)", "hai海(sea)", "he河(river)" and "shan山(mountain)" require initial description before being used as gene clusters to further describe other words.

For the description of natural geographical entities, we first predefine several core semantic genes: {[tu土(Soil)], [shi石(Stone)], [shui水(Water)], [shuiyu水域(Waters)], [lu路(Road)], [diqiu地球(Earth)], [diwu地物(Surface feature)]}. These are fundamental cognitive concepts that do not require or cannot be further analyzed at the linguistic level, as these genes involve a multitude of encyclopedic knowledge.

The more they are analyzed, the more complex they become, and this complexity does not aid in semantic understanding.

From the dictionary definitions of this group of words, several problems arise: (1) The definitions of "haiyang海洋" and "ludi陆地" encompass aspects such as area size, the proportion of area to the total surface area of the earth, regional divisions and naming, which are part of encyclopedic knowledge. In the description of word meaning, we omit this part of content, which does not affect the understanding of word meaning; (2) "hai海" refers to the area where the "yang洋" is adjacent to the continent and is a component of the "yang洋". Logically speaking, the two are not parallel relations. The explanation of "haiyang海洋" includes "a general term for both hai海 and yang洋", which is analogous to saying "a general term for table legs and tables". There is a flaw in the semantic logic. In practical usage, the preference for "haiyang海洋" over "hai海" or "yang洋" in certain contexts is not driven by semantic requirements but is constrained by prosodic and pragmatic factors. Therefore, in the description, "haiyang海洋 and "yang洋" are treated as synonyms.

$S_{洋} = S_{海洋}$ = {[地物]:{[水域]:{[构成]([i]of[[表面]of[地球]])}+{[范围]([广大])}}

$S_{洋} = S_{海洋}$ = {[Surface feature]:{[Waters]:{[Composition]([i] of [[Surface] of [Earth]])}+{[Scope]([Broad])}}

$S_{陆} = S_{陆地}$ = {[地物]:{[水域]:{[构成]([i]of[[表面]of[地球]])}+{[范围](![水域])}}

$S_{海}$ = {[地物]:{[水域]:{[构成]([i]of $_{Gs}$[洋])}+{[位置]([i]↑ $_{Gs}$[洋]([邻接]))}}

$S_{海}$ = {[Surface feature]:{[Waters]:{[Composition]([i] of $_{Gs}$[yang洋])}+{[Location]([i] ↑ $_{Gs}$[yang洋]([Adjacent]))}}

$S_{河}$ = {[地物]:{[水域]:{[构成]([i]of [路])}+{[状态]([流动])}+{[规模]([大])}+{[成因]([天然]∨[人工])}}

$S_{河}$ = {[Surface feature]:{[Waters]:{[Composition]([i] of [Road])}+{[State]([Flowing])}+{[Scale]([Large])}+{[Cause]([Natural]∨[Artificial])}}

$S_{山}$ = {[地物]:{[构成]([土]∧[石])}+{[处所]([[表面]of[地球]]}+{[外貌]([高]∧[大])}}

$S_{山}$ = {[Surface feature]:{[Composition]([Soil] ∧ Stone])}+{[Location]([[Surface] of [Earth]]}+{[Appearance]([High]∧Massive])}}

② {jiang江(river), heliu河流(river), chuan川(stream), hechuan河川(river), xi溪(brook)}.

Dictionary definition:

Jiang江: *The great river.*

Heliu河流: *A collective term for extensive natural watercourses on the Earth's surface, such as rivers and streams.*

Chuan川: *Rivers.*

Hechuan河川: *A general term encompassing all sizes of rivers and streams.*

Xi溪: *Originally referred to a small brook in the mountains, now it is used more broadly to denote any small brook.*

The core conceptual meanings of this group is "river", with various additional meanings. The analysis of the semantic genes of the word "river" has already been conducted above, so we can continue to analyze the others by using the gene cluster $_{Gs}$[he河(River)]:

$S_{江}$ = {[地物]:{$_{Gs}$[河]:{[规模]([大])}}
$S_{江}$ = {[Surface feature]:{Gs[River]:{[Scale]([Large])}}
$S_{河流}$ = {[地物]:{$_{Gs}$[河]:{[规模]([大])}+{[语用]([统称])}}
$S_{河流}$ = {[Surface feature]:{Gs[River]:{[Scale]([Large])}+
{[Pragmatic]([General term])}}
$S_{川}$ = {[地物]:{$_{Gs}$[河]:{[语体]([书])}}
$S_{川}$ = {[Surface feature]:{Gs[River]:{[Style]([Written])}}
$S_{河川}$ = {[地物]:{$_{Gs}$[河]:{[语用]([统称])}+{[语体]([书])}}
$S_{河川}$ = {[Surface feature]:{Gs[River]:{[Pragmatic]([General term])}+
{[Style]([Written])}}
$S_{溪}$ = {[地物]:{$_{Gs}$[河]:{[规模]([小])}}
$S_{溪}$ = {[Surface feature]:{Gs[River]:{[Large]([Small])}}

③ {niao鸟(bird), qin禽(fowl), shou兽(beasts), chong虫(bug), kunchong昆虫(insect), yu鱼(fish)}

Dictionary definition:

Niao鸟: *A class of vertebrates, characterized by a constant body temperature, oviparity, absence of teeth in the beak, feathers covering the entire body, a keel prominence on the chest, wings formed from the forelimbs, and walking ability in the hindlimbs. Most birds can fly, and some have degenerated wings and are unable to fly. Sparrows, swallows, eagles, chickens, ducks, and ostriches are all examples of birds.*

Qin禽: *Birds.*

Shou兽: *A general term for mammals. It typically refers to those with four legs and covered in fur.*

Chong虫: *Insect.*

Kunchong昆虫: *A class of arthropods, with their bodies divided into three parts: head, thorax, and abdomen. The head is equipped with antennae, eyes, and mouth-parts; the thorax has three pairs of legs and two or one pair of wings, with some lacking wings; the abdomen is segmented, with stigmata on both sides, serving as the respiratory organs. Most insects undergo developmental stages including egg, larva, pupa, and adult. Beneficial insects to humans include parasitic wasps and bees, whereas harmful insects include disease-carrying mosquitoes, flies, fleas, and crop-destroying locusts and aphids.*

Yu鱼: *Vertebrates living in water, whose body temperature varies with the external temperature. Generally, their bodies are laterally flattened, covered with scales and fins, and breathe through gills. The species of fish are extremely numerous, most of which are edible or can be used to produce fish glue.*

Analysis: Similar to the first group, the words in this group also serve as the foundation for describing other animal-related terms.

The semantic descriptions of terms referring to animals and plants are also quite complex, primarily facing the challenge of selecting the appropriate encyclopedic knowledge. The definitions of such terms in dictionaries typically encompass a considerable amount of specialized biological knowledge, indicating certain biological characteristics of the animals or plants they refer to, such as the biological feature of “birds” being “constant body temperature” and the biological feature of “fish” being “body temperature varying with the external temperature”. These knowledge have little impact on the ordinary people’s cognition of related concepts and understanding of word meanings. Most people are not aware of this knowledge, yet it does not hinder their comprehension of the meanings of these terms. Therefore, in the semantic description, we make the selection and discarding according to the actual circumstances, only choose representative features that can assist both humans and machines in understanding the meanings and distinguishing concepts. We employ a basic domain framework to describe the meanings of terms representing animals:

{[动物]:{[类]([a])}+{[结构]([b])}+{[颜色]([c])}+{[能力]([d])}+{[习性]([e])}}
{[Animal]:{[Category]([a])}+{[Structure]([b])}+{[Color]([c])}+{[Ability]([d])}+{[Habit]([e])}}

Here, the [lei类(Category)] function variable [a] takes the value of the biological classification name; the [jiegou结构(Structure)] function [b] generally has a composite value, including multiple groups of other feature functions, describing the typical body structure characteristics of the referent object; [yanse颜色(Color)] generally appears only when describing specific species with a typical and identifiable body color, such as “crows” and “flamingos”; the [nengli能力(Ability)] function describes the typical abilities of animals, such as “fish” being able to “swim” and “cats” being able to “catch mice”; the [xixing习性(Habit)] function describes the dietary habits, habitats, and other living habits of animals. In summary, except for the [Category] function, all other feature dimension functions only select representative content.

Based on the above understanding or convention, the semantic gene structures of words in this group can be described as follows:

$S_{\text{鸟}}$ = {[动物]:{[类](Gs[脊椎动物])}+{[结构](Gs[羽毛]∧[Gs[翅膀]([数量]([2]))]∧[Gs[牙齿]([φ])]}+{[能力](Gs[飞]([主体]([多数]of[i])))}}
$S_{\text{鸟}}$ = {[Animal]:{[Category](Gs[Vertebrate])}+{[Structure](Gs[feather]∧[Gs[Wing]([Quantity]([2]))] ∧[Gs[Tooth]([φ])]}+{[Ability](Gs[Fly]([Subject]([Most] of [i])))}}
$S_{\text{禽}}$ = {[动物]:{[类](Gs[脊椎动物])}+{[结构]([羽毛]∧[Gs[翅膀]([数量]([2]))]∧[[牙齿]([φ])]}+{[能力](Gs[飞]([主体]([多数]of[i])))}+{[语用]([统称])}}

$S_{\text{禽}}$ = {[Animal]:{[Category](Gs[Vertebrate])}+{[Structure](Gs[feather]∧[Gs[Wing]([Quantity]([2]))] ∧[Gs[Tooth]([φ])]}+{[Ability](Gs[Fly]([Subject]([Most] of [i])))}+{[Pragmatic]([General])}}

$S_{\text{兽}}$ = {[动物]:{[类](Gs[哺乳动物])}+{[结构]([Gs[腿]([数量]([4]))]∧ [[毛]([部位](Gs[全身]))]}+{[语用]([统称])}}

$S_{\text{兽}}$ = {[Animal]:{[Category](Gs[Mammal])}+{[Structure]([Gs[Leg]([Quantity]([4]))]∧ [[Fur]([Part](Gs[Whole body]))]}+{[Pragmatic]([General])}}

$S_{\text{昆虫}}$ = {[动物]:{[类](Gs[节肢动物])}+{[结构]({[头]:[结构](Gs[触角]∧Gs[眼睛]∧Gs[口])}∧{Gs[胸]:[结构]([Gs[足]([数量]([6]))]∧[Gs[翅膀]([数量]([4]∨[2]∨[0]))]}∧{Gs[腹]:[结构](Gs[节]∧[Gs[气孔]([功能](Gs[呼吸]))]}}}

$S_{\text{昆虫}}$ = {[Animal]:{[Category](Gs[Arthropod])}+{[Structure]({[Head]:[Structure](Gs[Antennae]∧Gs[Eye]∧Gs[Mouth])}∧{Gs[Thorax]:[Structure]([Gs[Foot]([Quantity]([6]))]∧[Gs[Wing]([Quantity]([4]∨[2]∨[0]))]}∧{Gs[Abdomen]:[Structure](Gs[Segment]∧[Gs[Spiracle]([Function](Gs[Breath]))]}}}

$S_{\text{鱼}}$ = {[动物]:{[类](Gs[脊椎动物])}+{[结构](Gs[鳞]∧Gs[鳍]∧[Gs[鳃]([功能](Gs[呼吸]))]}+{[能力](Gs[游泳]}}

$S_{\text{鱼}}$ = {[Animal]:{[Category](Gs[Vertebrate])}+{[Structure](Gs[Scale]∧Gs[Fins]∧Gs[Gill]([Function](Gs[Breath]))]}+{[Ability](Gs[Swim]}}

④ {shengchu牲畜(livestock), jiachu家畜(domestic animals), jiaqin家禽(poultry)}

Shengchu牲畜: *Domestic animal.*
Jiachu家畜: *Beasts domesticated by humans for economic or other purposes.*
Jiaqin家禽: *Birds domesticated by humans for economic or other purposes.*
Analysis: We can directly use the "beast" and "bird" analyzed in the previous group as gene clusters, and add other dimension feature functions to make the description.

$S_{\text{牲畜}}$ = $S_{\text{家畜}}$ = {[动物]:{[类](Gs[兽])}+{Gs[驯养]([施事]([人])∧[施事]([i]))}+{[用途]([经济]∨[u])}}

$S_{\text{牲畜}}$ = $S_{\text{家畜}}$ = {[Animal]:{[Category](Gs[Beast])}+{Gs[Domesticating]([Agent]([Human])∧[Patient]([i]))}+{[Purpose]([Economy]∨[u])}}

$S_{\text{家禽}}$ = {[动物]:{[类](Gs[禽])}+{Gs[驯养]([施事]([人])∧[施事]([i]))}+{[用途]([经济]∨[u])}}

$S_{\text{家禽}}$ = {[Animal]:{[Category](Gs[Poultry])}+{Gs[Domesticating]([Human]([Human])∧[Agent]([i]))}+{[Purpose]([Economy]∨[u])}}

⑤ {shu树(tree), shumu树木(trees), shucong树丛(grove), shulin树林(woods), conglin丛林(jungle), senlin森林(forest), linhai林海(immense forest)}

Shu树: *Common name for woody plants.*
Shumu树木: *Collective name for trees.*
Shucong树丛: *A thicket of trees.*
Shulin树林: *Many trees grow in patches, the area is smaller than the forest.*
Conglin丛林: *A dense, thickly wooded area.*
Senlin森林: *Generally refers to a large area covered with trees; in the context of forestry, it denotes a vast expanse of land where numerous trees grow, along with the animals and other plants that constitute the whole on this land.*
Linhai林海: *Metaphorically describes an endless forest that stretches out like an ocean.*

Analysis: The domain frameworks of nouns denoting plants and those denoting animals are similar, so the analysis is not delved into further here. This group of words primarily refers to different growth forms of "trees".The semantic gene structures of words in this group can be described as follows:

$S_{\text{树}}$ = {[植物]:{[类]($_{Gs}$[木本])}+{[语用]([通称])}}
$S_{\text{树}}$ = {[Plant]:{[Category]($_{Gs}$[Woody])}+{[Pragmatic]([General])}}
$S_{\text{树木}}$ = {[植物]:{[类]($_{Gs}$[木本])}+{[语用]([总称])}}
$S_{\text{树木}}$ = {[Plant]:{[Category]($_{Gs}$[Woody])}+{[Pragmatic]([Collective])}}
$S_{\text{树丛}}$ = {[植物]:{[类]($_{Gs}$[木本])}+{[形态]([密集])}}
$S_{\text{树丛}}$ = {[Plant]:{[Category]($_{Gs}$[Woody])}+{[Form]([Dense])}}
$S_{\text{树林}}$ = {[植物]:{[类]($_{Gs}$[木本])}+{[形态]([成片])}}
$S_{\text{树林}}$ = {[Plant]:{[Category]($_{Gs}$[Woody])}+{[Form]([Extensive])}{[Compare]([i]↑$_{Gs}$[Forest]([Smaller]))}}
$S_{\text{丛林}}$ = {[植物]:{[类]($_{Gs}$[木本])}+{[形态]([成片]∧[密集])}}
$S_{\text{丛林}}$ = {[Plant]:{[Category]($_{Gs}$[Woody])}+{[Form]([Dense]∧[Extensive])}}
$S_{\text{森林}}$ = {[植物]:{[类]($_{Gs}$[木本])}+{[形态]([成片])+{[范围]([广阔])}}
$S_{\text{森林}}$ = {[Plant]:{[Category]($_{Gs}$[Woody])}+{[Form]([Extensive])+{[Scale]([Vast])}}
$S_{\text{林海}}$ = {[植物]:{[类]($_{Gs}$[木本])}+{[形态]([成片])+{[范围]([广阔])}+{[比较]([i]↑$_{Gs}$[海]([相似]))}+{[修辞]([比喻])}}
$S_{\text{林海}}$ = {[Plant]:{[Category]($_{Gs}$[Woody])}+{[Form]([Extensive])+{[Scale]([Vast])}+{[Compare]([i]↑$_{Gs}$[Sea]([Similar]))}+{[Rhetoric]([Analogy])}}

⑥ {zhuangjia庄稼(crop), zuowu作物(crop), nongzuowu农作物(crop)}

Zhuangjia庄稼: *Crops grown on the fields, predominantly referring to food crops.*
Zuowu作物: *Abbreviation for agricultural crops.*
Nongzuowu农作物: *In agriculture, various plants cultivated, including food crops, oil crops, vegetables, fruit trees, as well as cotton and tobacco used as industrial raw materials. These plants are collectively referred to as crops.*

$S_{\text{农作物}}$ = $S_{\text{作物}}$ = {[植物]:{[类]([u])}+{[种植]([施事]([人])∧[施事]([i]))}+{[领域]([农业])}}
$S_{\text{农作物}}$ = $S_{\text{作物}}$ = {[Plant]:{[Category]([u])}+{[Planting]([Agent]([Human])∧[Agent]([i]))}+{[Field]([Agriculture])}}

$S_{庄稼}$ = {[植物]:{[类]([u])}+{[种植]([施事]([人])∧[施事]([i]))}+{[领域]([农业])}+{[状态]([生长])}+{[粮食]:[组成]([多数]of[i])}}
$S_{庄稼}$ = {[Plant]:{[Category]([u])}+{[Planting]([Agent]([Human])∧[Agent]([i]))}+{[Field]([Agriculture])}+{[State]([Growing])}+{[Grain]:[Composition]([Most]of[i])}}

Merging the above groups, we obtain part of the semantic set for nouns representing natural objects: {[tu土(Soil)], [shi石(Stone)], [shui水(Water)], [shuiyu水域(Waters)], [lu路(Road)], [diqiu地球(Earth)], [diwu地物(Surface Feature)], [liudong流动(Flowing)], [guimo规模(Scale)], [chengyin成因(Cause)], [tianran天然(Natural)], [rengong 人工(Artificial)], [goucheng构成(Composition)], [weizhi位置(Location)], [linjie邻接(Adjacent)], [waimao外貌(Appearance)], [tongcheng统称(General term)], [lei类(Category)], [yanse颜色(Color)], [nengli能力(Ability)], [xixing习性(Habit)], [shuliang数量(Quantity)], [duoshu多数(Most)], [buwei部位(Part)], [yongtu用途(Purpose)], [jingji经济(Economy)], [dongwu动物(Animal)], [zhiwu植物(Plant)], [xingtai形态(Form)], [miji密集(Dense)], [chengpian成片(Extensive)], [guangkuo广阔(Vast)], [bijiao比较(Compare)], [xiangsi相似(Similar)], [xiuci修辞(Rhetoric)], [biyu比喻(Analogy)], [zhongzhi种植(Planting)], [nongye农业(Agriculture)], [zhuangtai状态(State)], [shengzhang生长(Growing)], [liangshi粮食(Grain)]}, as well as the gene clusters Gs[jizhui dongwu脊椎动物(Vertebrate)], Gs[buru dongwu哺乳动物(Mammal)], Gs[jiezhi dongwu节肢动物(Arthropod)], Gs[yumao羽毛(Feather)], Gs[chibang翅膀(Wing)], Gs[yachi牙齿(Tooth)], Gs[fei飞(Fly)], Gs[tui腿(Leg)], Gs[quanshen全身(Whole body)], Gs[chujiao触角(Antennae)], Gs[yanjing眼睛(Eye)], Gs[kou口(Mouth)], Gs[xiong胸(Thorax)], Gs[zu足(Leg)], Gs[fu腹(Abdomen)], Gs[jie节(Segment)], Gs[qikong气孔(Spiracle)], Gs[huxi呼吸(Breath)], Gs[lin鳞(Scale)], Gs[qi鳍(Fins)], Gs[sha鳃(Gill)], Gs[youyong游泳(Swim)], Gs[xunyang驯养(Domesticating)], Gs[muben木本(Woody)] It can be observed that in the analysis of nouns denoting natural objects, a large number of gene clusters are remained, primarily due to the extensive use of nouns denoting body parts when describing animal names. These will be left for subsequent analysis.

5.2.3.2 Nouns Referring to Artificial objects

① {qiju器具(utensil), gongju工具(tool), yongju用具(implement), qixie器械(instrument), jixie机械(machinery), jiqi机器(machine), zhuangzhi装置(device)}

Qiju器具: *A general term for utensils or tools.*
Gongju工具: *Implements used in productive labor.*
Yongju用具: *Tools for daily use.*
Qixie器械: *Tools with specific functions or those with more intricate constructions.*
Jixie机械: *Devices constructed based on the principles of mechanics.*

Jiqi机器: *Devices that perform mechanical movements to transform or transmit energy, materials, and information.*

Zhuangzhi装置: *Objects with relatively complex structures and certain independent functions, found in machines, instruments, or other equipment.*

Analysis: Tools represent a typical category of artificial objects. The core framework of the semantic domain of this category can be expressed as:

{[人造物]:{[结构]([a])}+{[材料]([b])}+{[形状]([c])}+{[功能]([b])}
{[Artificial objects]:{[Structure]([a])}+{[Material]([b])}+{[Shape]([c])}+{[Function]([d])}

The analysis of dictionary definitions reveals that the three most fundamental core terms "qiju器具", "gongju工具", and "yongju用具" essentially exhibit circular interpretations. This indicates that these terms are difficult to explain independently of each other, suggesting that their meanings are not easily divisible. However, by utilizing the aforementioned domain framework, we can initially provide an independent description of the term with the broadest meaning, which is "qiju器具".

$S_{器具}$ = {[人造物]:{[结构]([u])}+{[材料]([u])}+{[形状]([u])}+{[功能]([u])}}
$S_{器具}$ = {[Artificial object]:{[Structure]([u])}+{[Material]([u])}+{[Shape]([u])}+{[Function]([u])}}

All feature functions are assigned universal values, which can be naturally expressed as "artificial objects made of certain materials, possessing certain structures, shapes, and functions". The term "yongju用具" can be reinterpreted as "daily-used utensils", while "tool" can be reinterpreted as "utensils used for productive labor". By adding the of dimension feature function [Place] to the semantic gene structure of the term "qiju器具", the circular interpretation is avoided.

$S_{用具}$ = {[人造物]:{[结构]([u])}+{[材料]([u])}+{[形状]([u])}+{[功能]([u])}+{[场所]([日常])}}
$S_{用具}${[Artificial object]:{[Structure]([u])}+{[Material]([u])}+{[Shape]([u])}+{[Function]([u])}+{[Place]([Daily])}}
$S_{工具}$ = {[人造物]:{[结构]([u])}+{[材料]([u])}+{[形状]([u])}+{[功能]([u])}+{[场所]([劳动]∨[生产])}}
$S_{工具}${[Artificial object]:{[Structure]([u])}+{[Material]([u])}+{[Shape]([u])}+{[Function]([u])}+{[Place]([Labor]∨[Procuce])}}
$S_{器具}$ = {[人造物]:{[结构]([精密])}+{[材料]([u])}+{[形状]([u])}+{[功能]([专用])}}
$S_{器具}$ = {[Artificial object]:{[Structure]([Precise])}+{[Material]([u])}+{[Shape]([u])}+{[Function]([Spesific])}}
$S_{装置}$ = {[人造物]:{[部件]([i]of $_{Gs}$[设备])}+{[结构]([复杂])}+{[功能]([u])}+{[方式]([独立])}}
$S_{装置}$ = {[Artificial object]:{[Component]([i]of $_{Gs}$[Equipment])}+{[Structure]([Complex])}+{[Function]([u])}+{[Way]([Independent])}}

$S_{\text{机械}}$ = {$_{Gs}$[装置]:{[原理]($_{Gs}$[力学])}}
$S_{\text{机械}}$ = {$_{Gs}$[Device]:{[Principle](Gs[Mechanics])}}
$S_{\text{机器}}$ = {$_{Gs}$[装置]:{[功能]([[转换]∨[传递]]([[能量]∨[信息]∨[物]]))}
$S_{\text{机器}}$ = {$_{Gs}$[Device]:{[Function]([[Transforming]∨[Transmiting]]([[Energy
]∨[Information]∨[Object]]))}

② {fangwu房屋(building), fangzi房子(house), fangjian房间(room), yuanzi院子(courtyard), zhuzhai住宅(residence), zhaiyuan宅院(messuage), zhaizi宅子(residence)}

Dictionary definition:
Fangwu房屋: *Houses (collective name).*
Fangzi房子: *A building with walls, a roof, doors, and windows, designed for human habitation or for other uses.*
Fangjian房间: *The various sections partitioned within the house.*
Zhuzhai住宅: *Housing, particularly referring to larger-scale accommodations.*
Zhaizi宅子: *(spoken) Residence.*
Yuanzi院子: *An open space enclosed by walls or fences in front and behind the house.*
Zhaiyuan宅院: *A residential building with an enclosed courtyard.*
Analysis: Buildings represent another typical artificial objects, with houses being a significant component of buildings. The basic descriptive framework for the "building" knowledge domain can be expressed as:

{$_{Gs}$[建筑物]:{[结构]([a])}+{[材料]([b])}+{[功能]([c])}+{[位置]([d])}+{[外形]([e])}}
{$_{Gs}$[Building]:{[Structure]([a])}+{[Material]([b])}+{[Function]([c])}+{[Location]([d])}+{[Appearance]([e])}}

Following this framework, semantic gene structures of words in this group can be described as follows:

$S_{\text{房子}}$ = {$_{Gs}$[建筑物]:{[结构]([顶])∧$_{Gs}$[门]∧$_{Gs}$[窗]∧$_{Gs}$[墙]}+{[功能]([居住]∨[u])}}
$S_{\text{房子}}$ =
{$_{Gs}$[Building]:{[Structure]([Roof])∧$_{Gs}$[Door]∧$_{Gs}$[Window]∧$_{Gs}$[Wall]}+{[Function]([Live]∨[u])}}
$S_{\text{房屋}}$ = {$_{Gs}$[建筑物]:{[结构]([顶])∧$_{Gs}$[门]∧$_{Gs}$[窗]∧$_{Gs}$[墙]}+{[功能]([居住]∨[u])}+{[语用]([总称])}}
$S_{\text{房屋}}$ =
{$_{Gs}$[Building]:{[Structure]([Roof])∧$_{Gs}$[Door]∧$_{Gs}$[Window]∧$_{Gs}$[Wall]}+{[Function]([Live]∨[u])}+{[Pragmatic]([General term])}}
$S_{\text{住宅}}$ = {$_{Gs}$[建筑物]:{[结构]([顶])∧$_{Gs}$[门]∧$_{Gs}$[窗]∧$_{Gs}$[墙]}+{[功能]([居住])}+{[规模]([大])}}
$S_{\text{住宅}}$ = {$_{Gs}$[Building]:{[Structure]([Roof])∧ $_{Gs}$[Door]∧ $_{Gs}$[Window]∧ $_{Gs}$[Wall]}+{[Function]([Live])}+{[Scale]([Large])}}

$S_{宅子}$ = {$_{Gs}$[建筑物]:{[结构]([顶])∧$_{Gs}$[门]∧$_{Gs}$[窗]∧$_{Gs}$[墙]}+{[功能]([居住])}+{[语体]([口])}}

$S_{宅子}$ = {$_{Gs}$[Building]:{[Structure]([Roof])∧$_{Gs}$[Door]∧$_{Gs}$[Window]∧$_{Gs}$[Wall]}+{[Function]([Live])}+{[Style]([Spoken])}}

$S_{院子}$ = {[空间]:{[结构]($_{Gs}$[墙])∧$_{Gs}$[栅栏]}+{[处所]($_{Gs}$[房屋]([前]∨[后]))}}

$S_{院子}$ = {[Space]:{[Structure](Gs[Wall])∧Gs[Fence]}+{[Location](Gs[House]([Front]∨[Back]))}}

$S_{宅院}$ = {[空间]:{[结构]($_{Gs}$[宅子])∧$_{Gs}$[院子]}}

$S_{宅院}$ = {[Space]:{[Structure]($_{Gs}$[Residence])∧$_{Gs}$[Courtyard]}}

In the aforementioned description, several gene clusters are employed, including $_{Gs}$[jianzhuwu建筑物(Building)], $_{Gs}$[qiang墙(Wall)], $_{Gs}$[men门(Door)],$_{Gs}$ [chuang窗(Window)] and $_{Gs}$[zhalan栅栏(Fence)]. By referencing their corresponding definitions in dictionaries, they are described as:

Jianzhuwu建筑物: *Man-made civil engineering structures, serve as spaces for human production, daily life, and various other pursuits.*

Qiang墙: *Intervals or protective barriers built with bricks, stones, earth,* etc., *perpendicular to the ground.*

Men门: *The entrances and exits of buildings or vehicles which can be opened and closed, or devices that can be opened and closed at the entrances and exits.*

Chuang窗: *A device for ventilation and light transmission on walls and other objects.*

Zhalan栅栏: *A sturdy fence-like enclosure made of iron bars, wooden sticks, bamboo,* etc.

$S_{建筑物}$ = {[人造物]:{[工程]:{[材料]([土]∧[木]∧[u])}+{[功能]([生产]∨[生活])}}}

$S_{建筑物}$ = {[Artificial object]:{[Engineering]:{[Material]([Soil]∧[Wood]∧[u])}+{[Function]([Production] ∨[Living])}}}

$S_{墙}$ = {[人造物]:{[材料]([土]∨[石]∨[砖])}+{[功能]([分隔]∨[保护])}+{[位置]([i]↑ $_{Gc}$[地面]([垂直]))}}

$S_{墙}$ = {[Artificial object]:{[Material]([Soil]∨[Stone]∨[Brick])}+{[Function]([Seperating]∨ [Protecting])}+{[Position]([i]↑ Gs[Ground]([Perpendicular]))}}

$S_{门}$ = {[人造物]:{[构成]([部分]([i]of $_{Gs}$[建筑物]∧$_{Gs}$[车]∨$_{Gs}$[船]))}+{[功能]([[进]∧[出]]([路径]([i]))}+{[操作]([开]∧[关])}}

$S_{门}$ = {[Artificial object]:{[Composition]([Part]([i]of $_{Gs}$[Building]∧$_{Gs}$[Vehicle]∨$_{Gs}$[Ship]))}+{[Function]([[In]∧[Out]]([Path]([i]))}+{[Operation]([Open]∧[Close])}}

$S_{窗}$ = $S_{窗户}$ = {[人造物]:{[处所]($_{Gs}$[墙]∨[顶])}+{[功能]([透]([主体]([光]∧[空气])∧[路径]([i]))}}

$S_{窗}$ = {[Artificial object]:{[Location]($_{Gs}$[Wall]∨[Roof])}+{[Function]([Permeable]([Main body]([Light] ∧[Air])∧[Path]([i]))}}

$S_{栅栏}$ = {[人造物]:{[材料]([铁]∨[木]∨[竹])}+{[功能]([分隔])}+{[性质]([坚固])}}
$S_{栅栏}$ = {[Artificial object]:{[Material]([Iron]∨[Wood]∨[Bamboo])}+{[Function]([Seperating])}+{[Nature]([Solid])}}

③ {shu书(book), shuji书籍(books), shuben书本(books), congshu丛书(series), zazhi杂志(magazine), qikan期刊(periodical), kanwu刊物(journal), shukan书刊(books and periodicals), baozhi报纸(newspaper), baokan报刊(newspapers and periodicals)}

Dictionary definition:
Shu书: *A written or illustrated work that is bound into a volume.*
Shuben书本: *Books (collective name).*
Shuji书籍: *Books (collective name).*
Congshu丛书: *A collection of books compiled into a set.*
Zazhi杂志: *Journal.*
Kanwu刊物: *A regular or irregular publication that publishes articles, pictures, music scores,* etc.
Shukan书刊: *Books and periodicals.*
Baozhi报纸: *A regular publication in the form of scattered pages, primarily containing news related to social, political, economic, and cultural events both domestically and internationally, and is generally understood to refer to daily newspapers.*
Baokan报刊: *The general term for newspapers and magazines.*

This group of words exhibits a complex entanglement of meanings, with the most central concepts being "book", "periodical", and "newspaper". All of them serve as carriers of various types of knowledge and information, such as graphic and textual works. The distinctions between them lie in two aspects: (1) "Book" and "periodical" are bound into volumes, whereas "newspaper" is in loose sheets and not bound, which we attribute to the [xingtai形态(Form)] dimension; (2) Both "newspaper" and "periodical" are publications, and they are continuous publications, which we also categorize under the [xingtai形态(Form)] dimension (this point is not mentioned in the definitions of dictionaries). Based on the above analysis, the semantic gene structures of words in this group are as follows:

$S_{书}$ = {[人造物]:{[功能]([载体]of[知识])}+[内容]([文字]∨[图])}+{[形态]([册])}}
$S_{书}$ = {[Artificial object]:{[Function]([Carrier]of [Knowledge])}+[Content]([Characters]∨[Picture])}+{[Form]([Volume])}}
$S_{书本}$ = $S_{书籍}$ = {[人造物]:{[功能]([载体]of[知识])}+{[内容]([文字]∨[图])}+{[形态]([册])}+{[语用]([统称])}}
$S_{书本}$ = $S_{书籍}$ = {[Artificial object]:{[Function]([Carrier]of[Knowledge])}+{[Content]([words]∨[Picture])}+{[Form]([Volume])}+{[Pragmatic]([General term])}}

$S_{丛书}$ = {[人造物]:{[功能]([载体]of[知识])}+[内容]([文字]∨ [图])}+{[形态]([册])}+{[数量]([多])}+{[形式]([套])}}

$S_{丛书}$ = {[Artificial object]:{[Function]([Carrier]of[Knowledge])}+{[Content]([Characters]∨[Picture])}+{[Form]([Volume]∧[Suite])}+{[Quantity]([Large])}}

$S_{刊物}$ = {$_{Gs}$[出版物]:{[功能]([载体]of[知识])}+[内容]([文字]∨[图])}+{[形态]([册])}+{[形式]([连续])}}

$S_{刊物}$ = {Gs[Publication]:{[Function]([Carrier]of[Knowledge])}+[Content]([Characters]∨[Picture])}+{[Form]([Volume]∧[Continuous])}}

$S_{期刊}$ = $S_{杂志}$ = {$_{Gs}$[出版物]:{[功能]([载体]of[知识])}+[内容]([文字]∨[图])}+{[形态]([册])}+{[形式]([连续])}+{[周期]([定期])}}

$S_{期刊}$ = $S_{杂志}$ = {$_{Gs}$[Publication]:{[Function]([Carrier]of[Knowledge])}+[Content]([Characters]∨ [Picture])}+{[Form]([Volume]∧[Continuous])}+{[Period]([Regular])}}

$S_{报纸}$ = {$_{Gs}$[出版物]:{[功能]([载体]of[知识])}+[内容]([文字]∨[图])}+{[形态](![册])}+{[形式]([连续])}+{[周期]([定期])}}

$S_{报纸}$ = {$_{Gs}$[Publication]:{[Function]([Carrier]of[Knowledge])}+[Content]([Characters]∨[Picture])}+{[Form](![Volume]∧[Continuous])}+{[Period]([Regular])}}

$S_{书刊}$ = {{$_{Gs}$[书]+$_{Gs}$[刊物]}+{[语用]([总称])}}

$S_{书刊}$ = {{$_{Gs}$[Books]+$_{Gs}$[Journal]}+{[Pragmatic]([General term])}}

$S_{报刊}$ = {{$_{Gs}$[报纸]+$_{Gs}$[刊物]}+{[语用]([总称])}}

$S_{报刊}$ = {{$_{Gs}$[Book]+$_{Gs}$[Journal]}+{[Pragmatic]([General term])}}

Incorporating the above groups, we obtain part of the semantic set for nouns representing artificial objects:{[cailiao材料(Material)], [xingzhuang形状(Shape)], [gongneng功能(Function)], [renzaowu人造物(Artificial object)], [jiegou结构(Structure)], [changsuo场所(Place)], [richang日常(Daily)], [laodong劳动(Labour)], [shengchan生产(Producing)], [jingmi精密(Precise)], [zhuanyong专用(Spesific)], [fuza复杂(Complex)], [fangshi方式(Way)], [duli独立(Independent)], [yuanli原理(Principle)], [zhuanhuan转换(Transforming)], [chuandi传递(Transmiting)], [nengliang能量(Energy)], [xinxi信息(Information)], [wu物(Object)], [ding顶(Roof)], [juzhu居住(Living)], [yuyong语用(Pragmatic)], [zongcheng总称(General term)], [chusuo处所(Location)], [kongjian空间(Space)], [qian前(Front)], [hou后(Back)], [gongcheng工程(Engineering)], [cailiao材料(Material)], [tu土(Soil)], [mu木(Wood)], [shenghuo生活(Living)], [shi石(Stone)], [zhuan砖(Brick)], [fenge分隔(Seperating)], [baohu保护(Protecting)], [weizhi位置(Position)], [chuizhi垂直(Perpendicular)], [jin进(In)], [chu出(Out)], [lujing路径(Path)], [caozuo操作(Operation)], [kai开(Open)], [guan关(Close)], [ding顶(Roof)], [tou透(Permeable)], [guang光(Light)], [kongqi空气(Air)], [tie铁(Iron)], [zhu竹(Bamboo)], [fenge分隔(Seperating)], [xingzhi性质(Nature)], [jiangu坚固(Solid)], [neirong内容(Content)], [xingtai形态(Form)], [xingshi形式(Modality)], [zaiti载体(Carrier)], [zhishi知识(Knowledge)], [wenzi文字(Characters)], [tu图(Picture)], [ce册(Volume)], [tao套(Suite)], [zhouqi周期(Period)], [dingqi定期(Regular)]}, as well as three gene clusters Gs[lixue

力学(Mechanics)], Gs[che车(Vehicle)] and Gs[chuan船(Ship)]for subsequent analysis.

5.2.3.3 Nouns Expressing Abstract Objects

① {zhishi知识(knowledge), kexue科学(science), lilun理论(theory), xuwen学问(erudition), jingyan经验(experience), xueshuo学说(doctrine), xueshu学术(academics), sixiang思想(thought), jishu技术(technology)}

Dictionary definition:

Zhishi知识: *The aggregate of knowledge and cognition acquired through human endeavors aimed at altering the world.*

Kexue科学: *A disciplinary knowledge system reflecting the objective laws of nature, society, and thought.*

Lilun理论: *The systematic conclusions derived from practice regarding the knowledge of nature and society.*

Xuewen学问: *The systematic knowledge formed through the study of objective laws, which correctly reflects objective realities, and is acquired through scholarly pursuits.*

Jingyan经验: *Knowledge or skills acquired through practice: He has extensive experience in grafting fruit trees.*

Xueshuo学说: *Systematic assertions or views in academia.*

Xueshu学术: *Systematic and specialized knowledge.*

Sixiang思想: *The result of cognitive activities, mirrors of objective existence reflected in human consciousness.*

Jishu技术: *The experiences and knowledge regarding production and labor accumulated by humans through the repeated practice of recognizing and altering the nature, also broadly refer to the skills in other operational aspects.*

Analysis: This group of words, on the whole, refers to the intellectual achievements of humans and carries relatively typical meta-conceptual meanings. Their meanings are intertwined, making it difficult to differentiate them from dictionary definitions. Generally speaking, when the definitions of a group of words in the dictionary are intermingled, it indicates that the concepts they express are often the most basic cognitive concepts. From these concepts, we can select the most core ones, which are capable of minimizing the circular interpretations, to serve as as the semantic genes. For example, "technology" is defined as "knowledge and experience of", while "knowledge" is further defined as "the aggregate of experiences of", and "experience" is then defined as "knowledge or skill of …" This leads to an infinite loop, making it impossible to resolve the meanings of the words. In fact, "technology" and "experience" are distinct. "Technology" not only accumulates "experience" and "knowledge" but also includes innovative solutions to problems based on "experience" and "knowledge". Therefore, we directly predefine [jingyan经验(Experience)] and [jishu技术(Technology)] as semantic genes without further analysis.

In order to further examine the meanings of this group of words, we have also selected [xitong系统(System)], [renzhi认知(Cognition)], [siwei思维(Thought)], [guilü规律(Law)], [shijian实践(Practice)] and [jielun结论(Conclusion)] as semantic genes. Based on these semantic genes, the following descriptions of the meanings of this group of words are provided:

S知识 = {[抽象物]:{[构成]([认知]∧[经验])}+{[来源]([实践])}}
S知识 = {[Abstract object]:{[Composition]([Cognition]∧ [Experience])}+{[Source]([Practice])}}
S科学 = {[抽象物]:{[构成]([系统]of Gs[知识])}+{[内容]([规律]([客观])}}
S科学 = {[Abstract object]:{[Composition]([System]of Gs[Knowledge])}+{[Content]([Law]([Objective])}}
S理论 = {[抽象物]:{[构成]([系统]of Gs[结论])}+{[内容](Gs[知识]}+{[来源]([实践])}}
S理论 = {[Abstract object]:{[Composition]([System]of Gs[Conclusion])}+{[Content](Gs[Knowledge]}+{[Source]([Practice])}}
S学问 = {[抽象物]:{[构成]([系统]of Gs[知识])}+{[来源]([研究]∨[学习]}+{[性质]([正确]}}
S学问 = {[Abstract object]:{[Composition]([System]of Gs[Knowledge])}+{[Source]([Research][Study]}+{[Nature]([True]}}
S学术 = {[抽象物]:{[构成]([系统]of Gs[知识])}+{[领域]([u]∧[专门]}}
S学术 = {[Abstract object]:{[Composition]([System]of Gs[Knowledge])}+{[Field]([u]∧ [Specialized]}}
S学说 = {[抽象物]:{[构成]([系统]of [Gs[主张]∨Gs[见解])}+{[领域](Gs[学术]}}
S思想 = {[抽象物]:{[构成]([结果]of[思维])}}
S学说 = {[Abstract object]:{[Composition]([System]of[Gs[Assertion]∨Gs[View])}+{[Field] Gs[Academics]}}
S思想 = {[Abstract object]:{[Composition]([Result]of[Thinking])}}

② {xiaoxi消息(message), yinxin音信(tidings), xinwen新闻(news), baodao报道(report), yaoyan谣言(rumor), chuanshuo传说(legend), gushi故事(story)}

Dictionary definition:
Xiaoxi消息: *Report on situations of human or objects.*
Yinxin音信: *Message or letter.*
Xinwen新闻: ❶*Various message about recently occurred events reported by the media.* ❷ *Significant or novel occurrences in society recently.*
Baodao报道: *News releases disseminated through media outlets.*
Yaoyan谣言: *Message concocted without basis or evidence.*
Chuanshuo传说: *Folk stories transmitted orally.*
Gushi故事: *Matters, either real or fictional, serve as the subject of narration, are coherent, attractive, and capable of moving people.*

Analysis: This is yet another example of circular interpretation. The interpretive path for "xiaoxi消息(message)"in is "xiaoxi消息(message) → baodao报道(report)

→ xinwen新闻(news) → xiaoxi消息(message)". From the interpretation of other words in this group, "message" appears to be a frequently used term for definition. Therefore, we predefine [xiaoxi消息(Message)] as a semantic gene. Moreover, "gushi故事(story)" can actually be considered a metacognitive concept. Children are accustomed to listening to various stories told by their parents from a young age, and their parents do not explain to them what a "story" is. However, this does not affect the children's cognition of the concept or their understanding of the word's meaning. Therefore, we also define [gushi故事(Story)] as a semantic gene, used to describe other words.

The semantic gene structures of words in this group can be described as follows:

$S_{\text{音信}}$ = {[抽象物]:[构成]([消息]∧$_{Gs}$[书信])}
$S_{\text{音信}}$ = {[Abstract object]:[Composition]([Message]∧ $_{Gs}$[Letter])}
$S_{\text{新闻1}}$ = {[消息]:{[内容]([事件])}+{[时间]([近])}+{[范围]([社会])}+{[渠道]($_{Gs}$[媒体])}}
$S_{\text{新闻1}}$ = {[Message]:{[Content]([Event])}+{[Time]([Recent])}+{[Scope]([Society])}+{[Channel]($_{Gs}$[Media])}}
$S_{\text{新闻2}}$ = {[事件]:{{[时间]([近])}+{[范围]([社会])}+{[性质]($_{Gs}$[新奇])}}
$S_{\text{新闻2}}$ = {[Event]:{{[Time]([Recent])}+{[Scope]([Society])}+{[Nature]($_{Gs}$[Novel])}}
$S_{\text{报道}}$ = {[抽象物]:{[构成]($_{Gs}$[稿件])}+{[内容]($_{Gs}$[新闻])}+{[渠道]($_{Gs}$[媒体])}}
$S_{\text{报道}}$ = {[Abstract object]:{[Composition]($_{Gs}$[Manuscript])}+{[Content]($_{Gs}$[News])}+{[Channel]($_{Gs}$[Media])}}
$S_{\text{谣言}}$ = {[消息]:{[性质]([假])}+{[极性]([贬])}}
$S_{\text{谣言}}$ = {[Message]:{[Nature]([False])}+{[Polarity]([Positive])}}
$S_{\text{传说}}$ = {[故事]:{[渠道]($_{Gs}$[口传])}+{[范围]($_{Gs}$[民间])}}
$S_{\text{传说}}$ = {[Story]:{[Channel]($_{Gs}$[Oral])}+{[Scope]($_{Gs}$[Folk])}}

③ {zhengce政策(policy), zhunze准则(criterion), yuanze原则(principle), celüe策略(strategy)}

Dictionary definition:

Zhengce政策: *Criterions and strategies formulated bynations or political parties to address issues and achieve objectives.*

Zhunze准则: *Principles on which speech, action,* etc. *are based.*

Yuanze原则: *Rules or standards on which speech or action is based.*

Celüe策略: *Tactics or stratagems. Generally, it denotes a set of plans that can be implemented to achieve a goal.*

Analysis: This set of terms also exhibits circular definitions. We have agreed to take the semantic genes [guize规则(Rule)] and [zhiding制定(Make)] as the descriptive benchmarks.

The semantic gene structures of words in this group can be described as follows:

$S_{\text{原则}}$ = {[抽象物]:{[规则]:{[[说]∨[行动]]([依据]([i])}}
$S_{\text{原则}}$ = {[Abstract object]:{[Rule]:{[[Speech]∨[Action]]([Basis]([i])}}

$S_{\text{准则}}$ = {[抽象物]:{[规则]:{[[说]∨[行动]]([依据]([i])}+{[性质]([标准])}}
$S_{\text{准则}}$ = {[Abstract object]:{[Rule]:{[[Speech]∨[Action]]([Basis]([i])}+{[Nature]([Standard])}}
$S_{\text{策略}}$ = {[抽象物]:[构成]([计划]$\wedge_{Gs}$[计谋])}
$S_{\text{策略}}$ = {[Abstract object]:[Composition]([Plan]$\wedge_{Gs}$[Stratagem])}
$S_{\text{政策}}$ = {[抽象物]:{[构成]($_{Gs}$[准则]$\wedge_{Gs}$[计谋])}+{[来源]([规定]([施事]([政党]∨[国家])∧[受事]([i]))}+[目的]([实现]([目标]$\wedge_{Gs}$[路线]))}
$S_{\text{政策}}$ = {[Abstract object]:{[Composition]($_{Gs}$[Principle]$\wedge_{Gs}$[Stratagem])}+{[Source]([Make]([Agent]([Party]∨[Country])∧[Ptient]([i]))}+[Objective]([Achieving]([Goal]$\wedge_{Gs}$[Path]))}

④ {nengli能力(ability), tianfu天赋(gift), tianfen天分(talent), tianzi天资(aptitude), caineng才能(capability), caihua才华(brilliance), caigan才干(competence), caizhi才智(intelligence)}

Dictionary definition:
Nengli能力: *The subjective condition to undertake a task.*
Tianfu天赋: ❶*Innate endowment; possessing from birth.* ❷*Aptitude.*
Tianfen天分: *Aptitude.*
Tianzi天资:*Innate ability or natural endowment..*
Caineng才能: *Knowledge and ability.*
Caihua才华: *Capability manifests as external abilities, particularly in the realm of arts.*
Caigan才干: *Ability to handle affairs.*
Caizhi才智: *Intellect and wisdom.*

Analysis: The objects described by this group of words are exclusively human. The dictionary definitions do not explicitly indicate this. To facilitate semantic reasoning by machines, it is necessary to clarify this in the description. We need to predefine three semantic gene [zizhi资质(Quality)], [nengli能力(Ability], and [tiansheng天生(Innate)] as the descriptive benchmarks. Among them, [Quality] serves as a dimension gene, [Innate] as an assignment gene, and [Ability] can function both as either of them.

The semantic gene structures of words in this group can be described as follows:

$S_{\text{天赋}}$ = $S_{\text{天分}}$ = $S_{\text{天资}}$ = {[抽象物]:{[资质]of[人]:{[构成]([能力])}+{[来源]([天生])}}}
$S_{\text{天赋}}$ = $S_{\text{天分}}$ = $S_{\text{天资}}$ = {[Abstract object]:{[Quality]of[Person]:{[Composition]([Ability])}+{[Source]([Innate])}}}
$S_{\text{才能}}$ = {[抽象物]:{[资质]of[人]:{[构成]($_{Gs}$[知识]∧[能力])}}}
$S_{\text{才能}}$ = {[Abstract object]:{[Quality]of[Person]:{[Composition]($_{Gs}$[Knowledge]∧[Capacity])}}}
$S_{\text{才华}}$ = {[抽象物]:{[资质]of[人]:{[构成]($_{Gs}$[知识]∧[能力])}}+{[形态]($_{Gs}$[外显])}}

$S_{才华}$ = {[Abstract object]:{[Quality]of[Person]{[Composition](Gs[Knowledge])}}+{[Form](Gs[Explicit])}}
$S_{才干}$ = {[抽象物]:{[资质]of[人]:{[构成]([能力]of[处理]([事务]))}}}
$S_{才干}$ = {[Abstract object]:{ [Quality]of[Person]:{[Composition]([Abality]of[Handling]([Affair]))}}}
$S_{才智}$ = {[抽象物]:{[资质]of[人]:{[构成](Gs[才能]∧[智慧])}}}
$S_{才智}$ = {[Abstract object]:{ [Quality]of[Person]:{[Composition](Gs[Intellect]∧[Wisdom])}}}

The above groups are summarized to obtain a set of semantic genes for describing virtual objects, which includes{[jingyan经验(Experience)], [jishu技术(Technology)], [xitong系统(System)], [renzhi认知(Cognition)], [siwei思维(Thought)], [guilü规律(Law)], [shijian实践(Practice)], [jielun结论(Conclusion)], [keguan客观(Objective)], [laiyuan来源(Source)], [yanjiu研究(Research)], [xuexi学习(Learning)], [xingzhi性质(Nature)], [zhengque正确(Correct)], [zhuanmen专门(Specialized)], [xiaoxi消息(Message)], [gushi故事(Story)], [shijian事件(Event)], [jin近(Near)], [shehui社会(Society)], [qudao渠道(Channel)], [jia假(False)], [jixing极性(Polarity)], [bian贬(Pejorative)], [guize规则(Rule)], [zhiding制定(Make)], [shuo说(Speech)], [xingdong行动(Action)], [yiju依据(Basis)], [biaozhun标准(Standard)], [goucheng构成(Composition)], [jihua计划(Plan)], [jiumou计谋(Stratagem)], [zhengdang政党(Party)], [guojia国家(Country)], [shixian实现(Achieving)], [mubiao目标(Goal)], [zizhi资质(Quality)], [nengli能力(Capacity)], [tiansheng天生(Innate)], [xingtai形态(Form)], [chuli处理(Handling)], [shiwu事务(Affair)], [zhihui智慧(Wisdom)]}, as well as gene clusters, Gs[主张zhuzhang(Assertion)], Gs[jianjie见解(View)], Gs[shuxin书信(Letter)], Gs[xinqi新奇(Novel)], Gs[gaojian稿件(Manuscript)], Gs[meiti媒体(Media)], Gs[kouchuan口传(Oral)], Gs[minjian民间(Folk)], Gs[jiumou计谋(Stratagem)], Gs[luxian路线(Path)], Gs[waixian外显(Explicit)], which are to be described later.

5.2.3.4 Nouns Expressing Virtual Objects

① {shenxian神仙(immortals), yaojing妖精(fairy), yaoguai妖怪(monster), yaomo妖魔(demon), gui鬼(ghost), mogui魔鬼(devil)}

Dictionary definition:
Shenxian神仙: *Characters in mythological legends, possessing superhuman abilities and capable of transcending the mundane world, achieving immortality and eternal youth.*
Yaoguai妖怪: *Spirits often depicted in myths, legends, and fairy tales, characterized by their grotesque and terrifying shapes, possession of supernatural powers, and propensity to harm humans.*
Yaojing妖精: *Monster.*
Yaomo妖魔: *Monster.*

Gui鬼: *Referring to the soul of a deceased person.*

Mogui魔鬼: *Malevolent spirits in religious or mythological narratives that deceive and harm human life, metaphorically representing evil forces.*

Analysis: This group of terms all denote fictional characters from mythology or religious culture, yet they exhibit differences in pragmatic usage and carry different emotional connotations. The word “shenxian神仙” conveys a positive, divine essence, whereas “yaoguai妖怪”, “yaomo妖魔(demon)”, “mogui魔鬼(devil)” are associated with evil. The dictionary definitions do not explicitly point out this distinction, which needs to be clearly stated in the semantic gene description. We can predefine several semantic genes [shenhua神话(Myth)], [zongjiao宗教(Religion)], [zhengyi正义(Justicial)], [xie’e邪恶(Evil)], and [linghun灵魂(Soul)] to describe them.

$S_{神仙}$ = {[虚拟物]:{[人物]:{[能力](Gs[超常]∧Gs[永生])}+{[领域]([神话])}+{[色彩]([正义])}}

$S_{神仙}$ = {[Virtual object]:{[Character]:{[Ability](Gs[Supernatural]∧Gs[Immortal])}+{[Field]([Myth])}+{[Connotation]([Justicial])}}

$S_{妖怪}$ = $S_{妖魔}$ = $S_{妖精}$ = {[虚拟物]:{[人物]:{[能力](Gs[法术])}+{[领域]([神话])}+{[习性](Gs[害人])}+{[色彩]([邪恶])}}

$S_{妖怪}$ = $S_{妖魔}$ = $S_{妖精}$ = {[Virtual object]:{[Character]:{[Ability](Gs[Supernatural])}+{[Field]([Myth])}+{[Habit](Gs[Harming])}+{[Connotation]([Evil])}}

$S_{鬼}$ = {[虚拟物]:{[灵魂]of[[人]([状态]([死亡]))]}+{[领域]([神话][8])}}

$S_{鬼}$ = {[Virtual object]:{[Soul]of[[Person]([State]([Death]))]}+{[Field]([Myth])}

$S_{魔鬼}$ = {[虚拟物]:{Gs[鬼]:{[领域]([神话]∨[宗教])}+{[习性](Gs[害人])}+{[色彩]([邪恶])}}

$S_{魔鬼}$ = {[Virtual object]:{Gs[Ghost]:{[Field]([Myth]∨[Religion])}+{[Habit](Gs[Harming])}+{[Connotation]([Evil])}}

② {tiantang天堂(paradise), tiangong天宫(celestial palace), diyu地狱(hell), difu地府(the underworld)}

Dictionary definition:

Tiantang天堂: *The pleasant place where the soul resides after death in certain religions (opposed to ‘hell’).*

Tiangong天宫: *The palace of the celestial deities in myths.*

Diyu地狱: *The place where the souls suffer after death in certain religions (opposed to ‘paradise’).*

Difu地府: *The place where the soul resides after death.*

Analysis: This group of words denotes the fictional places depicted in myths and legends. Description as follows: The description is as follows:

[8] 词典对“鬼”的释义用语“迷信”所指内容和“神话”基本相同，但该词有贬义色彩，有很大的主观性和不确定性，“神话”中的哪些部分属于“迷信”无法界定。所以我们采用中性基因[神话]，而不用[迷信]。下一组中“地府”的描写与此相同。

$S_{天堂}$ = {[虚拟物]:{[处所]:{[功能]([居住]([主体]([灵魂]of[[人]([状态]([死亡]))]))}+{[状况]([美好])}+{[领域]([宗教])}}

$S_{天堂}$ = {[Virtual object]:{[Location]:{[Function]([Living]([Subject]([Soul]of[[Person]([State]([Death]))]))}+{[Condition]([Fine])}+{[Field]([Religion])}}

$S_{地域}$ = {[虚拟物]:{[处所]:{[功能]([居住]([主体]([灵魂]of[[人]([状态]([死亡]))]))}+{[状况]([苦难])}+{[领域]([宗教])}}

$S_{地域}$ = {[Virtual object]:{[Location]:{[Function]([Living]([Subject]([Soul]of[[Person]([State]([Death]))]))}+{[Condition]([Miserable])}+{[Field]([Religion])}}

$S_{天宫}$ = {[虚拟物]:{$_{Gs}$[宫殿]:{[功能]([居住]([主体]($_{Gs}$[神仙]))}+{[领域]([神话])}}

$S_{天宫}$ = {[Virtual object]:{Gs[Palace]:{[Function]([Living]([Subject](Gs[Immortals]))}+{[Field]([Myth])}}

$S_{地府}$ = {[虚拟物]:{$_{Gs}$[宫殿]:{[功能]([居住]([主体]([灵魂]of[[人]([状态]([死亡]))]))}+{[领域]([神话])}}

$S_{地府}$ = {[Virtual object]:{[Location]:{[Function]([Living]([Subject]([Soul]of[[Person]([State]([Death]))]))}+{[Field]([Myth])}}

③ {long龙(loong), feng凤(phoenix), fenghuang凤凰(phenix), qilin麒麟(kylin)}

Dictionary definition:

Long龙: *A mythical creature in ancient Chinese legends, is characterized by its elongated body, scales, horns, and limbs, being able to walk, fly, swim, and even summon clouds and precipitate rain.*

Feng凤: *The phoenix.*

Fenghuang凤凰: *The king of all birds, as depicted in ancient legends, characterized by its exquisite feathers. The male is known as "feng 凤", while the female "huang 凰". It is commonly used to symbolize auspiciousness and good fortune.*

Qilin麒麟: *A mythical creature in ancient legends, resembling a deer in shape, with antlers and a tail,and scales covering its entire body. The ancients regarded it as a symbol of auspiciousness and good fortune.*

Analysis: This group of words denotes mythical virtual animals, and there are a considerable number of such terms in Chinese. These terms can be defined by borrowing the semantic knowledge domain of animal nouns:

{[虚拟物]:{[动物]:{[结构]([a])}+{[外貌]([b])}+{[能力]([d])}+{[色彩]([e])}}}

{[Virtual object]: {[Animal]: {[Structure]([a])}+{[Appearance]([b])}+{[Ability]([d])}{[Connotation]([e])}}}

$S_{龙}$ = {[虚拟物]:{[动物]:{[结构]($_{Gs}$[鳞]∧$_{Gs}$[角]∧$_{Gs}$[脚])}+{[外貌]($_{Gc}$[似蛇])}+{[能力]($_{Gs}$[行走]∧$_{Gs}$[飞]∧$_{Gs}$[游泳]∧$_{Gs}$[降雨])}}}

$S_{龙}$ = {[Virtual object]:{[Animal]:{[Structure]($_{Gs}$[Scale]∧$_{Gs}$[Horn]∧$_{Gs}$[Limb])}+

{[Appearance]($_{Gc}$[Snake-like])}+
{[Ability]($_{Gs}$[Walk]∧$_{Gs}$[Fly]∧$_{Gs}$[Swim]∧$_{Gs}$[Causing rain])}}}
$S_{凤}$ = {[虚拟物]:{[动物]:{[结构]($_{Gs}$[羽毛]([外观]([美])))}+{[外貌]($_{Gc}$[似鸟])}+{[地位]([王]of $_{Gs}$[鸟]}+{[性别]([雄]}+{[色彩]($_{Gs}$[祥瑞]}}}
$S_{凤}$ = {[Virtual object]:{[Animal]:{[Structure]($_{Gs}$[Feather]([Appearance]([Beautiful])))}+{[Appearance]($_{Gc}$[Bird-like])}+{[Status]([King]of $_{Gs}$[Bird]}+{[Gender]([Male]}+{[Connotation]($_{Gs}$[Auspiciousness]}}}
$S_{凰}$ = {[虚拟物]:{[动物]:{[结构]($_{Gs}$[羽毛]([外观]([美])))}+{[外貌]($_{Gc}$[似鸟])}+{[地位]([王]of $_{Gs}$[鸟]}+{[性别]([雌]}+{[色彩]($_{Gs}$[祥瑞]}}}
$S_{凰}$ = {[Virtual object]:{[Animal]:{[Structure]($_{Gs}$[Feather]([Appearance]([Beautiful])))}+[Appearance]($_{Gc}$[Bird-like])}+{[Status]([King]of $_{Gs}$[Bird]}+{[Gender]([Female]}+{[Connotation](Gs[Auspiciousness]}}}
$S_{凤凰}$ = {[虚拟物]:{[动物]:{[结构]($_{Gs}$[羽毛]([外观]([美])))}+{[外貌]($_{Gc}$[似鸟])}+{[地位]([王]of $_{Gs}$[鸟]}+{[色彩]($_{Gs}$[祥瑞]}}}
$S_{凤凰}$ = {[Virtual object]:{[Animal]:{[Structure]($_{Gs}$[Feather]([Appearance]([Beautiful])))}+{[Appearance]($_{Gc}$[Bird-like])}+{[Status]([King]of $_{Gs}$[Bird]}+{[Connotation](Gs[Auspiciousness]}}}
$S_{麒麟}$ = {[虚拟物]:{[动物]:{[结构]($_{Gs}$[鳞甲]∧$_{Gs}$[角]∧$_{Gs}$[尾巴])}+{[外貌]($_{Gc}$[似鹿])}+{[色彩]($_{Gs}$[祥瑞]}}}
$S_{麒麟}$ = {[Virtual object]:{[Animal]:{[Structure]($_{Gs}$[Scale]∧$_{Gs}$[Horn]∧$_{Gs}$[Tail])}+{[Appearance]($_{Gc}$[Deer-like])}+{[Connotation]($_{Gs}$[Auspiciousness]}}}

The description employs the abbreviated gene chain expressions $_{Gc}$[sishe似蛇(Snake-like)] and $_{Gc}$[silu似鹿(Deer-like)], as these gene units cannot form words and thus cannot be represented as gene clusters; they can only be denoted as gene chains. Such gene chains can be functionally expanded as follows:

{[X]:[比较]([a]↑[b]([相似]))}
{[X]:[Comparison]([a]↑[b]([Like]))}

In the given context, where "[a]" and "[b]" represent two objects being compared, and "[X]" denotes the aspect of comparison, the gene descriptions for "long龙(Loong)" and "qilin麒麟(Kylin)" can be expanded as follows:
{[外貌]:[比较]([i]↑$_{Gs}$[蛇]([相似]))}
{[Appearance]:[Comparison]([i]↑Gs[Snake]([Like]))} (where the reflexive gene [i] denotes the desribed object "Loong")
{[外貌]:[比较]([i]↑$_{Gs}$[鹿]([相似]))}
{[Appearance]:[Comparison]([i]↑Gs[Snake]([Like]))} (where the reflexive gene [i] denotes the desribed object "Loong")
By synthesizing the aforementioned groups, we obtain a set of semantic genes for the deecription of virtual objects, which includes {[shenhua神话(Myth)], [zongjiao宗教(Religion)], [zhengyi正义(Justicial)], [xie'e邪恶(Evil)], [linghun灵魂(Soul)], [secai色彩(Connotation)], [siwang死亡(Death)], [xixing习性(Habit)], [juzhu居住(Living)], [zhuangkuang状况(Condition)], [meihao美好(Fine)],

[kunan苦难(Miserable)], [dwei地位(Status)], [wang王(King)], [xingbie性别(Gender)], [xiong雄(Male)], [ci雌(Female)], [waiguan外观(Appearance)], [mei美(Beautiful)]}. Additionally, the gene clusters, Gs[chaochang超常(Supernatural)], Gs[yongsheng永生(Immortal)], Gs[hairen害人(Harming)], Gs[gongdian宫殿(Palace)], Gs[lin鳞(Scale)], Gs[jiao角(Horn)], Gs[jiangyu降雨(Causing rain)], Gs[xiangrui祥瑞(Auspiciousness)], Gs[weiba尾巴(Tail)]are reserved for subsequent analysis.

5.2.4 Semantic Analysis and Semantic Gene Extraction of Event Nouns

5.2.4.1 Natural Event Nouns

① {yu雨(rain), bayou暴雨(rainstorm), leiyu雷雨(thunderstorm), zhenyu阵雨(shower)}

Dictionary definition:

Yu雨: *The water that descends from the clouds towards the ground. When the tiny water droplets within the clouds increase in size to a point where they can no longer remain suspended in the air, they begin to fall as rain.*

Zhenyu阵雨: *The duration of rainfall is short, with significant variations in intensity, and both the onset and cessation are abrupt. Such rain is called a shower. Showers are often accompanied by lightning and thunder, and they are more commonly observed during the summer.*

Bayou暴雨: *Heavy and sudden rain.*

Leiyu雷雨: *The weather phenomenon produced by cumulonimbus clouds, characterized by precipitation accompanied by lightning and thunder, which typically occurs in the afternoon during summer.*

Analysis: Words such as "yu雨(rain)" and "xue雪(snow)" which refer to natural phenomena, actually encompass two layers of meaning. Firstly, they denote the natural phenomena themselves, such as "raining" or "snowing", which essentially represent an event. Secondly, they refer to the corresponding substances produced by these phenomena, i.e., the water droplets and ice crystals that fall from the sky. Therefore, these words can be categorized as event nouns. From the definitions provided in dictionaries, it can be observed that the interpretation of "rain" tends to emphasize its material meaning; whereas for compound words formed by the morpheme "yu雨", such as "zhenyu阵雨(shower)" and "baoyu暴雨(rainstorm)", the emphasis is more on their event meaning. The situation with "snow" is analogous.

As "yu雨" and "xue雪"are well-known cognitive basic concepts, the meanings of these two words, whether in terms of event meaning or material meaning, are the most fundamental lexical meaning units. Therefore, we do not analyze these two words and directly predefine them as core semantic gene [yu雨(Rain)] and [xue雪(Snow)], using them to describe other semantic structures.

Based on the above analysis, the semantic gene structures of words in this group are as follows:

$S_{阵雨}$ = {[自然事件]:{[现象]([天气])}+{[表现]([雨])}+{[持续]([短暂])}+{[程度]([强])}+{[性状]([突然]∧[变化])}+{[时间]([夏季])}}
$S_{阵雨}$ = {[Natural event]:{[Phenomenon]([Weather])}+{[Manifestation]([Rain])}+{[Duration]([Short])}+{[Degree]([Intense])}+{[Feature]([Sudden]∧[Change])}+{[Time]([Summer])}}
$S_{暴雨}$ = {[自然事件]:{[现象]([天气])}+{[表现]([雨])}+{[程度]([强])}+{[性状]([急]}}
$S_{暴雨}$ = {[Natural event]:{[Phenomenon]([Weather])}+{[Manifestation]([Rain])}+{[Degree]([Intense])}+{[Feature]([Sudden]}}
$S_{雷雨}$ = {[自然事件]:{[现象]([天气])}+{[表现]([雨])}+{[伴随]([雷]∧[闪电])}+{[时间]([夏季])}}
$S_{雷雨}$ = {[Natural event]:{[Phenomenon]([Weather])}+{[Manifestation]([Rain])}+{[Accompanied]([Thunder]∧[Lightning])}+{[Time]([Summer])}}

② {feng风(wind), fengbao风暴(storm), jufeng飓风(hurricane), taifeng台风(typhoon), longjuanfeng龙卷风(tornado)}

Dictionary definition:

Feng风: *The air flow parallel to the ground, is caused by the uneven distribution of atmospheric pressure. Generally, the wind is categorized into thirteen levels, ranging from zero to twelve, based on the intensity of the wind.*

Fengbao风暴: *A weather phenomenon characterized by strong winds accompanied by heavy rainfall.*

Jufeng飓风: *Tropical air vortices occurring over the Atlantic Ocean and the West Indies region, representing extremely intense storms that are analogous to typhoons in the western Pacific.*

Taifeng台风: *Tropical air vortices occurring over the western Pacific Ocean and the South China Sea, representing extremely violent storms with a force exceeding ten, accompanied by heavy rainfall. They are most frequent during the summer and autumn seasons.*

Longjuanfeng龙卷风: *Intense whirlwinds with a relatively small range, shaped like a large funnel. Their speeds often reach over one hundred meters per second, with immense destructive power. On land, they are capable of uprooting large trees, damaging various buildings and crops; at sea, they can draw seawater into the air, forming towering water columns. Tornadoes are relatively rare occurrences.*

Analysis: Similar to the previous group, the concept of [feng风(Wind)] is predefined as a semantic gene.

The semantic gene structures of words in this group can be described as follows:

$S_{风暴}$ = {[自然事件]:{[现象]([天气])}+{[表现]([风]∧[雨])}+{[强度]([大])}
$S_{风暴}$ = {[Natural Event]:{[Phenomenon]:([Weather])}+{[Manifestation]:([Wind]∧[Rain])} {[Intensity]([Great])}

$S_{\text{飓风}}$ = {[自然事件]:{[现象]([天气])}+{[表现](Gs[风暴])}+{[强度]([强烈])}+{[处所]([[大西洋]∨[印度群岛][9]]∧[方向]([西])}}
$S_{\text{飓风}}$ = {[Natural Event]:{[Phenomenon]([Weather])}+{[Manifestation](Gs[Storm])}+{[Degree]([Intense])}+{[Location]([[The Atlantic]∨[The Indies]∧[Direction]([West])}}
$S_{\text{台风}}$ = {[自然事件]:{[现象]([天气])}+{[表现](Gs[风暴])}+{[强度]([猛烈])}+{[速度]([>100米/秒])}+{[处所]([[太平洋]∧[方向]([西])]]∧[南海])}+{[伴随](Gs[暴雨]]+{[时间]([夏季]∧[秋季])}}
$S_{\text{台风}}$ = {[Natural Event]:{[Phenomenon]([Weather])}+{[Manifestation](Gs[Storm])}+{[Degree]([Intense])}+{[Speed]([>100 m/s])}+{[Location]([[The Pacific]∧[Direction]([West])]]∧[The South China Sea])}+{[Accompany](Gs[Storm]]+{[Time]([Summer]∧[Autumn])}}
$S_{\text{龙卷风}}$ = {[自然事件]:{[现象]([天气])}+{[表现](Gs[风暴])}+{[强度]([猛烈])}+{[量级]([>10])}+{[形状]:[比较]([i]↑Gs[漏斗]([相似]))}+{[范围]([小])}+{[危害]([大])}}
$S_{\text{龙卷风}}$ = {[Natural Event]:{[Phenomenon]([Weather])}+{[Manifestation](Gs[Storm])}+{[Degree]([Intense])}+{[Grade]([>10])}+{[Shape]:[Comparison]([i]↑Gs[Funnel]([Like]))}+{[Scope]([Small])}+{[Harm]([Big])}}

③ {dizhen地震(Earthquake), haixiao海啸(tsunami), rishi日食(solar eclipse), yueshi月食(lunar eclipse)}

Dictionary definition:

Dizhen地震: *The vibration of the earth's crust caused by interior movements within the Earth. It can be categorized into three types according to its cause: collapse earthquake, volcanic earthquake, and tectonic earthquake. Tectonic earthquakes account for ninety-five percent of all earthquakes globally.*

Haixiao海啸: *A series of powerful ocean waves generated by sudden disturbances, such as underwater earthquakes or storms. These waves can surge onto land, often resulting in catastrophic consequences.*

Rishi日食: *When the moon moves between the earth and the sun, the sunlight is obstructed by the moon, preventing it from reaching the earth, a phenomenon known as an eclipse. When the sun is completely obscured by the moon, it is called a total solar eclipse; when only a part is obscured, it is called a partial solar eclipse; and when only the central part is obscured, it is called an annular solar eclipse. All solar eclipses occur on the first day of the lunar calendar.*

Yueshi月食: *When the earth moves between the moon and the sun, thereby blocking the sunlight from reaching the moon. Consequently, a shadow appears on the moon's surface. This occurrence is referred to as a lunar eclipse. When the Earth completely obstructs the sunlight, it is called a total solar eclipse, while a*

[9] 七大洲四大洋名称、国家名、行政区划名、政党名、其他地名、人名等专有名词不作为基因簇，也不分析词义基因结构，语义计算中专门有命名实体识别技术处理。

partial obstruction results in a partial solar eclipse. Eclipses are always observed on or within a couple of days after the 15th day of the lunar calendar.

Analysis: This group of words encompasses a significant amount of encyclopedic knowledge. During the analysis of their meanings, it is essential to select the core conceptual meanings. The description is as follows:

$S_{地震}$ = {[自然事件]:{[现象]([地质])}+{[表现]([震动])}+{[部位]([地壳])}+{[原因]([变化]([主事]([内部]of[地球])))}

$S_{地震}$ = {[Natural Event]:{[Phenomenon]([Geology])}+{[Manifestation]([Vibration])}+{[Part]([Crust])}+{[Cause]([Change]([Agent]([Interior]of[Earth])))}

$S_{海啸}$ = {[自然事件]:{[现象]([地质])}+{[表现]([波动])}+{[部位]($_{Gs}$[海水])}+{[强度]([剧烈])}+{[原因]($_{Gs}$[地震])∧[部位]($_{Gs}$[海底])]∨[风暴])}}

$S_{海啸}$ = {[Natural Event]:{[Phenomenon]([Geology])}+{[Manifestation]([Vibration])}+{[Part]($_{Gs}$[Seawater])}+{[Degree]([Intense])}+{[Cause]($_{Gs}$[Earthquake])∧[Part]($_{Gs}$[Seabed])]∨[Storm])}}

$S_{日食}$ = {[自然事件]:{[现象]([天文])}+{[表现]([阴影])∧[部位]([地球])}+{[原因]([遮挡]([施事]([月球])∧[受事]($_{Gs}$[阳光])))}+{[[关系]of[位置]]([太阳]↑[月球]↑[地球]([直线]))}

$S_{日食}$ = {[Natural Event]:{[Phenomenon]([Astronomy])}+{[Manifestation]([Shadow])∧[Part]([Earth])}+{[Cause]([Block]([Agent]([Moon])∧[Patient]($_{Gs}$[Sunlight])))}+{[[Relation]of[Location]]([Sun]↑[Moon]↑[Earth]([Straight line]))}

$S_{月食}$ = {[自然事件]:{[现象]([天文])}+{[表现]([阴影])∧[部位]([月球])}+{[原因]([遮挡]([施事]([地球])∧[受事]($_{Gs}$[阳光])))}+{[[关系]of[位置]]([太阳]↑[地球]↑[月球]([直线]))}

$S_{月食}$ = {[Natural Event]:{[Phenomenon]([Astronomy])}+{[Manifestation]([Shadow])∧[Part]([Moon])}+{[Cause]([Blockg]([Agent]([Earth])∧[Patient]($_{Gs}$[Sunlight])))}+{[[Relation]of[Location]]([Sun]↑[Earth]↑[Moon]([Straight line]))}

The comprehensive analysis of the above groups yields a set of semantic genes for natural phenomena events, including {[xianxiang现象(Phenomenon)], [tianqi天气 (Weather)], [biaoxian表现(Manifestation)], [xingzhuang性状(Feature)], [bansui伴随(Accompanied)], [chusuo处所(Location)], [fangxiang方向(Direction)], [chixu持续(Duration)], [duanzan短暂(Short)], [qiangdu强度(Degree)], [liangji量级(Grade)], [xingzhuang形状(Shape)], [bijiao比较(Comparison)], [fanwei范围(Scope)], [buwei部位(Part)], [yuanyin原因(Cause)], [zhushi主事(Agent)], [guanxi关系(Relation)], [weizhi位置(Location)], [tianwen天文(Astronomy)], [bianhua变化(Change)], [dizhi地质(Geology)], [yu雨(Rain)], [xue雪(Snow)], [feng风(Wind)], [lei雷(Thunder)], [shandian闪电(Lightning)], [qiang强(Strong)], [qianglie强烈(Intense)], [turan突然(Sudden)], [xiaji夏季(Summer)], [dong东(East)], [nan南(South)], [xi西(West)], [bei北(North)], [menglie猛烈(Intense)], [sudu速度(Speed)], [chunji春季(Spring)], [xiaji夏季(Summer)], [qiuji秋季(Autumn)], [dongji冬季(Winter)], [xiangsi相似(Like)], [da大(Large)], [xiao小 (Small)], [weihai危害(Harm)], [zhendong震动(Vibration)], [diqiao地壳(Crust)], [neibu内部(Interior)], [diqiu地球(Earth)], [yueqiu月球(Moon)], [taiyang太阳(Sun)], [yinying阴影(Shadow)], [zheyang遮挡(Blocking)], [zhixian直线 (Straight line)}, as well as gene clusters Gs[loudou漏斗(Funnel)], Gs[haishui海水(Seawater)], Gs[haidi海底(Seabed)], Gs[yangguang阳光(Sunlight)], which are to be analyzed subsequently.

5.2.4.2 Disaster Event Nouns

① {zaihai灾害(disaster), zaihuang灾荒(famine), zaihuo灾祸(calamity), huohai祸害(bane), huoshi祸事(misfortune), zainan灾难(catastrophe), zaiqing灾情(disaster situation)}

Dictionary definition:
Zaihai灾害: *The damages caused by drought, flooding, insects, hail, war,* etc.
Zaihuang灾荒: *The damage caused by nature to human beings.*
Zaihuo灾祸: *Natural or man-made calamities.*
Huohai祸害: *Events of great harm.*
Huoshi祸事: *Events of great harm.*
Zainan灾难: *Severe damage and suffering caused by natural calamities and human-made disasters.*
Zaiqing灾情: *The extent and severity of the disaster-affected situation.*

Analysis: Disaster nouns are used to refer to various harmful events, with differences lying in the causes of the disasters and the extent of their damages. We employ a core gene cluster $_{\text{Gs}}$[youhai有害(Harmful)] to describe this class of event nouns.

$S_{祸害}$ = $S_{祸事}$ = {[事件]:{[性质]($_{\text{Gs}}$[有害])}+{[程度]([大])}}
$S_{祸害}$ = $S_{祸事}$ = {[Event]:{[Nature]($_{\text{Gs}}$[Harmful])}+{[Degree]([Large])}}
$S_{灾害}$ = {[事件]:{[性质]($_{\text{Gs}}$[有害])}+{[程度]([大])}+{[原因]([自然]∨$_{\text{Gs}}$[战争])}}
$S_{灾害}$ = {[Event]:{[Nature]($_{\text{Gs}}$[Harmful])}+{[Degree]([Large])}+{[Cause]([Nature]∨Gs[War])}}
$S_{灾荒}$ = {[事件]:{[性质]($_{\text{Gs}}$[有害])}+{[程度]([大])}+{[原因]([自然]}+{[结果]($_{\text{Gs}}$[荒年])}}
$S_{灾荒}$ = {[Event]:{[Nature]($_{\text{Gs}}$[Harmful])}+{[Degree]([Large])}+{[Cause]([Natural]}+{[Result](Gs[Lean year])}}
$S_{灾祸}$ = {[事件]:{[性质]($_{\text{Gs}}$[有害])}+{[程度]([大])}+{[原因]([自然]∨[人为])}}
$S_{灾祸}$ = {[Event]:{[Nature]($_{\text{Gs}}$[Harmful])}+{[Degree]([Large])}+{[Cause]([Natural]∨[Man-made])}}
$S_{灾难}$ = {[事件]:{[性质]($_{\text{Gs}}$[有害])}+{[程度]([大])}+{[原因]([自然]∨[人为])}+{[结果]([损失]∧[痛苦])}}
$S_{灾难}$ = {[Event]:{[Nature]($_{\text{Gs}}$[Harmful])}+{[Degree]([Large])}+{[Cause]([Natural]∨[Man-made])}+{[Result]([Loss]∧[Suffering])}}

$S_{\text{灾情}}$ = {[情况]:[原因](${}_{Gs}$[灾害])}
$S_{\text{灾情}}$ = {[Situation]:[Cause](${}_{Gs}$[Disaster])}

② {tianzai天灾(natural disaster), fengzai风灾(wind disaster), shuizai水灾(flood disaster), huozai火灾(fire disaster), chongzai虫灾(insect disaster), hanzai旱灾(drought disaster)}

Dictionary definition:
Tianzai天灾: *Natural disasters, such as floods, droughts, windstorms, and earthquakes.*
Fengzai风灾: *Disasters resulting from the passage of violent storms, typhoons, or hurricanes.*
Huozai火灾: *Disasters caused by a fire incident.*
Shuizai水灾: *Disasters caused by prolonged rainfall, sudden outbursts of mountain torrents, or the overflow of rivers,* etc.
Chongzai虫灾: *Disasters caused by significant pest damage.*
Hanzai旱灾: *Disasters caused by the prolonged absence of rainfall or insufficient rainfall, coupled with the lack of irrigation, which affects the normal growth of crops or leads to their withering, resulting in significant yield reductions.*
Analysis: This group of words primarily differentiates disasters caused by various causes. The semantic structure is simple, as described below:

$S_{\text{天灾}}$ = {${}_{Gs}$[灾害]:[原因]([自然])}
$S_{\text{天灾}}$ = {${}_{Gs}$[Disaster]:[Cause]([Natural])}
$S_{\text{风灾}}$ = {${}_{Gs}$[灾害]:[原因](${}_{Gs}$[暴风]∨${}_{Gs}$[台风]∨${}_{Gs}$[飓风]}
$S_{\text{风灾}}$ = {${}_{Gs}$[Disaster]:[Cause](${}_{Gs}$[Storm]∨${}_{Gs}$[Typhoon]∨${}_{Gs}$[Hurricane]}
$S_{\text{火灾}}$ = {${}_{Gs}$[灾害]:[原因](${}_{Gs}$[失火])}
$S_{\text{火灾}}$ = {${}_{Gs}$[Disaster]:[Cause](${}_{Gs}$[Fire])}
$S_{\text{水灾}}$ = {${}_{Gs}$[灾害]:[原因]({${}_{Gs}$[雨]:[时间]([长])}∨${}_{Gs}$[洪水]}
$S_{\text{水灾}}$ = {${}_{Gs}$[Disaster]:[Cause]({${}_{Gs}$[Rain]:[Time]([Long])}∨${}_{Gs}$[Floodwater]}
$S_{\text{虫灾}}$ = {${}_{Gs}$[灾害]:[原因](${}_{Gs}$[害虫])}
$S_{\text{虫灾}}$ = {${}_{Gs}$[Disaster]:[Cause](${}_{Gs}$[Pest])}
$S_{\text{旱灾}}$ = {${}_{Gs}$[灾害]:[原因](${}_{Gs}$[干旱])}
$S_{\text{旱灾}}$ = {${}_{Gs}$[Disaster]:[Cause](${}_{Gs}$[Drought])}

③ {renhuo人祸(man-made disaster), canhuo惨祸(frightful calamity), chehuo车祸(traffic accident), zhanhuo战祸(war disaster)}

Dictionary definition:
Renhuo人祸: *Calamities caused by human actions.*
Canhuo惨祸: *A severe disaster.*
Chehuo车祸: *Injury or death incidents occurring during the operation of vehicles, particularly automobiles.*
Zhanhuo战祸: *The calamities brought about by war.*
Analysis: The semantic structure is similar to the previous group. Description is as follows:

S人祸 = {Gs[祸害]:[原因]([人为])}
S人祸 = {Gs[Disaster]:[Cause]([Man-made])}
S惨祸 = {Gs[灾祸]:[结果]([惨]∧[重])}
S惨祸 = {Gs[Disaster]:[Result]([Miserable]∧[Severe])}
S车祸 = {Gs[灾祸]:{[原因](Gs[行车])}[结果]([伤]∨[亡]]([受事](Gs[人员])))}
S车祸 = {Gs[Disaster]:{[Cause](Gs[Driving])}[Result]([Injury]∨[Death]]([Patient](Gs[Personnel])))}
S战祸 = {Gs[祸害]:[原因](Gs[战争])}
S战祸 = {Gs[Disaster]:[Result](Gs[War])}

By integrating the above groups, we obtain the core semantic gene set for disaster events, which includes {[shijian事件(Event)], [xingzhi性质(Nature)], [chengdu程度(Degree)], [jieguo结果(Result)], [yuanyin原因(Cause)], [sunshi损失(Loss)], [tongku痛苦(Suffering)], [can惨(Miserable)], [yanzhong严重(Severe)], [da大(Large)], [shang 伤(Injury)], [wang亡(Death)], [ziran自然(Natural)], [renwei人为(Man-made)]}, as well as the gene clusters Gs[youhai有害(Harmful)], Gs[zhanzheng战争(War)], Gs[huangnian荒年(Lean year)], Gs[shihuo失火(Fire)], Gs[hongshui洪水(Floodwater)], Gs[haichong害虫(Pest)], Gs[ganhan干旱(Drought)], Gs[xingche行车(Traffic)], and Gs[renyuan人员(Personnel)] which are subject to further analysis.

5.2.4.3 War Event Nouns

① {zhanzheng战争(war), zhandou战斗(battle), zhanyi战役(campaign), zhanshi战事(warfare), zhanhuo战火(flames of war)}

Dictionary definition:

Zhanzheng战争: *Armed conflicts of a certain scale conducted between classes, ethnic groups, nations, states, or political groups for specific political objectives.*

Zhandou战斗: *Armed conflict between the opposing parties.*

Zhanyi战役: *A series of related military actions conducted concurrently within the same period and region to achieve a specific strategic objective.*

Zhanshi战事: *All activities related to war, broadly referring to the conduct of war.*

Zhanhuo战火: *The act of war or military conflict, emphasizing its destructive effects and the resultant calamities.*

Analysis: The amount of nouns pertaining to war-related events is quite large, and this group of words collectively refers to war from various perspectives. The core conceptual meaning of “war” means a conflict that occurs among multiple objects. To begin with, it is necessary to define three basic descriptive units: [canshi参事(Participant)], [zhijian之间(Between)]([x]), and Gs[douzheng斗争(Fight)]. [Participant] is a dimension gene, analogous to a semantic case of a verb, indicating the parties involved in the action or behavior. It cannot differentiate between the agent and the patient, or situations where they are mutually the agent and the patient. [Between]([x]) is a special function, which is considered unique because it differs from other functions in that it does not represent a feature dimension of the meaning, but rather serves as a composite assignment gene for other dimension feature functions, for example:

[参事]([之间]([双方]))
[Participant]([Between]([Both parties])).

The gene cluster $_{Gs}$ [douzheng斗争(Fight)] can be described as follows:
Douzheng 斗争: *The mutual confrontation between two conflicting parties, with one party striving to overcome the other.*

$S_{\text{斗争}}$ = {[事件]:{[内容]([冲突])}+{[参事]([之间]([双方]))}+{[目的]($_{Gs}$[取胜])}}
$S_{\text{斗争}}$ = {[Event]:{[Content]([Conflict])}+{[Participant]([Between]([Both parties]))}+{[Objective]($_{Gs}$[Winning])}}

The definitions of several terms providedin dictionaries have varying emphases.By mutually refering to each other, we select their key dimension features for description as follows:

$S_{\text{战争}}$ = {[事件]:{[内容]($_{Gs}$[斗争])}+{[参事]([之间]([国家]∨$_{Gs}$[民族]∨$_{Gs}$[阶级]∨[$_{Gs}$[集团]of[政治]]))}+{[目的]([政治])}+{[方式]([武力])}+{[规模]([大])}}
$S_{\text{战争}}$ = {[Event]:{[Content]($_{Gs}$[Fight])}+{[Participant]([Between]([Country]∨$_{Gs}$[Nation]∨$_{Gs}$[Class]∨ [$_{Gs}$[Group]of[Politics]]))}+{[Objective]([Politics])}+{[Way]([Force])}+{[Scale]([Large])}}
$S_{\text{战斗}}$ = {[事件]:{[内容]([冲突])}+{[参事]([之间]([双方]:[关系]($_{Gs}$[敌对]))}+{[方式]([武力])}}
$S_{\text{战斗}}$ = {[Event]:{[Content]($_{Gs}$[Conflict])}+{[Participant]([Between]([Both parties]:[Relation]($_{Gs}$[Hostility]))}+{[Way]([Force])}}
$S_{\text{战役}}$ = {[事件]:{[内容]($_{Gs}$[战争])}+{[形式]([系列])}+{[时间]:[区间]([相同])}+{[处所]:[范围]([相同])}+{[目的]([相同])}}
$S_{\text{战役}}$ = {[Event]:{[Content]($_{Gs}$[War])}+{[Form]([Series])}+{[Time]:[Range]([Same])}+{[Location]: [Area]([Same])}+{[Objective]([u])}}
$S_{\text{战事}}$ = {[事件]:{[内容]([活动]∧[事务])}+{[关涉]($_{Gs}$[战争])}}
$S_{\text{战事}}$ = {[Event]:{[Content]([Activity]∧[Affair])}+{[Involving]($_{Gs}$[War])}}
$S_{\text{战火}}$ = {[事件]:{[内容]($_{Gs}$[战争])}+{[结果]([破坏]∧$_{Gs}$[祸害])}}
$S_{\text{战火}}$ = {[Event]:{[Content]($_{Gs}$[War])}+{[Result]([Destruction]∧$_{Gs}$[Bane])}}

② {dazhang打仗(battle), sizhang死仗(life-and-death battle), yingzhang硬仗(tough battle), shengzhang胜仗(victorious battle), baizhang败仗(lost battle)}

Dictionary definition:
Dazhang打仗: *Engage in warfare; engage in combat.*
Sizhang死仗: *A battle where the participants are determined to fight to the death, deciding the outcome or the survival and extinction of both sides.*
Yingzhang硬仗: *Direct frontal confrontation,a hard-fought and intense battle.*

Shengzhang胜仗: *A victory in battle or campaign.*

Baizhang败仗: *A battle or campaign that results in defeat.*

Analysis: This group of words primarily focuses on depicting the feature of a specific dimension of war, such as its progression or outcomes. The semantic descriptions of this group of words are as follows:

$S_{\text{打仗}}$ = {[事件]:{[内容](Gs[战争]∧Gs[战斗])}}

$S_{\text{打仗}}$ = {[Event]:{[Content](Gs[War]∧Gs[Battle])}}

$S_{\text{死仗}}$ = {[事件]:{[内容](Gs[战斗])}+[影响]([[输]∨[赢]]∨[[生]∨[死]]}+{[强度]([激烈])}}

$S_{\text{死仗}}$ = {[Event]:{[Content](Gs[Battle])}+ [Impact]([[Wining]∨[Losing]]∨[[Living]∨[Death]]}+{[Intensity]([Fierce])}}

$S_{\text{硬仗}}$ = {[事件]:{[内容](Gs[战斗])}+[方式]([正面]}+{[强度]([激烈])}+{[过程]([艰苦])}+{[代价]([大])}}

$S_{\text{硬仗}}$ = {[Event]:{[Content](Gs[Battle])}+[Way]([Frontal]}+ {[Intensity]([Fierce])}+{[Process]([Arduous])}+{[Price]([Huge])}}

$S_{\text{胜仗}}$ = {[事件]:{[内容](Gs[战斗]∨Gs[战役])}+{[结果]([赢])}}

$S_{\text{胜仗}}$ = {[Event]:{[Content](Gs[Battle]∨Gs[Campaign])}+ {[Result]([Wining])}}

$S_{\text{败仗}}$ = {[事件]:{[内容](Gs[战斗]∨Gs[战役])}+{[结果]([输])}}

$S_{\text{胜仗}}$ = {[Event]:{[Content](Gs[Battle]∨Gs[Campaign])}+ {[Result]([Losing])}}

③ xiangzhan巷战(street battle), haizhan海战(naval battle), kongzhan空战(air battle)

Dictionary definition:

Xiangzhan巷战: *Combat conducted within urban alleyways and streets.*

Haihan海战: *Campaigns or battles conducted by the naval forces of the opposing sides in the ocean.*

Kongzhan空战: *Combat conducted by aircraft in the air.*

Analysis: This group of words primarily focuses on the specific methods of combat, encompassing features such as location and tools. The semantic gene structures of words in this group can be described as follows:

$S_{\text{巷战}}$ = {[事件]:{[内容](Gs[战斗])}+[处所](Gs[街道]∧Gs[巷子]}}

$S_{\text{巷战}}$ = {[Event]:{[Content](Gs[Battle])}+[Location](Gs[Street]∧Gs[Alley]}}

$S_{\text{海战}}$ = {[事件]:{[内容](Gs[战斗])}+{[参事]([之间](Gs[海军]of[双方]:[关系](Gs[敌对]))}+{[处所](Gs[海洋]}}

$S_{\text{海战}}$ = {[Event]:{[Content](Gs[Battle])}+{[Participant]([Between](Gs[Navy]of[Both parties]:[Relation](Gs[Hostile]))}+{[Location](Gs[Sea]}}

$S_{\text{空战}}$ = {[事件]:{[内容](Gs[战斗])}+{[参事]([之间](Gs[飞机]of[双方]:[关系](Gs[敌对]))}+{[处所]([天空]}}

$S_{\text{空战}}$ = {[Event]:{[Content](Gs[Battle])}+{[Participant]([Between](Gs[Aircraft]of[Both parties]:[Relation](Gs[Hostile]))}+{[Location](Gs[Sky]}}

The comprehensive analysis of the above groups yields the core semantic gene set for war event nouns:{[canshi参事(Participant)], [zhijian之间(Between)], [shuangfang双方(Both Parties)], [shijian事件(Event)], [neirong内容(Content)], [chongtu冲突(Conflict)], [mudi目的(Objective)], [guojia国家(Country)], [zhengzhi政治(Politics)], [fangshi方式(Way)], [wuli武力(Force)], [guimo规模(Scale)], [da大(Large)], [guanxi关系(Relation)], [xingshi形式(Form)], [xilie系列(Series)], [shijian时间(Time)], [qujian区间(Range)], [xiangtong相同(Same)], [chusu处所(Location)], [fanwei范围(Scope)], [mudi目的(Objective)], [shiwu事务(Affair)], [guanshe关涉(Involving)], [jieguo结果(Result)], [pohuai破坏(Destruction)], [yingxiang影响(Impact)], [shu输(Losing)], [ying赢(Winning)], [sheng生(Living)], [si死(Death)], [qiangdu强度(Intensity)], [jilie激烈(Fierce)], [zhengmian正面(Frontal)], [qiangdu强度(Intensity)], [jilie激烈(Fierce)], [guocheng过程(Process)], [jianku艰苦(Arduous)], [daijia代价(Price)], [tiankong天空(Sky)]}and some gene sets are left for further analysis: Gs[minzu民族(Nation)], Gs[jieji阶级(Class)], Gs[jituan集团(Group)], Gs[didui敌对(Hostile)], Gs[jiedao街道(Street)], Gs[xiangzi巷子(Alley)], Gs[feiji飞机(Aircraft)].

5.2.4.4 Nouns Expressing Exhibition and Celebration Events

① {huiyi会议(meeting), dahui大会(assembly), nianhui年会(annual meeting), lihui例会(regular meetings), shenghui盛会(grand gathering), wanhui晚会(evening party)}

Dictionary definition:

Huiyi会议: *A gathering convened by relevant organizations for the purposes of hearing reports, discussing issues, and assigning tasks.*

Dahui大会: ❶*General meetings held by national governmental bodies and organizations.* ❷*A mass gathering of a large number of people.*

Nianhui年会: *An annual gathering held by social organizations or similar entities.*

Lihui例会: *Regularly held meetings as stipulated by established schedule.*

Shenghui盛会: *A grand assembly.*

Wanhui晚会: *An evening gathering primarily centered around entertainment and cultural activities.*

Analysis: Several key elements are involved in the concept of gathering: participants, time or period, scale, and purpose. The basic descriptive framework for the knowledge domain of event nouns in this category can be defined as:

{[活动]:{$_{Gs}$[集会]:{[参事]([a])}+{[时间]([b])}+{[周期]([c])}+{[规模]([d])+{[目的]([e])}}}
{[Activity]:{Gs[Gathering]:{[Participant]([a])}+{[Time]([b])}+{[Period]([c])}+{[Scale]([d])+{[Purpose]([e])}}}

Initially, we describe the core gene cluster $_{Gs}$[jihui集会(Gathering)] based on dictionary definitions:

Jihui集会(gathering): *The act of gathering together for a meeting.*

Kaihui开会(Meeting): *A gathering of individuals for the purpose of conducting business, socializing, or attending lectures and reports.*

$S_{\text{集会}}$ = {[活动]:{[聚集]:{[参事]([人]:[数量]([若干]))}+{[目的](Gs[议事]∨Gs[联欢]∨[听](Gs[报告]))}}}
$S_{\text{集会}}$ = {[Activity]:{[Gathering]:{[Participant]([Person]:[Quantity]([u]))}+{[Purpose]([u])}}}

Based on this domain framework, the semantic gene structure of words in this group can be described as:

$S_{\text{会议}}$ = {Gs[集会]:{[参事]([u])}+{[目的](Gs[议事]∨[听]([情况])∨Gs[安排](工作))}}
$S_{\text{会议}}$ = {Gs[Gathering]:{[Participant]([u])}+{[Purpose](Gs[Discussing]∨[Listening]([Report])∨ Gs[Arranging]([Work]))}}
$S_{\text{大会1}}$ = {Gs[集会]:{[参事]([成员]:{[规模]([全体])})}+{[范围](Gs[机关]∨Gs[团体])}}
$S_{\text{大会1}}$ = {Gs[Gathering]:{[Participant]([Member]:{[Scale]([All])})}+{[Scope](Gs[Organs]∨Gs[Group])}}
$S_{\text{大会2}}$ = {Gs[集会]:{[参事]([群众]:{[数量]([多])})}}
$S_{\text{大会2}}$ = {Gs[Gathering]:{[Participant]([Masses]:{[Quantity]([Large])})}}
$S_{\text{年会}}$ = {Gs[集会]:{[范围]([团体])}+{[周期](Gc[每年])}}
$S_{\text{年会}}$ = {Gs[Gathering]:{[Scope]([Group])}+{[Period](Gc[Every year])}}
$S_{\text{例会}}$ = {Gs[集会]:{[周期]([固定])}}
$S_{\text{例会}}$ = {Gs[Gathering]:{[Period]([Fixed])}}
$S_{\text{盛会}}$ = {Gs[集会]:{[规模]([盛大])}}
$S_{\text{盛会}}$ = {Gs[Gathering]:{[Scale]([Grand])}}
$S_{\text{晚会}}$ = {Gs[集会]:{[时间]([夜晚])}+{[目的](Gs[联欢])}}
$S_{\text{晚会}}$ = {Gs[Gathering]:{[Time]([Evening])}+{[Purpose](Gs[Entertainment])}}

② {zhanlan展览(Exhibition), huazhan画展(art exhibition), huazhan花展(flower show)}

Dictionary definition:
Zhanlan展览: *Displaying for public viewing.*
Huazhan画展: *Painting exhibition.*
Huazhan花展: *Floral exhibition.*

This group of words has a simple semantic structure and can be directly described as follows:

$S_{\text{展览}}$ = {[活动]:{[陈列]([u])}+{[目的]([参观]([施事]([人])))}}
$S_{\text{展览}}$ = {[Activity]:{[Displaying]([u])}+{[Purpose]([Viewing]([Agent]([Person])))}}
$S_{\text{画展}}$ = {Gs[展览]:Gs[展品](Gs[画作])}
$S_{\text{画展}}$ = {Gs[Exhibition]:Gs[Showpiece](Gs[Painting])}
$S_{\text{花展}}$ = {Gs[展览]:Gs[展品](Gs[花卉])}
$S_{\text{花展}}$ = {Gs[Exhibition]:Gs[Showpiece](Gs[Flower])}

③ {dianli典礼(ceremony), qingdian庆典(celebration), shengdian盛典(pageantry), dadian大典(grand ceremony)}

Dictionary definition:
Dianli典礼: *A formal ritual.*
Qingdian庆典: *The grand celebration ceremony.*
Shengdian盛典: *A grand and solemn ceremony.*
Dadian大典: *The solemn ceremony.*
Analysis: The semantic differences among this group of words are relatively subtle, the description is as follows: The description is as follows:

$S_{典礼}$ = {[仪式]:[形式]([正式])}
$S_{典礼}$ = {[Ritual]:[Form]([Formal])}
$S_{庆典}$ = {$_{Gs}$[典礼]:[目的]([庆祝])}
$S_{庆典}$ = {$_{Gs}$[Ceremony]:[Purpose]([Celebrating])}
$S_{盛典}$ = {$_{Gs}$[典礼]:[规模]([盛大])}
$S_{盛典}$ = {$_{Gs}$[Ceremony]:[Scale]([Grand])}
$S_{大典}$ = {$_{Gs}$[典礼]:[气氛]([隆重])}
$S_{大典}$ = {$_{Gs}$[Ceremony]:[Atmosphere](Solemn])}

④ {hunli婚礼(wedding), zangli葬礼(funeral), jili祭礼(sacrificial rite)}

Dictionary definition:
Hunli婚礼: *Marriage ceremony.*
Zangli葬礼: *Burial rites.*
Jili祭礼: *A ritualistic ceremony of sacrifice or mourning.*

$S_{婚礼}$ = {[仪式]:[目的]($_{Gs}$[结婚])}
$S_{婚礼}$ = {[Ceremony]:[Purpose]($_{Gs}$[Marriage])}
$S_{葬礼}$ = {[仪式]:[目的]($_{Gs}$[殡葬])}
$S_{葬礼}$ = {[Ceremony]:[Purpose]($_{Gs}$[Funeral])}
$S_{祭礼}$ = {[仪式]:[目的]($_{Gs}$[祭祀]$\vee_{Gs}$[祭奠])}
$S_{祭礼}$ = {[Ceremony]:[Purpose]($_{Gs}$[Sacrifice]$\vee_{Gs}$[Mourning])}

The comprehensive analysis of the above groups yields the core semantic gene set for event nouns related to exhibition and celebration, which includes the following terms: {[huodong活动(Activity)], [juji聚集(Gathering)], [canshi参事(Participant)], [shijian时间(Time)], [zhouqi周期(Period)], [guimo规模(Scale)], [mudi目的(Purpose)], [shuliang数量(Quantity)], [ruogan若干(Several)], [anpai安排(Arranging)], [chengyuan成员(Member)], [guimo规模(Scale)], [quanti全体(All)], [fanwei范围(Scope)], [qunzhong群众(Masses)], [guding固定(Fixed)], [shengda盛大(Grand)], [yewan夜晚(Evening)], [chenlie陈列(Displaying)], [canguan参观(Viewing)], [yishi仪式(Ceremony)], [zhengshi正式(Formal)], [qingzhu庆祝(Celebrating)], [qifen气氛(Atmosphere)], [longzhong隆重(Solemn)]}. Additionally, there are several gene clusters awaiting further analysis, such as Gs[yishi议事(Discussing)], Gs[lianhuan联欢(Entertainment)], Gs[baogao报告(Report)], Gs[tuanti团体(Group)], Gs[jiguan机关(Organ)], Gs[zhanpin展

品(Showpiece)], Gs[huazuo画作(Painting)], Gs[huahui花卉(Flower)], Gs[jiehun 结婚(Marriage)], Gs[binzang殡葬(Funeral)], Gs[jisi祭祀(Sacrifice)], Gs[jidian祭奠(Mourning)]

The core semantic genes within the categories summarized above exhibit a significant degree of redundancy. The redundant elements are to be eliminated during the final consolidation and optimization stage. The residual semantic gene clusters will be analyzed at different stages of the entire project as it progresses.

5.3 Extraction of Semantic Genes for Verbs in Modern Chinese

5.3.1 Classification of Nouns and Selection of Analysis Samples

5.3.1.1 The Subclassification of Chinese Verbs

As with the subclassification of nouns, there are many different perspectives on the subclassification of Chinese verbs. The criteria for classification primarily stem from two angles: grammatical and semantic.

(1) Li 黎锦熙 (1924: 122–134) categorized verbs from the perspective of meaning into four types:

① Transitive verbs: "For the transitive verbs, the action extends to other objects." It is further subdivided into eight classes: disposing of objects, experience and methods, transferring items, dealing with affairs, identifying names, altering objects, expressing emotions and intentions, and indicating relationships.
② Intransitive verbs: "For the intransitive verbs, the action is condensed within itself." This category is further subdivided into five classes: typically action verbs, related to external objects, self-expression, emotional and volitional actions (which can also function as transitive verbs), and verbs indicating existence.
③ Copulative verbs: "For copulative verbs, there is no movement, yet imbued with dynamism." This category can be further subdivided into two classes: indicating determination and indicating comparison.
④ Auxiliary Verbs: They are divided into two subclasses: prefix auxiliaries and suffix auxiliaries.The prefix auxiliaries can be further divided into seven types: expressing possibility, volition, necessity, inevitability, contingency, passivity, and tendency. The suffix auxiliaries, on the other hand, are divided into three types: expressing possibility, completion, and continuation.

(2) Zhu 朱德熙 (1982: 58–61) categorized verbs into six types from the perspective of grammatical function:

① Transitive verbs: These verbs are capable of taking both true objects and quasi-objects.
② Intransitive verbs: These verbs can only take a quasi-object.
③ Nominal-object verbs: These verbs can only take nominal objects.
④ Predicative-object verbs: These verbs can take both nominal and predicative objects.
⑤ Nominal verbs: These verbs are capable of functioning as an object.
⑥ Auxiliary: They can only take predicate objects and cannot take nominal objects.

(3) Wang 王洪轩 (1987) categorized words based on their semantic features:

① Dynamic Features: Divided into stative verbs and dynamic verbs.
② Directional Features: Divided into, intro-orientational verbs, extro-orientational verbs, and bi-directional verbs.
③ Participant Features: Divided into collective verbs and individual verbs.
④ Volitional Features: Divided into non-volitional and volitional verbs.
⑤ Continuity Features: Divided intomomentary verbs verbs and durative verbs.
⑥ Beneficial Features: Divided into non-beneficial and beneficial verbs.
⑦ Dependency Features: Divided into non-dependent and dependent verbs.

(4) Ma 马庆株 (1992: 13) categorized verbs into two types: volitional and non-volitional, with non-volitional verbs further divided into change verbs and attribute verbs.
(5) Hu 胡裕树 & Fan 范晓 (1995: 156) categorized verbs into monovalent, bivalent, and trivalent types based on the verb valency principle. This classification is conducted within the context of the minimal subject-predicate structure that possesses semantic autonomy, where the categorization is determined by the number of syntactic components required by the verb.
(6) Yuan Yulin 袁毓林 (1998: 149–322) expanded the valency theory, discussing the valency coordination of verbs from four levels: link, item, position, and argument. He categorized verbs into four types of valences: monovalent, bivalent, quasi-bivalent, and trivalent.
(7) Guo 郭大方 (1994) categorized verbs into three semantic levels. The top level falls into five categories: ① human body, ② psychology, ③ society, ④ nature, and ⑤ comprehensive. Each primary category is further subdivided into several secondary and tertiary categories, ultimately resulting in a total of 255 tertiary categories.
(8) Liu 刘美君 & Wan 万明瑜 (2019) combined frame semantics and construction grammar to construct a verb word net for Chinese information processing, which collectively describes eight types of source frameworks for verbs: ① emotional, ② perceptual, ③ cognitive, ④ communicative, ⑤ evaluative, ⑥ automatic, ⑦ caused-motion, and ⑧ social interaction. Below the source frameworks, there are further divisions into primary frameworks, basic frameworks, and micro-frameworks. To date, the basic framework category has already encompassed over 80 types.

5.3.1.2 Selection of Analysis Samples for Semantic Gene Information of Verbs

By synthesizing various viewpoints on subclassification of verbs, we have selected several representative subclasses for semantic analysis and gene extraction.

(1) Displacement verbs
(2) Action Verbs
(3) Cognitive Verbs
(4) Change Verbs

5.3.2 Semantic Analysis and Semantic Gene Extraction of Displacement Verbs

① {lai来(come), qu去(go), daoda达到(arrive)}

Dictionary definition:
Lai来: *From elsewhere to the speaker's location (opposite to 'go').*
Qu去: *From the place of origin to another location (opposite to 'come').*
Daoda到达: *Arrived at (a location, a stage).*
Dao到: *Arrive at a certain point.*
Analysis: The semantics of displacement verbs encompass several key elements: the starting point, the endpoint, the direction, and the reference point, which are the spatial dimensions. Additionally, there are temporal dimensions, such as the starting and endpoint of time, for instance, "chufa出发(departure)" denotes that the time point at which the displacement occurs is either the moment of speaking or a time point specified in the utterance; while "daoda到达(arrive)" denotes the time point at which the displacement concludes, also either at the moment of speaking or at a time point specified in the utterance. This temporal dimension can be described independently or through a transformation from the spatial dimension. When the spatial reference point of the displacement coincides with the spatial starting point, it signifies "departure"; similarly, when the spatial reference point coincides with the spatial endpoint, it indicates "arrival". The semantic domain framework of "displacement" verbs can be represented as:

{$_{Gs}$[位移]:{[起点]([a])}+{[终点]([b])}+{[方向]([d])}+{[参照点]([d])}+{[时间起点]([e])}+{[时间终点]([f])}
{$_{Gs}$[Displacement]:{[Start Point]([a])}+{[Endpoint]([b])}+{[Direction]([d])}+{[Reference point]([d])}+{[Temporal starting point]([e])}+{[Temporal endpoint]([f])}.

The core gene cluster $_{Gs}$[weiyi 位移 (Displacement)] requires preliminary description:
Weiyi 位移: *The change in position of an object during its motion.*

$S_{\text{位移}}$ = {[变化]:{[对象]([人]∨[物])}+{[维度]([位置]of[空间])}}
$S_{\text{位移}}$ = {[Change]:{[Object]([Person]∨[Thing])}+
{[Dimension]([Position]of[Space])}}

Based on the above analysis, the semantic gene structures of words in this group are as follows:

$S_{\text{来}}$ = {Gs[位移]:{[起点]([u])}+{[终点]([处所]of Gs[说者])}}
$S_{\text{来}}$ = {Gs[Displacement]:{[Start Point]([u])}+{[Endpoint]([Location]of Gs[Speaker])}}
$S_{\text{去}}$ = {Gs[位移]:{[起点]([处所]of Gs[说者])}+{[终点]([u])}}
$S_{\text{去}}$ = {Gs[Displacement]:{[Start Point]([Location]of Gs[Speaker])}+
{[Endpoint]([u])}}
$S_{\text{到达}}$ = {Gs[位移]:{[起点]([u])}+{[终点]([参照点])}}
$S_{\text{到达}}$ = {Gs[Displacement]:{[Start Point]([u])}+{[Endpoint]([Reference point])}}

The gene cluster Gs[shuozhe 说者 (Speaker)] is not a fixed person, and its description is elaborated as follows:

$S_{\text{说者}}$ = {[人]:{[说]([施事](i))}
$S_{\text{说者}}$ = {[Person]:{[Speaking]([Agent](i))}

② {shangsheng上升(rise), xiajiang下降(fall), jiangluo降落(descend)}

Dictionary definition:
Shangsheng上升: *Ascending from a lower to a higher position.*
Xiajiang下降: *Descending from high to low.*
Jiangluo降落: *Falling down; to land; to alight.*
The description is as follows:

$S_{\text{上升}}$ = {Gs[位移]:{[起点](Gs[低处])}+{[终点](Gs[高处])}}
$S_{\text{上升}}$ = {Gs[Displacement]:{[Start Point](Gs[Low position])}+
{[Endpoint](Gs[High position])}}
$S_{\text{下降}}$ = {Gs[位移]:{[起点](Gs[高处])}+{[终点](Gs[低处])}}
$S_{\text{下降}}$ = {Gs[Displacement]:{[Start Point](Gs[High position])}+
{[Endpoint](Gs[Low position])}}
$S_{\text{降落}}$ = {Gs[位移]:{[起点](Gs[高处])}+{[方向]([下])}}
$S_{\text{降落}}$ = {Gs[Displacement]:{[Start Point](Gs[High position])}+
{[Direction]([Down])}}

The gene clusters Gs[gaochu高处(High position)] and Gs[dichu低处(Low position)] are described as follows:

$S_{\text{高处}}$ = {[处所]:[位置]([高])}
$S_{\text{高处}}$ = {[Location]:[Position]([High])}
$S_{\text{低处}}$ = {[处所]:[位置]([低])}
$S_{\text{低处}}$ = {[Location]:[Position]([Low])}

③ {jinlai进来(come in), jinqu进去(go in), jinru进入(enter), chulai出来(come out), chuqu出去(go out)}

Dictionary definition:
Jinlai进来: *Come from outside to the inside.*
Jinqu进去: *Go from outside to the inside.*
Jinru进入: *Step into a certain range or period.*
Chulai出来: *Come from inside to the outside.*
Chuqu出去: *Go from inside to the outside.*

Analysis: The feature dimension “canzhaodian参照点([Reference point])”is not utilized in the previous two groups. However, the characteristic of this group differs, with the [Reference point] being a key feature dimension. The description is as follows:

$S_{进来}$ = {$_{Gs}$[位移]:{[起点]($_{Gs}$[外面])}+{[终点]($_{Gs}$[里面])}+{[参照点]($_{Gs}$[里面])}}
$S_{进来}$ = {$_{Gs}$[Displacement]:{[Start Point]($_{Gs}$[Outside])}+{[Endpoint]($_{Gs}$[Inside])}+{[Reference point]($_{Gs}$[Inside])}}
$S_{进去}$ = {$_{Gs}$[位移]:{[起点]($_{Gs}$[外面])}+{[终点]($_{Gs}$[里面])}+{[参照点]($_{Gs}$[外面])}}
$S_{进去}$ = {$_{Gs}$[Displacement]:{[Start Point]($_{Gs}$[Outside])}+{[Endpoint]($_{Gs}$[Inside])}+{[Reference point]($_{Gs}$[Outside])}}
$S_{出来}$ = {$_{Gs}$[位移]:{[起点]($_{Gs}$[里面])}+{[终点]($_{Gs}$[外面])}+{[参照点]($_{Gs}$[外面])}}
$S_{出来}$ = {$_{Gs}$[Displacement]:{[Start Point]($_{Gs}$[Inside])}+{[Endpoint]($_{Gs}$[Outside])}+{[Reference point]($_{Gs}$[Outside])}}
$S_{出去}$ = {$_{Gs}$[位移]:{[起点]($_{Gs}$[里面])}+{[终点]($_{Gs}$[外面])}+{[参照点]($_{Gs}$[里面])}}
$S_{出去}$ = {$_{Gs}$[Displacement]:{[Start Point]($_{Gs}$[Inside])}+{[Endpoint]($_{Gs}$[Outside])}+{[Reference point]($_{Gs}$[Inside])}}

The gene clusters $_{Gs}$[limian里面(Inside)] and $_{Gs}$[waimian外面(Outside)] are described as follows:

$S_{里面}$ = {[处所]:[位置]([里])}
$S_{里面}$ = {[Location]:[Poition]([In])}
$S_{外面}$ = {[处所]:[位置]([外])}
$S_{外面}$ = {[Location]:[Poition]([Out])}

④ {zhuanyi转移(transfer), qianyi迁移(migrate), banqian搬迁(relocate), nuodong挪动(move)}

Dictionary definition:
Zhuanyi转移: *To change position, from one place to another.*
Qianyi迁移: *To leave one’s original location and relocating to another place.*
Banqian搬迁: *Referring specifically to the movement of residence or organization.*
Nuodong挪动: *To change the position slowly.*

$S_{\text{转移}}$ = {[变化]:{[对象]([人]∨[物])}+{[维度]([位置]∨[方向])}}
$S_{\text{转移}}$ = {[Change]:{[Object]([Person]∨[Thing])}+
{[Dimension]([Position]∨[Direction])}}
$S_{\text{迁移}}$ = {$_{\text{Gs}}$[位移]:{[起点]([原地])}+{[终点]([u])}}
$S_{\text{迁移}}$ = {$_{\text{Gs}}$[Displacement]:{[Start Point]([Original location])}+
{[Endpoint]([u])}}
$S_{\text{搬迁}}$ = {$_{\text{Gs}}$[转移]:[对象]($_{\text{Gs}}$[住所]∨[单位])}
$S_{\text{搬迁}}$ = {$_{\text{Gs}}$[Transfer]:[Object]($_{\text{Gs}}$[Residence]∨[Unit])}
$S_{\text{挪动}}$ = {$_{\text{Gs}}$[位移]:{[速度]([慢])}}
$S_{\text{挪动}}$ = {$_{\text{Gs}}$[Displacement]:{[Speed]([Slow])}}

5.3.3 Semantic Analysis and Semantic Gene Extraction of Action Verbs

① {da打(hit), peng碰(bump), zhuang撞(collide), qiao敲(knock), pai拍(slap)}

Dictionary definition:
Da打: *To strike an object with the hand or a tool.*
Pai拍: *To strike with the palm.*
Peng碰: *The motion of an object suddenly comes into contact with another object.*
Zhuang撞: *The crash of a moving object with another object abruptly.*
Qiao敲: *To Strike an object to produce a sound.*

Analysis: This is a group of verbs representing motion of hand. For verbs of human actions, when the body part involved in the action is specified, we categorize the body part under the dimension [canshi参事(Participant)] rather than the [shishi施事(Agent)], as the value of [Agent] refers to the person performing the action but not the specific body part.

The concept of "da打" is a difficult one to define. Examination of the definitions in multiple dictionaries reveals that the words "da打", "qiao敲", "zhuang撞" and "peng碰" exhibit a circular interpretation. Among them the definitions of "peng碰" and "zhuang撞" are relatively more independent. We will first analyze these two words and then use them as semantic genes to describe the meanings of the other terms.

$S_{\text{碰}}$ = {[动作]:{[接触]:{[参事]([物]:[数量]([2]))}+{[时间]($_{\text{Gc}}$[极短])}}}
$S_{\text{碰}}$ = {[Action]:{[Contacting]:{[Participant]([Thing]:[Quantity]([2]))}+
{[Time]($_{\text{Gc}}$[Extremely short])}}}
$S_{\text{撞}}$ = {[动作]:{$_{\text{Gs}}$[碰]:[力量]([大])}}
$S_{\text{撞}}$ = {[Action]:{$_{\text{Gs}}$[Bumping]:[Force]([Strong])}}
$S_{\text{打}}$ = {[动作]:{$_{\text{Gs}}$[撞]:[参事]([手])∨[工具]([器具])}}
$S_{\text{打}}$ = {[Action]:{$_{\text{Gs}}$[Colliding]:[Participant]([Hand])∨[Tool]($_{\text{Gs}}$[Utensil])}}
$S_{\text{拍}}$ = {[动作]:{$_{\text{Gs}}$[打]:[参事]($_{\text{Gs}}$[手掌])}}
$S_{\text{拍}}$ = {[Action]:{$_{\text{Gs}}$[Hitting]:[Participant]($_{\text{Gs}}$[Palm])}}
$S_{\text{敲}}$ = {[动作]:{$_{\text{Gs}}$[打]:{[受事]([表面]of[物])}+{[目的]([制造]([声音]))}}}

S敲 = {[Action]:{Gs[Hitting]:{[Patient]([Surface]of[Object])}+
{[Purpose]([Making]([Sound]))}}}

The gene chain Gc[jiduan极短(Extremely shor)t] and the gene cluster Gs[shouzhang手掌(Palm)] are generally described as follows:

S极短 = {[度量]:{[维度]([时间]∨{[空间]:[维度]([1])})+{[值]([小])}+{[程度]([极端])}
S极短 =
{[Measurement]:{[Dimension]([Time]∨{[Space]:[Dimension]([1])})+{[Value]([Small])}+{[Degree]([Extreme])}
S手掌 = {[部分]:{[构成]([u]of[人体])}+{[部位]([正面]of[手])}}
S手掌 = {[Part]:{[Composing]([i]of[Human body])}+
{[Part]([Frontal]of[Hand])}}

② {ti踢(kick), chuai踹(kick), cai踩(step on)}

Dictionary definition:
Ti踢: *The action of raising the leg and striking with the foot.*
Chuai踹: *The action of kicking outwards with the sole of the foot.*
Cai踩: *The contact of the sole with the ground or an object.*
Analysis: This group of words denotes actions of the foot, with "ti踢" being a composite action consisting of two consecutive movements: "lifting the leg" and "striking with the foot", which are performed in a sequential order. The description is as follows:

S踢 = {[动作]:{[抬]:[参事]([腿]) < Gs[撞]:[参事]([脚])}}
S踢 = {[Action]:{[Lifting]:[Participant]([Leg]) < Gs[Striking]:[Participant]([Foot])}}
S踹 = {Gs[踢]:{[参事]([底部]of[脚])}+{[方向]([外])}}
S踹 = {Gs[Kicking]:{[Participant]([Bottom]of[Foot])}+
{[Direction]([Outward])}}
S踩 = {[动作]:{[接触]:[参事]([底部]of[脚])}+{[目标](Gc[地面])∨[物体]}}
S踩 = {[Action]:{[Contacting]:[Participant]([Bottom]of[Foot])}+
{[Objective](Gs[Ground])∨[Object]}}

③ {diantou点头(nod), huishou回首(turn one's head)}

Dictionary definition:
Diantou点头: *The slight downward movement of the head,signifying consent, approval, comprehension, or a greeting.*
Huishou回首: *Turning the head towards the rear.*
Analysis: Verbs of head movement. The descriptive way is similar to the previous groups.

S点头 = {[动作]:{[移动]:{[参事]([头])}+{[方向]([下])}+{[功能](Gs[同意]∨Gs[问候])}}

$S_{点头}$ = {[Action]:{[Moving]:{[Participant]([Head])}+
{[Direction]([Downward])}+{[Function]($_{Gs}$[Agreement]∨$_{Gs}$[Greeting])}}
$S_{回首}$ = {[动作]:{[移动]:{[参事]([头])}+{[方向]([后])}}
$S_{回首}$ = {[Action]:{[Moving]:{[Participant]([Head])}+
{[Direction]([Backward])}}

④ {fei飞(fly), youyong游泳(swim), qianshui潜水(dive)}

Dictionary definition:
Fei飞: ❶*The action of birds, insects, and other creatures flapping their wings to move through the air.* ❷*The motion in the air by powered mechanical devices.*
Youyong游泳: *The movement of humans or animals through water.*
Qianshui潜水: *Entering below the water surface.*
Analysis: This group of verbs denote movements involved the whole body, with the performer of the action referred to as the [shishi施事(Agent)]. With the exception of a few verbs that indicate multiple body parts (such as "crawl"), the majority of these verbs do not specify the particular body part involved, i.e., the [canshi参事(Participant)]. The description is as follows:

$S_{飞}$ = {[动作]:{[移动]:{[施事]([动物]∨[器具])}+{[处所]([空中])}}
$S_{飞}$ = {[Action]:{[Moving]:{[Agent]([Animal]∨[Utensil])}+{[Location]($_{Gc}$[In the air])}}
$S_{游泳}$ = {[动作]:{[移动]:{[施事]([动物]∨[人])}+{[处所]($_{Gc}$[水中])}}
$S_{游泳}$ = {[Action]:{[Moving]:{[Agent]([Animal]∨[Person])}+
{[Location]($_{Gc}$[In the water])}}
$S_{潜水}$ = {[动作]:{$_{Gs}$[进入]:{[施事]([动物]∨[人])}+{[处所]($_{Gc}$[水下])}}
$S_{潜水}$ = {[Action]:{Gs[Entering]:{[Agent]([Animal]∨[Person])}+
{[Location]($_{Gc}$[Underwater])}}

5.3.4 Semantic Analysis and Semantic Gene Extraction of Cognitive Verbs

① {sikao思考(contemplate), sisuo思索(think), kaolü考虑(consider), zhenzhuo斟酌(weigh)}

Dictionary definition:
Sikao思考: *To conduct a profound and comprehensive cognitive activity.*
Sisuo思索: *To think and explore.*
kaolü考虑: *To think about something in order to make a decision.*
Zhenzhuo斟酌: *Consider whether things, words,* etc. *are feasible or appropriate.*
Analysis: "siwei思维(thinking)" is a complex psychological process that involves human perception and all cognitive or intellectual activities, serving as the foundational point for explaining other cognitive activities. Its meaning is also difficult to decompose, as one recursively analyzes its dictionary definitions,the complexity will

increases. Therefore, we conventionally use [siwei思维(Thinking)] as the semantic gene for describing the meanings of cognitive words.

$S_{\text{思考}}$ = {[[活动]of[认知]]:{[思维]:[方式]($_{Gs}$[深刻]∧$_{Gs}$[严密])}}
$S_{\text{思考}}$ = {[[Activity]of[Cognition]]:{[Thinking]:[Way]($_{Gs}$[Profound]∧$_{Gs}$[Rigorous])}}
$S_{\text{思索}}$ = {[[活动]of[认知]]:[构成]([思维]∧$_{Gs}$[探索])}}
$S_{\text{思索}}$ = {[[Activity]of[Cognition]]:[Composition]([Thinking]∧$_{Gs}$[Exploring])}}
$S_{\text{考虑}}$ = {[[活动]of[认知]]:{$_{Gs}$[思索]:[对象]([问题])}}
$S_{\text{考虑}}$ = {[[Activity]of[Cognition]]:{$_{Gs}$[Thinking]:[Object]([Problem])}}
$S_{\text{斟酌}}$ = {[[活动]of[认知]]:{$_{Gs}$[考虑]:[方式]([反复])}}
$S_{\text{斟酌}}$ = {[[Activity]of[Cognition]]:{$_{Gs}$[Considering]:[Way]([Repeatedly])}}

② {xiangxiang想象(imagine), tuice推测(speculate), tuiduan推断(infer), guji估计(estimate), caice猜测(guess)}

Dictionary definition:

Xiangxiang想象: ❶*In the context of psychology, it refers to the psychological process of creating new images through the combination of perceptual materials.* ❷*To mentally construct a detailed image of an object that is not present in the immediate environment.*

Tuice推测: *To imagine unknown matters based on what is already known.*

Tuiduan推断: *Speculate and determine.*

Guji估计: *To make general inferences about the nature, quantity, and changes of things based on certain conditions.*

Caice猜测: *Speculation; to estimate by imagination.*

Analysis: The semantic foundation of this group is "xiangxiang(想象imagining)". We will first describe it and then continue to describe other meanings using the gene cluster. "Imagining" is also a kind of thinking activity. Based on the analysis of the previous group, the description is as follows:

$S_{\text{想象}}$ = {[思维]:{[[目的]∨[结果]]([创造]([受事]([形象]))}+{[依据]({[材料]:[来源]([感知])}∨{[事物]:{[处所]($_{Gs}$[他处])}})}+{[领域]([心理])}}
$S_{\text{想象}}$ = {[Thinking]:{[[Purpose]∨[Result]]([Creating]([Patient]([Image]))}+{[Basis]({[Material]:[Source]([Perception])}∨{[Thing]:{[Location]($_{Gs}$[Elsewhere])}})}+{[Field]([Psychology])}}
$S_{\text{推测}}$ = {[思维]:{$_{Gs}$[想象]:{[对象]([事物]:[性质]([未知]))}+{[依据]([事物]:[性质]([已知]))}+{[方式]([分析])}}
$S_{\text{推测}}$ = {[Thinking]:{Gs[Imagining]:{[Object]([Thing]:[Nature]([Unknown]))}+{[Basis]([Thing]:[Nature]([Known]))}+{[Way]([Analysis])}}
$S_{\text{推断}}$ = {[思维]:{[获得]([结论])}+{[方式]($_{Gs}$[推测])}}
$S_{\text{推断}}$ = {[Thinking]:{[Obtaining]([Conclusion])}+{[Way]($_{Gs}$[Speculating])}}
$S_{\text{估计}}$ = {[思维]:{$_{Gs}$[推断]:{[对象]([[性质]∨[数量]∨[变化]]of[事物]))}+{[依据]([情况]:[性质]([已知]))}+{[方式]([大概])}}}
$S_{\text{估计}}$ = {[Thinking]:{$_{Gs}$[Inferring]:{[Object]([[Nature]∨[Quantity]∨[Change]]of[Thing]))}+{[Basis]([Condition]:[Nature]([Known]))}}}

$S_{猜测}$ = {[思维]:{$_{Gs}$[推测]:[依据]($_{Gs}$[想象])}}}
$S_{猜测}$ = {[Thinking]:{$_{Gs}$[Speculating]:[Basis]($_{Gs}$[Imagining])}}}

③ {yiwei以为(suppose), renwei认为(believe), gandao感到(feel), juede觉得 (feel)}

Dictionary definition:
Yiwei以为: *To believe.*
Renwei认为: *The act of forming a certain perspective or judgment about a person or thing.*
Gandao感到: *To feel.*
Juede觉得: *To believe(with a less affirmative tone.)*
Analysis: The core meaning of this group revolves around the concept of "judgment". "Judgment" is also a fundamental form of think, which is difficult to define. It is conventionally designated as the semantic gene [panduan判断(Judgment)].

$S_{以为}$ = $S_{认为}$ = {[思维]:{[判断]:[对象]([人]∨[事物])}∧{$_{Gc}$[使确定]([看法])}}
$S_{以为}$ = $S_{认为}$ = {[Thought]:{[Judgment]:[Object]([Person]∨[Thing])}∧{$_{Gc}$[Ensure]([View])}}
$S_{感到}$ = $S_{觉得}$ = {[思维]:{$_{Gs}$[认为]:[语气](![肯定])}}
$S_{感到}$ = $S_{觉得}$ = {[Thought]:{$_{Gs}$[Believing]:[Tone](![Affirmative])}}

A word-like gene chain $_{Gc}$[shi queding使确定(Ensure)] is employed, which represents a causative sense structure that is frequently used in the semantic description of verbs. The framework for the causative sense domain can be expressed as:

{[使役]:{[施事]([a])}+{[受事]([b])}+{[结果]([X])}}
{[Causative]:{[Agent]([a])}+{[Patient]([b])}+{[Result]([X])}}

In this construction, [X] is the is the meaning of the described verb. The gene chain Gc[shi queding使确定(Ensure)] can be expanded to describe as follows:

$S_{使确定}$ = {[使役]:{[施事]([u])}+{[受事]([b])}+{[结果]([确定])}}
$S_{使确定}$ = {[Causative]:{[Agent]([u])}+{[Patient]([b])}+{[Result]([Definite])}}

In the description of semantics, in order to simplify the expression of gene structure, the causative sense structure is reduced to a function: $_{Gc}$[使X]([b]) $_{Gc}$[Causing X]([b]).

④ {liaojie了解(understand), renshi认识(recognize), zhidao知道(know), lijie理解(comprehend)}

Dictionary definition:
Liaojie了解: *To know clearly.*
Renshi认识: *To identify that a particular person or thing is indeed the excat one but not something else.*
Zhidao知道: *To have a recognition of facts or principles.*
Lijie理解: *To understand; To know.*

Analysis: The core meaning of this group “zhidao知道(know)”, similar to the analysis of the preceding groups, this word is also difficult to define and is directly designated as the semantic gene [zhidao知道(Know)].

$S_{\text{了解}}$ = {[[活动]of[认知]]:{[知道]:[性质]([清楚])}}
$S_{\text{了解}}$ = {[[Activity]of[Cognition]]:{[Know]:[Nature]([Clearly])}}
$S_{\text{理解}}$ = {[[活动]of[认知]]:{[知道]:[性质]([清楚])}}
$S_{\text{理解}}$ = {[[Activity]of[Cognition]]:{[Know]:[Nature]([Clearly])}}
$S_{\text{认识}}$ = {[[活动]of[认知]]:{[区分]([人]∨[事物])}+{$_{Gc}$[使确定]([人]∨[事物])}}
$S_{\text{认识}}$ = {[[Activity]of[Cognition]]:{[Identify]([Person]∨[Thing])}+{$_{Gc}$[Ensure]([Person]∨[Thing])}}

⑤ {xiangnian想念(miss), dianj惦记(keep thinking about), huiyi回忆(recall)}

Dictionary definition:

Xiangnian想念: *One cannot forget persons who are revered or departed, or some certain environment, hoping to see them again.*

Dianji惦记: *To think about a person or thing constantly, with a sense of unease or restlessness.*

Huiyi回忆: *To think back.*

Analysis: This group of verbs denote psychological activities. Psychological activities are a type of cognitive activities; however, they differ in that psychological activities are often accompanied by some form of emotion or sentiment. This emotion or sentiment constitutes a part of the conceptual meaning of psychological activity verbs and generally cannot be further analyzed using semantic components beyond these components that denote emotions or sentiments.

$S_{\text{想念}}$ = {[[活动]of[心理]]:{{$_{Gc}$[使保留]([人]∨[事物])}+{[处所]([记忆])}}∧{{[希望]([见])}+{[程度]([强])}}}
$S_{\text{想念}}$ = {[[Activity] of [Psychology]]: {{Gc[Preservation]([Person] ∨ [Object]) {[Location]([Memory])}} ∧{{[Hope]([To see])} {[Degree]([Strong])}}}
$S_{\text{惦记}}$ = {[[活动]of[心理]]:{[想]:{[对象]([人]∨[事物])}+{[时间]([持续])}+{[情绪](!$_{Gs}$[放心])}}
$S_{\text{惦记}}$ = {[[Activity]of[Psychology]]:{[Thinking]:{[Object]([Person]∨[Thing])}+{[Time]([Constant])}+{[Emotion](!Gs[Reassured])}}
$S_{\text{回忆}}$ = {[[活动]of[心理]]:{[想]:{[对象]({[[人]∨[事物]]:[时间]([过去])}}}
$S_{\text{回忆}}$ = {[[Activity]of[Psychology]]:{[Thinking]:{[Object]({[[Person]∨[Thing]]:[Time]([Past])}}}

5.3.5 *Semantic Analysis and Semantic Gene Extraction of Change Verbs*

① {gaibian改变(change), biangeng变更(alter), genghuan更换(replace), gaige改革(reform)}

Dictionary definition:
Gaibian改变: *Significant differences emerge among occurrences.*
Biangeng变更: *To change.*
Genghuan更换: *To replace.*
Gaige改革: *To alter the outdated and unreasonable aspects of things to new ones that can adapt to the objective circumstances.*

Analysis: Change verbs denote certain events, with the core conceptual meaning being "bian变(change)". It is conventionally designated as the semantic gene[bianhua变化(change)]. "Change" involves the situations before and after the change, that is, the initial state and the final state of things. This knowledge domain framework can be represented as:

{[事件]:{[变化]:{[参事]([a])}+{[状态]([始]([a])∧[终]([b]))}}}
{[Event]: {[Change]: {[Participant]([a])}+{[State]([Initial]([b]) ∧ [End]([c]))}}}

According to this framework, these words are described as:

$S_{\text{改变}}$ = {[事件]:{[变化]:{[参事]([人]∨[事物]}+{[程度]([显著])}}
$S_{\text{改变}}$ = {[Event]:{[Change]:{[Participant]([Person]∨[Thing]}+{[Degree]([Rremarkable])}}
$S_{\text{变更}}$ = {[事件]:{[变化]:[参事]([人]∨[事物])}
$S_{\text{变更}}$ = {[Event]:{[Change]:[Participant]([Person]∨[Thing])}
$S_{\text{更换}}$ = {[事件]:{Gs[改变]∧Gs[替换]}}
$S_{\text{更换}}$ = {[Event]:{Gs[Change]∧Gs[Substituting]}}
$S_{\text{改革}}$ = {[事件]:{[变化]:{[参事]([事物])}+{[状态]([始]([旧]∧![合理]) ∧[终]([新]∧[合理]))}}}
$S_{\text{改革}}$ = {[Event]:{[Change]:{[Participant]([Thing])}+{[State]([Initial]([Old]∧![Reasonable]) ∧[End]([New]∧[Reasonable]))}}}

② {yanbian演变(evolve), yanhua演化(develop), bianqian变迁(experience vicissitude)}

Dictionary definition:
Yanbian演变: *To develop and change, which pertains to a relatively long span of time.*
Yanhua演化: *To evole, particularly in reference to natural phenomena.*
Bianqian变迁: *The change or transition of situations or stages.*

Analysis: This group of words denotes significant changes in nature or society, characterized by long duration and pronounced transformation. The description is as follows:

S演变 = {[变化]:{[参事]([事物])}+{[时间]([长])}+{[结果]([发展])}}
S演变 = {[Event]:{[Change]:{[Participant]([Thing])}+{[Time]([Long])}+{[Result]([Developed])}}}
S演化 = {[变化]:{[参事]([自然])}+{[时间]([长])}+{[结果](Gs[进化])}}
S演化 = {[Event]:{[Change]:{[Participant]([Nature])}+{[Time]([Long])}+{[Result](Gs[Evolved])}}}
S变迁 = {[变化]:{[参事]([情况]∨[阶段])}+{[时间]([长])}}
S变迁 = {[Event]:{[Change]:{[Participant]([Situation]∨[Stage])}+{[Time]([Long])}}}

③ {kuozhan扩展(expand), pengzhang膨胀(inflate), yanshen延伸(extend)}

Dictionary definition:
Kuozhan扩展: *To extend outward; To enlarge.*
Pengzhang膨胀: ❶*The increase in the length or volume of an object due to factors such as temperature rise or other causes.* ❷*The enlargement or growth of certain things.*
Yanshen延伸: *To lengthen; To stretch.*
Analysis: This group indicates an increase in quantity along the spatial dimension. Description as follows: The description is as follows:

S扩展 = {[变化]:{[参事]([范围])}+{[状态]([终]([大])}+{[方向]([外]}}
S扩展 = {[Change]:{[Participant]([Scope])}+{[State]([End]([Large])}+{[Direction]([Outward]}}
S膨胀 = {[变化]:{[参事]([空间]:([维度]([1]∨[3])))}+{[状态]([终]([大])}+{[原因](Gs[加热]∨[u])}}
S膨胀 = {[Change]:{[Participant]([Space]:([Dimension]([1]∨[3])))}+{[State]([End]([Large])}+{[Cause](Gs[Heating]∨[u])}}
S延伸 = {[变化]:{[参事]([空间]:([维度]([1]]))}+{[状态]([终]([大])}}
S延伸 = {[Change]:{[Participant]([Space]:([Dimension]([1]]))}+{[State]([End]([Large])}}

④ {zengjia增加(increase), dizeng递增(increase progressively), suoxiao缩小(decrease)}

Dictionary definition:
Zengjia增加: *To add more on the existing basis.*
Dizeng递增: *To Increase step by step.*
Suoxiao缩小: *To reduce the size of something.*
Analysis: This group denotes the variation in magnitude of a physical quantity. The description is as follows:

S增加 = {[变化]:{[参事]([数量])}+{[状态]([终]([大])}}

$S_{增加}$ = {[Change]:{[Participant]([Quantity])}+{[State]([End]([Large])}}
$S_{递增}$ = {[变化]:{[参事]([数量])}+{[状态]([终]([大])}+{[方式]($_{Gs}$[逐次])}}
$S_{递增}$ = {[Change]:{[Participant]([Quantity])}+{[State]([End]([Large])}+{[Way]($_{Gs}$[Progressively])}}
$S_{缩小}$ = {[变化]:{[参事]([u])}+{[状态]([始]([大])∧[终]([小])}}
$S_{缩小}$ = {[Change]:{[Participant]([u])}+{[State]([Initial]([Large])∧[End]([Small])}}

⑤ {gonggu巩固(consolidate), jiaqiang加强(strengthen), ruohua弱化(weaken)}

Dictionary definition:
Gonggu巩固: To make it sturdy.
Jiaqiang加强: To make it stronger or more effective.
Ruohua弱化: Become weak; To make it weaker.
Analysis: This group denotes the variation in intensity. They are causative verbs, which can be described using the causative framework nested within the variation framework.

$S_{巩固}$ = {[使役]:{[施事]([u])}+{[受事]([u])}+{[结果]([变化]:[状态]([终]($_{Gs}$[坚固])))}}
$S_{巩固}$ = {[Causative]:{[Agent]([u])}+{[Patient]([u])}+{[Result]([Change]:[State]([End](Gs[Sturdy])))}}
$S_{加强}$ = {[使役]:{[施事]([u])}+{[受事]([u])}+{[结果]([变化]:[状态]([终]([强]∨$_{Gs}$[有效])))}}
$S_{加强}$ = {[Causative]:{[Agent]([u])}+{[Patient]([u])}+{[Result]([Change]:[State]([End]([Strong]∨ $_{Gs}$[Effective])))}}
$S_{弱化}$ = {[使役]:{[施事]([u])}+{[受事]([u])}+{[结果]([变化]:[状态]([终]([弱])))}}
$S_{弱化}$ = {[Causative]:{[Agent]([u])}+{[Patient]([u])}+{[Result]([Change]:[State]([End]([Weak])))}}

By merging the above groups, the core semantic genes for the description of verb meanings are obtained, mainly including the following: {[qidian起点(StartPoint)], [zhongdian终点(Endpoint)], [fangxiang方向(Direction)], [canzhaodian参照点(Reference point)], [bianhua变化(Change)], [duixiang对象(Object)], [ren人(Person)], [wu物(Thing)], [dongwu动物(Animal)], [weidu维度(Dimension)], [weizhi位置(Position)], [shishi施事(Agent)], [shoushi受事(Patient)], [canshi参事(Participant)], [kongjian空间(Space)], [chusuo处所(Location)], [shuo说(Speaking)], [gao高(High)], [di低(Low)], [li里(Inside)], [wai外(Outside)], [shang上(Upward)], [xia下(Downward)], [biaomian表面(Surface)], [neibu内部(Interior)], [xiamian下面(Below)], [duixiang对象(Object)], [danwei单位(Unit)], [sudu速度(Speed)], [man慢(Slow)], [kuai快(Fast)], [dongzuo动作(Action)], [jiechu接触(Contacting)], [shuliang数量(Quantity)], [liliang力量(Force)], [shou手(Hand)], [gongju工具(Tool)], [qijü器具(Utensil)], [biaomian表面(Surface)], [mudi目的(Purpose)], [zhizao制造(Making)], [shengyin声音(Sound)], [duliang度量(Measurement)], [zhi值(Value)], [xiao小(Small)], [chengdu程度(Degree)], [jiduan极端(Extremely)], [bufen部分(Part)], [goucheng构成(Composition)], [rendi人体(Human Body)], [buwei部位(Part)], [zhengmian正面(Frontal)], [tai抬(Lifting)], [tui腿(Leg)], [jiao脚(Foot)], [dibu底部(Bottom)], [jiechu接触(Contacting)], [mubiao目标(Objective)], [wuti物体(Object)], [tou头(Head)], [gongneng功能(Function)], [kongzhong空中(Air)], [diqiu地球(Earth)], [siwei思维(Thinking)], [huodong活动(Activity)], [renzhi认知(Cognition)], [fangshi方式(Way)], [goucheng构成(Composition)], [duixiang对象(Object)], [fanfu反复(Repeatedly)], [jieguo结果(Result)], [chuangzao创造(Creating)], [xingxiang形象(Image)], [yiju依据(Basis)], [cailiao材料(Material)], [laiyuan来源(Source)], [ganzhi感知(Perception)], [lingyu领域(Field)], [xinli心理(Psychology)], [weizhi未知(Unknown)], [yizhi已知(Known)], [fenxi分析(Analysis)], [huode获得(Obtaining)], [jielun结论(Conclusion)], [qingkuang情况(Situation)], [dagai大概(General)], [kanfa看法(View)], [yuqi语气(Tone)], [kending肯定(Affirmative)], [zhidao知道(Knowledge)], [qingchu清楚(Clearly)], [qufen区分(Distinguishing)], [jiyi记忆(Memory)], [xiwang希望(Hoping)], [jian见(See)], [chengdu程度 (Degree)], [qiang强(Strong)], [qingxu情绪(Emotion)], [chixu持续(Constant)], [guoqu过去(Past)], [bianhua变化(Changing)], [shi始(Initial)], [zhong终(End)], [xianzhu显著(Remarkable)], [jiu旧(Old)], [xin新(New)], [heli合理(Reasonable)], [fazhan发展(Developing)], [tiaojian条件(Condition)], [jieduan阶段(Stage)], [shuliang数量(Quantity)], [ruo弱(Weak)]}, as well as some gene clusters Gs[tachu他处(Elsewhere)], Gs[shenke深刻(Profound)], Gs[yanmi严密(Rigorous)], Gs[tansuo探索(Exploring)], Gs[fangxin放心(Reassured)], Gs[yanmi严密(Rigorous)], Gs[tongyi同意(Agreement)], Gs[wenhou问候(Greeting)], Gs[zhusuo住所(Residence)], Gs[Jinhua进化(Evolving)], Gs[zhuci逐次(Progressively)], Gs[jiangu坚固(Sturdy)], Gs[youxiao有效(Effective)], which are to be further analyzed.

5.4 Extraction of Semantic Genes for Adjectives in Modern Chinese

5.4.1 Classification of Adjectives and Selection of Analysis Samples

5.4.1.1 The Subclassification of Chinese Adjectives

Compared to nouns and verbs, the subclassification of Chinese adjectives exhibits relatively less divergence.

(1) Li 黎锦熙 (1924: 149–164) categorized adjectives into four classes based on meaning.

① Qualitative Adjectives: Adjectives for distinguishing the qualities, states, shapes, or degrees of concrete things.
② Quantitative Adjectives: Adjectives for distinguishing the number or quantity of entities.
③ Indicative adjectives: Adjectives for distinguishing the denotation or scope of entities.
④ Interrogative Adjectives: Adjectives for distinguishing the types, properties, or quantities of concrete entities.

In the current classification of part of speech in Chinese, class② corresponds to the modern numerals, class③ corresponds to demonstrative pronouns, and class ④ corresponds to interrogative pronouns.

(2) Zhu 朱德熙 (1982: 72) categorized adjectives into two types: qualitative adjectives and stative adjectives.
(3) Lü 吕叔湘 (1979: 38) posited that the boundary between Chinese verbs and adjectives is not clearly defined. Adjectives that can function as predicates can be merged into the verb as a subclass, while those that cannot serve as predicates are categorized as a separate class, i.e., non-predicate adjectives.
(4) Hu 胡明杨 (1991) categorized adjectives into four types: qualitative adjectives, state adjectives, non-predicative adjectives, and only-predicative adjectives.

The subclass of "state", "qualitative", and "non-predicate" adjectives are currently widely accepted as a consensus. Other scholars have also explored the classification of adjective sunclassfication from multiple perspectives.

In the study of modern Chinese adjectives, there is a scarcity of research that focuses solely on the meaning of words. Most studies begin from the perspectives of function and usage, with an emphasis on exploring the morphological and syntactic manifestations of adjectives. This book aims to discuss the methods of semantic description, although it cannot completely avoid the discussion of morphology and syntax, which are not our primary focus of investigation. Therefore, by integrating various subclassification viewpoints, we have selected a sample of typical words based on the semantic nature of adjectives, categorizing them into three types: adjectives related to physical properties, adjectives related to human properties, adjectives related to event properties.

(1) Adjectives related to physical properties: Adjectives that describe the stability or temporary physical characteristics of objects, such as size, shape, color, taste, newness, and value assessment, etc.
(2) Adjectives related to human properties: Adjectives that describe the external and internal nature and state of a person, such as age, appearance, character, and abilities.
(3) Adjectives related to event properties Adjectives that describe the nature and state of various stages of events, such as their occurrence, development, change, and outcome, including aspects such as speed, time, duration, and correlation.

Anyway, the three subclassifications are not entirely distinct from each other. For instance, the word "beautiful" can denote both the nature of objects and the nature of human beings; "complex" can refer to both the nature of objects and the nature of events. It should be noted that some adjectives related to physical properties can describe the properties and states of human body parts or organs, such as "smooth" can modify "skin", and "bright" can modify the eyes. However, we do not categorize them as adjectives related to human properties because body parts still fall within the category of "objects". Additionally, some adjectives expressing human properties, such as "loyal", "smart", and "happy", can also be used to describe animals, but this is achieved through the rhetorical device of personification. Therefore, these words are neither classified as adjectives related to physical properties.

5.4.2 *Semantic Analysis and Semantic Gene Extraction of Adjectives Related to Physical Properties*

① {wuhei乌黑(pitch-black), fenhong粉红(pink), ganqing绀青(prune purple), cuilü翠绿(emerald green), jiaohuang焦黄(burnt yellow), huabai花白(grizzled), jiebai洁白(pure white)}

Dictionary definition:
Wuhei乌黑: *Deep black.*
Fenhong粉红: *A composite color of red and white.*
Ganqing绀青: *A deep red with a hint of black.*
Cuilü翠绿: *A green color similar to that of jade.*
Jiaohuang焦黄: *A color characterized by a yellowish hue with a dry and withered appearance.*
Huabai花白: *A mixed colour of black and white, describing hair and beard.*
Jiebai洁白: *Spotless white, a color that remains untainted by any other hues.*

Analysis: Color words constitute an essential component of adjectives related to physical properties. They are difficult to define, particularly basic color words. Dictionaries generally employ descriptive methods of interpretation, such as "象……一样的颜色"a color like that of…", for example:

Hong红(red): *The color like blood or pomegranate flowers.*

Not only is such an interpretive pattern adopted in Chinese dictionaries, but also in authoritative English dictionaries, for instance:

Red: *of the colour of fresh blood or a similar colour.* (*Oxford Advanced Learner's Dictionary)*

Red: *having the colour of blood.* (*Longman Dictionary of Contemporary English)*

Red: *Having a color resembling that of blood.* (*The American Heritage Dictionary of the English Language)*

Red: *Something that is red is the colour of blood or fire.* (*Collins Cobuild Advanced Learner's English Dictionary)*

The advantage of this interpretive method lies in its vivid and intuitive nature, offering a more accessible approach to understanding color concepts for the average reader than the physics-based explanation of spectral frequencies. However, it may sometimes lead to confusion, for instance:

Xinghong猩红(scarlet): *A red similar to that of a chimpanzee's blood; a crimson red.*

The majority of common people may be unaware of the specific color image of chimpanzee blood, and the distinctions between the colors "xinghong猩红(scarlet)" and "xuehong血红(blood red)" remain unclear.

In addition to this descriptive approach, the interpretive patterns of color words also include: "A色和B色合成 The combination of A color and B color", "深/浅X色Dark/Light X color", and "A色中带(透着)B色 A color with a trace of (through) B color". The descriptive frameworks for these interpretation patterns are defined as follows:

{[颜色]:[比较]([i]↑[[颜色]of$_{Gs}$[x]]([相似]))}
{[Color]:[Comparison]([i]↑[[Color]ofGs[x]]([Similar]))} (The variable x is the object of comparison).
{[颜色]:[融合]([a]∧[b]}
{[Color]:[Blend]([a]↑[b])} (The variables a and b represent the two base colors being blended).
{[颜色]:{[x]:[浓度]([深]∨[浅]}}
{[Color]: {[x]: [Concentration]([Dark]∨[Light])}} (The variable x denotes the base color).
{[颜色]:[构成]([主]([a])∨[次]([b])}
{[Color]:[Composition]([Primary]([a])∨[Secondary]([b])} (The [Primary]([a]) function denotes the dominant color presented in the composite color composition, and [Secondary]([b]) represents the secondary color, which is the subtle hue that appears to "filter through" or "carry" within).

In this study, we do not intend to describe all color words exhaustively. Instead, we first establish a set of basic color terms as semantic genes: [bai白(White)], [hei黑(Black)], [hong红(Red)], [lü绿(Green)], [lan蓝(Blue)], [huang黄(Yellow)], and [cheng橙(Orange)].

Based on the aforementioned analysis, the semantic gene structure of words in this group is described as:

S$_{乌黑}$ = {[颜色]:{[黑]:[浓度]([深])}}
S$_{乌黑}$ = {[Color]:{[Black]:[Concentration]([Dark])}}
S$_{粉红}$ = {[颜色]:[融合]([红]∧[白])}
S$_{粉红}$ = {[Color]:[Blend]([Red]∧[White])}
S$_{绀青}$ = {[颜色]:[构成]([主]([黑])∨[次]([红])}
S$_{绀青}$ = {[Color]:[Composition]([Primary]([Black])∨[Secondary]([Red])}
S$_{翠绿}$ = {[颜色]:{[绿]:[比较]([i]↑[[颜色]of$_{Gs}$[翡翠]]([相似]))}}
S$_{翠绿}$ = {[Color]:{[Green]:[Comparison]([i]↑[[Color] of $_{Gs}$[Jade]]([Similar]))}}
S$_{焦黄}$ = {[颜色]:{[黄]:[比较]([i]↑[[颜色]of$_{Gs}$[枯叶]]([相似]))}}

$S_{焦黄}$ = {[Color]:{[Yellow]:[Comparison]([i]↑[[Color] of $_{Gs}$[Withered leaf]]([Similar]))}}
$S_{花白}$ = {[颜色]:[混合]([黑]∧[白])}
$S_{花白}$ = {[Color]:[Mixture]([Black]∧[White])}
$S_{洁白}$ = {[颜色]:{[白]:[性质]([纯]∧!$_{Gs}$[污染])}}
$S_{洁白}$ = {[Color]:{[White]:[Nature]([Pure]∧!$_{Gs}$[Taint])}}

It is essential to clarify that the terms "pink" and "grizzled" are both composed of two colors, yet their synthesis methods differ. "Pink" is a new color produced through the fusion of the two colors, which is distinct from the original colors. Therefore, we represent it using the dimension gene [Blend]. On the other hand, "grizzled" is a hybrid of the two colors, with neither color altering its original hue; they merely mix together. Consequently, we denote it using the dimension gene [Mixture]. Although the semantic gene expressions for these two terms share the same structural form, their functions are distinct.

② {tuoyuan椭圆(oval), hunyuan浑圆(perfectly round), gunyuan滚圆(spherical), bian扁(flat), wanqu弯曲(bent), bizhi笔直(perfectly straight)}

Dictionary definition:
Tuoyuan椭圆: *An oblate or elongated shapes.*
Hunyuan浑圆: *A shape that is quite round.*
Gunyuan滚圆: *Extremely round.*
Bian扁(flat): *The distance between the top and bottom is smaller than the distance between the left and right sides; the thickness of an object is smaller than its length and width.*
Wanqu弯曲: *Not straight.*
Bizhi笔直: *Extremely straight.*

Analysis: This group of adjectives denotes the physical shape of objects. The shapes of all entities in the world are diverse and changeable, and their descriptions are difficult to be summarized into a unified framework. However, it it is indispensable to several fundamental elements: constituent units, including point, line, and surface; spatial relationships, such as horizontal and vertical; and fundamental geometric shapes, such as square, circular, straight, curved, and arc. From these elements, we can predefine several core semantic genes: [dian点(Point)], [xian线(Line)], [mian面(Surface)], [zhi直(Straight)], [fang方(Square)], [yuan圆(Circular)], [shuiping水平(Horizontal)] and [chuizhi垂直(Vertical)]. Based on these genes, referring to dictionary definitions, it is possible to carry out semantic descriptions of various physical adjectives that express shapes.

$S_{扁}$ = {[形状]:{[[量值]of[空间]]:[比较]([[垂直] → [水平]](小)}}
$S_{扁}$ = {[Shape]:{[[Magnitude]of[Space]]:[Comparison]([[Horizontal] → [Vertical]](Small)}}
$S_{椭圆}$ = {[形状]:[圆]∧$_{Gs}$[扁]∧[长]}
$S_{椭圆}$ = {[Shape]:[Circular]∧Gs[Flat]∧[Long]}
$S_{浑圆}$ = $S_{滚圆}$ = {[形状]:{[圆]:[[程度]of[标准]]([高])}}
$S_{浑圆}$ = $S_{滚圆}$ = {[Shape]:{[Circular]:[[Degree]of[Standard]]([High])}}

$S_{弯曲}$ = {[形状]:![直]}
$S_{弯曲}$ = {[Shape]:![Straight]}
$S_{笔直}$ = {[形状]:{[直]:[[程度]of[标准]]([高])}}
$S_{笔直}$ = {[Shape]:{[Straight]:[[Degree]of[Standard]]([High])}}

People's cognition of the daily concept associated with a same word may sometimes be at variance with the scientific concept it denotes, as illustrated by the example of "oval" discussed above. Similarly, "round" and "straight" are absolute concepts in the scientific domain, meaning that a geometric figure is either circular or not, and either straight or not straight. In daily language, when something is described as "very round" or "very straight", it actually implies that it may not be truly "round" or "straight", but rather that it is very close to the standards of "round" and "straight" in the scientific sense, indicating a high degree of standardization. Therefore, we employ the standard dimension function [[程度] of [标准]]([高]) [[Degree] of [Standard]]([High]) to describe this meaning.

③ {gao高(high), di低(low), ai矮(short), chang长(long), duan短(short)}

Gao高: *The distance from below to above is great.*
Di低: *The distance from below is small; closer to the ground (opposite to "high").*
Ai矮: *The height is small.*
Chang长: *The distance between two points is great (opposite to "short"), referring to space or time.*
Duan短: *The distance between the two ends is small (opposite to "long"),referring to space or time.*

Analysis: This group of words denotes the magnitude of one-dimensional linear measurements of objects. Among them, "di低" and "ai矮" exhibit pragmatic differences. "di低" can refer to the height of concrete entities or abstract objects (such as status, level, etc.), but generally does not refer to a person's stature; while "ai矮" can refer to a person's stature or the height of concrete entities, but generally does not refer to abstract objects. The dictionary definitions do not explicitly clarify this point, and we should supplement this in the semantic gene description. The depiction of one-dimensional spatial measurement values requires the use of a key gene cluster, $_{Gs}$[juli距离(Distance)].

We shall first describe it:

Juli 距离: *The separation in space or time; length of the separation.*

$S_{距离}$ = {[度量]:[维度]([[空间]∧[1]]∨[时间])}
$S_{距离}$ = {[Measurement]:[Dimension]([[Space]∧[1]]∨[Time])}

The semantic feature function [weidu维度(Dimension)]([x]) allows the variable x to assume values such as [shijian时间(Time)], [kongjian空间(Space)], [chuizhi 垂直(Vertical)], [shuiping水平(Horizontal)], as well as specific numbers [1], [2], [3], which respectively represent one-dimensional, two-dimensional, and three-dimensional spaces. These values can be combined; for instance, [Space]∧[1] denotes one-dimensional space, while [[Space]∧[1]]∨[time] signifies either one-dimensional space or time.

Based on the above analysis, the semantic gene structures of words in this group are as follows:

$S_{\text{高}}$ = {$_{\text{Gs}}$[距离]:{[维度]([空间]∧[垂直])}+{[值]([大]}}
$S_{\text{高}}$ = {$_{\text{Gs}}$[Distance]:{[Dimension]([Space]∧[Vertical])}+{[Value]([Large]}}
$S_{\text{低}}$ = {$_{\text{Gs}}$[距离]:{[维度]([空间]∧[垂直])}+{[值]([小]}+{[对象]([物])}}
$S_{\text{低}}$ = {$_{\text{Gs}}$[Distance]:{[Dimension]([Space]∧[Vertical])}+{[Value]([Small]}+{[Object]([Thing])}}
$S_{\text{矮}}$ = {$_{\text{Gs}}$[距离]:{[维度]([空间]∧[垂直])}+{[值]([小]}+{[对象]([人]∨ [物体])}}
$S_{\text{矮}}$ = {$_{\text{Gs}}$[Distance]:{[Dimension]([Space]∧[Vertical])}+{[Value]([Small]}+{[Object]([Person]∨ [Thing])}}
$S_{\text{长}}$ = {$_{\text{Gs}}$[距离]:{[维度]([[空间]∧[1]∧[水平]]∨[时间])}+{[值]([大]}}
$S_{\text{长}}$ = {$_{\text{Gs}}$[Distance]:{[Dimension]([[Space]∧[1]∧[Horizontal]]∨[Time])}+{[Value]([Large]}}
$S_{\text{短}}$ = {$_{\text{Gs}}$[距离]:{[维度]([[空间]∧[1]∧[水平]]∨[时间])}+{[值]([小]}}
$S_{\text{短}}$ = {$_{\text{Gs}}$[Distance]:{[Dimension]([[Space]∧[1]∧[Horizontal]]∨[Time])}+{[Value]([Small]}}

④ {xianmei鲜美(delicious), qingxiang清香(fragrant), gantian甘甜(sweet), kuse苦涩(bitter), xianjinjin咸津津(salty), lahuhu辣乎乎(spicy), xiangtian香甜(fragrant and sweet)

Xianmei鲜美: *(referring to dishes, fruits, and vegetables,* etc.*) Having a pleasant and appetizing taste.*
Qingxiang清香: *Light fragrance.*
Gantian甘甜: *Sweetness.*
Kuse苦涩: *Bitter and astringent taste.*
Xianjinjin咸津津: *The taste is slightly salty.*
Lahuhu辣乎乎: *The sensation of spiciness.*
Xiangtian香甜: *Tasting fragrant and sweet.*

Analysis: Words that describe the taste of things pertain to the sensory perceptions of humans towards food, encompassing both gustatory and olfactory experiences. These basic sensory information perceived by human is difficult to describe and define, exhibiting cognitive prototype characteristics. So they are directly predefined as semantic genes: [suan酸(Sour)], [tian甜(Sweet)], [ku苦(Bitter)], [la辣(Spicy)], [xian咸(Salty)], [ma麻(Numb)], [se涩(Astringent)], [xiang香(Fragrant)], [chou臭(Stinky)].

$S_{\text{鲜美}}$ = {[味道]:[[味觉]∧[嗅觉]]([好])}
$S_{\text{鲜美}}$ = {[Taste]:[[Gustatory]∧[Olfactory]]([Good])}
$S_{\text{清香}}$ = {[味道]:{[嗅觉]([香])}+{[浓度]([淡])}}
$S_{\text{清香}}$ = {[Taste]:{[Olfactory]([Fragrant])}+{[Concentration]([Light])}}
$S_{\text{甘甜}}$ = {[味道]:{[味觉]([甜])}+{[浓度]([浓])}}
$S_{\text{甘甜}}$ = {[Taste]:{[Gustatory]([Sweet])}+{[Concentration]([Strong])}}
$S_{\text{苦涩}}$ = {[味道]:{[味觉]([苦]∧[涩])}}

$S_{\text{苦涩}}$ = {[Taste]:{[Gustatory]([Bitter]∧[Stringent])}}
$S_{\text{咸津津}}$ = {[味道]:{[味觉]([咸])}+{[浓度]([淡])}+{[修辞]([摹状])}}
$S_{\text{咸津津}}$ = {[Taste]:{[Gustatory]([Salty])}+{[Concentration]([Low])}+ {[Rhetoric]([Description])}}
$S_{\text{辣乎乎}}$ = {[味道]:{[味觉]([辣])}+{[修辞]([摹状])}}
$S_{\text{辣乎乎}}$ = {[Taste]:{[Gustatory]([Spicy])}+{[Rhetoric]([Description])}}
$S_{\text{香甜}}$ = {[味道]:{[嗅觉]([香])}∧{[味觉]([甜])}}
$S_{\text{香甜}}$ = {[Taste]:{[Olfactory]([Fragrant])}∧{[Gustatory]([Sweet])}}

The reduplication suffixes attached to Chinese adjectives are frequently used to depict situations in a vivid manner. The semantic functions of reduplication suffixes falls into two types: the one solely serves the rhetorical function of depiction, such as "lahuhu辣乎乎" (spicy), "suanliuiu酸溜溜" (sour), and "meizizi美滋滋" (delighted); the other type, while depicting the situation, also indicates the degree of the attribute, for instance, "xianjinjin咸津津" (slightly salty) and "tiansisi甜丝丝" (slightly sweet) suggest a mild degree of "salty" and "sweet", respectively, while "xiangpenpen香喷喷" (fragrant) and "chouhonghong臭烘烘" (smelly) convey a strong degree of "fragrance" and "stench" respectively.

⑤ {jianying坚硬(hard), jiangu坚固(solid), rouruan柔软(soft), rouren柔韧(supple)}

Jianying坚硬: *Stiff.*
Jiangu坚固: *Tightly integrated and cannot be easily damaged;robust; firm.*
Rouruan柔软: *Gentle; not hard.*
Rouren柔韧: *Soft,pliable but strong.*

This group of words describes the physical appearances of things that are influenced by their internal structures.For their semantic description,there are several key sense element which are "ruan软(soft)", "ying硬(hard)" "ren韧(pliable)" and "cui脆(brittle)". According to dictionary definitions, we can initially describe these terms.

Ruan软: *The internal structure of objects is loose, making them susceptible to shape alteration upon the application of external forces (opposite to "hard").*

Ying硬: *The internal structure of objects is compact, making them resistant to shape alteration upon the application of external forces (opposite "soft").*

Ren韧: *Under the action of external forces, it deforms without being easily broken; soft yet robust (opposite to "brittle").*

Cui脆: *Something can be easily broken or shattered (opposite to "pliable").*

The interpretation in dictionary for "ruan软" and "ying硬" pertain to the internal structure of objects, which constitutes a form of encyclopedic knowledge that elucidates the reasons behind the material appearances of things. When people perceive the meanings of these words, their focus is on the appearances rather than the internal causes. The dictionary also exhibits variations in the ways it defines the four words, with the definitions of "ren韧" and "cui脆" not fully encompassing this aspect, which further supports this point. Therefore, in the description of semantic genes, we can dispense with this part.

$S_{\text{软}}$ = {[物性]:{[表象]({[变]([对象]([形状]))}+{[难度]([小])})}
$S_{\text{软}}$ = {[Physical property]:{[Manifestation]({[Change]([Object]([Shape]))}+{[Difficulty]([Small])})}
$S_{\text{硬}}$ = {[物性]:{[表象]({[变]([对象]([形状]))}+{[难度]([大])})}
$S_{\text{硬}}$ = {[Physical property]:{[Manifestation]({[Change]([Object]([Shape]))}+{[Difficulty]([Large])})}
$S_{\text{韧}}$ = {[物性]:{[表象]({[[碎]∨[断]]([对象]([物]))}+{[难度]([大])})}
$S_{\text{韧}}$ = {[Physical property]:{[Manifestation]({[[Crushed]∨[Fractured]]([Object]([Thing]))}+{[Difficulty]([Large])})}
$S_{\text{脆}}$ = {[物性]:{[表象]({[[碎]∨[断]]([对象]([物]))}+{[难度]([小])})}
$S_{\text{脆}}$ = {[Physical property]:{[Manifestation]({[[Crushed]∨[Fractured]]([Object]([Thing]))}+{[Difficulty]([Small])})}

The gene clusters $_{\text{Gs}}$[Soft], $_{\text{Gs}}$[Hard], $_{\text{Gs}}$[Pliable], and $_{\text{Gs}}$[Brittle] are employed to describe other words.

$S_{\text{坚硬}}$ = {[物性]:{[表象]($_{\text{Gs}}$[硬])}+{[程度]([大])}}
$S_{\text{坚硬}}$ = {[Physical property]:{[Manifestation]($_{\text{Gs}}$[Hard])}+{[Degree]([Large])}}
$S_{\text{坚固}}$ = {[物性]:{[表象]($_{\text{Gs}}$[硬]∧$_{\text{Gs}}$[稳])}}
$S_{\text{坚固}}$ = {[Physical property]:{[Manifestation]($_{\text{Gs}}$[Hard]∧$_{\text{Gs}}$[Stable])}}
$S_{\text{柔软}}$ = {[物性]:{[表象]($_{\text{Gs}}$[软])}+{[程度]([大])}}
$S_{\text{柔软}}$ = {[Physical property]:{[Manifestation]($_{\text{Gs}}$[Soft])}+{[Degree]([Large])}}
$S_{\text{柔韧}}$ = {[物性]:{[表象]($_{\text{Gs}}$[软]∧$_{\text{Gs}}$[韧])}}
$S_{\text{柔韧}}$ = {[Physical property]:{[Manifestation]($_{\text{Gs}}$[Soft]∧$_{\text{Gs}}$[Pliable])}}

The gene cluster $_{\text{Gs}}$[Stable], which shares a semantic structure akin to "soft" and "hard", is described as follows:

$S_{\text{硬}}$ = {[物性]:{[表象]($!$[变]([对象]([结构]∨[位置])))}
$S_{\text{稳}}$ = {[Physical property]:{[Manifestation]($!$[Change]([Object]([Structure]∨[Position])))}

5.4.3 Semantic Analysis and Semantic Gene Extraction of Adjectives Related to Human Properties

① {feipang肥胖(obese), miaotiao苗条(slender), kuiwu魁梧(burly), jianzhuang健壮(robust), qiangjian强健(strong), qiangzhuang强壮(muscular), jieshi结实(sturdy)}

Feipang肥胖: *Fat.*
Pang胖: *An excessive accumulation of body fat and muscle mass (opposite to "thin"),referring to human body.*

Miaotiao苗条: *A slim and graceful figure, referring to a woman's figure.*
Kuiwu魁梧: *Strong and tall, referring to human body.*
Jianzhuang健壮: *Strong.*
Qiangjian强健: *Sturdy, referring to human body.*
Qiangzhuang强壮: *Sturdy and strong, referring to human body.*
Jieshi结实: ❶*Robust and durable.* ❷*Strong.*

Analysis: This group of words describes the physical appearance of human, which belongs to the external manifestation of human properties. Among the words "jianzhuang健壮", "qiangjian强健", "qiangzhuang强壮" and "jieshi结实" there exists a circular interpretation. By analysis and comparison, we can find out that "jianzhuang健壮", "qiangjian强健" and "qiangzhuang强壮" are all based on the concept of "jieshi结实". "jieshi结实" has two pleremes, plereme❶ is a physical adjective, and plereme❷ is an extension of the original sense. Therefore, we predefine [Sturdy] as the semantic gene, for describing the meanings of the other words in the group.

$S_{\text{胖}}$ = {[体貌]:[表象]([Gs[脂肪]∨Gs[肉]]:[量]([多]))}
$S_{\text{胖}}$ =
{[Appearance]of[Person]:[Manifestation]([Gs[Fat]∨Gs[Muscle]]:[Quantity
]([Large]))}
$S_{\text{肥胖}}$ = {[体貌]:[表象](Gs[胖]:[程度]([大])}
$S_{\text{肥胖}}$ = {[Appearance]of[Person]:[Manifestation](Gs[Fat]:[Degree]([Large])}
$S_{\text{苗条}}$ = {[体貌]:[表象]({[身材]([高]∧!Gs[胖]}∧[美])}+{[对象]([人]:[性别]([
女]))}}
$S_{\text{苗条}}$ = {[Appearance]of[Person]:[Manifestation]({[Stature]([Tall]∧!Gs[Fat
]}∧[Pretty])}+{[Object]([Person]:[Sex]([Female]))}}
$S_{\text{强壮}}$ = {[体貌]:[表象]([结实]∧Gs[有力])}
$S_{\text{强壮}}$ = {[Appearance]of[Person]:[Manifestation]([Sturdy]∧Gs[Powerful])}
$S_{\text{强健}}$ = $S_{\text{健壮}}$ = {[体貌]:[表象](Gs[健康]∧Gs[强壮])}
$S_{\text{强健}}$ = $S_{\text{健壮}}$ =
{[Appearance]of[Person]:[Manifestation](Gs[Healthy]∧Gs[Muscular])}
$S_{\text{魁梧}}$ = {[体貌]:[表象](Gs[强壮]∧[高]∧[大])}
$S_{\text{魁梧}}$ =
{[Appearance]of[Person]:[Manifestation](Gs[Muscular]∧[Tall]∧[Large])}

② {zhongcheng忠诚(loyalty), zhengzhi正直(upright), xuwei虚伪(hypocritical), shanliang善良(kind)}

Zhongcheng忠诚: *Dedicate oneself with unwavering commitment to the nation, the people, the collective endeavor, the leaders, the friends, and other relevant entities.*
Zhengzhi正直: *Fair and straightforward.*
Xuwei虚伪: *Deceitful;insincerity; fake.*
Shanliang善良: *The purity of one's heart, devoid of malice.*

These words describe a person's moral character, and the depiction of such meanings is relatively challenging, as it lacks the tangible objects and reference standards that are present in physical appearance. Some basic cognitive concepts can be initially predefined as lexical semantic genes, such as: [zhong忠(Faithful)], [jian奸(Treacherous)], [shan善(Good)], [e恶(Evil)], [chengshi诚实(Honest)], [qianxu谦虚(Modest)], [gongzheng公正(Fair)], and so on. Moral character is an assessment of a person's intrinsic qualities from an external perspective and often carries polarity meanings, which is inherently contained within the conceptual meaning of these words, hence, the interpretation in dictionaries generally do not need to be explicitly stated. In the description of lexical semantic genes, we can add this feature dimension to facilitate semantic reasoning by machines.

$S_{忠诚}$ = {[品性]:{[评价]([忠]∧[诚])}+{[对象]([国家]$\vee_{Gs}$[人民]$\vee_{Gs}$[事业]$\vee_{Gs}$[领导]$\vee_{Gs}$[朋友])}+{[极性]([褒])}}
$S_{忠诚}$ = {[Character]:{[Evaluation]([Faithful]∧[Honest])}+
{[Object]([Nation]$\vee_{Gs}$[People]$\vee_{Gs}$[Cause] $\vee_{Gs}$[Leadership]$\vee_{Gs}$[Friend])}+
{[Polarity]([Positive])}}
$S_{正直}$ = {[品性]:{[评价]([公正]∧[诚实])}+{[极性]([褒])}}
$S_{正直}$ = {[Character]:{[Evaluation]([Fair]∧[Honest])}+
{[Polarity]([Negative])}}
$S_{虚伪}$ = {[品性]:{[评价](![诚实])}+{[极性]([贬])}}
$S_{虚伪}$ = {[Character]:{[Evaluation](![Honest])}+{[Polarity]([Negative])}}
$S_{善良}$ = {[品性]:{[评价]([善])}+{[极性]([褒])}}
$S_{善良}$ = {[Character]:{[Evaluation]([Good])}+{[Polarity]([Positive])}}

③ {kaixin开心(happy), cankui惭愧(ashamed), neijiu内疚(guilty), shangxin伤心(sad)}

Kaixin开心: *A state of mind characterized by joy and comfort.*
Cankui惭愧: *Feeling discomfort or unease due to personal shortcomings, errors committed, or inadequate fulfillment of duties.*
Neijiu内疚: *Feeling of guilt involves an inner sense of shame and unease.*
Shangxin伤心: *The feeling of sadness and distress in the heart.*

Analysis: This group of words describes human psychological states, expressing certain emotions or feelings, which are the intrinsic perceptions of one's own mood. Emotions or feelings also require the pre-definition of some core semantic genes, such as: {[xi喜(Joyful)], [nu怒(Angry)], [ai哀(Sorrowful)], [chou愁(Worried)], [bei悲(Sad)], and so on. These words also carry polarity meanings.

$S_{开心}$ = {[[状态]of[心理]]:{[感觉]([喜])}+{[极性]([正])}}
$S_{开心}$ = {[[State]of[Psychology]]:{[Feeling]([Joyful])}+
{[Polarity]([Positive])}}
$S_{惭愧}$ = {[[状态]of[心理]]:{[感觉](![安定])}+{[原因]($_{Gs}$[缺点]$\vee_{Gs}$[错误])}+{[极性]([负])}}
$S_{惭愧}$ = {[[State]of[Psychology]]:{[Feeling](![Settled])}+
{[Cause]($_{Gs}$[Shortcoming]$\vee_{Gs}$[Mistake])}+{[Polarity]([Negative])}}

S内疚 = {[[状态]of[心理]]:{[感觉]([安定])}+{[程度]([大])}+{[极性]([正])}}
S内疚 = {[[State]of[Psychology]]:{[Feeling]([Settled])}+{[Degree]([Large])}+{[Polarity]([Negative])}}
S伤心 = {[[状态]of[心理]]:{[感觉]([悲]∧[痛])}+{[极性]([负])}}
S伤心 = {[[State]of[Psychology]]:{[Feeling]([Sad]∧[Painful])}+{[Polarity]([Negative])}}

④ {xiuse羞涩(shy), ganga尴尬(embarrassed), dafang大方(natural and graceful), jujin拘谨(reserved)}

Xiuse羞涩: *Feeling awkward, displaying an unnatural demeanor.*
Ganga尴尬: *Inappropriate or unnatural (expressions or demeanor).*
Dafang大方: *A natural and unforced demeanor; free from constraint.*
Jujin拘谨: *Excessively cautious (speech or action); constrained. A manifestation of unease or discomfort in a certain situation due to a lack of confidence.*

Analysis: This group of words refers to the expressions and demeanor of individuals, depicting the unusual states that people exhibit in their behavior or facial expressions due to certain psychological activities. The meanings of these words are generally difficult to define or describe accurately, and the interpretations in dictionaries are usually quite general. For instance, the expressions of "xiuse羞涩" and "ganga尴尬" are both described as "unnatural", yet the actual semantic differences between these two words are significant. Sometimes, these differences are not due to the differences in the external expressions, but rather the psychological feelings that cause the depicted subject to exhibit such expressions, as well as the external causes that lead to these feelings. These factors often exceed the scope of the word meanings and require context to be manifested. For example, if someone appears to be "unnatural" or "blushed", without the context, we cannot determine whether they are "shy" or "embarrassed". In the description of these words, we combine internal causes with external manifestations. This group of words does not have a clear polarity meaning.

S羞涩 = {[神态]:{[表象](![自然])}+{[感觉]([羞])}}
S羞涩 = {[Expression]:{[Manifestation](![Natural])}+{[Feeling]([Shy])}}
S尴尬 = {[神态]:{[表象](![自然])}+{[原因](Gs[为难])}}
S尴尬 = {[Expression]:{[Manifestation](![Natural])}+{[Cause](Gs[Quandary])}}
S大方 = {[神态]:{[表象]([自然]∧!Gs[紧张])}
S大方 = {[Expression]:{[Manifestation]([Natural]∧!Gs[Nervous])}
S拘谨 = {[神态]:{[表象]([小心]∧![自然])}+{[原因](Gs![自信])}+{[程度]([高])}}
S拘谨 = {[Expression]:{[Manifestation]([Careful]∧![Natural])}+{[Cause](Gs![Confident])}+{[Degree]([High])}}

This group of words can also denote psychological states, such as "The situation made him feel extremely awkward." Similarly, the previous set of words expressing psychological states can also represent facial expressions or attitudes, such as "She looked sad." Although the functions of these two groups of words can intersect in specific contexts, their meanings themselves have distinct focal points.

The gene clusters $_{Gs}$[weinan为难(Quandary)], $_{Gs}$[jinzhang紧张(Nervous)] and $_{Gs}$[zixin自信(Confident)] are also categorized as psychological adjectives, and are analyzed as follows:

Dictionary definition:

Weinan为难: *Feeling difficult to cope with.*

Jinzhang紧张: *The mind is in a highly prepared state, restless and excited.*

Zixin自信: *Believe oneself.*

S$_{为难}$ = {[[状态]of[心理]]:{[感觉]([难])}+{[原因]([缺乏]([办法]))}}
S$_{为难}$ = {[[State]of[Psychology]]:{[Feeling]([Difficult])}+{[Cause]([Lack]([Method]))}}
S$_{紧张}$ = {[[状态]of[心理]]:{[感觉](![安定])}+{[原因]([精神]([兴奋]))}+{[程度]([高])}}
S$_{紧张}$ = {[[State]of[Psychology]]:{[Feeling](![Settled])}+{[Cause]([Spirit]([Excited]))}+{[Degree]([High])}}
S$_{自信}$ = {[[状态]of[心理]]:[感觉]([相信]([自己]))}
S$_{自信}$ = {[[State]of[Psychology]]:[Feeling]([Believing]([Oneself]))}

5.4.4 Semantic Analysis and Semantic Gene Extraction of Adjectives Related to Event Properties

① {shunli顺利(smooth), zhouzhe周折(arduous), fanrong繁荣(prosperous), xiaotiao萧条(depressed)}

Shunli顺利: *In the process of development of things or the progress of work, difficulties are rarely encountered or are virtually non-existent.*

Zhouzhe周折: *The process of a thing is fraught with obstacles, making it far from smooth.*

Fanrong繁荣: *Booming development (of economy or career); flourishing.*

Xiaotiao萧条: *Desolate and devoid of vitality.*

Analysis: This group of words describes the ongoing state of events, i.e., the phenomena presented in the development of things, reflecting the processuality and dynamism of events.

The description is as follows:

S$_{顺利}$ = {[[状态]of[发展]]:[表象]([困难]([少]∨![存在]))}
S$_{顺利}$ = {[[State]of[Developing]]:[Manifestation]([Difficulty]([Few]∨![Existing]))}
S$_{周折}$ = {[[状态]of[发展]]:[表象]([反复]∧!$_{Gs}$[顺利])}
S$_{周折}$ = {[[State]of[Developing]]:[Manifestation]([Repeated]∧!Gs[Smooth])}
S$_{繁荣}$ = {[[状态]of[发展]]:[表象]([速度]([快])∧[规模]([大]))}

$S_{繁荣}$ = {[[State]of[Developing]]:[Manifestation]([Speed]([Fast])∧[Scale
]([Large]))}
$S_{萧条}$ = {[[状态]of[发展]]:[表象](${}_{Gs}$[停滞]∧!${}_{Gs}$[活力])}
$S_{萧条}$ = {[[State]of[Developing]]:[Manifestation](${}_{Gs}$[Stagnation
]∧!Gs[Vitality])}

The aforementioned gene clusters, ${}_{Gs}$[tingzhi 停滞 (Stagnation)] and ${}_{Gs}$[huoli 活力 (Vitality)], are further elaborated as follows:

Dictionary definition:

Tingzhi停滞: *Due to hindrance, things cannot move or develop smoothly.*

Huoli活力: *Exuberant vigour.*

$S_{停滞}$ = {[[状态]of[运动]]:{[表象]([停])}+[原因]([阻力]))}
$S_{停滞}$ = {[[State]of[Moving]]:{[Manifestation]([Stopping])}+
[Cause]([Resistance]))}
$S_{活力}$ = {[抽象物]:{[力]of[生命]:[量]([充足])}
$S_{活力}$ = {[Abstract object]:{[Force]of[Life]:[Quantity]([Sufficient])}

② {chenggong成功(successful), shibai失败(failed), yuanman圆满(perfect), zhunque准确(accurate)}

Chenggong成功: *Refers to the satisfactory outcome of an event or endeavor.*

Shibai失败: *Refers to the outcome of an event that is unsatisfactory.*

Yuanman圆满: *Without any defects or shortcomings, meeting with satisfaction.*

Zhunque准确: *The outcome of the action is entirely in line with the actuality or the anticipation.*

Analysis:

These words describe the state at the end of an event, representing the outcome of its development, and demonstrating the phased nature, objectivity, and static aspect within the dynamics of the event.

The description is as follows:

$S_{成功}$ = {[[结果]of[事件]]:[表象](${}_{Gc}$[令人满意])}
$S_{成功}$ = {[[Result]of[Event]]:[Manifestation](${}_{Gc}$[Satisfactory])}
$S_{失败}$ = {[[结果]of[事件]]:[表象](!${}_{Gc}$[令人满意])}
$S_{失败}$ = {[[Result]of[Event]]:[Manifestation](!${}_{Gc}$[Satisfactory])}
$S_{圆满}$ = {[[结果]of[事件]]:[表象](${}_{Gc}$[令人满意]∧!${}_{Gs}$[瑕疵])}
$S_{圆满}$ = {[[Result]of[Event]]:[Manifestation](${}_{Gc}$[Satisfactory]∧!${}_{Gs}$[Defect])}
$S_{准确}$ = {[[结果]of[行动]]:[表象]([比较]([[结果] → [[实际]∨${}_{Gs}$[预期]]](同))}
$S_{准确}$ = {[[Result]of[Action]]:[Manifestation]([Comparing]([[Result] →
[[Reality]∨${}_{Gs}$[Expectation]]]([Same]))}

The gene chain ${}_{Gc}$[lingren manyi令人满意(Satisfactory)] constitutes an causative construction, which can be elaborated as follows:

$S_{令人满意}$ = {[使役]:{[施事]([u])}+{[受事]([人])}+{[结果]([满意])}}

$S_{令人满意}$ = {[Causative]:{[Agent]([u])}+{[Patient]([Person])}+
{[Result]([Satisfying])}}

The other two gene clusters $_{Gs}$ [xiaci瑕疵(Defect)] and $_{Gs}$ [yuqi预期(Expectation)] used in the description are described together as follows:

Xiaci瑕疵: *Minor flaws.*

Yuqi预期: *Anticipated expectations.*

$S_{瑕疵}$ = {[抽象物]:{[缺点]:[量]([微])}}
$S_{瑕疵}$ = {[Abstract object]:{[Flaw]:[Quantity]([Tiny])}}
$S_{预期}$ = {[活动]of[心理]:{[希望]:[性质]([预设])}}
$S_{预期}$ = {[Activity]of[Psychology]:{[Hoping]:[Nature]([Presupposed])}}

③ {gongping公平(fair), heli合理(reasonable), huangmiu荒谬(absurd)}

Gongping公平: *Dealing with things in a reasonable and impartial manner, without showing favoritism to any particular side.*

Heli合理: *Conforming to reason or logic.*

Huangmiu荒谬: *Extremely erroneous; Extremely unreasonable.*

Analysis: This group of words describes the evaluation of the process and structure of an event, reflecting the subjectivity of the event (as perceived from an external viewpoint). Core genes need to be predefined, including [zhengque正确(True)], [cuowu错误(False)], and [gongzheng公正(Fair)].

The description is as follows:

$S_{公平}$ = {[评价]:[处置]([受事]([事])∧[方式]([公正])}
$S_{公平}$ = {[Evaluation]:[Handling]([Patient]([Thing])∧[Way]([Fair])}
$S_{合理}$ = {[评价]:[比较]([u] → [情理]([同]))}
$S_{合理}$ = {[Evaluation]:[Comparing]([u] → [Reason]([Same]))}
$S_{荒谬}$ = {[评价]:[性质]([错误])∧[程度](深)}
$S_{荒谬}$ = {[Evaluation]:[Nature]([False])∧[Degree](Deep)}

By combining the aforementioned groups, we can get the core semantic gene set for adjectives: {[yanse颜色(Color)], [bai白(White)], [hei黑(Black)], [hong红(Red)], [lü绿(Green)], [lan蓝(Blue)], [huang黄(Yellow)], [cheng橙(Orange)], [bijiao比较(Comparison)], [xiangsi相似(Similar)], [ronghe融合(Blending)], [hunhe混合(Mixture)], [nongdu浓度(Concentration)], [shen深(Dark)], [qian浅(Light)], [zhu主(Primary)], [ci次(Secondary)], [dian点(Point)], [xian线(Line)], [mian面(Surface)], [zhi直(Straight)], [fang方(Square)], [yuan圆(Circular)], [shuiping水平(Horizontal)], [chuizhi垂直(Vertical)], [xingzhuang形状(Shape)], [liangzhi量值(Magnitude)], [kongjian空间(Space)], [biaozhun标准(Standard)], [gao高(High)], [duliang度量(Measurement)], [weidu维度(Dimension)], [shijian时间(Time)], [duixiang对象(Object)], [jiegou结构(Structure)], [weizhi位置(Position)], [wu物(Thing)], [ren人(Person)], [wuti物体(Object)], [weidao味道(Taste)], [weijue味觉(Gustatory)], [xiujue嗅觉(Olfactory)], [suan酸(Sour)], [tian甜(Sweet)], [ku苦(Bitter)], [la辣(Spicy)], [xian咸(Salty)], [ma麻(Numb)], [se涩(Stringent)], [xiang香(Fragrant)], [chou臭(Stinky)], [hao好(Good)], [dan淡(Light)], [nong

浓(Strong)], [xiuci修辞(Rhetoric)], [mozhuang摹状(Description)], [wuxing物性(Physical property)], [biaoxiang表象(Manifestation)], [nandu难度(Difficulty)], [bian变(Changing)], [timao 体貌(Appearance)], [shencai身材(Stature)], [gao高(Tall)], [mei美(Pretty)], [xingbie性别(Gender)], [nü女(Female)], [nan男(Male)], [jieshi结实(Sturdy)], [zhong忠 (Faithful)], [jian奸(Treacherous)], [shan善(Good)], [e恶(Evil)], [chengshi诚实(Honest)], [qianxu谦虚(Modest)], [gongzheng公正(Fair)], [pinxing品性(Character)], [pingjia评价(Evaluation)], [jixing极性(Polarity)], [xi喜(Joyful)], [nu怒(Angry)], [ai哀(Sorrowful)], [chou愁(Worried)], [bei悲(Sad)], [xiu羞(Shy)], [xinli心理(Psychology)], [ganjue感觉(Feeling)], [anding安定(Settled)], [shentai神态(Expression)], [ziran自然(Natural)], [yuanyin原因(Cause)], [xiaoxin小心(Cautious)], [nan难(Difficult)], [quefa缺乏(Lack)], [banfa办法(Method)], [jingshen精神(Spirit)], [xingfen兴奋(Excited)], [xiangxin相信(Believing)], [ziji自己(Self)], [zhuangtai状态(State)], [fazhan发展(Developing)], [kunnan困难(Difficulty)], [shao少(Few)], [cunzai存在(Existing)], [fanfu反复(Repeated)], [sudu速度(Speed)], [kuai快(Fast)], [guimo规模(Scale)], [yundong运动(Moving)], [biaoxiang表象(Representation)], [ting停(Stoping)], [yuanyin原因(Cause)], [zuli阻力(Resistance)], [chouxiangwu抽象物(Abstract object)], [li力(Force)], [shengming生命(Life)], [liang量(Quantity)], [chongzu充足(Sufficient)], [shijian事件(Event)], [manyi满意(Satisfaction)], [quedian缺点(Flaw)], [liang量(Quantity)], [wei微(Tiny)], [xiwang希望(Hoping)], [xingzhi性质(Nature)], [yushe预设(Presupposed)], [zhengque正确(True)], [cuowu错误(False)], [chuzhi处置(Handling)], [fangshi方式(Way)], [qingli情理 (Reason)], [tong同(Same)], [da大(Large)], [xiao小(Small)], [bao褒(Commendatory)], [bian贬(Pejorative)], [zheng正(Positive)], [fu负(Negative)]}.

5.5 Data Validation and Optimization

5.5.1 Statistical Analysis of Semantic Gene Data

5.5.1.1 The Merging and Deduplication of Semantic Gene Sets

This chapter provides a representative description of 452 words, selected from the three fundamental word classes of modern Chinese (nouns, verbs, and adjectives). For each class, a certain number of basic semantic genes have been extracted, as shown in the table below (Table 5.1).

The semantic gene sets, after merging and deduplication, were ultimately reduced to a primary set of 527 semantic genes in modern Chinese. As the number of analyzed words increases, the quantity of extracted genes from this primary set will gradually escalate. However, as more words are analyzed later on, the utilization rate of semantic genes tends to be higher, resulting in a slower pace of growth for the gene set.

Table 5.1 Statistical data on the extraction of semantic genes

Word Class		Word Groups Described	Words Described	Genes Extracted
Nouns	Nouns Referring to People	25	309	382
	Nouns Referring to Objects	16		
	Nouns Referring to Event	13		
Verbs	Displacement Verbs	4	74	120
	Action Verbs	4		
	Cognitive Verbs	5		
	Change Verbs	5		
Adjectives	Adjectives Related to Physical Properties	5	69	130
	Adjectives Related to Human Properties	4		
	Adjectives related to Event Properties	3		

5.5.1.2 Frequency Statistics of Semantic Genes

The frequency of semantic genes refers to the frequency and the relative frequency at which each semantic gene extracted in the semantic analysis appears in the entire semantic description. By excluding genes with low frequency (twice or less), only 165 semantic genes were extracted from the noun part, 42 from the verb part, and 41 from the adjective part. After summarizing the three categories, a total of 224[10] semantic genes with a frequency of 3 times or more were obtained, which is less than half of the total number of primary semantic genes.This is not a simple addition of the three categories, but a re-calculation after merging and optimizing the three sets of data. The high-frequency semantic genes in each category, as shown in the following tables (Tables 5.2, 5.3, 5.4 and 5.5), are as follows:

The frequency distribution of semantic genes holds significant importance for our subsequent optimization of gene sets. High-frequency genes constitute the core components of the semantic structure of the entire vocabulary system of Modern Chinese. For low-frequency genes, we should, based on the actual circumstances, carry out segmentation and merging to minimize the scale of the semantic gene set as much as possible.

It should be noted that, the statistical results above are based on an analysis of a small-scale dataset and do not fully reflect the true distribution of semantic genes in modern Chinese. Here in this book we have only analyzed a portion of the data

[10] This is not a simple summation of the three data sets, but rather the result of re-counting after the merging and optimization of them.

Table 5.2 High-frequency semantic genes for the description of noun (Top 30)

Semantic Gene	Frequency	Relative Frequency	Order	Semantic Gene	Frequency	Relative Frequency	Order
[人]	120	0.0518583	1	[口]	17	0.0073466	23
[称谓]	76	0.0328436	2	[类]	16	0.0069144	24
[性别]	74	0.0319793	3	[自然]	16	0.0069144	24
[亲属]	67	0.0289542	4	[职业]	16	0.0069144	24
[辈分]	47	0.0203111	5	[能力]	14	0.0060501	25
[族系]	47	0.0203111	5	[近系]	14	0.0060501	25
[血缘]	47	0.0203111	5	[性质]	13	0.005618	26
[男]	45	0.0194468	6	[虚拟物]	13	0.005618	26
[血亲]	41	0.0177182	7	[人造物]	13	0.005618	26
[大]	39	0.0168539	8	[目的]	13	0.005618	26
[领域]	38	0.0164218	9	[来源]	12	0.0051858	27
[施事]	37	0.0159896	10	[形态]	12	0.0051858	27
[内容]	37	0.0159896	10	[母系]	12	0.0051858	27
[语体]	36	0.0155575	11	[动物]	12	0.0051858	27
[关系]	33	0.014261	12	[级别]	12	0.0051858	27
[事件]	32	0.0138289	13	[语用]	11	0.0047537	28
[长幼]	30	0.0129646	14	[表现]	11	0.0047537	28
[功能]	27	0.0116681	15	[状态]	11	0.0047537	28
[女]	27	0.0116681	15	[规模]	11	0.0047537	28
[旁系]	25	0.0108038	16	[冲突]	11	0.0047537	28
[结构]	24	0.0103717	17	[现象]	11	0.0047537	28
[处所]	23	0.0099395	18	[地点]	11	0.0047537	28
[构成]	23	0.0099395	18	[地物]	10	0.0043215	29
[语气]	21	0.0090752	19	[生产]	10	0.0043215	29
[范围]	21	0.0090752	19	[商品]	10	0.0043215	29
[小]	21	0.0090752	19	[方式]	10	0.0043215	29
[受事]	20	0.008643	20	[居住]	9	0.0038894	30
[身份]	20	0.008643	20	[数量]	9	0.0038894	30
[父系]	19	0.0082109	21	[对方]	9	0.0038894	30
[原因]	19	0.0082109	21	[书]	9	0.0038894	30
[抽象物]	18	0.0077787	22	[植物]	9	0.0038894	30

samples. Moreover, in order to authentically demonstrate the potential issues that may arise in the extraction of semantic genes, the sample words are selected with an uneven distribution sampling approach, which facilitates the observation of data bias under extreme scenarios. From the data, we have found that:

Table 5.3 High-frequency semantic genes from analysis of verb (Top 15)

Semantic Gene	Frequency	Relative Frequency	Order	Semantic Gene	Frequency	Relative Frequency	Order
[参事]	21	0.052764	1	[方式]	6	0.015075	12
[变化]	18	0.045226	2	[方向]	6	0.015075	12
[处所]	15	0.037688	3	[受事]	6	0.015075	12
[事物]	14	0.035176	4	[参照点]	5	0.012563	13
[人]	13	0.032663	5	[物]	4	0.01005	14
[动作]	12	0.030151	6	[数量]	4	0.01005	14
[活动]	11	0.027638	7	[心理]	4	0.01005	14
[起点]	11	0.027638	7	[空间]	4	0.01005	14
[终]	10	0.025126	8	[依据]	4	0.01005	14
[位置]	10	0.025126	8	[移动]	4	0.01005	14
[终点]	10	0.025126	8	[使役]	4	0.01005	14
[状态]	10	0.025126	8	[事件]	4	0.01005	14
[对象]	9	0.022613	9	[知道]	3	0.007538	15
[思维]	9	0.022613	9	[外]	3	0.007538	15
[认知]	8	0.020101	10	[动物]	3	0.007538	15
[施事]	8	0.020101	10	[表面]	3	0.007538	15
[性质]	7	0.017588	11	[长]	3	0.007538	15
[结果]	7	0.017588	11	[清楚]	3	0.007538	15
[大]	7	0.017588	11	[脚]	3	0.007538	15
[时间]	7	0.017588	11	[水体]	3	0.007538	15
[维度]	6	0.015075	12	[程度]	3	0.007538	15

(1) The imbalance in data will severely affect the frequency values of the distribution of semantic genes. The samples we analyzed consist predominantly of nouns, among which the proportion of nouns referring to people is the largest. This results in a high frequency and rate of semantic genes related to "people" in the gene pool, such as [ren人(Person)], [xingbie性别(Gender)], [chengwei称谓(Address)], [qinshu亲属(kinship)], etc. In fact, with the exception of [da大(Large)], the top five in Table 5.5 basically belong to the bias data. After the top five, with the exception of a few genes such as [zhangyou长幼(Age order)], [fuxi父系(Paternal)], [muxi母系(Maternal)], [jinxi近系(Close)], etc., the distribution values of other semantic genes are relatively close to linguistic facts and have statistical significance. Bias data is not meaningless. In the subsequent applications of semantic computation, when assigning weights to different dimensions of semantic features, different weighting strategies can be adopted according to different application scenarios. For example, in the computational analysis of interpersonal relationships, these data can be assigned a higher weight, while in

Table 5.4 High-frequency semantic genes for the description of adjective (Top 10)

Semantic Gene	Frequency	Relative Frequency	Order	Semantic Gene	Frequency	Relative Frequency	Order
[表象]	28	0.078652	1	[值]	5	0.014045	8
[状态]	12	0.033708	2	[维度]	5	0.014045	8
[大]	10	0.02809	3	[结果]	5	0.014045	8
[程度]	9	0.025281	4	[发展]	4	0.011236	9
[物性]	9	0.025281	4	[垂直]	4	0.011236	9
[颜色]	9	0.025281	4	[神态]	4	0.011236	9
[心理]	8	0.022472	5	[对象]	4	0.011236	9
[感觉]	8	0.022472	5	[品性]	4	0.011236	9
[极性]	8	0.022472	5	[自然]	4	0.011236	9
[形状]	7	0.019663	6	[难度]	4	0.011236	9
[味道]	7	0.019663	6	[浓度]	4	0.011236	9
[评价]	7	0.019663	6	[变]	3	0.008427	10
[高]	6	0.016854	7	[事件]	3	0.008427	10
[原因]	6	0.016854	7	[嗅觉]	3	0.008427	10
[味觉]	6	0.016854	7	[褒]	3	0.008427	10
[小]	6	0.016854	7	[物]	3	0.008427	10
[体貌]	6	0.016854	7	[黑]	3	0.008427	10
[空间]	6	0.016854	7	[性质]	3	0.008427	10
[比较]	5	0.014045	8	[量]	3	0.008427	10
[参事]	5	0.014045	8	[白]	3	0.008427	10

the computational analysis of events, properties, and materiality, the weighting weight should be reduced.

(2) The distribution of the same semantic gene across different parts of speech exhibits significant differences in positions. For instance, the semantic gene[fangshi方式(Way)] occupies the 29th position in the noun semantic gene pool,12th in the verb semantic gene pool, and has no appeared in the adjective semantic gene pool, and is ranked 25th in the overall pool. It reflects the differences in the dimensions of semantic features across different parts of speech. These differences also serve as important references for assigning weights to the dimensions of semantic features in specific semantic computation applications.

Table 5.5 High-frequency semantic genes for the description of three basic word classes (Top 30)

Semantic Gene	Frequency	Relative Frequency	Order	Semantic Gene	Frequency	Relative Frequency	Order
[人]	135	0.043988	1	[自然]	21	0.006843	22
[性别]	75	0.024438	2	[身份]	20	0.006517	23
[称谓]	75	0.024438	2	[变化]	20	0.006517	23
[亲属]	67	0.021831	3	[结果]	20	0.006517	23
[大]	56	0.018247	4	[抽象物]	20	0.006517	23
[血缘]	47	0.015314	5	[父系]	19	0.006191	24
[族系]	47	0.015314	5	[程度]	19	0.006191	24
[辈分]	47	0.015314	5	[时间]	17	0.005539	25
[施事]	45	0.014663	6	[口]	17	0.005539	25
[男]	45	0.014663	6	[方式]	17	0.005539	25
[血亲]	41	0.013359	7	[职业]	16	0.005213	26
[事件]	39	0.012708	8	[类]	16	0.005213	26
[领域]	39	0.012708	8	[事物]	15	0.004888	27
[处所]	38	0.012382	9	[位置]	15	0.004888	27
[内容]	37	0.012056	10	[动物]	15	0.004888	27
[语体]	36	0.01173	11	[目的]	15	0.004888	27
[参事]	34	0.011079	12	[近系]	14	0.004562	28
[状态]	33	0.010753	13	[能力]	14	0.004562	28
[关系]	33	0.010753	13	[活动]	14	0.004562	28
[长幼]	30	0.009775	14	[对象]	14	0.004562	28
[小]	29	0.009449	15	[数量]	13	0.004236	29
[女]	28	0.009123	16	[人造物]	13	0.004236	29
[表象]	28	0.009123	16	[虚拟物]	13	0.004236	29
[功能]	28	0.009123	16	[来源]	13	0.004236	29
[受事]	27	0.008798	17	[形态]	12	0.00391	30
[原因]	26	0.008472	18	[心理]	12	0.00391	30
[构成]	26	0.008472	18	[形状]	12	0.00391	30
[结构]	25	0.008146	19	[规模]	12	0.00391	30
[旁系]	25	0.008146	19	[空间]	12	0.00391	30
[性质]	23	0.007494	20	[母系]	12	0.00391	30
[语气]	22	0.007168	21	[动作]	12	0.00391	30
[范围]	22	0.007168	21	[级别]	12	0.00391	30

5.5.2 Verification of the Description of Semantic Gene Structures

5.5.2.1 Manual Verification of Description Consistency

In order to ensure the accuracy of semantic analysis and the extraction of semantic genes in engineering practice, we employ two manual or semi-manual verification methods:

(1) Three-person cross-verification: The annotators are divided into groups of three, each analyzing and annotating different words within the same domain. After completion, their annotations are reviewed by the other two annotators. In case of discrepancies, a discussion is held among the three annotators until a consensus is reached.
(2) Human–Machine Combined Verification: In this process, three individuals form a group to annotate the same dataset. The annotated results are then submitted to a computer for analysis and comparison.If there are discrepancies in annotations, the three individuals will collaborate in discussions until a consensus is achieved.

The first method is employed in the preliminary stage of semantic analysis, where annotators are not yet proficient in the process or are not well-versed in the semantic features of a particular domain. Additionally, the number of predefined semantic genes available for analysis is limited, resulting in incomplete coverage. Therefore, the annotations made by three annotators often exhibit significant discrepancies. Manual verification and discussion are the necessary means to ensure the correct annotation of word meaning structure and the extraction of semantic genes. In the intermediate stage of annotation, an increasing number of reusable semantic genes become available. Through continuous iterative stages of deduplication and merging, annotators become proficient in the techniques of lexical meaning analysis, and the discrepancies among the three annotators diminish. The application of computer verification can greatly enhance the efficiency of annotation. By the later stages of the project, the same dataset can be annotated by only one or two annotators, with the machine randomly sampling for manual review to further improve work efficiency.

5.5.2.2 Machine Verification of Circular Interpretation

To avoid circular interpretation in lexical meaning analysis, once a certain scale of analysis annotations for the same category of words is reached, computer-based circular interpretation verification is conducted to correct any deviations. After the entire project is completed, a comprehensive circular interpretation verification is performed. The basic computational principle for machine verification is as follows:

Assume that the semantic gene structure of word X contains semantic gene clusters {Gs [Y1], Gs [Y2], Gs [Y3],… Gs [Yn]}:

(1) If any of the clusters Y1 to Yn equals the word X, it is determined that the word X exhibits circular interpretation.
(2) Search for the semantic gene structures of the words Y1 to Yn, if the semantic gene structure of any word among them contains the semantic gene cluster Gs[X], it is determined that there exists a circular interpretation between the word X and the word Yn.

All words with circular interpretations are reanalyzed and described; after completion of the description, a verification is conducted once again, until all cases of circular interpretation are excluded.

5.5.3 Optimization of the Semantic Gene Set and the Semantic Structures Description

5.5.3.1 Merging of Semantic Genes

To effectively limit the total amount of data in the semantic gene set, the extracted semantic genes are reasonably merged in stages to achieve optimization of the gene set. The merging methods are categorized into three types:

(1) Merging of Synonym or Near-synonym Semantic Genes For instance, [zhong终(End)] and [zhongdian终点(Endpoint)] are merged into [zhong终(End)], with [zhongdian终点(Endpoint)] being excluded; [secai色彩(Color)], [se色(Color)], and [yanse颜色(Color)] are merged into [se色(Color)], with [yanse颜色(Color)] and [secai色彩(Color)] being excluded; [bianhua变化(Change)] and [bian变(Change)] are merged into [bian变(Change)], with [bianhua变化(Change)] being excluded. During the process of synonym or near-synonym gene merging, it is preferable to adopt monosyllabic genes (characters) as much as possible.
(2) Merging Antonym Semantic Genes By employing the negation logical operator "!", semantic genes of opposite meanings are merged, such as merging [sheng生(Living)] and [si死(Dead)] into [sheng生(Living)] and! [sheng生(Living)], eliminating [si死(Dead)]. It should be noted that only absolute antonyms, that is, mutually exclusive antonyms, can be merged; polar antonyms, which are relative antonyms with intermediate states between the two poles, cannot be merged. For instance, there exists intermediate states [wen温(Warm)] or [liang凉(Cool)] between [leng冷(Cold)] and [re热(Hot)], it is not advisable to conflate them.
(3) Splitting of Semantic Genes. Splitting is also a method of merging, which involves decomposing a semantic gene into two or more (usually two) functions, gene combinations, or gene chains of already extracted higher-frequency genes. For instance, the gene [xiamian下面(Below)] can be split into a function [fangwei方位(Orientation)]([xia下(Down)]), as both [Orientation] and [Down] have already been extracted and are of higher frequency;

[dibiao地表(Earth's surface)] can be split into the gene combination [biaomian表面(Surface)]of[diqiu地球(Earth)]; and [nongdu浓度(Concentration)] can be split into the gene chain {[chengdu程度(Degree)]:[weidu维度(Dimension)]([nong浓(Density)])}.

After the merging of semantic genes, for words that have employed the discarded genes in semantic description, a new method is adopted for their re-description.

5.5.3.2 Optimization of Semantic Descriptive Expressions

To reduce redundant data, the expression for describing the semantic gene structure can be further refined and optimized, while maintaining logical comprehensiveness.

(1) Simplification of Feature Function

① For nested feature functions with variables taking another function as the values, the value function can be simplified to a composite gene or a gene cluster, depending on the specific situation, with the relevant gene clusters described separately. For instance: [参事]([之间]([双方]:[关系]($_{Gs}$[敌对])) [Participant]([Between]([Both parties]:[Relation]($_{Gs}$[Hostility]))can be simplified to[参事]([双方]of$_{Gs}$[敌对]) [Participant]([Between]of$_{Gs}$[Hostility]); [人]([状态]([死亡])) [Person]([State]([Death])) can be simplified to [人]([死亡])[Person](! [sheng 生 (Living)]), or further simplified to the gene cluster Gs[siren死人(The dead)].
② For complex feature functions with variables taking the value of composite genes, the value function can be simplified according to specific circumstances. For instance, the expression [维度]([空间]∧[1]) [Dimension]([Space]∧[1]) can be simplified to [维度](1) [Dimension](1). Originally, [weidu 维度 (Dimension)] is divided into [kongjian 空间 (Space)] and [shijian时间(Time)], but in the present human cognition and linguistic expression, [Space] is divided into one-dimensional, two-dimensional, or three-dimensional, while [Time] is only one-dimensional. The logical AND operator "∧" and the dimension value [1] within this function value already imply that the dimension is spatial, thus the gene [Space] can be omitted. Moreover, since the specific number "1" is not treated as a semantic gene, the gene boundary symbol "[]" can also be omitted. Such omissions will not cause computational ambiguity under the premise of defining computational rules.
③ For nested composite functions with variable values that involve both nested functions and composite genes, it is possible to alter the function structure by transforming a unary function into a bivariate function. For instance, the expression [Verb]([Agent]([x]) ∧[Patient]([y])) can be simplified to [Verb]([x], [y]). The original function value [Agent]([x])∧[Patient]([y]) is a composite value formed by two functions, which is formally a composite nested function composed of three univariate functions. After simplification, it becomes a binary function. It should be noted that this function has two variants, namely, the form without a patient,

as [Verb]([Agent]([x])) and the form without an agent,as [Verb]([Patient]([y])). Both of them can still be simplified to [Verb]([x], [φ]) and [Verb]([φ], [y]), and even further simplified to [Verb]([x],) and [Verb](, [y]). It is essential to note with particular emphasis that in this ultimate simplified form, the comma must not be omitted, as it is the crucial and unique marker for the machine to make a judgments between [Agent] and [Patient].

(2) Simplification of Semantic Gene Chain

① For the subchains that can be represented by gene clusters within a long semantic gene chain, the gene clusters are directly used to replace the subchains, for instance:

$S_{灾害}$ = {[事件]:{[性质]($_{Gs}$[有害])}+{[程度]([大])}+{[原因]([自然]∨$_{Gs}$[战争])}}
$S_{灾害}$ = {[Event]:{[Nature](Gs[Harmful])}+{[Degree]([Large])}+{[Cause]([Nature]∨Gs[War])}}

can be simplified as:

$S_{灾害}$ = {[事件]:$_{Gs}$[祸害]:[原因]([自然]∨$_{Gs}$[战争])}
$S_{灾害}$ = {[Event]:Gs[Bane]:[Cause]([Natural]∨Gs[War])}

Here because the subchain {[事件]:{[性质]($_{Gs}$[有害])}+{[程度]([大])} {[Event]:{[Nature]($_{Gs}$[Harm -ful])}+{[Extent]([Large])} has been separately described as: $S_{祸害}$ = {[事件]:{[性质]($_{Gs}$[有害])}+{[程度]([大])}} $S_{祸害}$ = {[Event]:{[Nature](Gs[Harmful])}+{[Extent]([Large])}} and can be directly invoked as the gene cluster Gs[huohai祸害(Bane)].

② For those semantic gene chains that contain nested constant genes, it may be permissible to omit the constant gene at a higher-level in the semantic classification tree, depending on the specific circumstances, such as:

$S_{飞}$ = {[动作]:{[移动]:{[主体]([动物]∨[器具])}+{[处所]([空中])}}
$S_{飞}$ = {[Action]:{[Moving]:{[Agent]([Animal]∨[Utensil])}+{[Location]([In the air])}}

Here the first constant gene [Action] can be omitted, simplifying to:

$S_{飞}$ = {[移动]:{[主体]([动物]∨[器具])}+{[处所]([空中])}
$S_{飞}$ = {[Moving]:{[Agent]([Animal]∨[Utensil])}+{[Location]([In the air])}

Constant genes serve as a crucial basis for semantic reasoning. "Flying" is a mode of "moving", and the semantic category of "moving" is [Action]. Therefore, computers can infer that "flying" is an action. However, due to the pre-established semantic inheritance mechanism, all the semantic genes of the superordinate words can be completely transmitted as family genes to the subordinate terms. "Action" is the superordinate word of "moving", and "moving" is the superordinate term of "flying". Thus, when "flying" inherits the semantic genes of "moving", it also inherits its semantic category gene [Action]. Therefore, the "gene" [Action] can be omitted in the semantic description of the word "fly".

Similarly, the semantic description of the term "zaihai 灾害 (disaster)" can also be further simplified as follows:

$S_{灾害} = \{_{Gs}[祸害]:[原因]([自然] \vee _{Gs}[战争])\}$
$S_{灾害} = \{_{Gs}[Bane]:[Cause]([Nature] \vee _{Gs}[War])\}$

Through the discussion of the semantic gene merging and the simplification rules for the expression of semantic descriptions, the majority of the semantic gene expressions described in this chapter can be further optimized. There are also certain changes in the extracted gene sets and the frequency values of gene distribution. The optimized final results are no longer listed one by one in this chapter.

References

Fan, X. 范晓. (2001). Nouns and Their Reclassification in Modern Chinese [现代汉语的名词及其再分类]. In Shanghai Language Association (Eds.)., *Proceedings of Language Studies* (Vol. 7) [语文论丛]. Shanghai Education Press.

Feng, H. 冯海霞, & Zhang, Z. 张志毅. (2006). Establishment and Improvement of the Defining System for The Contemporary Chinese Dictionary: Reading Notes on the Fifth Edition [《现代汉语词典》释义体系的创建与完善——读《现代汉语词典》第5版]. *Chinese Language* [中国语文], (05), 455–461+480.

Fillmore, C. J. (1968). The case for case. In E. Bach & R. T. Harms (Eds.), *Universals in Linguistic Theory* (pp. 1–88). Holt, Rinehart, and Winston.

Fu, H. 符淮青. (1992). The Defining Method of Words in Chinese Dictionaries [语文词典中词的释义方式]. In *Compilation Experience of Dictionaries* [辞书编纂经验荟萃](pp. 120–138). Shanghai Dictionary Society [上海辞书学会].

Guo, D. 郭大方. (1994). *Verb Classification Dictionary of Modern Chinese* [现代汉语动词分类词典]. Jilin Education Press.

Hu, M. 胡明扬. (1991). Reclassification of Adjectives in Mandarin [北京话形容词的再分类]. In *Collection of Linguistic Studies* [语言学论文集]. China Renmin University Press.

Hu, Y. 胡裕树, & Fan, X. 范晓. (1995). *Study on Verbs* [动词研究]. Henan University Press.

Ji, W. 吉文玉. (2003). Dictionary of Chinese Synonyms 中华同义词词典. Changchun: Jilin Literature and History Publishing House 长春: 吉林文史出版社.

Li, J. 黎锦熙. (1924). *New Grammar of National Language* [新著国语文法]. Commercial Press.

Li, Q. 李强, & Yuan, Y. 袁毓林. (2016). On Dictionary Definitions of Nouns from the Perspective of Generative Lexicon Theory [从生成词库论看名词的词典释义]. *Lexicographical Studies* [辞书研究], (04), 12–26+93.

Li, Q. 李强. (2018). Supplement to "On Dictionary Definitions of Nouns from the Perspective of Generative Lexicon Theory" - A Response to Shang Jian (2017) [《从生成词库论看名词的词典释义》补议——对尚简(2017)的回应]. *Lexicographical Studies* [辞书研究], (01), 34–41+93–94.

Liu, M. 刘美君, & Wan, M. 万明瑜. (2019). Research on Chinese Verbs and Their Classification: Construction and Application of the Chinese Verb Lexical Semantic Network [中文动词及分类研究: 中文动词词汇语义网的构建及应用]. *Lexicographical Studies* [辞书研究], (02), 42–60+110.

Liu, S. 刘顺. (2003). *Modern Chinese Nouns: A Multidimensional Study* [现代汉语名词的多视角研究]. Xuelin Publishing House.
Lü, S. 吕叔湘. (1942). *Outline of Chinese Grammar* [中国文法要略]. The Commercial Press.
Lü, S. 吕叔湘. (1979). *Problems in the Analysis of Chinese Grammar* [汉语语法分析问题]. The Commercial Press.
Ma, J. 马建忠. (1898). *Mashi Wen Tong* [马氏文通]. Commercial Press.
Ma, Q. 马庆株. (1992). *Verbs and Verbal Structures in Chinese* [汉语动词和动词性结构]. Beijing Language Institute Press.
Peng, R. 彭睿. (1996). Nouns and the Reclassification of Nouns [名词和名词的再分类]. In M. Hu 胡明扬 (Ed.), *An Examination of Word Class Issues* [词类问题考察]. Beijing Language and Culture University Press.
Wang, H. 王惠. (2004). *A Syntagmatic Study on Noun Senses in Contemporary Chinese* [现代汉语名词词义组合分析]. Peking University Press [北京大学出版社].
Wang, H. 王洪轩. (1987). A Summary of Semantic Classification of Verbs [动词语义分类举要]. *Journal of Hebei University (Philosophy and Social Science)* [河北大学学报(哲学社会科学版)], (02), 86–91.
Wang, J. 王珏. (2001). *A Study on Nouns of Modern Chinese* [现代汉语名词研究]. East China Normal University Press.
Wang, L. 王力. (1985). *Grammar of Modern Chinese* [中国现代语法]. Commercial Press.
Yuan, Y. 袁毓林. (1998). *Studies on the Valency of Chinese Verbs* [汉语动词的配价研究]. Jiangxi Education Press.
Yuan, Y. 袁毓林. (2014).On a Descriptive System of Qualia Structure of Chinese Nouns and Its Application in Parsing Complex Chinese Grammatical Phenomena [汉语名词物性结构的描写体系和运用案例]. *Contemporary Linguistics* [当代语言学], *16*(01), 31–48.
Zhang, Z. 张志毅, & Zhang, Q. 张庆云. (2001). *Lexical Semantics* [词汇语义学]. The Commercial Press.
Zhao, Y. 赵元任. (1970). *A Grammar of Spoken* Chinese. University of California Press.
Zhu, D. 朱德熙. (1982). *Lectures on Grammar* [语法讲义. Commercial Press.

Chapter 6
Epilogue

6.1 The Genetic Laws and Word Formation of Semantic Genes

In the introduction, we integrated holographic theory to explore the genetic metaphor within the domain of natural language semantics, which draws upon the principles of holography to illuminate the underlying mechanisms and structures of meaning in natural languages. From a macro perspective, the three classic genetic laws of biology: the law of segregation, the law of independent assortment, and the law of linkage and crossing-over of genes, are all reflected in a similar manner in natural semantics. From a micro perspective, the operation mechanism of gene inheritance in the semantic system is not entirely identical to the genetic inheritance laws of organisms, and there are many subtle differences between them.

6.1.1 The Similarities between Semantic Genetic Inheritance and Biological Genetic Inheritance

6.1.1.1 The Heritability of Genes

The heritability of both semantic genes and biological genes serves as the starting point for the research presented in this book.

Biological organisms propagate the next generation and expand their population through genetic inheritance. Similarly, the semantic genetic inheritance can also generate new words, thereby expanding the vocabulary.

D. Hu, *Lexical Semantic Gene Structure of Modern Chinese*,
https://doi.org/10.1007/978-981-96-6425-2_6

6.1.1.2 The Recombinability of Genes

Recombination of genes is the primary means for the generation of new individuals. In sexually reproducing organisms, offspring undergo gene recombination by acquiring different genes from their paternal and maternal ancestors, thereby producing new biological individuals. Different recombination patterns of certain genes result in individuals with varying phenotypes, making gene recombination a significant factor in the generation of biodiversity. In the lexical system, the recombination of semantic genes can also lead to the creation of new words. For instance, a set of dimension genes {[duliang度量(Measurement)], [weidu维度(Dimension)], [zhi 值(Value)]} and a set of assignment semantic genes {[da大(Large)], [xiao小(Small)], [chuizhi垂直(Vertical)], [shuiping水平(Horizontal)], [xianxing线性(Linear)]} can be combined in various ways to yield multiple distinct words:

① {[度量]([值]([大]))}+{[维度]([水平]∧([线性]))}
{[Measurement]([Value]([Large]))}+{[Dimension]([Horizontal]∧([Linear]))}.
The combination results in the word "chang 长 (long)".
② {[度量]([值]([小]))}+{[维度]([水平]∧([线性]))}.
{[Measurement]([Value]([Small]))}+{[Dimension]([Horizontal]∧([Linear]))}.
The combination results in the word "duan 短 (short)".
③ {[度量]([值]([大]))}+{[维度]([垂直]∧([线性]))}.
{[Measurement]([Value]([Large]))}+{[Dimension]([Vertical]∧([Linear]))}.
The combination results in the word "gao 高 (High)".
④ {[度量]([值]([小]))}+{[维度]([垂直]∧([线性]))}.
{[Measurement]([Value]([Small]))}+{[Dimension]([Vertical]∧([Linear]))}.
The combination results in the word "ai 矮 (short)".

In any language, there exists a vast array of synonyms and near-synonyms, and the subtle differences between these meanings are often produced by the combination and variation of individual semantic genes along a certain feature dimension. It is the presence of these synonyms and near-synonyms that endows language with a rich and varied expressions in practical usage. While fulfilling the basic function of information transmission, language also possesses aesthetic value and artistic charm. Therefore, akin to biodiversity, the recombination of semantic genes is an important factor contributing to the diversity of linguistic expression.

6.1.1.3 The Variability of Genes

Biological genes often undergo variations during the process of inheritance. Variations in biological genes can lead to two outcomes:

① The emergence of pathogenic genes weakens the biological constitution, resulting in illness and even death in individual organisms; or it makes it difficult for organisms to adapt to the natural environment of survival, thereby gradually being eliminated in the process of evolution.

② The enhancement of biological constitution leads to the need for resistance to diseases and pests, as well as high yields, which are essential for adapting to the natural environment of survival. Therefore, these traits are preserved and continuously evolve through the process of evolution. This is "Natural Selection, Survival of the Fittest."

The semantic genes are also subject to variation during the development of the lexical system. Variations in semantic genes can lead to two outcomes:

① The lifecycle of neologisms generated by variation of semantic genes is short, and they gradually fade away with the changes of the times, unable to survive in the linguistic system for a long period. In a specific period, different countries and regions may have certain universally concerned issues, leading to the creation of a batch of new words to express these matters, which are known as buzzwords. For instance, the terms "niuguisheshen牛鬼蛇神(the monsters and freaks)" and "niupeng牛棚 (cowshed)" in the 1950s and 1960s, "xunhu寻呼(paging)", "xunhuji 寻呼机(pager)", and "dageda大哥大(cellular phone)" in the 1980s and 1990s, were all generated through the variation of semantic genes. These words have now basically lost their vitality and are only preserved in historical documents.
② The neologisms generated by variation possess a strong vitality and gradually enter the basic vocabulary system, ensuring their long-term retention with high circulation and productivity. For instance, the extended meanings of words arise from the genetic variation of their basic meanings, and some extended meanings even exceed the basic meanings, becoming the central plereme of the word.

6.1.2 The Differences Between Semantic Genetic Inheritance and Biological Genetic Inheritance

6.1.2.1 The Temporal and Spatial Dimensions of Genetic Inheritance

To be strictly, genetic inheritance follows a temporal sequence, where the genes of the parents are passed on to their offspring, with the parents being born before the offspring, which is a fundamental biological law. However, the inheritance of semantic genes does not follow this pattern entirely.

The inheritance of semantic genes is divided into two dimensions: temporal and spatial.

(1) The temporal inheritance, i.e., the genetic inheritance of word meanings from their basic to extended senses: the extension of word meanings is an essential mode of development within the lexical system. Extended senses emerge after the basic meanings, and they cannot be separated from the basic meanings. Instead, they are produced through variation after acquiring a portion of the basic meaning's semantic genes through inheritance. For example:

The word "jie结(tie)" originally functions as a verb, as annotated in the "Shuo Wen(说文)", "jie, means to tie." In the "Yi Xi Ci Xia(易·系辞下)", it is mentioned that "in ancient times, people governed by tying knots", with *The Contemporary Chinese Dictionary (7th Edition)* interpreting it as "to tie knots on rods or to create items in this manner." Subsequently, it has been extended to the concrete noun sense of "a knot made from a rod", as "jie结(knot)" is generally not easy to untie, and further to the sense of "a difficult problem to solve", as in "xinjie心结(a knot in heart)". The first extension from the verb sense to the noun sense involves the semantic gene [jie结(Tie)] and gene cluster Gs [geda疙瘩(Knot)] of the verb sense being inherited to the noun sense, which then combines with a new semantic gene [jieguo结果(Result)] to form the extended sense "the result of the act of tying knots", i.e., "knot". The second extension involves the combination of the semantic genes with a new semantic gene [yinyu隐喻(Metaphor)] during inheritance, resulting in genetic variation through a mechanism, thereby obtaining a new sense of the word.

The semantic inheritance along the sole dimension of time does not exhibit a hierarchical relationship between the extended and basic pleremes in the semantic spatial distribution.

(2) The spatial inheritance: Hypernyms emerge later than hyponyms; however, in the spatial distribution of semantic hierarchical trees, hyponyms inherit all the semantic genetic genes from hypernyms. In the temporal dimension, the sequence of inheritance between the inherited terms and the inheriting terms is reversed; they are not truly in the sense of offspring and ancestors. This phenomenon can be explained by the theory of category hierarchy (Hu 胡惮, 2011: 27–36).

Categorization is one of the most fundamental and important advanced cognitive activities through which humans recognize the world. The entities that constitute the objective world are complex and multifaceted, each possessing inherent and extrinsic multidimensional characteristics. In the process of cognition, humans continuously judge and analyze the characteristics of these entities, identify similarities among different entities, and classify and categorize them accordingly, thereby forming concepts. This cognitive activity involving the interaction between the subjective and objective aspects is referred to as categorization. The outcomes of categorization result in cognitive categories, which correspond to concepts.

Cognitive categories do not exist in a disordered manner; instead, they form an inherently organic and hierarchical network system. The most typical members within a category belong to the prototype category, while the members of the basic-level category exhibit the greatest familial similarity, which is indicative of the prototype category.

The outcomes of categorization, i.e., concepts, are generally represented in the linguistic system by words or phrases. The vocabulary corresponding to the basic level categories forms the core part of the lexical system and is classified as basic vocabulary. When children acquire language, they also begin from the basic level categories. This is because the concepts corresponding to the basic level categories often possess a holistic gestalt, which is easy to form a clear mental image, such as "cat", "dog", "tree", "grass", "apple", and "banana". The superordinate categories of the basic level categories are often more abstract in meaning, such as "animal", "plant", and "fruit", which can only be formed by classifying them based on a certain number of basic level categories through the induction of their common or similar features. Therefore, they generally appear later in the sequence of language acquisition than the basic vocabulary. The subordinate categories are too specific in meaning, containing features that require more encyclopedic knowledge to differentiate, such as "Persian cat", "ginger cat", "willow", "poplar", "orchid", and "Chinese alpine rush", etc. Therefore, the acquisition of these words also occurs later than that of the basic vocabulary.

The superordinate and subordinate categories are both parasitic categories at the basic level, which depend on the existence of the basic level categories. From the perspective of the chronological order of their emergence, both the superordinate and subordinate categories, as well as the corresponding vocabulary in the linguistic system, generally appear later than the basic level categories.

Therefore, in the semantic hierarchical tree, although words that belong to the basic level categories possess all the semantic gene traits of their superordinate terms, they are not the offspring in terms of the temporal dimension. Their semantic genes are not truly acquired through inheritance, but rather, their structural organization of semantic genes and the manifestation of genetic inheritance are identical. This is what we refer to as the semantic inheritance along the spatial dimension.

(3) The semantic genetic inheritance across both temporal and spatial dimensions is manifested in the process of morpheme-based word formation: when constructing new words through morpheme combination, the new words emerge later than the morphemes themselves. They acquire the semantic genes of different superordinate morphemes through inheritance, and then, through genetic recombination and variation, new word meanings are generated. For instance:

Ji机(Machine) → {feiji飞机(aircraft), dianji电机(electrical machinery), erji(耳机headphone), fadongji发动机(engine), zhengqiji蒸汽机(steam engine), jichuang机床 (machine tool), jichang机场(airport), jijing机井(motor-pumped well), jijian机件(machine part)……}.

ai爱(Love) → {reai热爱(devotion), xiai喜爱(affection), guanai关爱(care), jingai敬爱(esteem), aixi爱惜(cherish), aihu爱护(care for), aiqing爱情(romantic love), airen 爱人(beloved), aihao爱好(hobby)……}.

bai白(White) → {xuebai雪白(snow-white), huabai花白(grizzled), canbai惨白(pale), cangbai苍白(pallid), baihua白桦(white birch), baiguo白果(ginkgo), baijin白金 (platinum), baigu白骨(bones of the dead), baifen白粉(heroin)……}.

This semantic gene inheritance across the temporal dimension aligns with the chronological sequence of the biological gene inheritance in new and old individuals. In terms of semantic spatial distribution, some new words and original words (morphemes) exhibit a hierarchical relationship. In terms of the new words that cannot serve as offsprings of original words (morphemes), such as "jijing机井(motor-pumped well)", "jijian机件(machine part)", "airen爱人(beloved)", "aiqing爱情(romantic love)", "baigu白骨 (bones of the dead)", and "baijin白金(platinum)", it's because their semantic gene origins from multiple ancestors, and the semantic genes obtained from the current ancestor word (morpheme) are not the main part of the new word's semantic gene, they can only function as the hyponyms of another ancestor word (morpheme) as the gene source.

6.1.2.2 Origin of Genes

The genes of organisms originates from both existing genes of their parents and the newly generated genes. The fundamental route for the production of new genes is gene mutation. In asexually reproducing organisms (such as new plants produced by cutting branches), since there is only one parent, the genes of the parent are completely replicated to the offspring. If no genetic mutation takes place, the offspring and the parent will share identical genes. In sexually reproducing organisms, individuals obtain a portion of their genes from both the paternal and maternal parents and then undergo recombination. Recombination does not generate new genes but only new genotypes. A genotype refers to the sum of all genes inherited by an organism from its parents, and in genetics, the specific genotype often refers to the combination of genes that control the phenotype of a certain trait in an organism. New genes in sexually reproducing organisms are also produced through gene mutation.

The origin of semantic genes is more complex. We cannot simply attribute the creation of new words to sexual or asexual reproduction, nor can we stipulate that the semantic genes of new words can only derive from one or two parent terms. In fact, we are fundamentally unable to define how many parent terms a new word has. Many new semantic genes do not originate from any parent term, such as the generation of new semantic genes through metaphor. We can only attribute the source of this new gene to a mutation in semantic genes. This is the first difference between the origin of biological genes and semantic genes.

The second distinction lies in the fact that for organisms with sexual reproduction, offspring can only inherit a portion of the genes from each parent, rather than all the genes from either parent. In contrast, the inheritance of semantic genes operates differently: for offspring words that have explicit superior parent words, they often acquire all the genes of one parent as the primary part of their semantic genes, while part of genes of the other parent occupies a secondary position on the offspring's gene chain. For instance:

The terms "nainiu奶牛(cow)" and "niunai牛奶(milk)" share a clear and identical hypernym, "niu牛(cattle)", and "nai奶(milk)", respectively. However, "nainiu奶牛(cow)" genetically inherits all the semantic genes of "niu牛(cattle)", fully possessing all the semantic dimension features of "niu牛(cattle)". In contrast, the semantic gene of "nai奶 (milk)" constitutes only a minor part of the "nainiu奶牛(cow)" semantic genotype, and the semantic of "nainiu奶牛(cow)" lacks the dimension features of "nai奶(milk)". Conversely, "niunai牛奶(milk)" possesses the complete semantic dimension features of "nai奶(milk)" but lacks the semantic dimension features of "niu牛(cattle)". Therefore, in the semantic hierarchical tree, "nainiu奶牛(cow)" can only serve as a hyponym of "niu牛(cattle)cattle", while "milk" can only serve as a hyponym of "nai奶(milk)".

Similar instances encompass: "xuebai雪白(snow-white)" versus "baixue白雪(white snow)", "虫害(insect pest)" versus "haichong害虫(pest insect)", "shigu事故(accident)" versus "gushi故事(story)", "cansha蚕沙(silkworm excrement)" versus "shacan沙蚕(silk worm)", "jisuan计算(calculation)" versus "suanji算计(conspiracy)", and the like.

Words formed by reversing the sequence of two identical morphemes may not always differ in meaning significantly. In fact, a considerable number of them are synonyms or even equivalents. In lexicology, these words are categorized as inverse morphemes synonyms. For instance, "shibing士兵(soldier)" and "bingshi兵士(soldier)", "jidu忌妒 (jealousy)" and "duji妒忌(jealousy)", "hengman横蛮(brutal)" and "manheng蛮横(brutal)", "chajue察觉(perceive)" and "juecha觉察(perceive)", "pandeng登攀(climb)" and "dengpan登攀(climb)", "bieli别离(parting)" and "libie离别(parting)", "daiti代替(replace)" and "tidai替代(replace)", "huxiang互相(mutual)" and "xianghu相互(mutual)". Unlike the above examples, the two constituent morphemes of these words originally have similar meanings, with most of their semantic genes being identical. However, in modern Chinese, many of these morphemes can no longer stand alone as words but can only function as components of words, i.e., morphemes.

Therefore, in terms of temporal order, the newly created words come into existence after their two superior morphemes. Semantic inheritance is evident during the process of word formation. Nevertheless, from a semantic spatial perspective, these morphemes do not qualify as the superordinates for the newly formed words. For instance, while the morpheme "bing兵" can stand alone as a word, it is not the superordinate for "bingshi兵士(soldier)" or "shibing士兵(soldier)"; rather, it is a synonym. This is because the semantic genes of them are largely identical.

6.1.2.3 Heritable Genes and Non-Heritable Genes

Not all genetic information in organisms is heritable; mutations induced by environmental factors cannot be passed on to the next generation. In contrast, the semantic genes are distinct. On the semantic hierarchical tree, all genes of the superordinate terms, whether they are inherited genetic genes from the lexical family or individual genes resulting from variation, are fully inherited by the subordinate terms. The genetic law of semantic genes for words that are in the relationship of superordination and subordination on the semantic hierarchical tree are illustrated as follows (Fig. 6.1).

New pleremes arise through extension, and the genetic inheritance of semantic genes between extended meanings and their basic meanings is typically not overall. Temporally, the extended meanings can be seen as the descendants of the original meanings, but spatially, within the semantic hierarchical tree, they do not exhibit a strict hierarchical relationship of superordinate and subordinate. Therefore, the extended meanings inherit only a portion of the semantic genes from the basic

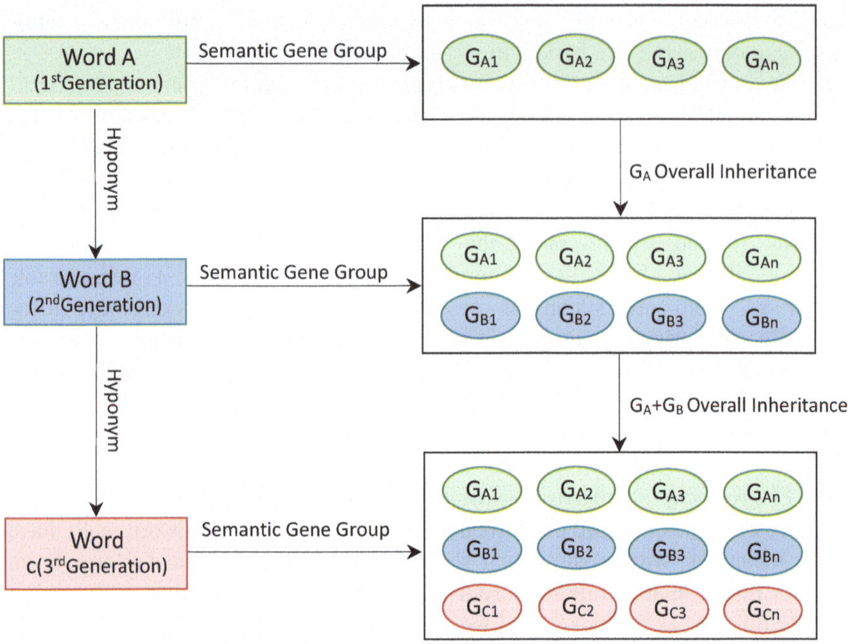

Fig. 6.1 Overall inheritance law of smantic genes on the semantic hierarchical tree

meanings, and new meanings are acquired either through genetic variation or by recombining semantic genets from other sources. There are two types of semantic extension:

(1) Starting from the original meaning, various new senses are generated, each of which inherits semantic genes of one or more feature dimensions from the original meaning. For instance, in *The Contemporary Chinese Dictionary (7th Edition)*, the word "shen深(deep)" encompasses nine different pleremes:

Shen深(Deep): ❶ Great distance from top to bottom or from outside to inside (opposite to 'shallow', as in ❸–❻). ❷ shendu深度(Depth). ❸ shenao深奥(Profound). ❹ shenke深刻(Impressive). ❺ (Emotiona) strong or(relationship) close. ❻ (Color) intense. ❼ Long time since the start. ❽ Very; extremely. ❾ A surname.

The plereme ❾ has no extension relationship with the original meaning. The extension relationships and the semantic genetic inheritance among the other eight pleremes are as follows:

"shen深(Deep)" originally meant the name of a river. According to the 'Shuo Wen《说文》', it is described as: "深水。出桂陽南平。西入營道。Deep water. Originating from Nanping in Guangyuan, flowing west into Yingdao." This meaning is now obsolete, not included in *The Contemporary Chinese Dictionary*. In the《古汉语字典》*Ancient Chinese Dictionary* compiled by Wang 王力, the first plereme of "shen深" is "The water is deep", which is taken as the basic plereme in modern Chinese. The gene structure description is as follows:"

S 深 = {[距离]:{[程度]([大])}+{[维度]([空]∧[垂直])}+{[方向]([起]([上])∧[止]([下]))}+{[对象]([水])}}

S 深 = {[Distance]:{[Degree]([Large])}+{[Dimension]([Space]∧[Vertical])}+{[Direction]([Start]([Top])∧ [End]([Bottom]))}+{[Object]([Water])}}

The first plereme is actually composed of two pleremes, namely, a long vertical dimension distance from top to bottom and a long horizontal distance from outside to inside. These two pleremes respectively inherit the semantic genes of the basic plereme of "deep", which includes [juli距离(Distance)], [chengdu程度(Degree)] and [da大(Large)].

The plereme ❷ is derived from the adjective meaning and extended to the nominal meaning, inheriting all the semantic genes of the basic plereme except for [Large], and then recombined with the semantic gene [duliang度量(Measurement)]. It loses the object dimension gene chain {[duixiang对象(Object)]([shui水(Water)])}, representing the measurement of "distance from top to bottom or from outside to inside".

The plereme ❼ is derived from the extension of the spatial dimension to the temporal dimension, inheriting the semantic genes of the basic plereme [juli距离(Distance)], [chengdu程度(Degree)] and [da大(Large)]. The assignment genes of the object dimension feature function undergo mutation.

The plereme ❸–❻ are derived from the extension of concrete meanings to abstract meanings and have only inherited two semantic genes of the basic plereme, [chengdu程度 (Degree)] and [da大(Large)], while the assignment genes of the object feature function of the dimension gene chain undergo mutation. The transition from concrete to abstract meanings is achieved through the metaphorical mechanism, resulting in semantic variation.

The plereme ❽ is also involves the extension of abstract meanings from concrete ones, with a semantic variation pattern similar to plereme ❸–❻, but it lacks the object dimension gene chain.

To summarize, the extension of the word "shen深(deep)" from its basic plereme "shuishen水深" to its eight other pleremes constitutes a network of semantic radial extension. In conjunction with its original meaning as a river name in ancient Chinese, the extension path of the meaning of "shen深(deep)" can be illustrated as follows (Fig. 6.2).

Extended from the basic plereme, a first-level extended plereme is generated, which in turn produces a second-level extended plereme, gradually forming a recursive pattern. This recursive chained extension is relatively common in ancient Chinese. For instance, in the extension of the word "shen 深 (deep)", if tracing back to its original meaning in ancient Chinese, the sequence "river name → water is deep → various pleremes in modern Chinese" constitutes multiple recursive chains of extension. For another example, the word "bing 秉" has nine pleremes in the《汉语大词典》*Great Chinese Dictionary*:

bing 秉 (bundle): ❶ A bunch of gramineae.❷ Quantifier,sixteen bushels.❸ Hold.❹ Preside over; master.❺ Yield to; comply with.❻ Bear; endure.❼ Equivalent to "bing 柄 (handle)". Authority.❽ Equivalent to "bang谤(slander)".❾ A surname.

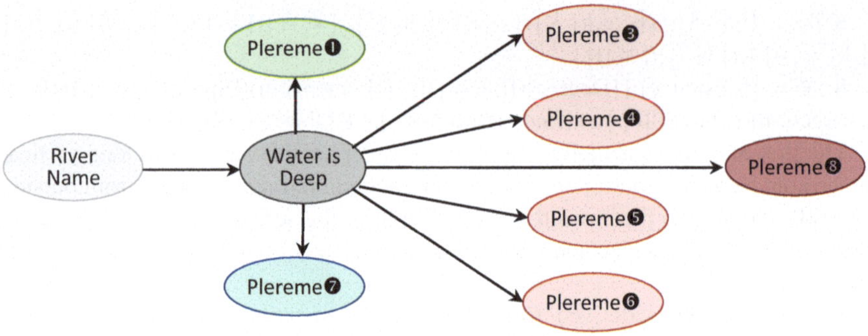

Fig. 6.2 Illustration of the meaning extension of the word "deep"

Among them, there is a recursive chained extension: Plereme❶ → Plereme❸→ Plereme❹ → Plereme❼. The extension and genetic inheritance path analysis are as follows:

"bing秉"originally means" "a bundle (a sheaf) of gramineae". According to the shuowen jiezi 说文解字: "秉,禾束也。a bundle of gramineae." This aligns with the first plereme in the *Great Chinese Dictionary.* Therefore, the semantic gene structure of the basic meaning of "bing秉" can be described as follows:

S 秉 = {[禾]:[度量]([单位](Gs[把])∧[数量](1))}

S 秉 = {[Gramineae]:[Measurement]([Unit](Gs[Bunch])∧[Quantity](1))}

The second plereme of the explanation for "ba 把 (bunch)" in the *Great Chinese Dictionary* is: *The measure of the thickness or quantity that can be held in one palm.*

The structure of the semantic gene can be described as:

S 把 = {[单位]of[量]:[[方式]of[度量]]([握]([工具]([掌]))}

S 把 = {[Unit]of[Quantity]:[[Method]of[Measurement]]([Hold]([Tool]([Palm]))}

By combining the two semantic gene expressions, it can be observed that the basic plereme of the character "bing秉(bundle)" encompasses the following semantic genes: [he 禾(Gramineae)], [duliang度量(Measurement)], [danwei 单位(Unit)], [shuliang数量(Quantity)], [fangshi方式(Method)], [wo握(Hold)], [gongju工具(Tool)], [zhang掌 (Palm)].

By inheritance, the plereme❸ inherits only three genes [wo握(Hold)], [gongju 工具(Tool)] and [zhang掌(Palm)] from the basic plereme, rejecting other genes. It undergoes a semantic variation through the transformation from noun to verb, and is then combined with the semantic gene chain {[duixiang对象(Object)]([jutiwu具体物(Concrete Entity)])} to generate a new sense.

The plereme❹ inherits all the genes of plereme❸, but on the feature dimension gene chain {[duixiang对象(Object)]([jutiwu具体物(Concrete Entity)])}, the assignment gene of the dimension function varies, changing from [{[duixiang对象(Object)]([jutiwu具体物(Concrete Entity)])}] to [chouxiangwu抽象物(Abstract Entity)].

The plereme❼ only inherits and acquires one gene [Abstract Entity] from plereme❹, which then undergoes variation, becoming a specific object within [Abstract Entity]. The part of speech also varies again, with verbs reverting to nouns.

It can be seen that in the recursive process of chained extension,each recursive iteration of a word results in variations of its semantic genes. The later the sense, the less the semantic genes it inherits from the basic plereme, and the last sense no longer possesses any semantic genes of the basic plereme.

Obviously, the genetic inheritance resulting from semantic extension is not the overall genetic inheritance of the basic plereme. However, theoretically, any part of the genes within the basic plereme could potentially be inherited by the extended pleremes. The genes that are not inherited are not related to whether there has been genetic variation in the basic plereme; rather, it represents part of the dimension feature function gene chain discarded by the extended pleremes. In other words, even if some genes within the basic plereme has undergone variation, it can still be inherited. This differs from the case in biological genetics, where variant genes are not inherited. For instance, in the analysis of the extended meanings of "shen 深(deep)", "shuishen水深(water is deep)" itself arises from the basic meaning of "shen深(deep)" as a river name. In the various chained extended pleremes of "bing 秉(bundle)", the variant semantic genes have been inherited continuously in the chain.

All in all, the vocabulary system is dynamically changing. The lifespan of words varies, with some buzzwords appearing and disappearing in a flash, while others seem almost eternal. The transient words are not really dead,in fact,they are still dormant in historical literature, ready to be temporarily reborn at any moment when there is a need for expression, though they are no longer widely used. Due to their dormancy, the changes in their semantic genes are relatively minor, essentially fixed at the point of their dormancy. In contrast, eternal words do not remain unchanged in meaning; they continuously evolve and change with the development of society and the expansion of human cognitive scope. Their semantic genes undergo continuous evolution, including: the addition of semantic genes leading to the expansion of meaning; the reduction of semantic genes resulting in the narrowing of meaning; the splitting of semantic genes to produce new senses; and the mutation of semantic genes causing semantic variations. Semantic variations are the manifestation of the evolution of meaning over the long river of time, and are an inevitable outcome of the interaction between the vocabulary system and the external objective and subjective world during the process of genetic inheritance and recombination. Semantic variations include two types: self-variation, where the symbol remains unchanged but the meaning it carries changes; and composite variation, where the original symbol's meaning changes during the process of combining with other morphological components to form new words.

6.2 Vision for the Application of Semantic Gene Resources

6.2.1 Computational Application of Semantic Gene Resources

Based on the database of semantic genes and the semantic gene structure description, numerous fundamental semantic computation tasks can be conducted. For instance:

(1) Automatic Generation of Language Ontology

The Ontology serves as a crucial foundation for the realization of artificial general intelligence. The most influential Ontologies in semantic computation are domain Ontologies, common-sense Ontologies, and linguistic Ontologies. Currently, in the research of knowledge ontologies, the achievements and the available resources for computational invocation of domain Ontologies are relatively abundant, while common-sense Ontologies and linguistic Ontologies remain underdeveloped, indicating a gap in this area of research. The most renowned linguistic Ontology worldwide is the Wordnet developed by Princeton University. Wordnet describes various semantic relationships, including synonymy, antonymy, hyponymy, meronymy, entailment, causation, and so on, and has become the most important public semantic resource in NLP today. The Chinese version of Wordnet includes the CCD (Chinese Concept Dictionary) developed by Peking University and the SinicaBOW (The Academia Sinica Bilingual Ontological Wordnet) developed by the Academia Sinica. At present, we do not have a true Chinese linguistic Ontology.

The semantic gene structure description database of modern Chinese under this study has already incorporated the structural thought of the Ontology during its development. Each word's semantic gene structure expression already encompasses various types of semantic relationship information. Once all the basic vocabulary has been described, the computer should then be employed to automatically learn these semantic relationships, thereby constructing the linguistic Ontology of modern Chinese.

(2) Semantic similarity computation

Semantic similarity computation is a most fundamental semantic processing technique that is indispensable in a variety of NLP tasks. There are currently two main computational strategies: the node distance algorithm based on semantic trees and the statistical algorithm based on contextual information. Generally speaking, the former calculates the semantic similarity between two words by determining the shortest distance between their respective nodes in a Ontology or semantic tree; the latter computes the distance between the meanings of words by calculating the similarity of their spatial vectors in the context. Both strategies have several specific computational methods.

These two strategies, in essence, are indirect methods of addressing the problem. The semantic distance between words is determined by their spatial relationships with other words, rather than directly based on the internal features of their meanings themselves. Based on the premise of the lexical meaning gene resource library, we provide the third strategy for solving the problem: calculating the semantic similarity between two words based on the shared and distinct features of their semantic genes and gene structures.

$$\mathrm{Sim}(A, B) = \frac{\log(G(a, b) \times p + L(a, b) \times q)}{\log((Ga + Gb) \times p + (La + Lb) \times q)}$$

In the formula, A and B denote any two words. Sim(*A*,*B*) represents the semantic similarity between the two words. *G*(*a*,*b*) signifies the count of shared semantic genes, while *L*(*a*,*b*) denotes the number of shared dimension gene chains. *Ga*, *Gb*, *La*, and *Lb* refer to the respective counts of semantic genes and dimension gene chains for words *A* and *B*. The variables p and q serve as weights. However, this formula offers only a general depiction of the computational strategy; the precise parameters must be validated and fine-tuned within extensive semantic gene datasets.

(3) Automatic Generation of Semantic Networks

The Semantic Network is a modeled representation of human associative memory, a structured knowledge representation method that employs directed graphs to depict semantic relationships among concepts, and it has extensive applications in artificial intelligence. As illustrated in Fig. 6.3.

In the semantic gene structure database, we have conducted a structured description of the features of all semantic dimensions for words. Then the computer can employ these features for analyzing matching, enabling the automatic generation of multiple analogous semantic networks.

(4) Automatic Description of semantic gene structure

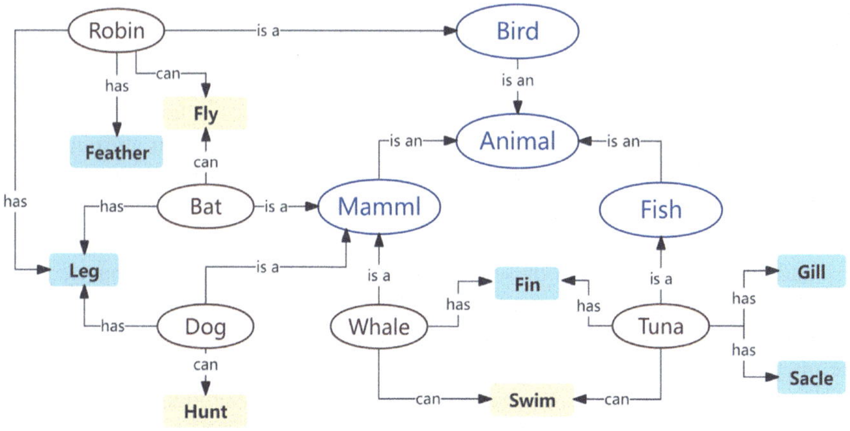

Fig. 6.3 The semantic network of some animals

According to the specifications of expression for the semantic genetic structure in existing databases, computers can automatically describe the semantic genetic structure of new words by combining features extracted from large-scale text corpora through deep learning. After manual correction, the descriptions are then incorporated into the database.

These computational technologies and the semantic resources derived from them are instrumental in a range of artificial intelligence applications, including semantic reasoning, automated question-answering systems, text clustering and classification, information extraction, and automatic text summarization.

6.2.2 Traditional Application of Semantic Gene Resources

The semantic gene database can also find extensive applications in traditional fields such as language teaching, linguistic research, and lexicography.

(1) Automated Construction of Visualized Lexical-Semantic Knowledge Graph

Lexical-semantic knowledge graph plays a significant role in language teaching and research, particularly in the study of vocabulary teaching. The following figure (Fig. 6.4) illustrates a visualized local part of the lexical-semantic knowledge graph of modern Chinese.

In the semantic gene bank, based on the genes and gene chain structures of each word's meaning, computers can automatically construct similar visual knowledge graph starting from any word. The principle and algorithm for automatically constructing such knowledge graphs from the gene database are similar to those of the aforementioned automatic construction of semantic networks in the previous section on computational applications.

(2) Lexicology and Semantics Research

The study of semantic genes and their genetic laws explored in this research can offer a novel perspective for observing and interpreting issues in lexical semantics, such as the evolution of lexical systems, the structure of word meanings, the pursuit of semantic motivations, the syntagmatic and paradigmatic laws of words, the semantic features of words, the meaning relationships between words, and the qualitative and quantitative analysis of word meanings, etc. The semantic gene bank can provide rich and detailed materials for these studies. Moreover, as the data in semantic gene bank are highly structured, it is very conducive for automatic retrieval and processing by computers. With the assistance of corresponding research tools, it may facilitate the integration of information technology and modern techniques into the study of traditional lexical semantics, thereby enhancing the research methodologies and tools employed in this field.

(3) Compilation of New Dictionaries

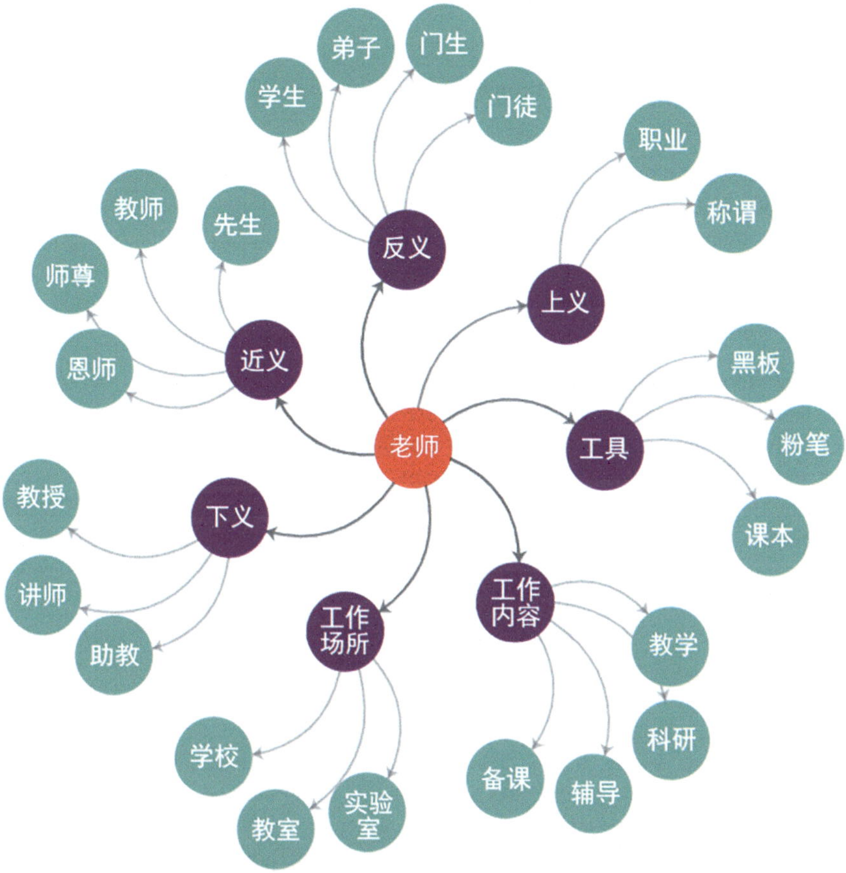

Fig. 6.4 Lexical-Semantic Knowledge Graph of the Chinese Word "laoshi老师(teacher)"

To date, we are still in need of a Modern Chinese Dictionary akin to the Longman Dictionary of English, which explains all basic vocabulary using a limited set of primitive words. The issue of circular interpretations within the current Chinese dictionaries remains difficult to effectively control. Based on the semantic gene database, we are hopeful to achieve this grandiose goal.

Furthermore, the semantic gene structure expressions in the database is a highly formalized and structured data representation method, which not only allows for direct invocation by computers for semantic computation but also can be translated into definitional natural language statements through simple NLP techniques. These statements can serve as the definitions of entries, thereby facilitating the automatic generation of the preliminary draft of human-readable dictionaries, achieving a semi-automated approach to dictionary compilation.

6.3 Summary and Prospect

6.3.1 The Main Work of This Book

In this study, we set out to investigate the computational features of natural language as symbolic intelligence within artificial intelligence, and elaborate on the significance of semantic formalization representation for NLP. Guided by the holographic theory and genetic theory, we aim to explore the theories, methods, and engineering implementation technologies for the formal description of lexical meanings. The main viewpoints of this book can be summarized as:

(1) The internal micro-structural components of word meaning exhibit holographic isomorphism with the genetic structure of organisms. The operational mechanism of the semantic system follows similar genetic inheritance, recombination, and variation laws as biological systems.
(2) The fundamental structural unit of meaning is the semantic gene, which governs certain semantic features of words. Semantic genes can be manipulated through processes of inheritance, recombination, and variation to construct new terms.
(3) Each plereme of a word constitutes a multi-dimensional semantic space composed of various semantic features, with each dimension's feature being represented by a feature function. A semantic feature function of a word is a semantic gene chain formed by the arrangement of several semantic genes according to certain structural rules. Multiple semantic gene chains, in turn, are combined according to specific structural rules to constitute the entire semantic space of a plereme. There exists a relationship of semantic gene inheritance and variation among the various pleremes of a word.
(4) The number of words in a language is open and infinite, whereas the set of semantic genes that constitute meanings of all the words is finite and controllable in terms of quantity. Words of different semantic types exhibit distinct genetic structures. The framework for describing the semantic domain of word meanings serves as the fundamental rule of the semantic gene structure and also the norm we adhere to when describing the expression of semantic gene structures. Through predefining and semantic gene structure analysis, we can extract all the semantic genes present in a language.
(5) The lexical family is analogous to a biological family, where all members within a family share a common set of semantic genes, while each individual within the family possesses its own unique semantic genes. The development and evolution of the lexical system, as well as the emergence of new words and meanings, are the outcomes of the inheritance, recombination, and variation of these semantic genes. The development of vocabulary system and the emergence of new words in a language is the result of the inheritance, recombination, and variation of semantic genes.

Based on these perspectives, we have taken the three fundamental parts of speech in modern Chinese, as examples to conduct a thorough investigation, namely nouns, verbs, and adjectives. We have selected a portion of representative basic vocabulary and conducted detailed semantic gene analysis and extraction. This has led to the preliminary establishment of a primary database for the semantic gene database of modern Chinese. Furthermore, we have initially explored the basic rules of semantic gene inheritance and the construction of new words.

6.3.2 The Limitation and Future Work

While this study has provided valuable insights, it is not without limitations. These identified deficiencies are also the primary focus of our subsequent endeavors.

(1) The theoretical system requires further refinement: ① The categorization of types of semantic feature functions and the description framework of semantic knowledge domains currently exhibit certain imperfections. ② The genetic inheritance, recombination, and variation laws of semantic genes require deeper exploration. These tasks necessitate the summary and induction based on a larger volume of data.
(2) The scale of engineering practice needs to be further expanded: the number of entries analyzed and the quantity of semantic genes extracted at present is insufficient, necessitating a continuous allocation of human resources to increase the number and scale of entries analyzed. Only when the data volume reaches a sufficient scale can the refinement of the theoretical system and the development of practical applications proceed more smoothly.
(3) The development of practical applications remains insufficient. Based on the semantic gene database, numerous computational applications and language teaching research applications can be derived, including relevant algorithms, tools, databases, and dictionaries. This aspect of work requires further enhancement.

In conclusion, the semantic gene analysis and extraction represents a significant genetic engineering endeavor within linguistics. The scale of this project is vast, and its implications and value are as profound as those of the genome sequencing projects in biology, marking a long and challenging journey.

Reference

Hu, D. 胡惮. (2011). *Alloconcepts and Their Formalized Description* [概念变体及其形式化描写]. China Social Sciences Press.

References

An, H. 安华林. (2005). *Research on Definition Primitives of Modern Chinese* [现代汉语释义基元词研究]. China Social Sciences Press.

An, H. 安华林. (2005). Forming of Metalanguage Theory and Linguistics Metalanguage View [元语言理论的形成和语言学的元语言观]. *Inner Mongolia Social Sciences* [内蒙古社会科学], *26*(01), 104–108.

An, H. 安华林. (2013). On the Definition of Chinese Explanatory Primitive Words [关于汉语释义基元词的界定问题]. *Lexicographical Studies* [辞书研究], (03), 15–20.

Arnauld, A., & Nicole, P. (1996). Foreword. In J. V. Buroker (Ed.), *Antoine Arnauld and Pierre Nicole: Logic or the Art of Thinking*. Cambridge Texts in the History of Philosophy. Cambridge University Press.

Bai, L. 白丽芳. (2006). *A Comparative Study of English and Chinese Metalanguage* [英汉元语言比较研究]. Nanjing Normal University [南京师范大学].

Beaugrande, R., & Dressler, W. U. (1981). *Introduction to Text Linguistic*. Longman.

Bloomfield, L. (1933). *Language*. George Allen & Unwin Ltd.

Bussmann, H. (Ed.). (1996). *Routledge Dictionary of Language and Linguistics* (G. P. Trauth & K. Kazzazi, Trans. & Ed.). Routledge.

Cai, S. 蔡曙山, & Zou, C. 邹崇理. (2010). Research on Formal Theories of Natural Language [自然语言形式理论研究]. Beijing: People's Publishing House.

Cai, Z. 蔡自兴, & Xu, G. 徐光祐. (2004). Artificial Intelligence and Its Applications [人工智能及其应用 (第四版)] (4th Edition). Tsinghua University Press.

Cao, W. 曹炜. (2001). *Lexical Semantics of Modern Chinese* [现代汉语词义学]. Xuelin Press.

Cen, Y. 岑运强. (1994). Further Exploration on Semantic Fields and Sememe Analysis [语义场和义素分析再探]. *Foreign Languages in Fujian* [福建外语], (Z2), 1–7.

Chen, B. 陈保亚, & Yu, D. 余德江. (2017). Arbitrariness of Signs: Linguistic Foundation of Cognitive Relativity [符号的任意性: 认知相对性的语言基础]. *Journal of Guizhou Minzu University (Philosophy and Social Science)* [贵州民族大学学报 (哲学社会科学版)], (4), 82–95.

Chen, D. 陈端吕, & Li, J. 李际平. (2010). Interpretation of the Connotation of Holographic Theory [全息论的内涵解读]. *Journal of Southwest University of Agriculture (Social Sciences)* 西南农业大学学报(社会科学版), *8*(01), 73–75.

Chen, Q. 陈全献. (2009). Philosophical Reflections on the Theory of Language Holography [语言全息论的哲学思考]. *Data of Culture and Education* [文教资料], (1), 96–98.

Chen, Y. 陈勇. (2008). Semiotic Characteristics of Texts [篇章的符号学特征]. *Journal of PLA University of Foreign Languages* [解放军外国语学院学报], (05), 42–49.

Cheng, Q. 程琪龙. (1997). Jackendoff's Theory of Conceptual Semantics Jackendoff [的概念语义学理论]. *Foreign Language Teaching and Research* [外语教学与研究], (02), 9–14+81.

Chomsky, N. (1987). Language in a psychological setting. *Sophia Linguistica, 1987*(22), 1–73.

Crystal, D. (2008). *A Dictionary of Linguistics and Phonetics* (6th ed.). Blackwell Publishing.

D. Hu, *Lexical Semantic Gene Structure of Modern Chinese*,
https://doi.org/10.1007/978-981-96-6425-2

Dong, Z. 董志铁. (2018). The Relationship Between Logic and Language from the Perspective of Ancient Chinese Dialectics [从中国古代名辩学看逻辑与语言的关系]. *Chinese Journal of Language Policy and Planning* [语言战略研究], *3*(1), 12–13.

Dong, Z. 董振东, & Dong, Q. 董强. (1999). An Introduction to HowNet [知网导论]. http://www.keenage.com/Theory-and-practice-of-HowNet/03.pdf

Evans, V., & Melanie, G. (2006). *Cognitive Linguistics: An Introduction.* New Jersey: Lawrence Erlbaum Associates.

Fan, X. 范晓. (2001). Nouns and Their Reclassification in Modern Chinese [现代汉语的名词及其再分类]. In Shanghai Language Association (Eds.)., *Proceedings of Language Studies* (Vol. 7) [语文论丛]. Shanghai Education Press.

Feng, Z. 冯志伟. (2007). Notes on Advantages and Disadvantages of Rationalism and Experimenralism in Natural Language Processing [自然语言处理中理性主义和经验主义的利弊得失]. *Yangtze River Academic* [长江学术], (2), 79–85.

Feng, H. 冯海霞, & Zhang, Z. 张志毅. (2006). Establishment and Improvement of the Defining System for The Contemporary Chinese Dictionary: Reading Notes on the Fifth Edition [《现代汉语词典》释义体系的创建与完善——读《现代汉语词典》第5版]. *Chinese Language* [中国语文], (05), 455–461+480.

Feng, Q. 冯契. (Ed.). (2001). *Encyclopedia of Philosophy* (Revised Edition) [哲学大辞典(修订本)]. Shanghai Dictionary Press.

Feng, Z. 冯志伟. (2018). In the Field of Artificial Intelligence, Those Who Master Language Will Master the World [人工智能领域: 得语言者得天下]. *Chinese Journal of Language Policy and Planning* [语言战略研究], *3*(05), 1.

Fillmore, C. J. (1968). The Case for Case. In E. Bach & R. T. Harms (Eds.), *Universals in Linguistic Theory* (pp. 1–88). New York: Holt, Rinehart, and Winston.

Fu, H. 符淮青. (1988). Componential Analysis and Lexical Definition [构成成分分析和词的释义]. *Lexicography Research* [辞书研究], (01), 48–55.

Fu, H. 符淮青. (1995). The Division of Semantic Units and Pleremes [词义单位的划分和义项]. *Lexicographical Studies* [辞书研究], (01), 75–83.

Fu, H. 符淮青. (1996). *Analysis and Description of Lexical Meaning* [词义的分析和描写]. Language & Culture Press.

Fu, H. 符淮青. (2002). Symbolic Meaning: Its Nature and Definition [指号义的性质和释义]. *Lexicographical Studies* [辞书研究], (5), 1–10.

Fu, H. 符淮青. (1998). The Division of Semantic Units [词义单位的划分]. *Chinese Language Learning* [汉语学习], (04), 26–32.

Fu, H. 符淮青. (1992). The Defining Method of Words in Chinese Dictionaries [语文词典中词的释义方式]. In *Compilation Experience of Dictionaries* [辞书编纂经验萃萃] (pp. 120–138). Shanghai Dictionary Society [上海辞书学会].

Gao, M. 高名凯, & Shi, A. 石安石. (1963). *Introduction to Linguistics* [语言学概论]. Zhonghua Book Company.

Gao, S. 高圣林. (2000). The Deconstruction of Linguistic Forms and the Emergence of Semantics—One of the Structural Patterns of Humor [语形的解构与语义的隐现——幽默的结构模式之一]. *Contemporary Rhetoric* [修辞学习], (Z1),16–18.

Ge, B. 葛本仪. (2001). *Lexicology of Modern Chinese* [现代汉语词汇学]. Shandong People's Publishing House.

Ge, B. 葛本仪. (1992). *Practical Chinese Linguistics Dictionary* [实用中国语言学词典]. Qingdao Publishing House [青岛出版社].

Ge, H. 葛宏伟. (2006). *The Research of Some Optimization Problems Based on Computational Intelligence* [基于计算智能的若干优化问题研]. Jilin University.

Goddard, C., & Wierzbicka, A. (Eds.). (2002). *Meaning and Universal Grammar: Theory and Empirical Findings* (2 vols.). John Benjamins.

Goddard, C. (1998). *Semantic Analysis: A Practical Introduction.* Oxford University Press.

Greimas, A. J.(1986). *Sémantique structurale.* Presses Universitaires de France.

Grice, H. P. (1957). Meaning. *Philosophical Review, 66*(3), 377–388.

Grice, H. P. (1968). Utterer's Meaning, Sentence-Meaning, and Word-Meaning. *Foundations of Language, 4*(3), 225–242.

Grice, H. P. (1969). Utterer's Meaning and Intentions. *Philosophical Review, 78*(2), 147–177.

Guo, D. 郭大方. (1994). *Verb Classification Dictionary of Modern Chinese* [现代汉语动词分类词典]. Jilin Education Press.

Han, X. 韩秀娟. (2005). *The Research Report of the Prior Set of Modern Chinese Basic Words* [现代汉语基本词汇先验集的考察分析研究]. In *Proceedings of the Eighth National Joint Conference on Computational Linguistics* (JSCL-2005) (pp. 219–225).

Hao, N. 郝宁湘. (2003). Philosophy of Computation: The New Tendency of the 21st Century's Philosophy of Science [计算哲学: 21世纪科学哲学的新趋向]. *Journal of Dialectics of Nature* [自然辩证法通讯], *25*(06), 37–42+110.

Hartmann, R. R. K., & Stork, F. C. (1972). *Dictionary of Language and Linguistics*. John Wiley & Sons.

He, L. 贺林, Ma, D. 马端, & Duan, T. 段涛. (2013). *Clinical Genetics* [临床遗传学]. Shanghai Scientific & Technical Publisher.

Hou, C. 侯成亚. (2003). The Holistic Theory and Its Methodological Significance [全息论及其方法论意义]. *New Horizons from Tianfu* [天府新论], (3), 11–13.

Hu, D., & Gao, J. (2009). Semantic Genes and the Semantic Composition of Adjectives in Modern Chinese. In *2009 International Conference on Asian Language Processing*. IEEE CPS.

Hu, D. 胡惮, Gao, J. 高精炼, & Zhao, L. 赵玲. (2011). Semantic Genes and the Formal Expression of Lexical Semantics [语义基因与词义结构的形式化表达初论]. *Yangtze River Academic* [长江学术], (4), 138–143, 168.

Hu, D. 胡惮. (2009). On Category Hierarchy and Ontology [略论范畴层次与知识本体]. *Journal of Shenyang Normal University (Social Science Edition)* [沈阳师范大学学报 (社会科学版)], *33*(06), 32–34.

Hu, D. 胡惮. (2011). *Alloconcepts and Their Formalized Description* [概念变体及其形式化描写]. China Social Sciences Press.

Hu, D. 胡惮. (2014). *Research on Modern Chinese Lexical Primitives for Natural Language Processing* [面向自然语言处理的现代汉语词义基元结构研究]. World Publishing Corporation.

Hu, M. 胡明扬. (1991). Reclassification of Adjectives in Mandarin [北京话形容词的再分类]. In *Collection of Linguistic Studies* [语言学论文集]. China Renmin University Press.

Hu, Y. 胡裕树, & Fan, X. 范晓. (1995). *Study on Verbs* [动词研究]. Henan University Press.

Huang, B. 黄伯荣, & Liao, X. 廖序东. (2008). *Modern Chinese* [现代汉语上册]. Higher Education Press.

Huang, H. 黄华新, & Hong, Z. 洪峥怡. (2019). Exploring a New Approach to Combine Language Logic with Information Processing: A Review of Logical Semantics on Natural Language Processing [探索语言逻辑与信息处理结合的新路径—《自然语言信息处理的逻辑语义学研究》评介]. *Journal of Chongqing Institute of Technology (Social Science)* [重庆理工大学学报 (社会科学版)], *33*(4), 13–16

Huang, Z. 黄曾阳. (1998). *Hierarchical Network of Concepts - A New Approach to Research on Computer Understanding of Language* HNC [概念层次网络理论—计算机理解语言研究的新思路]. Tsinghua University Press [清华大学出版社].

Huang, Z. 黄曾阳. (2004). *Basic Theorems and Mathematical-Physical Representations of Language Concept Space* [语言概念空间的基本定理和数学物理表示式]. Marine Press [海洋出版社].

Jackendoff, R. (1983). *Semantics and Cognition*. The MIT Press.

Jackendoff, R.(1990). *Semantic Structures*. The MIT Press.

Jackendoff, R. (2002). *Foundations of Language: Brain, Meaning, Grammar, Evolution*. Oxford University Press.

Jia, Y. 贾彦德. (1992). *Chinese Semantics* [汉语语义学]. Peking University Press.

Jiang, Z. 姜兆梓. (2012). The Development of Natural Language Processing from a Philosophical Perspective [哲学视阈中自然语言处理及发展]. *The Northern Forum* [北方论丛], (3), 47–49.

Jiang, Z. 姜照昶, Su, Y. 苏宇, & Ding, K. 丁凯孟. (2019). Advances in Multidisciplinary Methods of Swarm Computelligence [群体智能计算的多学科方法研究进展]. *Computer and Digital Engineering* [计算机与数字工程], *47*(12), 3053–3058.

Kittay, E. F. (1987). *Metaphor: Its Cognitive Force and Linguistic Structure*. New York: Oxford University Press.

Lakoff, G., & Johnsen, M.(2003). *Metaphors We Live By*. The University of Chicago press.

Lakoff, G. (1987). *Women, Fire, and Dangerous Things: What Categories Reveal about the Mind*. Chicago University Press.

Leech, G. (1974). *Semantics: The Study of Meaning*. Penguin Books.

Lei, Z. 雷子宸. (2018). Understanding and Application on the Nature of Mendel' s Law [关于孟德尔遗传定律的本质理解和应用]. *Journal of Anhui Vocational College of Metallurgy and Technology* [安徽冶金科技职业学院学报], *28*(1), 72–75.

Li, J. 黎锦熙. (1924). *New Grammar of National Language* [新著国语文法]. Commercial Press.

Li, B. 李葆嘉. (2002). The Study of Metalanguage System of Chinese: An Analysis Project of Language Gene Atlas [汉语元语言系统研究的理论建构及应用价值]. *Journal of Nanjing Normal University (Social Science Edition)* [南京师大学报(社会科学版)], (04), 140–147.

Li, B. 李葆嘉. (2003). Theories of Semantic Grammar and Meta-language System: Their Researche [语义语法学理论和元语言系统研究]. *Journal of Shenzhen University (Humanities and Social Sciences)* [深圳大学学报(人文社会科学版)], (02), 105–110.

Li, J. 李炯英. (2005). The Poland Semantic School: A Review [波兰语义学派概述]. *Foreign Language Teaching and Research* [外语教学与研究], (05), 377–382+401.

Li, J. 李炯英. (2006). A Comparison of the Semantic Theories of Wierzbicka and Jackendoff from Perspective of Semantic Primitives [从语义基元的视角比较] Wierzbicka [与] Jackendoff [的语义学理论——波兰语义学派研究之三]. *Foreign Language Education* [外语教学], *27*(05), 16–18.

Li, J. 李炯英. (2011). The Philosophical Foundation and Six Core Ideas of the Polish Semantic School [波兰语义学派的哲学基础及其六大核心思想——波兰语义学派研究之五]. *Contemporary Foreign Language Studies* [当代外语研究], (11), 8–11+51+60.

Li, Q. 李强. (2018). Supplement to "On Dictionary Definitions of Nouns from the Perspective of Generative Lexicon Theory" - A Response to Shang Jian (2017) [《从生成词库论看名词的词典释义》补议——对尚简(2017)的回应]. *Lexicographical Studies* [辞书研究], (01), 34–41+93–94.

Li, J. 李炯英, & Li, B. 李葆嘉. (2007). An Examination of the Objectives, Principles and Methodology of Natural Semantic Metalanguage Approach NSM [理论的研究目标、原则和方法]. *Contemporary Linguistics* [当代语言学], (01), 68–77+94.

Li, J. 李炯英, Liu, P. 刘鹏辉, & Ding, J. 丁洁. (2014). Research Into NSM Theory in China: A Review [国内自然语义元语言理论研究: 现状与思考]. *Journal of Nanjing University of Posts and Telecommunications (Social Science)* [南京邮电大学学报 (社会科学版), *16*(03), 87–93.

Li, Q. 李强, & Yuan, Y. 袁毓林. (2016). On Dictionary Definitions of Nouns from the Perspective of Generative Lexicon Theory [从生成词库论看名词的词典释义]. *Lexicographical Studies* [辞书研究], (04), 12–26+93.

Liu, C. 刘承华. (1994). On the Holographic Effect of the Three Major Harmonies [试论三大和谐的全息效应]. *Journal of Anhui University (Philosophy and Social Sciences)* [安徽大学学报(哲学社会科学版)], (3), 51–54.

Liu, D. 刘道英. (2002). Several Thoughts on the Theory of Morpheme in the Cognizance [谈义素理论认知上的几个问题]. *Journal of Qinghai Nationalities Institute (Social Sciences)* [青海民族学院学报], (03), 100–103.

Liu, G. 刘桂芳. (1995). A Brief Discussion on Sememe Analysis [义素分析略说]. *Journal of Shanxi Normal University (Social Sciences)* [山西师大学报(社会科学版)], (02), 96–98.

Liu, G. 刘桂芳. (2006). My Opinions on Types of Sememe and Its Analysis [义素类型及分析之我见]. *Academic Exchange* [学术交流], (12), 141–143.

Liu, S. 刘叔新. (1995). Descriptive Lexicology of Chinese [汉语描写词汇学]. The Commercial Press.

Liu, S. 刘顺. (2003). *Modern Chinese Nouns: A Multidimensional Study* [现代汉语名词的多视角研究]. Xuelin Publishing House.

Liu, X. 刘晓林. (2006). A Review of Jackendoff's Conceptual Semantics Jackendoff [概念语义学述评]. *Foreign Language Education* [外语教学], *27*(02), 12–15.

Lin, Y. 林奕欧, Lei, H. 雷航, Li, X. 李晓瑜, & Wu, J. 吴佳. (2017). Deep Learning in NLP: Methods and Applications [自然语言处理中的深度学习: 方法及应用]. *Journal of University of Electronic Science and Technology of China* [电子科技大学学报], *46*(6), 913–919.

Liu, M. 刘美君, & Wan, M. 万明瑜. (2019). Research on Chinese Verbs and Their Classification: Construction and Application of the Chinese Verb Lexical Semantic Network [中文动词及分类研究: 中文动词词汇语义网的构建及应用]. *Lexicographical Studies* [辞书研究], (02), 42–60+110.

Liu, W. 刘伟, Tian, E. 田娥, & Tan, M. 谭苗苗. (2016). Research and Application of Information Processing Technology Based on Computational Intelligence [基于计算智能的信息处理技术的研究与应用]. *Video Engineering* [电视技术], *40*(12), 51–56.

Lü, S. 吕叔湘. (1942). *Outline of Chinese Grammar* [中国文法要略]. The Commercial Press.

Lü, S. 吕叔湘. (1979). *Problems in the Analysis of Chinese Grammar* [汉语语法分析问题]. The Commercial Press.

Lü, S. 吕叔湘. (1981). *Preface to the Concise Thesaurus* [简明同义词词典.序》]. Shanghai Lexicographical Publishing House.

Lü, H. 吕鹤. (2010). On Evolution of Meanings of Chinese word Chi [汉语"吃"字系列的古今词义演变]. *Journal of Jixi University* [鸡西大学学报], *10*(05), 127–128.

Lyons, J.(1968). *Introduction to Theoretical Linguistic*. Cambridge University Press.

Lyons, J.(1977). *Semantics*. Cambridge University Press.

Ma, J. 马建忠. (1898). *Mashi Wen Tong* [马氏文通]. Commercial Press.

Ma, Q. 马庆株. (1992). *Verbs and Verbal Structures in Chinese* [汉语动词和动词性结构]. Beijing Language Institute Press.

Miao, C. 苗传江, & Liu, Z. 刘智颖. (2010).The Lexical Knowledge Base of Modern Chinese Based on HNC Theory [基于HNC的现代汉语词语知识库建设]. *Journal of Yunan Normal University(Humanities and Social Sciences)* [云南师范大学学报(哲学社会科学版)], *42*(4), 15–18.

Newell, A., & Simon, H. A. (1976). Computer Science as Empirical Inquiry: Symbols and Search. *Communications of the ACM, 19*(3), 113–126.

Peng, R. 彭睿. (1996). Nouns and the Reclassification of Nouns [名词和名词的再分类]. In M. Hu 胡明扬 (Ed.), *An Examination of Word Class Issues* [词类问题考察]. Beijing Language and Culture University Press.

Peng, Y. 彭业飞, Feng, Z. 冯智鑫, & Zhang, W. 张维继. (2017). Bionic Intelligent Algorithm Research Status and Military Applications Review [仿生智能算法研究现状及军事应用综述]. *Techniques of Automation and Applications* [自动化技术与应用], *36*(02), 5–8+14.

Pu, D. 蒲冬梅. (2008). Analysis on Validity of Natural Semantic Metalanguage [自然语义元语言有效性评析]. *Foreign Language Research* [外语学刊], (4), 55–59.

Pu, D. 蒲冬梅. (2012). Natural Semantic Metalanguage: Rationales and Prospects [自然语义元语言的理论基础及研究前景]. *Foreign Language Research* [外语学刊], (04), 45–49.

Pylyshyn, Z. W. (1986). *Computation and Cognition: Toward a Foundation for Cognitive Science*. The MIT Press.

Qian, G. 钱冠连. (1998). Outline of the Law of Language Holography [语言全息律纲要]. *Foreign Languages and Their Teaching* [外语与外语教学, (08), 3–7+56.

Qian, G. 钱冠连. (2002a). *The Theory of Language Holography* [语言全息论]. The Commercial Press.

Qian, G. 钱冠连. (2002b). On the Theory of Language Holography [何为语言全息论]. *Foreign Languages Research* [外语研究], (2), 20–26.

Qiu, Q. 邱庆山. (2018). Description and Construction of the Attribute Sense Ontology of Chinese Nouns of "bi" Class [汉语笔类名词的属性义知识本体描写与构建]. *Journal of*

Hubei University (Philosophy and Social Science) [湖北大学学报(哲学社会科学版)], *45*(05), 152–159.

Qiu, X. 邱雪玫, & Li, B. 李葆嘉. (2016). The Formation Process and Academic Background of Semantic Analysis Methods—Unveiling the Second Mystery of Structural Semantics [语义解析方法的形成过程及其学术背景—揭开结构主义语义学的第二个谜]. *Jianghai Academic Journal* [江海学刊], (03), 65–73.

Richards, J. C., & Schmidt, R. (2010). *Longman Dictionary of Language Teaching and Applied Linguistics* (4th ed.). Longman.

Saussure, F. de (1916). *Cours de linguistique générale*. Payot.

Shi, A. 石安石, & Zhan, R. 詹人凤. (1988). *Introduction to Linguistics* [语言学概论]. Higher Education Press.

Shi, Q. 施启良. (1991). Prospects for the Research of Holographic Theory [全息论研究展望]. *Science, Technology and Dialectics* [科学技术与辩证法], (02), 54–55.

Shi, D. 石定栩. (2002). *Chomsky's Theory of Syntax* [乔姆斯基的形式句法]. Beijing Language and Culture University Press.

Snustad, D. P., & Simmons, M. J. (2011). *Principles of Genetics* (6th ed.). New York: John Wiley & Sons.

Su, B. 苏宝荣. (2000). *A Study on Lexical Semantics and Lexicographical Interpretation* [词义研究与辞书释义]. The Commercial Press.

Su, X. 苏新春. (2003). Three Interpretations of Metalanguage and Different Researches on Defining Metalanguage [元语言研究的三种理解及释义型元语言研究评述]. *Journal of Jiangxi Normal University (Philosophy and Social Sciences Edition)* [江西师范大学学报(哲学社会科学版)], (06), 93–102.

Su, X. 苏新春. (2005). *Studies on Chinese Definitional Metalanguage* [汉语释义元语言研究]. Shanghai Education Press [上海教育出版社].

Su, X. 苏鑫. (2019). On the Logical Relationships in Language [浅论语言中的逻辑关系]. *Shenzhou* [神州], (9), 67.

Sun, Y. 孙毅. (2019). Constructing Theoretical Paradigms of Contemporary Metaphorology [当代隐喻学的理论范式构念]. *Journal of HaiNan University(Humanities & Social Sciences)* [海南大学学报(人文社会科学版)], *37*(6), 126–134.

Sun, D. 孙道功, & Li, B. 李葆嘉. (2008). On Marker Set Construction of Analysis Metalanguage [试论析义元语言标记集的建构]. *Applied Linguistics* [语言文字应用], (02), 132–138.

Tang, X. 唐兴全. (2001). The Quintuple of HNC Theory and Part of Speech HNC [理论的五元组与词性]. In *Natural Language Understanding and Machine Translation - Proceedings of the Sixth National Joint Academic Conference on Computational Linguistics* [自然语言理解与机器翻译——全国第六届计算语言学联合学术会议论文集] (pp. 263–268). China Society of Chinese Information Processing [中国中文信息学会].

Tian, M. 田明明. (2016). On the Impact of Cognitive Levels in Different Eras on Lexical Meaning through the Development of Terminological Semantics [从术语义的发展演变看不同时代人们的认知水平对词义的影响]. *Modern Chinese Language (Language Research)* [现代语文(语言研究)], (9), 38–39, 40.

Turing, A. M. (1950). Computing Machinery and Intelligence. *Mind, 59*(236), 433–460.

Wang, F. 王芳. (2015). Generation of Natural Language Logic and Knowledge Representation in Artificial Intelligence [自然语言逻辑的产生与人工智能中的知识表示]. *Journal of Fujian Agriculture and Forestry University (Philosophy and Social Sciences)* [福建农林大学学报(哲学社会科学版)], *18*(05), 98–101.

Wang, H. 王洪轩. (1987). A Summary of Semantic Classification of Verbs [动词语义分类举要]. *Journal of Hebei University (Philosophy and Social Science)* [河北大学学报(哲学社会科学版)], (02), 86–91.

Wang, J. 王珏. (2001). *A Study on Nouns of Modern Chinese* [现代汉语名词研究]. East China Normal University Press.

Wang, J. 王军. (2005). *Research on the Semantic System of Chinese Words* [汉语词义系统研究]. Shandong People's Publishing House.

Wang, L. 王力. (1985). *Grammar of Modern Chinese* [中国现代语法]. Commercial Press.

Wang, N. 王宁. (1996). *Principles of Chinese Exegetics* [训诂学原理]. China International Broadcasting Press.

Wang, W. 王文庆, & Han, C. 韩崇昭. (2004). Holographic Control Design for Complex Systems Based on Fuzzy Logic Systems [基于模糊逻辑的一类复杂系统全息控制设计]. *Systems Engineering and Electronics* [系统工程与电子技术], *26*(8), 1097–1101.

Wang, D. 王德春. (1983). *Studies on Lexicology* [词汇学研究]. Shandong Education Press.

Wang, H. 王红卫. (2010). The Semantic View of Encyclopedia Knowledge and Its Enlightenment for English Vocabulary Teaching [百科知识语义观及其对英语词汇教学的启示]. *Journal of Liaoning University of Technology (Social Science Edition)* [辽宁工业大学学报(社会科学版)], *12*(3), 124–126, 135.

Wang, H. 王惠. (2004). *A Syntagmatic Study on Noun Senses in Contemporary Chinese* [现代汉语名词词义组合分析]. Peking University Press [北京大学出版社].

Wang, J. 王今铮, et al. (1985). *Concise Linguistics Dictionary* [简明语言学词典]. Inner Mongolia People's Publishing House [内蒙古人民出版社].

Wang, N. 王宁. (1988). On the Explanation of Word Meaning [论词义训释]. *Lexicographical Studies* [辞书研究], (01), 2–11.

Wierzbicka, A. (2004). Conceptual Primes in Human Languages and Their Analogues in Animal Communication and Cognition. *Language Sciences, 26*(5), 413–441.

Wierzbicka, A. (1996). *Semantic: Prime and Universals.* Oxford University Press.

Wierzbicka, A. (1972). *Semantic Primitives.* Athenäum-Verl.

Wittgenstein, L. (1922). *Tractatus Logico-Philosophicus.* London: Routledge & Kegan Paul.

Wu, T. 伍铁平. (1979). A Review of the Etic and Emic Theory in Gao Mingkai's *On Language* [评高名凯《语言论》中的位素理论]. *Language Teaching and Linguistic Studies* [语言教学与研究], (02), 135–151.

Xiao, G. 萧国政, Xiao 肖珊, & Guo, T. 郭婷婷. (2011). The Mapping from Space of Concept Primitives to Space of Word Meaning Primitives [从概念基元空间到语义基元空间的映射——HNC联想脉络与词汇语义结构表述研究]. *Journal of East China Normal University (Philosophy and Social Sciences)* [华东师范大学学报(哲学社会科学版), *43*(01), 139–143+156.

Xiao, G. 萧国政, & Hu, D. 胡惮. (2007). The Constructive State of Prospective on the Chinese Semantic Resources of Information Processing [信息处理的汉语语义资源建设现状分析与前景展望]. *Yangtze River Academic* [长江学术], (2), 86–91.

Xie, X. 谢晓明.(2008). A Multi-angle Investigation of Semantically Related Verbs with Objects: A Case Study of "Eat" and "Drink" with Objects [语义相关动词带宾语的多角度考察 "吃""喝"带宾语个案研究]. Central China Normal University Press.

Xing, F. 邢福义, & Wu, Z. 吴振国. (2002). *Introduction to Linguistics* [语言学概论]. Central China Normal University Press.

Xu, J. 徐晋麟, Xu, Q. 徐沁, & Chen, C. 陈淳. (2001). *Principles of Modern Genetics* [现代遗传学原理]. Science Press.

Xu, L. 徐烈炯. (1995). *Semantics* [语义学(修订本)]. The Education Press.

Xu, S. 徐思益. (1984). On the Semantic Structure of Sentences [论句子的语义结构]. *Journal of Xinjiang University (Philosophy and Social Sciences)* [新疆大学学报(哲学社会科学版)], (01), 96–105.

Xu, W. 许威汉. (1987). *Introduction to Exegetics* [训诂学导论]. Shanghai Education Press.

Yan, C. 严春友, & Wang, C. 王存臻. (1988). Hegel and the Holographic Unity Theory [黑格尔与宇宙全息统一论]. *Journal of Tianjin Normal University (Social Sciences)* [天津师大学报(社会科学版)], (05), 11–20.

Yan, C. 严春友. (2008). Introduction to Holographic Philosophy [全息哲学引论]. *Tribune of Social Sciences* [社会科学论坛], (23), 31–47.

Yang, S. 杨升初. (1982). Issues in the Sememe Analysis of Modern Chinese [现代汉语的义素分析问题]. *Journal of Xiangtan University(Philosophy and Social Sciences)* [湘潭大学学报(哲学社会科学版)], (03), 49–57+93.

Ye, B. 叶斌, & Xie, G. 谢国剑. (2007). The Summary of Domestic "Sememe Theory" in Recent Twenty Years 20 [多年来国内义素论综述]. *Journal of Hangzhou Teachers College (Social Sciences Edition)* [杭州师范学院学报(社会科学版)], *29*(5).

Ye, F. 叶蜚声, & Xu, T. 徐通锵. (1993). *Outline of Linguistics* (3rd ed.) [语言学纲要第3版]. Peking University Press.

Ye, T. 叶眺新, & Lu, B. 陆丙甫. (1994). Linguistics and the Biological Holographic Law 语言学和生物全息律. *Journal of Hebei Normal University (Philosophy and Social Sciences)* [河北师范大学学报(社会科学版)], (02), 12–19.

Yuan, Y. 袁毓林. (1998). *Studies on the Valency of Chinese Verbs* [汉语动词的配价研究]. Jiangxi Education Press.

Yuan, Y. 袁毓林. (2014).On a Descriptive System of Qualia Structure of Chinese Nouns and Its Application in Parsing Complex Chinese Grammatical Phenomena [汉语名词物性结构的描写体系和运用案例]. *Contemporary Linguistics* [当代语言学], *16*(01), 31–48.

Zeng, L. 曾利沙. (2005). On Theoretical and Methodological Characteristics of the Theory of Language Holography: Theoretic Categorization and Innovational Academic Researches [论《语言全息论》的理论与方法论特征—也谈学术创新研究的途径: 理论范畴化]. *Shandong Foreign Language Teaching Journal* [山东外语教学], (3), 15–18.

Zhan, R. 詹人凤. (1997). *Semantics of Modern Chinese* [现代汉语语义学]. The Commercial Press.

Zhang, D. 张道民. (1995). On the Principle of Correlation [论相关性原理]. *Journal of Systemic Dialectics* [系统辩证学学报, *3*(1), 48–53.

Zhang, S. 张双棣, Zhang, L. 张联荣, Song, S. 宋绍年, et al. (2002). *A Course in Ancient Chinese Language Knowledge* [古代汉语知识教程]. Peking University Press.

Zhang, S. 张嗣瀛, & Yang, G. 杨光红. (1996). Holographic Control of Complex Systems [一类复杂控制系统的全息控制]. *Control and Decision* [控制与决策], (04), 501–505.

Zhang, T. 张廷远. (2007). An Analysis of the Implied Semantic Components and Their Pragmatic Value [隐含义素的剖析及其语用价值]. *Chinese Linguistics* [汉语学报], (03), 44–52+96.

Zhang, Z. 张志毅, & Zhang, Q. 张庆云. (2001). *Lexical Semantics* [词汇语义学]. The Commercial Press.

Zhang, G. 张国英, & He, Y. 何元娇. (2010). Subject and Knowledge System Review of Artificial Intelligence [人工智能知识体系及学科综述]. *Computer Education* [计算机教育], (08), 25–28.

Zhang, J. 张津, & Huang, C. 黄昌宁. (1997). Method of Deriving Definition Primitives from a Monolingual Dictionary [从单语词典中获取定义原语的一种方法]. *Journal of Tsinghua University (Science and Technology)* [清华大学学报(自然科学版)], (03), 29–34.

Zhang, N. 张能甫. (1999). Review and Prospect of Research on Chinese Basic Vocabulary [汉语基本词汇研究的回顾与展望]. *Journal of Sichuan Normal University (Social Sciences Edition)* [四川师范大学学报(社会科学版)], (02), 90–95.

Zhang, R. 张韧弦, & Liu, N. 刘乃实. (2004). Towards a Formal Approach to Semantics [语义学的形式化研究]. *Shandong Foreign Languages Teaching Journal,* (2), 18–21.

Zhang, W. 张万有. (2001). A Brief Talk About Semantic Analysis [义素分析略说]. *Language Teaching and Linguistic Studies* [语言教学与研究], (01), 61–65.

Zhang, Y. 张勇, Gen, G. 耿国华, Zhou, M. 周明全, & Chen, L. 陈丽萍. (2017). Survey of Computational Intelligence [计算智能研究综述]. *Application Research of Computers* [计算机应用研究], *34*(11), 3201–3203+3213.

Zhang, Z. 张喆. (2007). *Natural Semantic Metalanguage: Theory and Practice* [自然语义元语言: 理论与实践]. Science Press 科学出版社.

Zhang, Z. 张志平. (2007). *Research on Automatic Extraction of Chinese Basic Vocabulary Based on Genetic Algorithm* [基于遗传算法的汉语基本词汇自动提取研究]. Inner Mongolia Normal University [内蒙古师范大学].

Zhao, Y. 赵彦春. (2004). *Philosophical Critique of Linguistics* [语言学的哲学批判]. Chongqing Publishing House.

Zhao, X. 赵小兵. (2007). *A Study on Recognition and Extraction Method of Contemporary Chinese Basic Vocabulary Based on Dynamic Circuit Corpus* [基于动态流通语料库的现代汉语基本词汇自动识别与提取方法研究]. Beijing Language and Culture University [北京语言大学].

Zhao, Y. 赵元任. (1970). *A Grammar of Spoken* Chinese. University of California Press.

Zheng, J. 郑捷. (2017). *Principles and Practices of Chinese Natural Language Processing* NLP [汉语自然语言处理原理与实践]. Publishing House of Electronics Industry.

Zhong, C. 仲崇山. (2010). Grammar: Structural Rule Between Language Signs [语法: 语言符号之间的结构规律]. *Academic Exchange* [学术交流], (10), 157–159.

Zhou, Y. 周洋. (2011). A Review of Semantic Feature Analysis [义素分析法评述]. *Journal of Hotan Teachers College* [和田师范专科学校学报], *30*(4), 65–67.

Zhou, Y. 周一民. (1995). Types of Sememes and Their Analysis [义素的类型及其分析]. *Chinese Language Learning* [汉语学习], (06), 34–36.

Zhou, Z. 周祖谟. (1959). *Lectures on Chinese Lexicology* [汉语词汇讲话]. People's Education Press.

Zhu, D. 朱德熙. (1982). *Lectures on Grammar* [语法讲义. Commercial Press.

Zou, C. 邹崇理. (2000). *Research on Logical Semantics of Natural Language* [自然语言逻辑研究]. Peking University Press.

The manufacturer's authorised representative in the EU is Springer
Nature Customer Service Centre GmbH, Europaplatz 3, 69115 Heidelberg,
Germany. If you have any concerns regarding our products, please
contact ProductSafety@springernature.com

Printed and bound by CPI Group (UK) Ltd, Croydon, CR0 4YY
01/10/2026
02225922-0008